Facebook®

7th Edition

by Carolyn Abram
with Amy Karasavas

for
dummies®
A Wiley Brand

Facebook® For Dummies®, 7th Edition

Published by **John Wiley & Sons, Inc.**, 111 River Street, Hoboken, NJ 07030-5774, www.wiley.com

Copyright © 2018 by John Wiley & Sons, Inc., Hoboken, New Jersey

Media and software compilation copyright © 2018 by John Wiley & Sons, Inc. All rights reserved.

Published simultaneously in Canada

For general information on our other products and services, please contact our Customer Care Department within the U.S. at 877-762-2974, outside the U.S. at 317-572-3993, or fax 317-572-4002. For technical support, please visit https://hub.wiley.com/community/support/dummies.

Wiley publishes in a variety of print and electronic formats and by print-on-demand. Some material included with standard print versions of this book may not be included in e-books or in print-on-demand. If this book refers to media such as a CD or DVD that is not included in the version you purchased, you may download this material at http://booksupport.wiley.com. For more information about Wiley products, visit www.wiley.com.

Library of Congress Control Number: 2018932655

ISBN: 978-1-119-45386-4; ISBN (ePDF): 978-1-119-45384-0; ISBN (ePub): 978-1-119-45383-3

Manufactured in the United States of America

10 9 8 7 6 5 4 3 2 1

Contents at a Glance

Table of Contents

Introduction

Facebook connects you with the people you know and care about. It enables you to communicate, stay up-to-date, and keep in touch with friends and family anywhere. It facilitates your relationships online to help enhance them in person. Specifically, Facebook connects you with the *people* you know around *content* that is important to you. Whether you're the type to take photos or look at them, or write about your life, or read about your friends' lives, Facebook is designed to enable you to succeed. Maybe you like to share websites and news, play games, plan events, organize groups of people, or promote your business. Whatever you prefer, Facebook has you covered.

Facebook offers you control. Communication and information sharing are powerful only when you can do what you want within your comfort zone. Nearly every piece of information and means of connecting on Facebook come with full privacy controls, allowing you to share and communicate exactly how — and with whom — you desire.

Facebook welcomes everyone: students and professionals; grandchildren (as long as they're at least age 13), parents, and grandparents; busy people; socialites; celebrities; distant friends; and roommates. No matter who you are, using Facebook can add value to your life.

About Facebook For Dummies

Part 1 of this book teaches you all the basics to get you up and running on Facebook. This information is more than enough for you to discover Facebook's value. Part 2 teaches you about the basics of using Facebook — the sorts of things millions of people log in and do every day. Part 3 explains how to find friends and all the ways you can interact with them. Part 4 explores some of the special ways you might find yourself using Facebook once you're up and running. Finally, Part 5 explores the creative, diverse, touching, and even frustrating ways people have welcomed Facebook into their lives.

Here are some of the things you can do with this book:

- **Find out how to represent yourself online.** Facebook lets you create a profile (called a Timeline) that you can share with friends, co-workers, and people-you-have-yet-to-meet.

- **Connect and share with people you know.** Whether you're seeking close friends or long-lost ones, family members, business contacts, teammates, businesses, or celebrities, Facebook keeps you connected. Never say, "Goodbye" again . . . unless you want to.

- **Discover how the online tools of Facebook can help enhance your relationships offline.** Photo sharing, group organization, event planning, and messaging tools all enable you to maintain an active social life in the real world.

- **Take Facebook with you when you're not at your computer.** Facebook's mobile tools are designed to make it easy to use Facebook wherever you are.

- **Bring your connections off Facebook and on to the rest of the web.** Many websites, games, apps, and services on the Internet can work with your Facebook information to deliver you a better experience.

- **Promote a business, fundraiser, or yourself to the people who can bring you success.** Engaging with people on Facebook can help ensure that your message is heard.

Foolish Assumptions

In this book, we make the following assumptions:

- You're at least 13 years of age.

- You have some access to the Internet, an email address, and a web browser that is not Internet Explorer 6 (Internet Explorer 7, Safari, Chrome, Firefox, and so on are all good).

- There are people in your life with whom you communicate.

- You can read the language in which this sentence is printed.

Facebook pages and features — such as the Facebook Groups or the Settings page — are called out with capital letters. Brackets like <*this*> denote generic text that will be different on your screen, such as looking at <*Your Name*>.

Amy and Carolyn often state our opinions throughout this book. Though we have worked for Facebook in the past, the opinions expressed here represent only our own perspectives, not that of Facebook. We were avid Facebook users long before either one of us worked for Facebook.

Icons Used in This Book

What's a *For Dummies* book without icons pointing you in the direction of great information that's sure to help you along your way? In this section, I briefly describe each icon used in this book.

The Tip icon points out helpful information that is likely to improve your experience.

The Remember icon marks an interesting and useful fact — something that you may want to use later.

The Technical Stuff icon indicates interesting and probably unnecessary information that may prove useful at some later point.

The Warning icon highlights lurking danger. With this icon, we're telling you to pay attention and proceed with caution.

Beyond the Book

In addition to what you're reading right now, this product also comes with a free access-anywhere Cheat Sheet that helps you build your Friends List; communicate with your friends in the many ways available on Facebook; and stay on top of important Facebook dates, such as friends' birthdays and events. To get this Cheat Sheet, simply go to www.dummies.com and search for "Facebook For Dummies Cheat Sheet" in the Search box.

1
Getting Started with Facebook

Chapter **1**

The Many Faces of Facebook

Think about the people you interacted with throughout the past day. In the morning, you may have gone to get the paper and chatted with a neighbor. You may have asked your kids what time they'd be home and negotiated with your partner about whose turn it is to cook dinner. Perhaps you spent the day at the office, chatting, joking, and (heaven forbid) getting things done with your co-workers. In the midst of it all, you may have sent an email to all the people in your book club, asking them what book should be next, and what date works for the most people. Maybe while you sat on the bus you read the newspaper or called your mom to wish her a happy birthday or searched on your phone for a good restaurant to go to for drinks with friends. This is your world, as it revolves around you.

Each of us has our own version of the world, and as we interact with each other, those worlds intertwine, interplay, and interlock. Maybe your best friend from college was the one to introduce you to the book club, and then someone from the book club recommended a good restaurant. This network of people you interact with — your friends, acquaintances, and loved ones — exists online. Facebook is the online representation of the web of connections between people in the real world. Facebook (and other Internet companies) likes to call this network the *social graph*.

Now, you may be asking, if this graph or network exists in the real world, why do I need it online, too? Good question (gold stars all around). The answer is that having it online facilitates and improves all your social relationships. In other words, Facebook makes your life easier and your friendships better. It can help with very practical things like remembering a friend's birthday or coordinating a party. It can also help with the more abstract aspects of relationships, things like staying close with family you aren't physically near or talking about your day with friends.

Getting set up and familiar with Facebook does take a little work (which you know, or else you wouldn't be starting out on this book-length journey). It may feel a little overwhelming at times, but the reward is worth it — I promise you.

So . . . What Is Facebook, Exactly?

"Yes, Carolyn," you're saying. "I know it's going to help me stay in touch with my friends and communicate with the people in my life, but what *is* it?"

Well, at its most basic, Facebook is a website. You'll find it through a web browser like Safari, Google Chrome, Firefox, or Internet Explorer, the same way you might navigate to a search engine like Google or to an airline's website to book tickets. (You can also access it using an app on your smartphone or tablet, but more on Facebook Mobile in Chapter 7.) Figure 1-1 shows what you will probably see when you navigate to www.facebook.com.

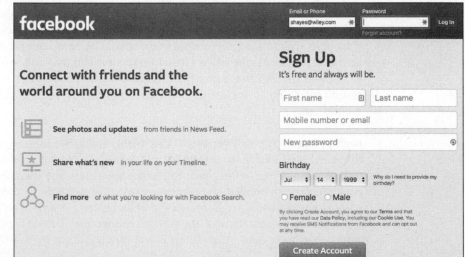

FIGURE 1-1:
Welcome to Facebook. Would you like fries with that?

If you're already a Facebook user and choose to stay logged in on your computer, www.facebook.com will likely look more like Figure 1-2, which shows an example of News Feed and your Home page.

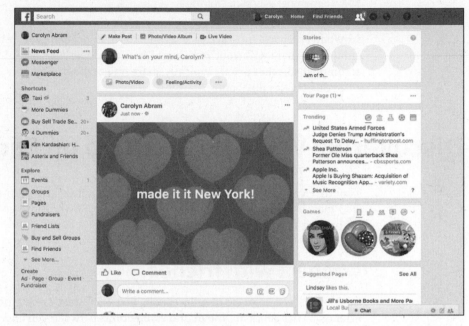

FIGURE 1-2:
Welcome back
to Facebook,
old friend.

Facebook is a website where you go to connect and share with friends. And just as there are a lot of different ways you interact with friends in the real world, there are a lot of ways to do so on Facebook. For example, you may go to Facebook to

» Check out what your friends are up to today.

» Tell your friends and family about your recent successes, show them your photos, or let them know you're thinking of them.

» Share a tidbit from your day, something you've been thinking about, or an article you found interesting

» Show off the pictures from your latest vacation.

» Share a live video of a concert, event, or whatever is going on right now.

» Make a contact in a city you're moving to or at a company where you're applying for a job.

» Plan an event.

» Get in touch with an old friend.

>> Garner support for a cause.

>> Get recommendations from friends for movies, books, music, and restaurants.

>> Remember everyone's birthday.

So what Facebook *is*, exactly, is a website built to help you represent yourself online and share with your real-world friends online. The rest of it — how that's accomplished, what people typically share on Facebook, and how it all works — is what this book is all about.

Discovering What You Can Do on Facebook

Now that you know Facebook is a means by which you can connect with people who matter to you, your next question may be, "How?" More gold stars for you! In the next few sections, I give you an overview.

Connect with friends

As soon as you sign up for Facebook, you will start seeing prompts to "Add Friends." *Friendships* are the digital connections between you and your real-world friends and acquaintances. On Facebook, it's common to refer to *friending* people you know. This just means establishing the virtual connection. Friending people enables you to communicate and share with them more easily. Friends are basically the reason Facebook can be so powerful and useful to people. Facebook offers the following tools to help you find your friends:

>> **People You May Know:** Shows you the names and pictures of people you likely know. These people are selected for you based on commonalities like where you live or work or how many friends you have in common.

>> **Personal Contacts Importer:** Enables you to scan the email addresses in your email address book to find whether those people are already on Facebook. Selectively choose among those with whom you'd like to connect.

>> **Search:** Helps you find the people in your life by name. Chances are they are already using Facebook.

After you establish a few friendships on Facebook, use those friendships to find other people you know by searching through their connections for familiar names. Chapter 8 explains how to find people you know on Facebook.

Learn what's going on with your friends

Whenever you log into Facebook, you'll see your *News Feed.* News Feed is the constantly updating list of stories by and about your friends. In less vague terms, every time one of your friends adds something to Facebook — a photo, a post about her day, a link to an article he liked — it creates a story that may appear when you log in. In this way, News Feed becomes an ongoing update about your friends. News Feed is how I know when my friends have gotten engaged, moved, or had a baby. It's how I know who had a funny thought while they were waiting for their coffee, and whose kid just said something bizarre and profound. It's how I know that there was an earthquake in California (don't worry, everyone's fine) and that people were disappointed by the way the Seattle Seahawks played over the weekend. You can see a snippet of a News Feed in Figure 1-2. Chapter 4 provides much more detail about News Feed.

Establish a Timeline

When you sign up for Facebook, one of the first things you do is establish your *Profile,* or *Timeline.* The reason Facebook uses both terms to refer to the same thing is because a Facebook Profile is much more than an at-a-glance bio. Instead, your profile is centered on your Timeline, which updates every time you add something to Facebook. Your Timeline becomes an ongoing history of your life on Facebook. When you (or your friends) are feeling nostalgic, you can explore your history the same way you might flip through an old photo album.

At first, the thought of putting a photo album of your entire life online may feel sort of scary or daunting. After all, that stuff is personal. But one of the things you'll discover about Facebook is that it's a place to be personal. The people who will see your Timeline are, for the most part, the people you'd show a photo album to in real life. They are your friends and family members.

REMEMBER

That "for the most part" is an important part of Facebook, too. You will encounter other people on Facebook, including potential employers or professional contacts, more distant friends, and casual acquaintances. This distinction — between your close friends and everyone else — is an important one to be aware of.

The Timeline, shown in Figure 1-3, is set up with all kinds of privacy controls to specify *whom* you want to see *which* information. The safest rule here is to share on your Timeline any piece of information you'd share with someone in real life. The corollary applies, too: Don't share on your Timeline any information that you wouldn't share with someone in real life.

Chapter 5 provides lots of detail about the Timeline and what you might choose to share there. For now, think of it as a personal web page that helps you share with your friends on Facebook.

Communicate with Facebook friends

As Facebook grows, it becomes more likely that anyone with whom you're trying to communicate can be reached. Chances are you'll be able to find that person you just met at a dinner party, an old professor from college, or the childhood friend you've been meaning to catch up with. Digging up a person's contact information could require calls to mutual friends, a trip to the white pages (provided you know enough about that person to identify the right contact information), or an email sent to a potentially outdated email address. Facebook streamlines finding and contacting people in one place. If the friend you're reaching out to is active on Facebook, no matter where she lives or how many times she's changed her email address, you can reach each other.

And Facebook isn't just about looking up old friends to say hi. Its messaging system is designed to make it easy to dash a quick note off to friends and get their reply just as fast. The comments people leave on each other's photos, status updates, and posts are real conversations that you will find yourself taking part in.

Share your thoughts

You have something to say. I can just tell by the look on your face. Maybe you're proud of the home team, maybe you're excited for Friday, or maybe you can't believe what you saw on the way to work this morning. All day long, things are happening to all of us that make us just want to turn to our friends and say, "You know what? . . . That's what." Facebook gives you the stage and an eager audience. Chapter 4 shows how you can make short or long posts about the things happening around you and how they're distributed to your friends in an easy way.

Share your pictures and videos

Since the invention of the modern-day camera, people have been all too eager to yell, "Cheese!" Photographs can make great tour guides on trips down memory lane, but only if you remember to develop, upload, or scrapbook them. Many memories fade away when the smiling faces are stuffed into an old shoe box, remain on undeveloped rolls of film, or are left to molder in obscurity on your phone's camera roll.

Facebook offers three great incentives for uploading, organizing, and editing your photos and videos:

>> **Facebook provides one easy-to-access location for all your photos and videos.** Directing any interested person to your Facebook Timeline is easier than e-mailing pictures individually, sending a complicated link to a photo site, or waiting until the family reunion to show off the my-how-the-kids-have-grown pics. You can share videos alongside your photos, so people can really get a feel for all parts of your vacation.

>> **Every photo and video you upload can be linked to the Timelines of the people in the photo or video.** For example, you upload pictures of you and your sister and link them to her Timeline. On Facebook, this is called *tagging* someone. Whenever someone visits your sister's Timeline, he sees those pictures; he doesn't even have to know you. This is great because it introduces longevity to photos. As long as people are visiting your sister's Timeline, they can see those pictures. Photo albums no longer have to be something people look at right after the event and maybe then again years later.

>> **Facebook gives you the power to control exactly who has access to your photos and videos.** Every time you upload a photo or create a new photo album on Facebook, you can decide whether you want everyone on Facebook to see it, just your friends, or even just a subset of your friends based on your comfort level. You may choose to show your wedding photos to all your friends, but perhaps only some friends see the honeymoon. This control enables you to tailor your audience to those friends who might be most interested. All your friends might enjoy your baby photos, but maybe only your co-workers will care about photos from the recent company party.

Chapter 11 shows how to share your photos and videos.

Plan Events

Events are just what they sound like: a system for creating events, inviting people to them, sending out messages about them, and so on. Your friends and other guests RSVP to events, which allows the event organizers to plan accordingly and allows attendees to receive event reminders. Facebook Events can be used for something as small as a lunch date or something as big as a march on Washington, D.C. Sometimes events are abstract rather than physical. For example, someone could create an event for Ride Your Bike to Work Day and hope the invitation spreads far and wide (through friends and friends of friends) to promote awareness. I use Events to plan barbecues for my friends as well as to put together a larger reading series. Chapter 13 covers Events in detail.

Join and create Groups

Groups are also what they sound like: groups of people organized around a common topic or real-world organization. One group may be intimate, such as five best friends who plan several activities together. Another group could be practical — for example, PTA Members of Denver Schools. Within a group, all members can share relevant information, photos, or discussions. My groups include one for my son's daycare classroom where parents can share information and coordinate playdates, one for my *For Dummies* editorial team so we can update each other on how the writing is going, and one for a group of friends who are all planning to take a trip together next year. Groups are covered in detail in Chapter 10.

Whenever you choose to share content to Facebook, you can choose to share it only with members of a certain group. So if you just had a baby and know how much your family is jonesing for new photos, you can just share photos with your family group without inundating the world at large.

Facebook and the web

Facebook Photos, Groups, and Events are only a small sampling of how you can use Facebook to connect with the people you know. Throughout this book, you find information about how Facebook interacts with the greater Internet. You might see articles recommended by friends when you go to *The New York Times* website, or information about what music your friends like when you use Spotify, an Internet radio website. Chapter 15 explains in detail the games, apps, and websites that you can use with your Facebook information.

Many of these websites and applications have been built by outside developers who don't work for Facebook. They include tools to help you edit your photos; create slideshows; play games with friends across the globe; divvy up bills among people who live or hang out together; and exchange information about good movies, music, books, and restaurants. After you become a little more comfortable with the Facebook basics, you can try some of the thousands of applications and websites whose services allow you to interact with your Facebook friends.

Promote a cause or business

Every day, you interact with your friends and family. You also interact with other beings: a newspaper or magazine, your favorite coffee shop, a celebrity whose marriage travails you can't help but be fascinated by, a television show that has you on the edge of your seat, or a cause that's near and dear to your heart. All these entities can be represented on Facebook through Pages (with a capital P). These Pages look almost exactly like Timelines, just for the not-quite-people among us. Instead of becoming friends with Pages, you can like them. So when you like a television show (say, *The Daily Show with Trevor Noah*), you'll start to see updates from that Page *(The Daily Show)* in your News Feed. Liking Pages for businesses or causes helps you stay up-to-date with news from them. You can also fundraise for a cause you care about by promoting it on your Timeline and asking for donations towards a goal.

If you're the one managing something like a small business, a cause, or a newsletter, you can also create a Page. After you've created that Page, your users/customers/fans can like it, and then you can update them with news about whatever's going on in the world of your store/cause/thing. Chapter 14 covers all the ins and outs of Pages.

Keeping in Mind What You Can't Do on Facebook

Facebook is meant to represent real people and real associations; it's also meant to be safe. Many of the rules of participation on Facebook exist to uphold those two goals.

TECHNICAL STUFF

There are things you can't do on Facebook other than what's listed here. For example, you can't look at the photos of someone who has tight privacy settings; you can't prevent ads from showing up from time to time; you can't spin straw into gold. These rules may change how you use Facebook, but probably won't change *whether* you use it. The following four rules are highlighted in this section because if any are a problem for you, you probably won't get to the rest of the book.

You can't lie

Okay, you can, but you shouldn't, especially not about your basic information. Facebook's community standards include a commitment to use an "Authentic Identity." What this means is that Facebook wants you to create only one Timeline for yourself. You don't *have* to use your real name, but I recommend that you do. (I have a few exceptions to this rule, including teachers wanting to keep some professional distance from their students by using an alias.) However, if you create multiple accounts or fake accounts, there is a good chance these will be flagged, disabled, and removed from Facebook.

You can't be twelve

Or younger. Seriously. Facebook takes very seriously the U.S. law that prohibits minors under the age of 13 from creating an online Timeline for themselves. This rule is in place for the safety of minors, and it's a particular safety rule that Facebook does enforce. If you or someone you know on Facebook is under 13, deactivate (or make him deactivate) the account now. If you're reported to the Facebook Community Operations team and they confirm that you're underage, your account will be disabled.

You can't troll, spam, or harass

On the Internet, *trolling* refers to posting deliberately offensive material to websites to get people upset. *Spamming* refers to sending out bulk promotional messages. When I talk about *harassment,* I mean deliberately tormenting or bothering another person or group of people. If you do any of these things on Facebook, there's a good chance your posts will be removed, and your account can be shut down.

The logic for this is that Facebook is about real people and real connections. It's one thing to message a mutual friend or the occasional stranger whose Timeline implies being open to meeting new people if the two of you have matching interests. However, between Facebook's automatic detection systems and user-generated reports, sending too many unsolicited messages is likely to get your account flagged and disabled.

Similarly, Facebook aims to be a "trusted" environment for people to exchange ideas and information. If people deliberately disturb the peace with pornographic, hateful, or bullying content, that trust is pretty much broken. While there are many places on Facebook where you can find spirited public discussion of controversial topics, Facebook does respond to reports of offensive material and will take down anything it deems hate speech.

Chances are that you have no intention of engaging in hate speech, so keep in mind that if you see trolling, spam, or harassment taking place, you can report the content or person to Facebook (you see how to report a photo, for example, in Chapter 11), and its Community Operations team investigates the report. If you're getting warnings about things like spamming, chances are you just need to tweak *how* you're using Facebook. For example, you may need to create a Page instead of using your personal account for mass messaging. You see how to promote your business (or yourself) in Chapter 14.

You can't upload illegal content

Facebook users live in virtually every country in the world, so Facebook is often obligated to respect the local laws for its users. Respecting these laws is something Facebook must do regardless of its own position on pornography (where minors can see it), copyrighted material, hate speech, depictions of crimes, and other offensive content. However, doing so is also in line with Facebook's value of being a trusted place for people 13 and older. Don't confuse this with censorship; Facebook is all about freedom of speech and self-expression, but the moment that compromises anyone's safety or breaks any law, disciplinary action is taken.

Realizing How Facebook Is Different from Other Social Sites

Lots of social sites besides Facebook try to help people connect. Some popular sites are Twitter, LinkedIn, Instagram, Tumblr, SnapChat, WhatsApp, and many others.

I'll start with the biggest reason Facebook is different. Literally, the biggest: Facebook has over *two billion* users across the world (yes, billion with a *b*). Other social sites might be popular in one country or another, but Facebook is popular pretty much everywhere.

REMEMBER

If you're going to use only one social networking site, choose Facebook — everyone you want to interact with is already there.

You'll see a lot of similar functionality across different sites: establishing connections, creating Timelines, liking content, and so on. However, each site brings a slightly different emphasis in terms of what is important. LinkedIn, for example, helps people with career networking, so it puts emphasis on professional information and connections. Twitter encourages its members to share short *tweets*, 280-character posts with their connections. Instagram (which is owned by Facebook) encourages its members to share cool photos taken with mobile phones.

SnapChat allows people to have video chats with friends while applying silly filters to their image in the video.

You might find some or all these sites useful at different points in time, but Facebook wants to be the one that is always useful in one way or another — so it tries to offer all the functionality I just mentioned . . . *and more.*

How You Can Use Facebook

Now that you know what you can do, generally, on Facebook, it's time to consider some of the specific ways you may find yourself using Facebook in the future. The following list is by no means comprehensive, and I've left out some of the things already mentioned in this chapter (things like sharing photos and events and groups). These are more specific-use cases than an advertisement for Facebook's features.

REMEMBER

Two billion people use Facebook, but not all of them can see your whole Timeline. You can share as much or as little with as many or as few people as you so desire. Put under lock and key the posts or parts of your Timeline you *don't* want to share with everyone. Chapter 6 goes into much greater detail on how to protect yourself and your information.

Getting information

At any age, you may need to find someone's phone number or connect with a friend of a friend to organize something. Facebook can make these very practical tasks a little bit easier. If you can search for someone's name, you should be able to find her on Facebook and find the information you're looking for.

Keeping up with long-distance friends

These days, families and friends are often spread far and wide across state or country lines. Children go to college; grandparents move to Florida; people move for their job or because they want a change of scenery. These distances make it hard for people to interact in any more significant way than gathering together once per year to share some turkey and pie (pecan, preferably). Facebook offers a place where you can virtually meet and interact. Upload photos of the kids for everyone to see; write posts about what everyone is up to. Even the more mundane information about your life ("I'm at jury duty") can make someone across the world feel like, just for a second, she's sitting next to you and commiserating with you about your jury summons.

AM I SIGNING UP FOR A DATING SITE?

Throughout this book, you read about ways to communicate: messages, chatting, poking, liking, and commenting. These neutral activities can take on a whole new meaning and spark when they happen between two people interested in each other.

Although Facebook is not technically a dating site, plenty of people do take advantage of its social nature to boost their dating lives in different ways:

- You can inform people through your Timeline whom you're looking to meet (women, men, or both).

- You can certainly use Facebook's systems to flirt, get to know, and yes, do a little background research on dating prospects.

- If you're happily ensconced in couple-dom, listing your relationship status and linking to your partner's Timeline is an easy way to broadcast, "Move along; I'm taken."

Moving to a new city

Landing in a new city with all your worldly belongings and an upside-down map can be hugely intimidating. Having some open arms or at least numbers to call when you arrive can greatly ease the transition. Although you may already know some people who live in your new city, Facebook can help connect with all the old friends and acquaintances you either forgot live there or have moved there since you last heard from them. These people can help you find doctors, apartments, hair stylists, Frisbee leagues, and restaurants.

As you meet more and more new friends, you can connect with them on Facebook. Sooner than you thought possible, when someone posts about construction slowing down his commute, you know exactly the street he means, and you may realize, *I'm home.*

Getting a job

Plenty of people use Facebook as a tool for managing their careers as well as their social lives. If you're looking at a company, find people who already work there to get the inside scoop or to land an interview. If you're thinking about moving into a particular industry, browse your friends by past jobs and interests to find someone to connect with. If you go to a conference for professional development, you can keep track of the other people you meet there as your Facebook friends.

Reunions

Thanks to life's curveballs, your friends at any given time may not be the people in your life at another. The memories of people you consider to be most important in your life fade over the years so that even trying to recall a last name may give you pause. The primary reason for this lapse is a legitimate one: There are only so many hours in a day. While we make new, close friends, others drift away because it's impossible to maintain many intense relationships. Facebook is an extremely powerful tool; however, it hasn't yet found a way to extend the number of hours in a day, so it can't exactly fix the problem of growing apart. Facebook can, however, lessen the finality and inevitability of the distance.

Because Facebook is only about thirteen years old (and because you're reading this book), you probably don't have your entire social history mapped out. Some may find it a daunting task to create connections with everyone they've ever known, which I don't recommend. Instead, build your graph as you need to or as opportunity presents. Perhaps you want to upload a photo taken from your high school graduation. Search for the people in the photo on Facebook; form the friend connection; and then *tag*, or mark, them as being in the photo (you can learn about photo tagging in Chapter 11). Maybe you're thinking about opening a restaurant, and you'd like to contact a friend from college who was headed into the restaurant business after graduation. Perhaps you never told your true feelings to the one who got away. For all these reasons, you may find yourself using the Facebook Search box.

TIP

Frequently, I receive reports from adopted children who connect with their biological parents or estranged siblings who find each other on Facebook. I once heard from my sixth-grade bully, who found me on Facebook and apologized for his behavior as a kid. I, in turn, used it to apologize to someone I treated terribly around the same time.

Organizing movements

In the summer of 2014, you couldn't look at a News Feed without encountering a video of someone dumping a bucket of ice water over their head. It wasn't some sort of bizarre hazing ritual; it was the ALS ice bucket challenge, designed to raise awareness of amyotrophic lateral sclerosis (also known as Lou Gehrig's disease). This awareness campaign hinged entirely on social sites like Facebook to spread. People would "challenge" their friends to either donate to an ALS-related charity or dump ice water over their heads and post the video of it to Facebook (or, ideally, do both). One person would post her ice-bucket video, challenge five friends, and then those five friends would post their ice-bucket videos, and so on and so on. The campaign spread through Facebook and the ALS association reported that it had more than doubled the amount of money raised over the previous summer.

The term *movement*, here, can apply to anything. People have used Facebook to agitate against terrorist groups, to raise money for victims of natural disasters, to spark conversation about suicide clusters at elite schools. Whatever the cause or movement may be, Facebook can be used to bring support and spread the word.

THE BIRTH OF THE 'BOOK

In ye olden days, say, the early 2000s, most college freshmen would receive a thinly bound book containing the names and faces of everyone in their matriculating class. These *face books* were useful for matching names to the students seen around campus or for pointing out particular people to friends. There were several problems with these face books. If someone didn't send his picture in, the books were incomplete. They were outdated by junior year because many people looked drastically different, and the books didn't reflect the students who had transferred in or who were from any other class. Finally, they had little information about each person.

In February 2004, Mark Zuckerberg, a sophomore at Harvard, launched an online "book" to which people could upload their photos and personal information, a service that solved many of these problems. Within a month, more than one-half of the Harvard undergraduates had signed up.

Zuckerberg was then joined by others to help expand the site into other schools. I was the first Stanford student to receive an account. During the summer of the same year, Facebook moved to Palo Alto, California, where the site and the company kept growing. By December 2004, the site had grown to one million college students. Every time Facebook opened to a new demographic — high school, then work users, then everyone — the rate at which people joined the site continued to increase.

At the end of 2006, the site had more than 10 million users; 2007 closed out with more than 50 million active users. At the time of this book's publication in 2018, that final count has grown to in excess of two billion people across the globe using Facebook to stay in touch.

Communicating in times of trouble

It is a sad fact of life that sometimes events happen beyond our control. Disasters great and small befall everyone at one time or another. While Facebook tends to be a place for sharing the good stuff, its tools also work very well to help with some of the logistics of recovering from certain types of disasters. *Safety Check* is a feature that gets turned on in certain geographic regions after natural disasters or security attacks. This feature allows people to easily notify their wider Facebook community that they are okay and can even help them coordinate with the services they might need. Facebook's Groups feature was used to help coordinate civilian boat evacuations after a hurricane flooded Houston, TX, in 2017. Because people live so much of their lives on Facebook, Facebook winds up being there for both the good and the bad.

Chapter **2**

Adding Your Own Face to Facebook

C hapter 1 covers why you might want to join Facebook. In this chapter, I get you signed up and ready to go on Facebook. Keep a couple of things in mind when you sign up. First, Facebook becomes exponentially more useful and more fun when you start adding friends. Without friends, it can feel kind of dull. Second, your friends may take a few days to respond to your Friend Requests, so be patient. Even if your first time on Facebook isn't as exciting as you hope, be sure to come back and try again over the following weeks. Third, you can have only one account on Facebook. Facebook links accounts to email addresses or phone numbers, and your email address (or number) can be linked to only one account. This system enforces a world where people are who they say they are on Facebook.

Signing Up for Facebook

Officially, all you need to join Facebook is a valid email address or phone number. When I say *valid email,* I just mean that you need to be able to easily access the messages in that account because Facebook emails you a registration confirmation. A *valid phone number* means a mobile phone number that can send and receive text messages, since Facebook will text you your registration confirmation. Figure 2-1 shows the crucial part of the sign-up page, which you can find by navigating to www.facebook.com.

As you can see, you need to fill out a few things:

>> **First and Last Name:** Facebook is a place based on real identity. Sign up with the name people know you by. I don't recommend signing up with a fake name or alias because that will make it hard for you to be found by friends. After you've signed up, you can add nicknames or maiden names to your Timeline to make it even easier for friends to find you. But for now, just use your real first and last names.

>> **Mobile Number or Email:** You need to enter your valid email address or phone number here. Facebook asks you to enter this information twice to make sure that there are no typos and your emails or texts will get to you.

If you're signing up for Facebook with a phone number, it needs to be a mobile phone number. Your home phone number can't get texts, so it won't help you sign up for Facebook.

REMEMBER

>> **New Password:** As with all passwords, using a combination of letters, numbers, and punctuation marks is a good idea for your Facebook password. It's probably not a good idea to use the same password for every site you join, so I recommend using something unique for Facebook. Facebook requires passwords to be at least six characters long.

>> **Birthday:** Enter your date of birth. If you're shy about sharing your birthday, don't worry: You'll be able to hide this information on your Timeline later.

>> **Sex (Female or Male):** Facebook uses your gender information to construct sentences about you on the site. For example, you might see a News Feed story that reads "Carolyn updated her profile picture." If you are transgender or use a nonstandard gender pronoun, you'll have the ability to change this in your settings.

After you fill out this information, click Create Account (that's the big green button). Congratulations: You officially joined Facebook!

REMEMBER

When you click Create Account, you're agreeing to Facebook's Terms of Service and Data Policy. Most websites have similar terms and policies, but if you're curious about just what Facebook's are, you can always follow the Terms and Data Policy links just above the big green Create Account button.

Getting Started

Although you have this book to help guide you through the ins and outs of Facebook, lots of Facebook users do not. (How sad for them!) That's why Facebook puts all its users through a Getting Started Wizard to help start them out on the right foot. In certain cases, depending on whether you were invited to join Facebook by a friend or you joined with an email address from your workplace or school, you may get slightly different steps than those detailed in the following sections. You may be asked to confirm your email address (which is covered in the "What to Expect In Your Inbox" section). You may not even see a Getting Started Wizard as it appears in the screenshots. Don't worry; the same principles apply: You want to find your friends and set up your profile. This section covers the most basic parts of getting started: finding your friends and making yourself recognizable to friends by adding a profile picture.

Step 1: Find Your Friends

The Find Your Friends step, shown in Figure 2-2, is first because it's that important to enjoying Facebook. Without friends, Facebook can feel a little bit like going to an amusement park alone. Sure, the rides were fun, and the food was greasy, but no one was there to appreciate it with you.

REMEMBER

You have many ways to find friends on Facebook. All of them are covered in Chapter 8, as well as talking more about what friendship really means on Facebook. The method Facebook is highlighting in this step is the *Friend Finder.*

The Friend Finder works by allowing Facebook access to your email account. Facebook then combs through your email contacts and matches the emails it finds with emails attached to the Facebook accounts of the people you email. So if Joe Smith, your friend, emailed you from jsmith@email.com and had a Facebook account he created with that email address, the Friend Finder presents you with Joe's name and profile picture and asks if you want to be friends on Facebook.

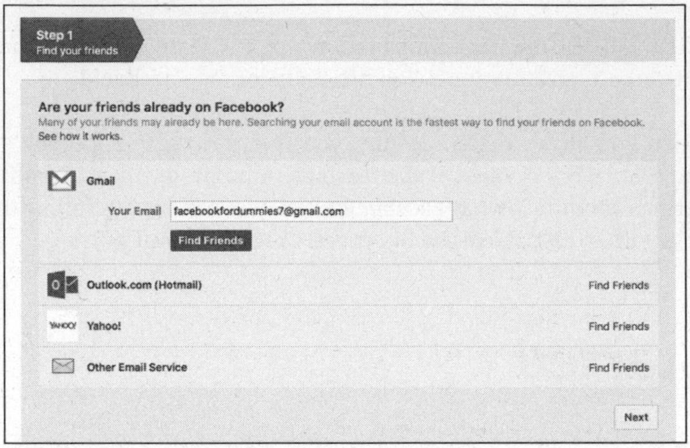

Step 1
Find your friends

Are your friends already on Facebook?
Many of your friends may already be here. Searching your email account is the fastest way to find your friends on Facebook.
See how it works.

M **Gmail**

Your Email facebookfordummies7@gmail.com

Find Friends

O **Outlook.com (Hotmail)**   Find Friends

YAHOO! **Yahoo!**   Find Friends

✉ **Other Email Service**   Find Friends

Next

FIGURE 2-2:
Find your friends
early and often.

To use the Friend Finder, follow these steps:

1. **Select the email provider you're using.**

   This may be Outlook.com (or Hotmail), Gmail, Yahoo!, AOL, or another email client. Facebook automatically selects a provider based on the email you used to register.

   TIP

   Depending on what email service you use, importing your contacts and looking for friends may entail a few extra steps. You may need to export your email contacts into a .csv file. You may be brought to the website of your email provider to log in to your email account. Log in and follow any necessary prompts to allow Facebook to access your contacts list.

2. **Enter your email address and email password.**

   Remember to enter your email password, not the password you just created for Facebook.

3. **Click Find Friends.**

   Behind the scenes, Facebook searches your contact list and presents you with the people in your email Contacts list who are already on Facebook. By default, all these people are selected to be your friends.

4. **Look through the list and choose the people you want to be friends with on Facebook by clicking their names.**

   I talk more about *who,* exactly, should be your Facebook friends in Chapter 8, but for now, a good rule is to look for people you're friends with or related to in real life. You can deselect the people you don't want to add by clicking their faces or the check boxes.

This isn't your only opportunity to use the Friend Finder. If you aren't sure about adding a lot of people right away, that's okay. Chapter 8 shows you how to get back to these steps at any point in time.

5. **Click Add Friends.**

   This sends *Friend Requests* to all the people you selected in Step 4. On Facebook, all friendships must be agreed to by both people. A request to your friend needs to be approved by her before you are officially Facebook friends.

   After you add friends, Facebook looks at the email addresses it didn't find matches for and asks you whether you want to invite those people to join Facebook.

6. **Select people you want to invite to join Facebook.**

   By default, all your friends are selected to be invited. You can click the Select all/None box at the top of the list to deselect everyone. You can also deselect people individually by clicking the boxes next to their names.

   If you don't want to invite anyone to join Facebook just yet, look on the bottom right of the screen for a Skip link. It's right next to the Send Invites button.

7. **Click Send Invites to send out invitations to your friends via email.**

   They'll receive emails from Facebook letting them know you invited them to join.

The Friend Finder is very useful when you're just getting started on Facebook because it allows you to find a whole bunch of friends all at once. If you had to look for each of your friends by name, it could take a while. Friend Finder allows you to speed up that process.

Step 2: Profile Picture

Your *Facebook Profile,* or *Timeline,* is the online representation of who you are. Most likely, you have online profiles for various websites. Facebook Timelines tend to be a little more comprehensive and dynamic, for reasons that I detail in Chapter 5.

Your Profile Picture is one of the most important parts of your Timeline. It's a good first step towards starting to tell your friends all about you. And, significantly, it helps your friends identify you. Remember all those friend requests you sent while you were using the Friend Finder? When those friends see your request, it will be much easier for them to verify that you're *you* if they can see a photo of you. Step 2, adding a profile picture, is shown in Figure 2-3.

Upload a profile picture

Add Picture

— OR —

Take a Photo
With your webcam

FIGURE 2-3:
Add a profile
picture to get
your own face
on Facebook.

TIP

If you've already been through the Getting Started Wizard or aren't seeing the wizard as it appears in Figure 2-3, click the Edit Profile link on the right side of the screen and then click Add Profile Picture when you arrive on the Edit Profile page. The instructions below assume you are looking at the Getting Started Wizard, so may not match the steps you take from the Edit Profile page exactly, though they are very similar.

You can add a profile picture in one of two ways. You can either upload a photo from your computer's hard drive or, if you have a computer with a built-in webcam, you can take a photo you want to use.

To add a profile picture from your hard drive, make sure you have a photo you want to use saved somewhere you can find it, and follow these steps:

1. **Click Add Picture.**

   This opens a window for browsing your computer's hard drive. Use it to navigate to wherever you saved the photo you wanted to use as a profile picture.

2. **Select your desired photo and click Choose or OK.**

   This brings you back to the Getting Started Wizard, except now there's a preview of your new profile picture.

3. **Click Next.**

If you want to use your computer's webcam to take a profile picture, follow these steps:

1. **Click the Take a Photo link.**

   This opens a dialog box for accessing your computer's webcam. You may have to click Allow before Facebook is able to work with your computer to show an image of you.

2. **Strike a pose and click the Take Photo button.**

   Once the photo has been taken, it displays in the dialog box. You can choose to retake the photo if you don't like the way your smile looks.

3. **Click Save.**

I talk a lot about your profile picture and the many ways it's used on Facebook in Chapter 5, but here are a few quick tips on selecting a profile picture:

>> **Make a good first impression.** Your profile picture is one of the first ways people interact with your Timeline and how you choose to represent yourself. Most people pick pictures that are flattering or that represent what's important to them. Sometimes, profile pictures include other people — friends or significant others. Other times, the location matters. If the first photo you see of someone is at the beach versus at a party or sitting at his desk, you may draw different conclusions about that person. What picture represents you?

>> **Consider who will see your profile picture.** By default, your profile picture appears in search results that are visible to all of Facebook and can even be made available to the larger Internet population. So, generally, people who search for your name can see that picture. Make sure it's something you're comfortable with everyone seeing.

>> **Pick a photo _you_ like.** As you use Facebook, you wind up seeing your own photo quite often. Small versions appear wherever you make a comment, post something, or are part of a group. So pick a photo you like looking at.

>> **You're not stuck with it.** After I put all this pressure on you to pick the perfect photo, keep in mind that you can easily change your profile picture at any time. Is it the dead of winter, and that photo of you on the beach last summer is just too depressing to look at? No problem; simply edit your profile picture, which you can find out how to do in Chapter 5.

What to Expect in Your Inbox

After you sign up for Facebook, you will immediately see an email arrive in your Inbox asking you to confirm your account. This will be the first of many emails Facebook sends you as it helps you get fully integrated into the Facebook world. Read on to learn how to respond to these emails and why they are important.

Confirmation

Confirmation is Facebook's way of trying to make sure that you are really you and that the email address you used to sign up is really yours.

When you click the Create Account button (as I describe earlier), Facebook sends you an email asking you to confirm your account. In other words, Facebook is double-checking that you are the person who owns your email address.

If Facebook is asking you to confirm your email but you aren't seeing that email in your Inbox, try checking your spam or trash folders. Sometimes Facebook emails can wind up there by accident.

To confirm that you are, in fact, you, and that the email address is, in fact, yours, go to your email, look for that message, and open it. (It will usually have a subject like *Welcome to Facebook* or *Facebook Confirmation*.) That email contains a link or button. Click the link or button in that email, and you will be confirmed. Your confirmation email may also contain a confirmation code that you will be asked to enter on Facebook's website.

You may have already confirmed your email address by using the Friend Finder or other normal activities. If Facebook isn't bugging you about it with banners or follow-up emails, you can pretty much assume you're good to go.

Email outreach

Once you've confirmed your email address and added a few friends, Facebook considers you a full-fledged member of the site. However, it doesn't want you to just show up once and leave; as a result, after you sign up, it may email you to remind you that you are now a Facebook user. These outreach emails have various subject lines, ranging from a notice that one of your new Facebook friends has updated his status, to a general notice that "You have more friends on Facebook than you think." Clicking the links in these emails will open Facebook in your browser.

If you don't like receiving these emails, you can unsubscribe by clicking the "Unsubscribe" link in the bottom of any individual email. This will also open Facebook in your browser, asking if you are sure you want to unsubscribe from that type of email. Click Confirm to make it official.

When Facebook asks whether you want to unsubscribe from "this type" of email, it is being very specific. Email updates about your friends (Carolyn added new photos on Facebook) are a different type than general prompts to find more friends. You may have to click unsubscribe from more than one email before you stop receiving emails altogether.

Your New Home Page

After you complete your Getting Started Wizard, you arrive at your Home page. This is where Facebook starts to look like the Facebook you would see if you'd been using the site for a while already. The Home page is what you see when you log in to Facebook.

What's interesting about the Facebook Home page is that while some parts remain the same (such as the big blue bar on top, and the menu on the left-hand side), the bulk of what you see is constantly changing. This is because the Home page (also known as the News Feed) updates to show you what your friends are posting, sharing, and talking about on Facebook.

At the beginning of this chapter, I point out that Facebook gets exponentially better once you have friends. This is absolutely true on the Home page. Until your friends respond to your requests, you may not see much here except prompts to learn more about Facebook, find more friends, or fill out more profile information beyond your profile picture. After you add the people you know as friends, take a break. Stretch. Take a walk. Drink some water. Come back over the next few days to see the interesting photos, status updates, and links your friends are sharing.

TIP

As you navigate around Facebook for the first time, you may notice small boxes popping up in different parts of the screen (there's an example of one such box in Figure 2-4). Don't ignore these guys! They are trying to teach you tips and tricks to get you comfortable using Facebook.

FIGURE 2-4:
These little boxes point out how and why to use different Facebook features.

AM I TOO OLD FOR FACEBOOK?

No. Most emphatically, no. This is a common misconception, mainly because Facebook was originally exclusive to college students. Facebook's origins, even its name, are rooted in college campuses, but its utility and nature aren't limited to being useful to only college students.

Everyone has networks of friends and people with whom they interact on a day-to-day basis. Young or old, in college or working, this is true. Facebook tries to map these real-world connections to make it easier for people to share information with their friends.

If you're reading this section and thinking maybe you're just too old for Facebook, you're wrong. More and more people in older age demographics are signing up for Facebook every day to keep in touch with old friends, share photos, create events, and connect with local organizations. Almost everything I discuss in the book is non-age-specific.

Obviously, how people use the site can be very different at different ages, but you will discover these nuances when you use Facebook more and more. Generally, you should feel confident that you and your friends can connect and use Facebook in a meaningful way.

More than two billion people are using Facebook, and that number isn't made up of "a bunch of kids." Rather, it's a bunch of people from every age group, every country, and every walk of life.

Adding More Friends

As a new user logging into Facebook, there seems to be one overwhelming thing that Facebook wants you to do — add more friends. You may be seeing the updates of friends in your News Feed, but you are almost certainly seeing previews of people you may know with big buttons prompting you to Add Friend. You may see these previews on the right side of your Home page, in your News Feed, even on your Timeline.

Facebook finds people to recommend you add as friends based largely on the people you are already friends with (this is a vastly oversimplified explanation of the find friends algorithm, but the longer explanation involves more math). Each time you see a "Person You May Know" you can choose to ignore the suggestion by clicking the tiny X button in the upper-right corner or click the Add Friend button.

I always hesitate to give too much advice in terms of whether or not you should add someone as a friend. In general, especially when you are just starting out, I lean towards adding everyone you know and care about. Family, friends, coworkers, teammates, classmates — add 'em all. Adding more friends will make your News Feed more interesting, and Facebook will learn over time whom, exactly, you find most interesting.

REMEMBER

On Facebook, friendships are *reciprocal*. You don't officially become Facebook friends with others until they have approved your friend request.

On the flip side, I would not recommend adding people you don't like as friends. Yes, I mean that one person from your last job who was always super nice to you but secretly drove you insane. Or that second cousin twice removed who always asks you inappropriate questions about your love life. Don't feel obligated to click Add Friends simply because you *know* someone.

WARNING

Categories of people you may not want to add as friends are teachers, doctors, students, or other people you know and like but who you would like to maintain a more professional distance from. Facebook is often a place where people are casual, let their (virtual) hair down, and don't censor. It can be weird or even inappropriate to see your therapist venting about her patients or for your boss to see photos of you relaxing at the beach when you claimed you were home sick.

Chapter 8 provides much more information about the nuances of friendship and how to know whom to add.

Filling out Your Profile Information

Getting your Timeline set up is not a requirement for starting to use Facebook. In fact, your Timeline is something that gets built up over time (and doing so is covered in Chapter 5), so I wouldn't give you such a Herculean task right away.

However, there are a few basic pieces of information that will help you find your friends on Facebook, as well as helping your friends identify you when you send them a friend request. These are your current workplace, current city, any schools you've attended, and your hometown. Especially if you have a common name, this information can really help someone who is regarding a friend request figure out if you are in fact Jane Smith from Portland (who they definitely want to be friends with) or Jane Smith from Seattle (who, maybe not so much).

To add this basic profile information, follow these steps:

1. **From your Home page, click your name in the big blue bar on top of the screen.**

This takes you to your profile.

2. **Click the About tab.**

It is located underneath your name. Clicking it takes you to the About section of your profile, which is likely empty at this time.

3. **Click Add a workplace or Add a school.**

Clicking any of these links opens an interface for typing in the name of your workplace, college, or high school, respectively.

4. **Start typing the name of your workplace or school.**

Facebook *autocompletes*, or attempts to guess at what you're typing as you type. So, for example, if you start typing "m-i-c" Facebook will display a menu of possible company matches — Microsoft, Mic Media, Michael Kors, and so on.

5. **Select your workplace or school when you see it appear in the autocomplete menu.**

If your workplace doesn't appear in the autocomplete menu, simply finish typing its name and press Enter.

6. **(Optional) Add more details about your work or school.**

You can add information like your specific job title, major, year of graduation, and more.

7. **Click Save Changes.**

The blue Save Changes button is at the bottom of the section you are editing.

TIP

To the left of the Save Changes button, a small globe icon and the word "Public" lets you know that once you save it, this information is publicly available. Anyone can see it. I talk more about what this means in Chapter 6.

To add your hometown and current city from the About section of your profile, click the Places You've Lived link on the left side of the page (underneath Work and Education). You can then click to add your current city and hometown the same way you added your work and education information. You can also edit this information from the Overview section.

Chapter **3**

Finding Your Way Around Facebook

ere's the thing about using Facebook: It has a lot of options. Now, this is actually one of the best things about Facebook. You can upload photos, look at photos, chat with a friend, message a friend, read updates from friends . . . the list goes on and on. What does get a little confusing is that there's no one way to do anything on Facebook. Depending on the page you're on, you'll see slightly different things. Depending on who your friends are, you'll see slightly different things. Using Facebook can't exactly be broken down into ten easy steps.

You can learn, however, to recognize a few more constant places. Starting from when you log in, you will always start on your *Home page,* which is where you'll find one of Facebook's most defining features, *News Feed.* Though News Feed is always different (more on that later) the home page has a few constants that are detailed in this chapter. If you ever find yourself lost on Facebook (it happens; trust me), click the Home link, or the Facebook logo, in the blue bar on top of any page to go to the Home page, where you'll be able to reorient yourself.

Figure 3-1 shows a sample Home page. This chapter details the elements of the Home page that you're likely to see, too: menus and links to other parts of the site. Some of these links can be found no matter where you are on Facebook, some appear only when you're on your Home page, and some will be there, well, sometimes. Learning about these links helps you understand how to find your way around Facebook and enables you to work with some of Facebook's features and options.

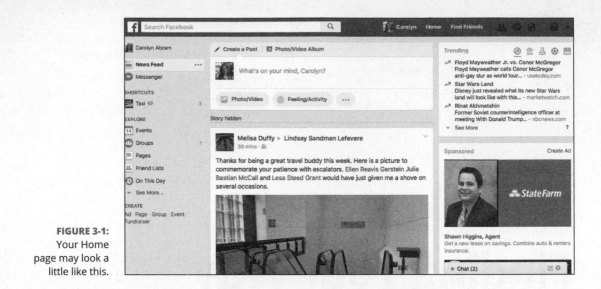

FIGURE 3-1:
Your Home
page may look a
little like this.

Checking Out the Blue Bar on Top

I happen to spend a lot of time in coffee shops working alongside writers, students, businesspeople, and hobbyists — all drinking steamy beverages and manning laptops. I can always tell at a glance when someone is browsing Facebook by the big blue bar across the top of the page. The blue bar is home to many of the important navigational links on Facebook. And anytime you're looking at a Facebook page, you'll have the blue bar accompanying you, like a really loyal puppy. Figure 3-2 shows the blue bar.

FIGURE 3-2:
The blue bar
at the top.

Here's what you need to know about the different parts of the blue bar:

>> **Facebook logo:** The "f" Facebook logo on the left of the blue bar serves two purposes. First, it reminds you what website you're using. Second, no matter where you are on Facebook, if you click this icon, you're back at the Facebook Home page.

>> **Search:** The big white box next to the Facebook logo is the search box. This text area is where you can type any sort of search query. Simply click that text and start typing what you're looking for. After you click, Facebook opens a menu with suggested searches. I talk more about how to find people and other Facebook content later in the "Search" section of this chapter.

TIP

The text within the search box will change depending on where you are on Facebook. For example, when you're on a friend's Timeline, it will show your friend's name. When you're exploring a group, it will show the group's name. This can help you from getting lost.

>> **<Your Name> and Profile Picture:** If you share a computer with other people, glancing at this link whenever you use Facebook is an easy way to make sure you're using your Facebook account and not your spouse's or kid's account. Clicking this link brings you to your Timeline.

>> **Home:** This link is always there to bring you back to the Home page. When in doubt, just go Home and start over.

>> **(New Users) Find Friends:** If you're a new user of Facebook or don't have very many friends, Facebook adds this link to your blue bar to make it as easy as possible for you to go get more friends. Clicking it brings you to the Find Friends page, where you can use Facebook's various tools for finding and adding your friends. Chapter 8 covers all the ways to find friends.

>> **Friend Requests:** Next to the Home link is an icon of two people, intended to depict friends. Clicking this icon reveals a menu that shows you any pending Friend Requests you may have. Whenever you receive brand-new Friend Requests, a little red number totaling the number of new requests shows up on top of this icon. When you view the new requests, regardless of whether you respond to them, the red flag goes away. Chapter 8 covers sending and receiving Friend Requests in more detail.

>> **Messages:** An icon depicting a speech bubble lets you access a preview of your Messages Inbox. Clicking it shows you snippets from your most recent messages, as well as links to use if you want to send a new message or go to your Inbox. As with the Friend Requests, a little red flag appears to show you how many new messages you have. When you click that flag and view the preview of the new messages, the flag disappears. Chapter 9 covers Facebook Messages.

>> **Notifications:** When someone on Facebook has taken an action that involves you, you're notified by a red flag on top of the next icon — the globe. Maybe the person has tagged you in a photo, posted to your Timeline, liked a comment you made, or posted something to a group you belong to. Click the globe to scroll through your most recent notifications. You can also click links to change your notification settings or see all your notifications on another page.

>> **Quick Help:** An icon depicting a question mark in a circle marks where you can click if you ever have a question that you need answered. If you ever have a problem and you can't find the answer in this book, the Quick Help menu

and the Help Center are good places to start. Clicking this icon opens a menu of options for you:

- *Help Center*: The Help Center is where Facebook maintains various FAQs, video tutorials, and other content to help you use Facebook more confidently. Click this link to be taken there.

- *Search Help*: Start typing a question or keyword into this search box to find answers to any Facebook-related questions that may be on your mind. As you type, Facebook will display frequently asked questions that match your search terms. If you see one that looks like your question, click it to see the answer.

- *Help With This Page*: Depending on what you are doing when you click the Quick Help icon, you will see different topics displayed in this space. For example, when you're looking at your profile, you see links to information about topics like adding a cover photo or updating your info. When you're looking at a group, you see links to information about posting to a group or managing your group.

- *Privacy Checkup:* Privacy checkup is a tool that you can use to make sure that your privacy settings are adjusted the way you want them to be. It's covered in more depth in Chapter 6.

- *Privacy Shortcuts:* Privacy shortcuts are links to the most commonly adjusted privacy settings, which allow you to control the answers to three main questions: Who can see my stuff, Who can contact me, and How do I stop someone from bothering me. These questions (and more) are covered in Chapter 6.

- *Support Inbox:* The Support Inbox is where you'll go if you ever have a problem that requires you contacting Facebook's Help team. Any correspondence with that team will take place in your Support Inbox.

- *Report a Problem*: If you ever see something on Facebook you think you shouldn't (such as harassment or porn), you can go to the help menu and choose to Report a Problem.

» **Account menu (down arrow):** In this book, I reference the *Account menu.* That's the menu that appears when you click this arrow. Here's a rundown of some of the categories you can find on the Account menu:

- *Your Pages:* Chapter 14 shows you how to create a *Page,* or special profile for businesses or organizations. If you create or manage Pages, you'll be able to find links to use Facebook on behalf of your Pages from the Account menu. You can also find links to create new Pages or manage your existing Pages.

- *Groups:* Chapter 10 explains how to create and use Groups to communicate and share with smaller groups of people within Facebook. The Account menu contains links to create groups, check out your new groups, and manage any groups you have created.

- *Create Fundraiser:* We delve into fundraisers in Chapter 12. This is a way for you to raise money for causes near and dear to your heart.

- *Ads:* If you create an ad to be shown on Facebook, you'll find links to manage and create more ads in this menu. If you're looking to advertise on Facebook, you might want to check out some more specific Dummies books like Facebook Marketing for Dummies.

- *Activity Log:* I talk about Activity Log when I talk about privacy in Chapter 6. It's a way to keep track of all the actions you have taken recently on Facebook and who may be able to see those actions. You can get to your Activity Log from this menu.

- *News Feed Preferences:* Your News Feed is a constantly updated list of stories by and about your friends. It's what you see front and center on your Home page every time you log in to Facebook. In Chapter 4, I talk about how you can influence what you see in News Feed using the News Feed Preferences.

- *Settings:* Choosing this brings you to the Settings page, where you can change your name, your email address or password, your mobile information, or the language you want to use on the site. This is also where you go to find privacy settings (detailed in Chapter 6), notification settings, and to deactivate your account.

- *Send Money:* Some users see an option to send money. Clicking this link lets you send payments from your debit card directly to a friend. This comes in handy when you owe a friend for the dinner she paid for the other night or your roommate for the monthly cable bill.

- *Log Out:* Clicking this ends your Facebook session. If you share your computer with others, always be sure to log out to ensure that another person can't access your Facebook account.

WARNING

If you have the Remember Password option selected when you log in, you won't ever be logged out until you click Log Out. Remember Password keeps you logged in despite closing the browser; therefore, I recommend using the Remember Password option only on a computer you don't share with others.

Search

Search has become an integral part of using the Internet. It's the way we find the info we need — whether that's a business' address, a person's contact info, or the year of the great San Francisco earthquake. Facebook's search is also important, though it works a bit differently from the way a search engine like Google or Bing does.

Most of the time, you will use Search to hop quickly to a friend's Timeline or to check out a Page you follow. Simply start typing your friend's name into the search box in the blue bar on top of the page. Facebook displays an *auto-complete menu* as you type, showing possible matches as you add more and more letters. When you see the name of the person you are looking for, click on her name or picture to go to her Timeline.

Even though the simplest use of Search is what you'll use most of the time, it's worth noting that Facebook has an incredible database of information that you can search through at any time. You can search through friends' posts, photos, and videos simply by entering a search term into the search box. Given the amount of information you might see in your News Feed on any given day, it can be incredibly helpful to search to find that one piece of information you are looking for (I *know* someone posted a link to the best place to pick apples in the fall, but I can't remember when . . .). The search results page allows you to filter for the latest results, or to look only at people, photos, videos, Pages, or places.

The Left-side Menu

The left side of the Facebook Home page is taken up by what Facebook calls the *left-side menu.* The sidebar is the menu on the left side of the page that provides links to frequently used areas of the site (see Figure 3-3).

The sidebar is divided into a few sections. The top section provides links to your own Timeline, News Feed, and Messenger. You may also see Watch, and Marketplace links here. Watch brings you to a page with original video content. Marketplace brings you to a digital home for buying and selling goods and services. Clicking News Feed when you are already looking at News Feed will refresh the page and possibly display new stories for you to read.

The Shortcuts section provides links to the parts of Facebook you use most. These are often the groups you visit the most often, Pages you manage, and games you play most often. You can edit the order of the items that appear in your Shortcuts section.

The Explore section provides links to other, lesser used parts of Facebook. This includes things like links you've saved, friend lists you've created, Events, Groups, fundraisers, and any other apps that you use on Facebook.

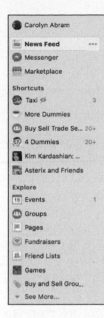

FIGURE 3-3:
A sample sidebar.

The Shortcuts section

Facebook adds items to this section as you use Facebook. For example, if you start to spend a lot of time posting and commenting on a particular group, Facebook will automatically add it to your Shortcuts section. Over time, you may wind up with more shortcuts than easily fit in this space, at which point Facebook will choose the five shortcuts you click most often to display, and the rest will be hidden behind a blue "See More" link at the bottom of the Shortcuts section. Click on that link to see a full list of your shortcuts.

In all my time using Facebook, I've never found that I needed to adjust the items in the Shortcuts menu, since Facebook automatically adds the links I use most to the top of the shortcuts menu. However, if Facebook's failed you in this regard, you can choose to pin certain shortcuts to the top of the menu. *Pinning* is the digital equivalent of keeping something stuck to the top of a list. Facebook also gives you the ability to both hide and unpin shortcuts. When you hide a shortcut, you no longer see it at all in the Shortcuts section. When you pin a shortcut, it stays visible in your side menu. It's the digital equivalent of pinning a list of your most called phone numbers to a bulletin board. When you unpin a shortcut, it still appears in the Shortcuts section after you click the See More link.

To hide or unpin a link from the Shortcuts section, follow these steps:

1. **Hover your mouse over the item you want to remove or unpin.**

An ellipsis icon appears to the right of the link.

2. **Click the ellipsis.**

A menu opens just beneath the shortcut. Depending on whether it is a group, Page or game, you may see more than two options, but each item has at least two options: Unpin from Top, and Hide from Shortcuts (see Figure 3-4).

3. **Click Hide from Shortcuts or Unpin from Top.**

The menu closes, and the link disappears from the Favorites section.

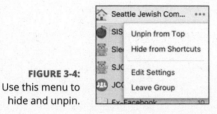

FIGURE 3-4:
Use this menu to
hide and unpin.

If you find yourself needing to click the See More link more often than you'd like to get to one of your shortcuts, you may want to pin that shortcut to the top of your Shortcuts section. To pin a shortcut, follow these steps:

1. **Click See More at the bottom of the Shortcuts section.**

This expands the Shortcuts section to display your full list of shortcuts.

2. **Hover your mouse over the item you want to pin.**

An ellipsis icon appears to the right of the shortcut.

3. **Click the ellipsis.**

A menu opens just beneath the shortcut. Depending on whether the shortcut is for a group, Page, or game, you may see more than two options, but every shortcut shows at least two options: Pin to Top, and Hide from Shortcuts.

4. **Click Pin to Top.**

The shortcut will immediately appear at the top of your Shortcuts section.

Explore

The Explore section of the sidebar lists items that you may want to, well, explore. These cover a huge range of features, tools, and destinations. At least five items appear in your sidebar all the time, the rest you can view by clicking the See More link at the bottom of the list.

Most users won't use all these features, but every user will wind up loving at least one of them. The items listed below are not comprehensive; I tried to focus on some of the most popular items, as well as ones that give you a sense of the many possibilities Facebook offers to you.

» **Groups:** Groups are a way for (you guessed it) groups of people to communicate and share with each other. Groups can be small or large and can represent real world groups or not. Groups you join are added to the Shortcuts section of the sidebar. Clicking Groups in the Explore section brings you to an overview of your groups. Groups are covered in detail in Chapter 10.

» **Events:** Facebook's Events feature allows people to easily organize and invite people to an event. You can view events you've been invited to or created by clicking this Events link in your sidebar. You can learn more about creating, managing, and finding events in Chapter 13.

» **Pages:** *Pages* are Timelines for everything that's not a regular person. Public figures like Neil deGrasse Tyson or Lady Gaga have Pages, as do small businesses, fictional characters, television shows and movies, pets of all hues and stripes, and pretty much everything else you can think of. If you are a Page owner (meaning you use Facebook to represent something other than yourself), your specific Pages appear in the Shortcuts section. Clicking to explore Pages brings you to a page where you can view all your Pages as well as tabs where you can view the Pages you have liked or find local Pages you may want to like. Chapter 14 covers creating and managing Pages.

» **Friend Lists:** Friend Lists are a feature that allows you to create clusters (or lists) of friends and then easily share directly with those friends. Think of sharing with a list as more like sending out an email blast and sharing with a group as more of a post to a message board. Facebook automatically creates certain lists (such as Close Friends) and you can create your own lists that you find useful to using Facebook. Clicking to explore Friend Lists brings you to a page where you can view and edit your lists.

» **Find Friends:** Clicking this item in your sidebar brings you to a page where you can access various tools for finding friends. Chapter 8 covers these tools in depth.

» **On This Day:** On this Day is a tool that works best once you've been on Facebook for a while. Much like a newspaper callback to notable moments in history on any given day, On this Day calls out any notable moments from your own personal history — on this day two years ago you posted a photo of the snake your cat caught in your backyard. Four years ago, you became friends with someone you later married. Clicking "On This Day" is a great way to access some quick nostalgia, if you are ever in need.

>> **Live Video:** Facebook's Live Video is pretty much what it sounds like; it's a way for all users to stream video live from their phones or other cameras. You can use it to bring your friends with you wherever you go, whether that's on a hike or to the grocery store. Many news organizations use Live Video to provide extra segments to their viewers, and often public figures will use it to share with fans. Clicking to explore Live Video allows you to select from currently streaming live videos and see what people are publicly sharing.

>> **Games:** Every day, people play various online games through Facebook. Playing on Facebook means that you can play games directly with your Facebook friends (who are, as I've mentioned before, your real-life friends). Clicking to explore Games allows you to browse the games that you can play and continue playing games you've played in the past. Interacting with games and other apps is covered in Chapter 15.

>> **Fundraisers:** People often use Facebook to promote causes they care about. In response to that, Facebook added the ability to fundraise for a cause. You can fundraise for a personal reason, or for a nonprofit. Facebook handles processing your friends' donations and getting them to the organization you select. Clicking to explore Fundraisers guides you through the process of starting your fundraising and allows you to check out other people's fundraisers. For more information on fundraising with Facebook, see Chapter 12.

>> **Saved:** Often when you're perusing News Feed (which is covered in more depth in Chapter 4) you will see a link to an article or a video that, for whatever reason, you can't fully appreciate at the moment. You can click to save that link, and then get to it later by clicking Saved in the Explore section of your sidebar.

>> **Photos:** Photos is one of Facebook's most popular features and has been for a very long time. You can share as many photos as you want with your friends, completely free. The many options available to you when you're sharing photos, such as tagging, albums, privacy, and editing are covered in depth in Chapter 11. Clicking to explore Photos in the sidebar brings you to a page displaying all the photos you have already added.

>> **Pokes:** Pokes are the original *easter egg,* or silly secret, of Facebook. It is a simple feature: you click a button to "poke" a friend. They are then informed they have been poked, and they can poke back. That's it. Click to explore pokes and you'll see a list of friends you can poke and view any pokes you've received.

>> **Buy/Sell/Trade Groups:** Buy/Sell/Trade Groups way are a popular way that people use Facebook in their communities to buy and sell used items. It's easy to create listings for anything you may be selling, communicate with potential buyers, and even use Facebook to pay one another. Clicking Buy/Sell Groups will allow you to choose from any local Buy/Sell/Trade groups that you might

be interested in. For example, I am a member of a Buy/Sell/Trade group focused on Children's Items in Seattle. You can learn more about buying and selling on Facebook in Chapter 12.

>> **Recommendations:** Ever asked a friend to recommend a dentist? Or a restaurant? Or the best place to eat in Whitefish, Montana? You can ask for recommendations on Facebook from friends informally, or slightly more formally through the Recommendations feature. When you use the recommendations feature, you add a location to your post, which lets people know *where* you're going to be when you need that information, which allows them to be the most helpful friends they can be.

>> **Town Hall:** Town Hall is a relatively new Facebook feature that uses your location information to connect you to your elected officials' Facebook Pages, from your local council-member all the way up to your president. You can follow and send messages to these public officials. You can also turn on voting reminders from Facebook.

Create

Beneath the Explore section is a short section of little links. There are all links that get you directly into the process of creating something new. Since there are so many things happening on your Home page, and so many ways to navigate around Facebook, you may find it helpful to be able to circumvent a few clicks when you know exactly what it is you want to do. You can click on any of the links in this section to immediately get started making an ad, Page, group, event, or fundraiser.

Viewing News Feed

This chapter is about navigating Facebook, which is why the blue bar and the sidebar are so important. At the same time, these menus aren't really the focus of the Home page. Instead, these menus serve as a bit of a background to the main event in the center of the page: News Feed. As I mention earlier, News Feed is really what you pay attention to when you go to the Home page.

So what is News Feed? Imagine that your morning paper, news show, or radio program included an additional section that featured articles solely about the specific people you know. That's what News Feed is. As long as the people you know are active on Facebook, you can stay up-to-date with their lives via your News Feed. A friend may post photos from his recent birthday party, another may write a post about her new job, and another may publish a public event for her upcoming art show. These may all show up as stories in your Facebook News Feed. A News Feed bonus: You can often use it to stay up-to-date on current events just by seeing what your friends are talking about or by liking the Pages of real-world news organizations and getting their updates in your News Feed. When there's unusual weather, I find out about it on Facebook first because I see a flurry of posts asking if that was really hail.

News Feed is possibly one of the best and most interesting things about Facebook, but also one of the hardest to explain. This is because no matter how I describe seeing a photo of my friend and her new baby pop up in my News Feed, it won't be as exciting as when *your* friend posts those photos. I do my best to capture at least a bit of this excitement in Chapter 4.

At the very top of News Feed is what's called the *Publisher* or *share box*, shown in Figure 3-5. This box is what you use to add your own content to Facebook: status posts, photos, links to articles you find interesting, and so on. These posts also go into News Feed and may appear in your friends' News Feeds. Your friends can then comment, like, and generally interact with you about your post. I go into more detail about how to use the Publisher in Chapter 4.

FIGURE 3-5:
Share what's on your mind from the Publisher.

Right On

Much like the left sidebar, the items you see on the right side of the page change depending on how you use Facebook. If you're a new user, you may see different things than if you have been using Facebook for a long time. People with many friends may see something different than people with fewer friends. Here are some of the items you may see on the right side of your Home page:

>> **Reminders:** You may see reminders for things like upcoming events, friends' birthdays, or requests you need to respond to.

>> **Trending:** Trending topics shows a taste of what *everyone* is talking about on Facebook. For example, if everyone is talking about a presidential candidate or a particularly hilarious video of a rat stealing a pizza slice, those topics will appear under the heading of Trending. You can click on any of the trending

topics to learn more about them. You can also click to see more or use the filters next to the word Trending to see trending topics in politics (state building icon), science and technology (beaker icon), sports (soccer ball icon), or entertainment (clapperboard icon).

>> **Ticker:** Earlier in this chapter, I mention News Feed and how it is a constantly updated list of posts from your friends and Pages you like. Well, one of the things to know about Facebook is that it isn't *all* your friends' posts. For most people, it would be overwhelming to get an update every time every friend did something on Facebook. News Feed tries to show you the best of the best. Ticker, on the other hand, shows you everything. Ticker itself shows an abbreviated summary of what happened (for example, Juliana likes Martha's link). You can then hover your mouse over that item to see details about the link Martha shared and who else likes or commented on it.

>> **Facebook Suggestions:** Facebook's suggestions are generally ways for you to continue to find and interact with people and things you may find interesting. Facebook may suggest people it thinks you would want to add as friends, Pages you might like, groups you might want to join, and so on. These suggestions are based on people, Pages, and groups you already have interacted with.

>> **Sponsored Ads:** Ads on the right side of the page appear in a section labeled "Sponsored." Facebook is 100% free for you to use, and one of the ways it pays the bills is by selling ads like these.

The Littlest Links

At the very bottom of the rightmost column are a handful of important, but infrequently needed links. These links all appear in grey text.

>> **English (US):** If you signed up for Facebook on a computer in the United States, Facebook defaults to English. If for any reason you want to change the language in which you use Facebook, click the suggested Language links next to English or the + button to open the entire list of language options.

>> **Privacy:** Details the Facebook Data Use Policy, if you're looking for a little light bedtime reading.

>> **Terms:** This link takes you to a page where you can view all of Facebook's Terms and Policies, including the Statement of Rights and Responsibilities (which you agreed to when you signed up), the Data Policy, and its Community Standards.

>> **Advertising:** Click this link to create or manage ads that you've posted to Facebook.

>> **Ad Choices:** Clicking this link brings you to the Facebook Help pages where you can learn more about how Facebook targets ads to you, and what you can do to adjust what ads you see.

>> **Cookies:** Sadly, clicking this link doesn't make chocolate chip cookies suddenly appear in your hand. Instead, it brings you to a page that explains how Facebook uses *web cookies,* or stored data on your web browser. Cookies are used on many websites to keep your experience more convenient, and to deliver ads to you.

>> **More:** Clicking this link opens a menu of still more links. Click any of these options to navigate to different parts of Facebook:

- **About:** Facebook's About page is where you can learn more about Facebook's products, the company, and what it's been doing in the news lately.

- **Careers:** If you're considering applying for a job at Facebook, check out its careers page first.

- **Create Page:** If you want to create a Page for a band, brand, celebrity, or other non-person entity, you can use this link.

- **Create Fundraiser:** If you want to create a fundraiser for any sort of cause, you can start from here.

- **Developers:** If you are a software engineer looking for ways to build apps that use Facebook, click this link to learn more about the Facebook Platform.

- **Help:** A duplicate of the link in your Account menu, this takes you to the Facebook Help Center.

>> **Chat:** At the very bottom of the right side of the Home page, you may see a box that says Chat with a green dot. Clicking on this opens a window where you can quickly send Facebook messages to your friends who are listed in the window. You can turn off Chat by clicking the gear symbol in the upper-right corner of the window and choosing Turn Off Chat. You can always turn it back on by clicking Turn On Chat from the same menu. We go over Chat in Chapter 9.

2

Day-to-Day Facebook

IN THIS PART . . .

Logging in and reading News Feed

Sharing your status, photos, and links

Checking out what's going on with friends

Interacting via comments, likes, and sharing

Using Facebook on your mobile phone

Managing your privacy

Chapter **4**

The Daily Facebook: News Feed and Posting

Sometimes after I've explained the basics of Facebook to someone — it's a website that lets you connect and share with your friends — they follow up with an obvious question: But what do you *do* with it?

The answer to that question is both very simple — you keep up with your friends — and somewhat complicated. There are so many tiny actions and interactions on Facebook that add up to a sense of being surrounded by your friends. It's that sense of friendship that keeps people coming back to Facebook day after day (and, with smartphones, minute after minute).

This book tells you how to do virtually everything you could ever want to do on Facebook, but chances are you won't create a photo album or plan an event every single day. Chances are that as you go about your day online — reading articles, watching videos, shopping, and more — you'll check in on Facebook, find out news big and small from your friends and the Pages you follow, share a few of your own thoughts or observations, and go on your way. This chapter covers those very basic activities in depth.

The main way people find out news and generally keep in touch on Facebook is through News Feed, the constantly updating list of stories about content people are posting to their Timelines. I talk about News Feed at length in this chapter, and about the ways you interact with what you see there. News Feed isn't just about reading the posts you see there; it's also about comments and likes.

You can also keep up with friends by sharing your own content — things like status updates, photos, and links to articles you read. You can post your own content from the top of News Feed and your friends will, in turn, be able to see it, like it, and comment on it.

Your Daily News . . . Feed

News Feed is the centerpiece of your Home page. When you log in to Facebook, you see the familiar blue bar on top and the left-side menu but mostly you see News Feed.

So what is News Feed? It's a constantly updating list of stories by and about your friends. *Stories* here refers to actions that your friends have taken on Facebook — things like writing a status update, sharing a photo or link, or fundraising for charity (in fact, there are a lot of different types of stories that are all detailed below in the "Common story types" section). You may also see stories from Pages that you follow. Facebook sometimes refers to stories as posts, and I use the terms interchangeably here as well.

Back in the day, a common refrain around the Facebook office was, "News Feed is a robot." More accurately, News Feed is an algorithm. It doesn't show you *everything* from your friends; instead, it tries to show you things it thinks you will find interesting. News Feed makes its selections based on a complicated calculus of who is posting what and when. News Feed will likely show you more stories from people you interact with more often on Facebook. It also tends to show you "big events" like engagements or new babies even from more distant acquaintances. News Feed also learns the sorts of stories you are likely to click on, like, or comment on, and will try to show you more of those. Simply browsing News Feed and interacting with the things you see helps News Feed to improve. There are ways for you to manually fine-tune News Feed as well, which I cover in the "Adjusting News Feed" section.

Because News Feed tries to show you what it thinks you'll find most interesting, stories might not always appear from newest to oldest. There is some bias toward new stories (especially if you log into Facebook frequently), but you might see a popular photo that a friend posted several days ago appear at the top of your News Feed instead of one from this morning if it got a lot of likes or comments. Additional likes or comments can also cause a post to reappear in your News Feed even if you've already seen it.

Anatomy of a News Feed story

Figure 4-1 shows a sample News Feed story. In this case, it's a status update from a friend. In Facebook world a *status update* refers to any text people post that answers the question "What's on your mind?"

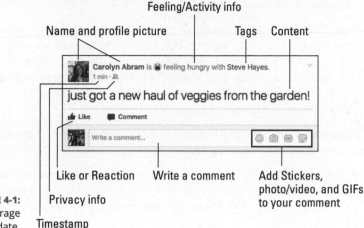

Feeling/Activity info

Name and profile picture   Tags   Content

Carolyn Abram is 😋 feeling hungry with Steve Hayes.
1 min · 👥

just got a new haul of veggies from the garden!

👍 Like   💬 Comment

Write a comment...   😊 📷 GIF 💬

Like or Reaction   Write a comment   Add Stickers,
                                                    photo/video, and GIFs
Privacy info   to your comment

Timestamp

FIGURE 4-1: Just your average status update.

Even in this tiny example, there are lots of things to pay attention to, though the first things you'll probably pick up on when you're scanning News Feed are "who" and "what":

>> **Name and profile picture:** The first part of any story is who it's about or who wrote it. Both the name and picture are links to that person's Timeline. In addition, if you hover the mouse cursor over a person's name, you'll see a miniaturized preview of the person's Timeline with information about your relationship (that you are friends and following her, in most cases) as well as a button you can click to message her.

Hovering the mouse cursor over any bolded text in a News Feed story generates a preview for a Timeline, Page, or interest with specific buttons for adding friends, liking, or following.

TIP

>> **Content:** The content section of a News Feed story is the most variable. It might be a preview of an article, or a video, or a photo album. It could also be a location where someone has *checked in,* or marked her location (the Golden Gate Bridge, her local coffee shop, etc.) when she posted. The content is the part of the story that is the most important; it's the whole reason for the story existing. In Figure 4-1, the content is a status update about my garden.

After you've got the basics and who and what down, you can focus on some of the other details to be found in a simple status update:

>> **Feeling/Activity info:** Not every status includes this, but Facebook provides a list of emotions and activities that can be appended to any status update or post. In this case, the emoji (and words) depict that I was "feeling hungry" when I wrote this status update.

>> **Tags:** Tags are a way of marking who or what is with you when you post something to Facebook. You might tag a person who is with you when you write a post, or you might tag a TV show you are watching. Tags in posts are displayed as links in blue text. You can hover the mouse cursor over these tags to view more info about that person, Page, place, or thing. In the status update shown in Figure 4-1, I tagged my friend Steve.

>> **Timestamp:** The little gray text near the profile photo in the post tells you how long ago this post was added.

>> **Privacy info:** The gray icon next to the timestamp represents the privacy of that post. Hover the mouse cursor over the icon to see who else can see the post. Usually posts are visible either to everyone (Public) or just to that person's friends.

>> **Like, Comment, and (Share):** These links allow you to interact with your friends about the content they've posted. In addition, you can see how many people have already liked a post, and you can see any comments that have been made beneath the post itself. You may also see a text box next to your own profile picture prompting you to "Write a comment . . . ." I talk more about commenting, liking, and sharing in the "Interacting with News Feed" section later in this chapter.

Common story types

News Feed is made up of all sorts of stories. Although the basic anatomy is the same, here are some of the common story types you might encounter:

>> **Status updates:** The status update post appears in Figure 4-1. Status updates are the short little posts that your friends make about what's going on in their lives.

>> **Links:** Figure 4-2 shows a post sharing a link. This is one of the chief ways I get my news: Friends share links to articles, and the previews are so interesting to me I have to read the whole article. Click the links (or the article's title) to go to the articles.

- » **Photos and Videos:** Figure 4-3 shows a photo album story. When people add photos or are tagged in photos, Facebook creates this type of story, with information about who was tagged and a sample of the photos that were added. You can include videos in photo albums (the "Play" arrow indicates a video). Click the photos or videos to see bigger versions, browse albums, and watch videos.

- » **Live Videos:** Figure 4-4 shows a Live Video story. Live Videos are just what they sound like — videos that are being streamed live from wherever the poster is. You might see a friend streaming live video from the tide pools she is exploring, or you might see live video from a celebrity at a red-carpet event. Many news organizations share live video feeds of formal press conferences, as well as more casual live videos of behind the scenes footage. Hover the mouse cursor over the video to display the video's progress bar and other controls. Click the volume icon to turn on the sound and tune in.

- » **Timeline Posts:** Figure 4-5 shows a Timeline post story between two friends. In the example here, Carolyn wrote the message on Steve's Timeline.

- » **Group and event posts:** When people post to a group or event you're a member of, it may show up in your News Feed. These stories look very similar to the Timeline posts; the second friend's name is simply replaced with the group or event name.

- » **Life Events:** People can create Life Events from their Timelines. These events can be for an event as small as buying a new pair of sunglasses, but in my experience people use them to mark big moments: weddings, babies, moving, getting a pet, buying a house, and other things that tend to be truly major developments in one's life. Figure 4-6 shows a Life Event post.

- » **Check-ins:** A check-in is a way of marking where you are. Stories about check-ins show a map of their location, as well as a preview of information about the location where that person checked in. They also may show a list of other friends who have checked in there in the past.

- » **Tags:** Stories about tags let you know what photos or posts your friends have recently been tagged in and include a preview of the photos with your friend in them. Because of the way tags work, you may be seeing photos or posts that were added by someone who is not your friend.

- » **Likes and comments:** Stories about likes and comments let you know what Pages, posts, or articles your friends have liked or commented on recently. Usually whatever your friend has interacted with is shown and linked so that you can check it out for yourself.

- » **Friendships:** Friendship stories might be about just two people becoming friends or about one person becoming friends with lots of different people.

>> **Changed cover and profile pictures:** These stories often look very similar to a regular photo story. Click through to look at the new photos on your friends' Timelines in their full-sized glory.

>> **Events:** Stories about events (usually letting you know which friends have RSVP'd *yes* to an event) include a link to the event, so if you're looking for someplace to go, you can say *yes,* too. Only public events show up here, so if you've added a private event, don't worry about people who weren't invited seeing it in News Feed.

>> **Recommendation requests:** Sometimes friends may be looking for help creating a vacation itinerary or finding a good place to buy new soccer cleats. They can ask their wise Facebook friends for help answering these sorts of questions by requesting recommendations. Recommendation request stories usually include location information and a map (like check-in stories) so that you can quickly figure out if you'll be able to help.

>> **Fundraisers**: Fundraisers are ways for people to raise money toward any sort of goal. They might be associated with a nonprofit or trying to round up some cash for a personal goal or on behalf of a friend. When you see stories about your friends' fundraisers, you get some information about the organization or cause, as well as links to learn more or donate.

>> **Read/Watch/Listen:** Certain services and websites, such as the book-reading site Goodreads, may be allowed to automatically post specific actions people take on their site to Facebook. See Chapter 15 for more information about how these applications work.

>> **Sponsored and suggested:** Suggested and sponsored stories are ads. Ads are what keep Facebook free to use, so there's no way to remove them. These ads are hopefully relevant to you and your life and may even help you find Pages or services you find interesting.

FIGURE 4-2:
Use your status
to share links
to articles.

FIGURE 4-3:
A photo story featuring the dynamic duo

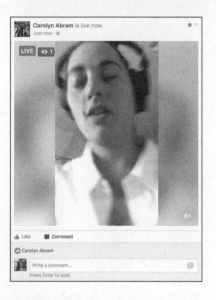

FIGURE 4-4:
Live videos let you connect with people in real time.

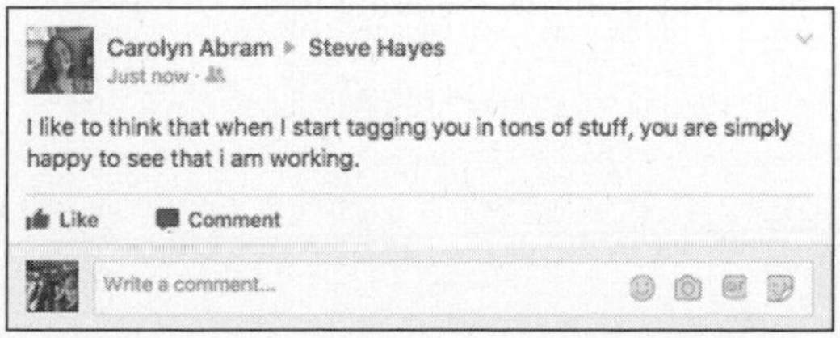

FIGURE 4-5:
A Timeline post between friends.

FIGURE 4-6:
A Life Event
post about
cutting out meat.

Trending

If you consider yourself a news junkie or are just someone who likes to know what everyone's talking about these days, you'll probably enjoy paying attention to the box labeled Trending on the right side of your News Feed, shown in Figure 4-7.

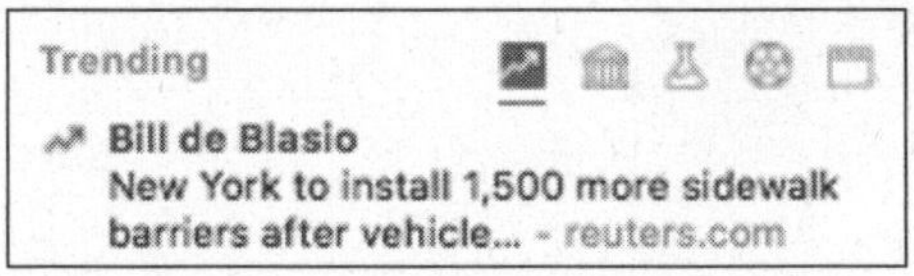

FIGURE 4-7:
Check out what
people are
sharing most.

Trending topics shows headlines that people are talking about across *all* of Facebook. So even if no one in your group of friends is posting about the latest episode of *Game of Thrones*, if enough people on Facebook are talking about it, you'll see a headline about it in the Trending box.

Clicking on any of the trending topics opens a Facebook page that compiles the articles that are being shared about any given topic, as well as related videos and photos, as well as some public posts about it.

Usually trending topics focus on pop culture or major headlines. You can filter trending topics by various categories using the icons in the upper right of the Trending box. By default, you see trending topics, signified by an arrow climbing up and to the right. You can also select from Politics (town hall icon), Science and Technology (beaker icon), Sports (soccer ball icon), or Entertainment (clapper-board icon).

Interacting with News Feed

Unlike the newspaper on your doorstep in the morning, News Feed is not just a method of delivering news. It's more of a starting place, meant to facilitate more interactions between you and your friends. Each story has at least two options at the bottom of it: Like and Comment. Many stories also have a third option: Share. Each of these options allows you to interact with your friend and their content. You can also save content you see on Facebook to go back to later.

Liking

Liking is one of the simplest actions on Facebook. Here's how you like something:

1. Click Like.

It really is that easy. Anytime you see something that is just good, you can click Like to let the person who shared it know that you liked seeing it. Like buttons may appear as text or as a thumbs up icon (or both). When you like something, the person who shared it will be notified (and trust me, being notified that someone liked something you shared is a great feeling). Additionally, other people seeing that story may see that you have liked it. If you ever like something by accident, simply click Unlike to undo it.

I don't want to overcomplicate liking by over-explaining when you might like something, when you might like something instead of commenting on it, when you might like something *and* comment on it. Suffice it to say that if you enjoyed something you saw, or that you agree with something your friend said, or that, well, you liked that content, then clicking Like communicates the sentiment loud and clear.

Reacting

Liking is the simplest way to let someone know you saw and appreciated something they posted. Sometimes, however, Like just doesn't seem appropriate. People often post stressful or sad things on Facebook; it would be insensitive to respond to "My dog had to be put down today" with *Like*. On the other side of things, sometimes Like isn't a strong enough term. Do you like that baby smiling, or do you *love it so much you want to eat its face?* Historically, you might see people commenting on these sorts of posts with one-word responses: Love. Dislike. LOL. Sad. Reactions is Facebook's way of providing more than just one button to express your sentiment. To leave a Reaction other than a Like, simply hover the mouse cursor over the Like button or link and wait for the Reactions menu to open. You can then choose your Reaction from the following options:

>> **Like:** The old standby. Click on the thumbs up icon to let your friend know you liked their post.

>> **Love:** The heart icon lets your friend know you loved their post.

>> **Haha:** The laughing smiley face lets your friend know you thought what they posted was funny.

>> **Wow:** The smiley face gaping in awe lets your friend know that you were impressed if not flabbergasted by their post.

>> **Sad:** Express a little empathy by clicking the crying smiley face. It is the virtual equivalent of a gentle pat on the back.

>> **Angry:** The virtual equivalent of a little "grrrrr," clicking the glowering smiley face lets your friend know that you are angry.

When you click any of these reactions, your friend receives a notification that you reacted to their post.

Liking Pages

You can like almost anything on Facebook. You can like a photo or a status; you can even like a comment on a photo or status. But there's a slight difference between liking this sort of content and liking Pages.

Pages are sort of official profiles that companies, bands, and public figures make to represent themselves on Facebook. They mostly work like Timelines (the key differences are covered in Chapter 14), except instead of friending Pages, you like them.

This sort of liking has one big implication you should be aware of. It means you may start seeing posts and updates from the Page in your News Feed, alongside stories from your friends. These sorts of updates can be interesting and cool if you're into the company or brand (for example, Disneyland or *The New York Times*). If they start to bother you, you can always hide that Page from your News Feed.

Commenting

Liking something is the quickest and easiest way to let your friend know that you saw what they had to say and enjoyed it. Commenting is also simple, and it takes you from a reaction — I liked this! — to a conversation. The only requirement for a comment is that you to have something to say. The comment box appears under most content on Facebook. You can see an example of it in Figure 4-8.

FIGURE 4-8:
Share your own thoughts with a comment, and it may spark a conversation.

Carolyn Abram
July 28 at 4:14pm ·

Just doing some thinking

👍 Like   💬 Comment   ➤ Share

Carolyn Abram what are you thinking about?
Like · Reply · Just now

Carolyn Abram Oh, you know, the world at large. Also the weekend
Like · Reply · Just now

Write a reply...

Write a comment...

REMEMBER

When you comment on something on Facebook, anyone who can see that item—whether it is a post, a photo, or something else—will be able to see and respond to your comment. By the same token, you can see comments from people you aren't friends with.

Adding a comment

Commenting isn't much harder than liking something. To comment on anything on Facebook, follow these steps:

1. **Click Comment.**

   The comment box expands. Frequently, this box is already expanded, in which case you can simply go on to Step 2.

2. **Click in the text box that appears.**

3. Type what you want to say.

4. Press Enter.

Pressing Enter posts your comment beneath the post. Whoever posted the item will be notified of your comment and will be able to respond.

After you comment on something, you'll be notified about subsequent comments so that you can keep up on the conversation.

Adding a comment with extras

Adding a comment is meant to be easy, but sometimes you need more than words to express yourself. For example, I once posted a photo of a fully unrolled tube of toilet paper, courtesy of my two-year-old. The comments from my friends included their own photos of toddler-toilet paper mayhem. You can add emojis, photos, *GIFs* (quick animations on loop), and stickers to comments.

» **Emojis:** Click on the smiley face icon in the comment box to open a menu of emojis you can add to your comment. Emojis range from faces to flags to food. Simply click on the emoji you want to add, and it will appear in the comment box.

» **Photos:** Click the camera icon to open a window that allows you to select photos and videos from your computer's hard drive. Click on the photo or video you want to add, then select "Choose" or "Open" at the bottom of that window. When you post your comment, the photo or video will be included.

» **GIFs:** A *GIF* is technically a type of file format for images, but people also use it to refer to short animated clips that play on a loop. These clips are often pulled from pop culture (a repeated loop of a character from a TV show rolling her eyes, for example) and can be used as a sort of visual shorthand or punctuation in text. Click on the GIF icon in the comment box to open a menu of GIFs you can add to a comment. These are sorted by trending, meaning the first few GIFs you see are the ones currently being used the most. You can use the search box to find a GIF for virtually any emotion, complex thought, or cultural meme. Simply click on the GIF you want to post it as a comment.

» **Stickers:** Like Emojis and GIFS, stickers are a way for you to add an extra visual element to your comments. Stickers are meant to be the same as their real-world counterparts, a decorative little image that brightens someone's day. Click the Stickers icon (It looks a little like a sticky note being peeled) to open a menu for choosing stickers. You can pick a category (such as Happy or Sleepy) or search by keyword for the sticker you want. Click on the sticker to post it as a comment.

One other commenting extra you can try is *tagging* a friend in your comment. Tagging is a way of creating a link between something you post and your friend's

Timeline. In this case, people often tag friends to bring their comments (or the original post) to the attention of other friends, as tagging someone sends them a notification. You can tag a friend in a comment by typing the @ symbol (that's Shift+2) and then typing your friend's name. Facebook will auto-complete as you type, and you will be able to select the person's name from a menu that appears.

Editing and Removing comments

If you decide, on second thought, your comment was a poor choice, all is not lost! You can edit or delete a comment at any time.

1. **Hover your mouse over the comment that you'd like to change or remove.**

   A small ellipsis icon appears in the upper-right corner of the comment.

2. **Click the ellipsis icon.**

   This opens a small menu with two options, "Edit" or "Delete."

3. **Select Edit to make changes to your original comment or Delete to simply remove it.**

   If you choose Edit, the comment box will reopen as if you had just finished typing your comment but not yet hit enter. If you choose to delete, you will need to confirm that you want to delete the comment.

TIP

You can delete any comments, from anyone, on your own content, by following these same steps.

REMEMBER

If you make multiple edits to a comment, you can see all your previous edits you've made by clicking the Edited link under that comment. Others may be able to see that same Edited link on your comment, especially the person who posted the content, but they won't be able to click or see any changes you've made.

Replying to and liking comments

As I mention earlier, commenting on something is a way of starting a conversation, and the way to continue that conversation is by liking or replying to comments. At the bottom of any comment, you can see two small links to Like or Reply.

Liking a comment is generally a way of saying "I agree" or "Right on!" or "That's funny." Click Like next to any comment to let the commenter know how much you enjoyed what he had to say.

Replying to a comment is as easy as clicking the Reply link beneath the comment you want to respond to. This opens a text box that says Write a reply . . . . You can then follow the same commenting steps detailed earlier.

Replies show up indented from the original comment, as shown previously in Figure 4-8.

Sharing

You've probably noticed the word *Share* being used a lot on Facebook. In addition to the Share box (also called the *Publisher*) at the top of your News Feed and Timeline, Facebook has a specific Share feature, designed to make it easy to post and send content that you find both on Facebook and on the web.

TIP

Sharing is a variation of using the Publisher, or Share box. I go over using the Publisher in the "Sharing Your Own News" section of this chapter.

Perhaps you've already noticed the little Share links all over Facebook. They show up on albums, individual photos, events, groups, News Feed stories, and more. They help you share content quickly without having to copy and paste.

If you're looking at content on Facebook that you want to show someone, simply click the Share link near it. This opens a small menu with several options:

>> **Share Now (<Privacy>):** This is the quickest way to share something. Choosing this option simply posts the content to your own Timeline (and, by extension, your friends' News Feeds). The <Privacy> notice reminds you who normally sees content that you share on Facebook. It might say "Public" or "Friends" or "Custom" depending on your privacy settings.

>> **Share:** This option opens a full Share box that allows you to add your own commentary on the content you are sharing before you share it. Use the drop-down menu at the top (shown in Figure 4-9) to choose how you'd like to share the content.

- **Share on Your Timeline:** This option posts the content to your Timeline the same way you post a link or a photo from your Share box. This means it will go into your friends' News Feeds as well. This is redundant with the Share Now option, except you also get to add any comments to your post about your friend's post before you share it.

- **Share on a Friend's Timeline:** This option is the same as copying and pasting a link into a post you leave on your friend's Timeline (but it's much easier than all that copy/paste nonsense).

- **Share in a Group:** This option allows you to post the content to a specific group you're a member of. You can find more about sharing with groups in Chapter 10.

- **Share in an Event:** This option allows you to post the content to an Event you are attending.

- **Share on a Page You Manage (for Page owners only):** If you're the admin of a Page — a Timeline for non-people — you can share things as a post from your Page.

- **Share in a Private Message:** This accomplishes the same thing as copying and pasting a link into a message to a friend. In other words, only the friend you send it to will see the link, whereas sharing via the Timeline means anyone viewing your friend's Timeline can also see the content. I talk about messages in Chapter 9.

REMEMBER

If you're choosing to share on your own Timeline, you can click the privacy drop-down menu next to the Post button to change who can see the post.

>> **Send as Message:** This option opens a message box where you can type in names you would like to message with your friend's post. You can also add a comment to the "Say something about this" section to let your friend(s) know why you are sharing it with them (yes, this is the same as the Share in a Private Message option, above).

>> **Share on a friend's Timeline:** This option lets you post the content to a friend's Timeline. Again, it is fundamentally a shortcut that accomplishes the same thing as copying and pasting a link on your friend's Timeline (and yes, it's the same as the Share on a Friend's Timeline option, above).

>> **Share to a Page:** If you're a Page owner or admin, you can use this link to share something as a post from your Page. When you click this option, you can add your commentary and decide if you want it attributed directly to the Page or from you. Followers of your Page will then be able to see that content (yes, this is the same as the Share on a Page You Manage option, above).

FIGURE 4-9:
Share here.

TIP

If you click Share on a friend's post, the friend who originally shared it is given a credit. So if you reshare an article, the post that your friends see will say Shared *<Friend's Name>*'s Post so that everyone knows where you found it.

Sharing across the Internet

If you're a reader of blogs, or a viewer of videos, or an online shopper, you probably know that virtually everything you look at has links to share it. Almost any content you share can easily be shared directly through Facebook if you are logged in to Facebook in your browser. Next time you are reading an article on your favorite site, look to see if you can spot a Facebook logo (you may need to click "share" first, and then select Facebook from a menu of options).

When you choose to share on Facebook, a Share box opens in its own window. You can then view the post, add any of your own comments, adjust the privacy, and post it to your Timeline without ever having to leave the page you were on.

Saving

For me, News Feed is one of the best sources I have for articles, videos, and legitimate old-fashioned news that I might find interesting. I follow several Pages for newspapers and magazines, and my friends are the nerdy type who read and share articles that they find interesting as well. The only problem with this is that sometimes I see articles that look interesting when I don't have time to click through and read them. That's why the Save feature is one of my favorite hidden Facebook features. Saving articles, videos, and other posts is an effective way to make a reading list for later, when you have more time. This is also a good way to bookmark helpful websites you might need later (like a list of the best pumpkin patches to visit in the fall).

To save a post, click the small down arrow in the upper right corner of the post you want to save. This opens the News Feed menu (see Figure 4-10). Click the Save post option (usually in the middle of the menu). This automatically adds the post to your Saved section. You can get to your saved posts at any time by clicking Saved in the menu on the left side of the window. Facebook may also occasionally show you a selection of your saved items in your News Feed in case you forgot about them.

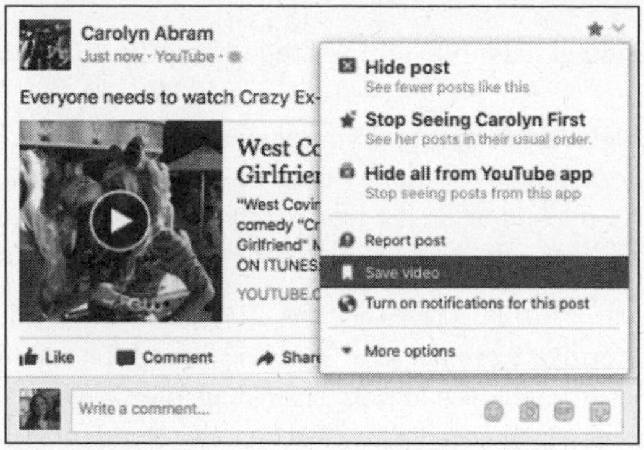

FIGURE 4-10:
Saving a video
for later.

Adjusting News Feed

News Feed is designed to learn about what you like and whom you care about and to show you stories accordingly. As you use News Feed, it learns what you like based on your clicks, comments, and likes. You can give News Feed more information to work with to make News Feed even better for you.

Hiding posts and people

There are ways to tell News Feed explicitly who you do and don't want to see (and I go over these in the "News Feed Preferences" section). But chances are you might not know what you like or don't like until you see it. Sometimes you'll realize that you will simply explode if you have to see another baby photo from a particular coworker. Sometimes someone you know just won't stop posting political screeds. And sometimes one post will just bug you and you won't want to see it anymore.

As soon as you realize you don't like what you are seeing, you can easily give this feedback to News Feed using the menu of options found as part of any News Feed story. To open this menu, click on the small down arrow in the upper right corner of any News Feed story. This menu is shown in Figure 4-11.

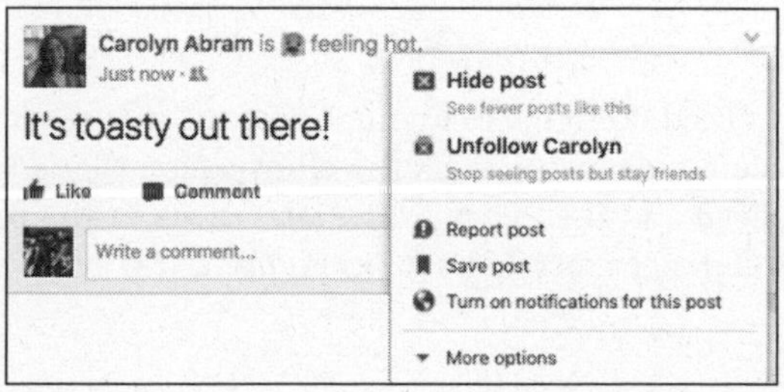

FIGURE 4-11:
Use this menu
to hide posts
and people.

This menu gives you at least two options regarding the story you are looking at

>> **Hide post:** Selecting this option will immediately hide that post from your News Feed. Additionally, Facebook will try to show you fewer posts "like this." In other words, depending on the type of story you are hiding (such as a photo story or life event) Facebook will try not to show you as many of that story type.

>> **Unfollow <Friend or Page Name>:** Selecting this option will semi-permanently prevent stories from this friend from appearing in your News Feed at all. I say semi-permanently because you will be able to undo this option later if you wish.

Selecting either option will hide the story you are looking at and display a small confirmation message to let you know that you have successfully hidden that post or unfollowed your friend. You can click the blue Undo here if you regret your actions.

If you are looking at a post that involves multiple people, such as a story about Sansa (your friend) tagged in a photo by Petyr (not your friend), you may see additional options to Hide All from Petyr. If someone is sharing a post from a Page or an App, you may also see options to hide posts from that Page or App.

REMEMBER

Unfollowing friends is different from unfriending them. Unfriending them severs the link between your Timelines and may mean you are no longer able to see certain parts of their Timeline. Unfollowing simply removes their posts from your News Feed.

News Feed preferences

Hiding posts and people is a good way to incrementally adjust your News Feed over time. But if you're looking to make a bigger impact right away, you may want to adjust your News Feed preferences instead. Your News Feed preferences allow you to choose friends you want to see first, unfollow friends you already know you don't want in your News Feed, and reconnect with people you may have unfollowed in the past.

To get to the News Feed Preferences menu, hover the mouse cursor over the News Feed link in your left-side menu. Click the ellipsis icon that appears to the left of the words News Feed and then click Edit Preferences in the menu that appears. This opens the Preferences menu shown in Figure 4-12.

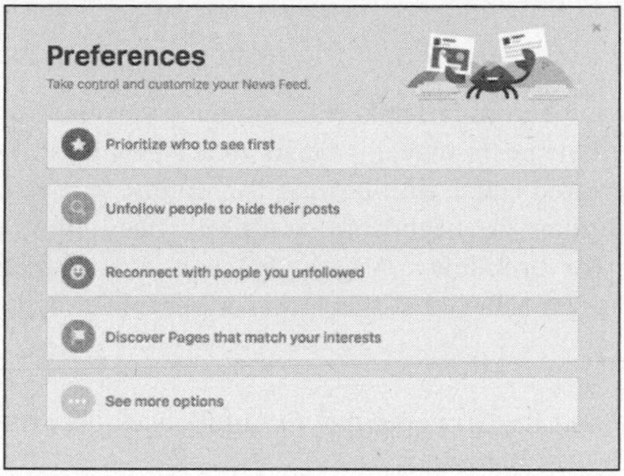

FIGURE 4-12:
The News Feed
Preferences
menu.

There are four sections of preferences you can use to influence News Feed. (The fifth option, "See more options" is simply a way to keep track of any apps you may have hidden from News Feed).

Prioritize

Prioritizing friends is a way of designating people you *always* want to see in News Feed. I prioritize people like my best friends and my husband. I also have prioritized a more distant friend who I think posts hilarious stuff, so I want to make sure I don't miss what she has to say.

Posts from prioritized friends will always be at the top of your News Feed when you log in. Unfortunately, if your friends don't post very often, there still won't be anything to show you. News Feed needs something to work with. You can see a prioritized post in Figure 4-13. The only thing that differentiates such a post (other than the fact that it's at the top of News Feed when you log in) is a tiny blue star in the upper right corner of the post.

FIGURE 4-13:
A prioritized post
in News Feed.

Click Prioritize Who to See First to open a menu for choosing people from your friend list. Facebook displays the people it thinks you'll likely want to see first at the top, you may have to scroll down a bit to find whom you're looking for. Click on any friend's face to select them (and click again to deselect them). When you're finished, click the blue Done button to save your choices.

Unfollow

By default, when you become friends with someone you also start following them. This means that their posts may appear in your News Feed. However, as not all friendships are created equal, unfollowing is a simple way to stop seeing stories while still maintaining the friendship. You don't need any particular reason to unfollow people (or unfollow a Page). You can do it because they post too frequently, or you don't like what they post, or because they just broke your best friend's heart.

To select people (and Pages) you'd like to unfollow, follow these steps from the News Feed Preferences menu:

1. **Click the Unfollow People to Hide Their Posts section.**

   This opens an interface for selecting people and Pages.

2. **Click on the people or Pages you want to unfollow.**

   When you have selected someone to unfollow, that person's profile picture will be outlined in blue and the word "Unfollowed" will appear below her name.

3. **Click Done to save your selections.**

Reconnect

If your News Feed is ever feeling a little stale or bland, you might want to consider refollowing people you had previously unfollowed. Clicking this section of the Preferences menu opens a menu for choosing from people whom you have previously unfollowed. Click on any face to add them back into the News Feed mix and then click Done.

Discover

If you don't have many friends yet, or you don't like the type of stuff your friends post, you may be able to make your News Feed more interesting to you by following Pages. Pages post all the same types of content that people do, and you may find that certain Pages actually post your favorite links or articles or top ten lists. Clicking this section of the Preferences menu opens a display of Pages your friends have liked (or are popular across Facebook). Click on any of the Page names to actually go visit that Page and see what sort of stuff they post. You can also click the like button (thumbs up icon) to immediately like and follow that Page. You can always unlike or unfollow the Page later if it turns out you don't like the things posted there.

Sharing Your Own News

While there are millions of things to do on Facebook (and this book tries to cover every single one of them), the most basic action on Facebook is sharing. The previous parts of this chapter cover how you see and interact with the things your friends have shared. Now it's time to put yourself out there and start sharing things for yourself.

First things first: Take a look at the *Publisher* (also called the Share box) at the top of your News Feed. It's shown in Figure 4-14. A very similar box appears at the top of your Timeline, and the top of most Groups and Pages. The Publisher is what you use to create and share posts with your friends. Any posts you make from the Publisher will go on your Timeline and may appear in your friends' News Feeds.

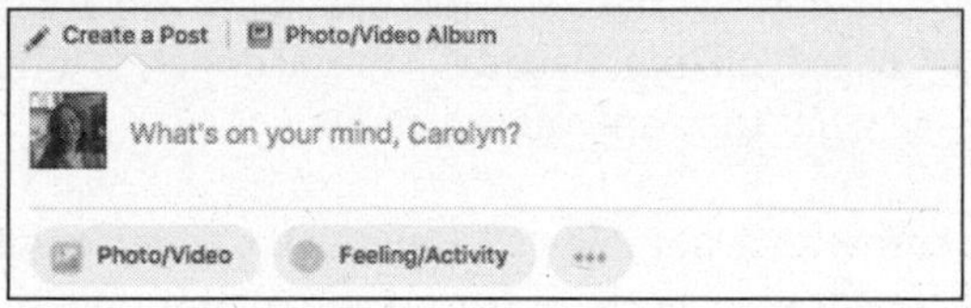

FIGURE 4-14: Start sharing here.

Like much of Facebook, there's a lot packed into this little box. Before going into all the details of what you can share and how, I start with the most basic type of post: a status update.

Status updates

A status update is a way of reporting what's going on with you right now. Facebook uses the phrase "What's on your mind?" to prompt a status update. So you can share what you're thinking about, what you're doing, or really anything. To update your status, follow these steps:

1. **Click into the Publisher, where it says, "What's on your mind?"**

   The Publisher expands and the rest of the screen fades away so that you can focus on your post.

2. **Type your status.**

   If you're experiencing writer's block, check out the upcoming section, "What should I say?"

3. **Click Post.**

   It's the blue button in the lower-right corner of the Publisher.

Like I said, sharing on Facebook is meant to be easy.

Once you've shared your status, your friends will likely see it in their News Feeds and they will be able to like and comment on your status.

What should I say?

There isn't a simple answer to the question of what you should or shouldn't post as a status update. The question "What's on your mind?" is meant to provoke whatever it is you'd like to share.

In general, sharing where you are or what you're doing are basic status reports that make sense as status updates. When I see updates from my friends they often are sharing a random thought that passed through their heads as they were out and about during the day. If there's a football game on I can often figure out what's happening based on my friends' status updates. Check out your own friends' posts to see what they are talking about.

You might share something notable you saw recently; you might tell a quick and funny story (or a longer one, as there isn't a word limit on status updates) about your day. Originally, status updates all started with the words "<Carolyn> is. . ." and for the most part status updates tend to be about what you're doing or think-ing about right now. All the examples captured in the figures in this chapter are the sorts of posts I see regularly on Facebook. If you're feeling uninspired, feel free to post that you are reading *Facebook For Dummies*.

Beyond the basic status update

Now that you know the basics of posting a status update, you can learn more about all the other buttons and options you see in the Publisher. Adding links to your updates allows you to share interesting things you've found all over the Internet. You can also click any of the buttons at the bottom of the Publisher to add a pop of color to your post, or you can add photos, tags, and details about what you're doing and where you are. You can combine almost all these additions to your posts, for example adding first an emoji, then a photo. However, you can't add both links and photos from your hard drive at the same time.

Adding a background

Adding a background color or design is a fun way to add some personality to a post. When you add a background color it also changes the format and font size of your post, so it gives your words a certain amount of emphasis that they don't always have in a traditional status update. You can see the difference between a regular status update and one with a background color, as shown in Figure 4-15.

FIGURE 4-15:
Adding a
background color
gives your words
a little more pop.

To add a background color, simply click on one of the colorful squares that appear beneath your text when you start typing a status. As soon as you click on a color, your text will appear on that background. You can then play around with what you want to say, as well as clicking between the different colors and designs to find the one that fits your post best. When it's to your liking, click Post.

TIP

If you ever start creating a post and decide you don't like it, click the X in the upper right corner of the Publisher to cancel everything you've done and go back to News Feed.

Adding links

To add content from another website to your post, simply copy and paste the link into the Publisher. Facebook will automatically generate a preview for the content based on the link. Previews usually include an image, a headline, and a description. Depending on the content you are sharing, you may be able to choose from different thumbnail photos. You can also hover over the thumbnail image and click the X that appears in the upper-right corner to remove the image entirely.

Once you get your preview looking the way you want, you can delete the original link (the preview will remain) and use the space above to share your thoughts about your link. When you're ready to share, click Post.

Adding an emoji

An *emoji* is a smiley face icon or other small-sized image that you can insert into your post. To select from a menu of emoji, click on the smiley face icon on the right side of the Publisher's text box. When you see the emoji you want to add, click it. You can add emoji to text or simply create a post made entirely of emojis. You can see an example of emoji in Figure 4-16.

FIGURE 4-16: Emojis help you express all the feels.

Adding a photo or video

Click the Photo/Video button in the lower half of the Publisher to add a photo to your post. When you click this, it opens an interface for navigating your computer's hard drive to find the photo you want to add.

TIP

Often some of the best photos you want to share on Facebook are on your phone. You can learn how to share photos directly from your smartphone in Chapter 7.

Once you've selected the photo (or photos) you want to add, click Choose or Open. This brings you back to the Publisher. The photos you've added will appear as small square thumbnails within your post. Hovering the mouse cursor over this thumbnail causes three new icons to appear. Click the X in the upper-right corner of the thumbnail to remove that photo from your post. Select the left icon (a person with a tag) to *tag* the people who are in that photo. Tagging is a way of linking a photo to one of your friends' Timelines. That way people will know who is in your photo, and your friend's friends will be able to see the photo as well.

Select the Paintbrush icon (on the right side of the photo thumbnail) to edit your photo. Clicking this opens a larger preview of your photo with editing options along the left of the screen. The options for editing are: filters, tag, crop, add text, and add stickers. For more information on these options, see Chapter 11.

TIP

Click the +Album button at the bottom of the Publisher to add these photos to one of the albums you've already created on Facebook. They will be added to the end of that album in addition to creating a new post with them.

When you're happy with the photos you've chosen, you can add more text or other information to the post, or simply click Post to share.

Adding a tag

A *tag* is a way of linking someone or something else to your own content on Facebook. Most often tags are used to let people know who is in a photo, but tags can also be used in status updates to let people know who is with you. People also use tags to bring certain friends' attention to something they are posting. For example, you might see a status update that says something like "Who's up for going climbing? **Jon, Ygritte?**" Each bolded name links to a friend's Timeline. Additionally, those friends get notified when the post is published, which means they definitely see the invitation to go climbing.

There are two ways to tag someone in your post. The first is to type the @ symbol (that's Shift + 2) and begin typing the name of the person you want to tag. Facebook auto-completes as you type. When you see your friend's name highlighted, hit Enter or select it with your mouse. When you tag someone this way, the tag appears as part of the post: "Way better than **Tyrion** at brooding."

The second way that you can add a tag is by clicking the Tag Friends button at the bottom of the Publisher. Clicking this opens a small text field at the bottom of the Publisher that asks, "Who are you with?" Again, start typing your friend's name and press Enter when you see it highlighted in the auto-complete menu. When you tag people this way, their name gets appended to the top of the post: "Get busy brooding — with **Tyrion**." You can see both types of tags in Figure 4-17.

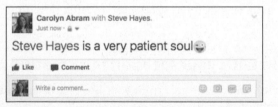

TIP

In addition to people, you can tag Pages. For example, you might want people to know that you are very excited about the latest episode of *Game of Thrones*. Type the @ sign and start typing **Game of Thrones**, and you'll find that it also appears in the auto-complete menu.

Adding what you're doing or feeling

Clicking the Feeling/Activity button opens a menu of choices to explain what you are doing, thinking, or feeling while writing your status update. You may be feeling blessed, or baking cookies, or traveling to the Grand Canyon. The options here are virtually endless. The information you enter here gets appended to your post, often with a tiny *emoji,* or icon, that further illustrates what you are doing or feeling. Additionally, if something you are doing has a page or information about it on Facebook, Facebook may add a preview of that information to your post. Figure 4-18 shows an example of a post with information about what I am celebrating. There is an emoji of confetti and a horn to signify New Year's Eve.

FIGURE 4-18: A post with activity information.

You can only add one thing you are doing or feeling to a post, so unfortunately you cannot be both feeling conflicted and watching *Game of Thrones* at the same time, as far as your posts go.

Adding a sticker

Stickers are a way to add a slightly more detailed visual element to your post. Much like their real-world counterparts they run the gamut from a simple image to a complicated drawing. They are bigger than the emojis that you can add and appear at the top of your post. To add a sticker, click the Sticker button in the lower half of the Publisher. This opens a menu for choosing stickers. You can click on a topic that piques your interest or enter a search term to find the sticker that best reflects your post.

Checking in with your location information

Facebook uses information it gets from your browser to automatically append at least a small amount of location information (usually your city) to your posts. You can click Check In to add more specific location information. Clicking Check In opens a small text field that asks, "Where are you?" Start typing where you are — that might be a place like a coffee shop or an airport, or a city or a landmark. Facebook auto-completes as you type; when you see your desired location highlighted, press Enter to check in there.

Controlling who sees your posts

The big question people often have before they share something on Facebook is "Who is going to see this?" Facebook makes it easy to know who will see a post as you are creating it. In the bottom left corner of the Publisher is the Privacy menu, shown in Figure 4-19.

FIGURE 4-19:
The Privacy
menu.

The Privacy menu has four very basic options that allows you to simply decide who will see your post. There are some more advanced options I touch on briefly here but that will be covered in more detail in Chapter 6.

Public posts

By default, when you sign up for Facebook, your posts are public. When something is public, it means that anyone can see it. It doesn't mean, however, that everyone *does* see it. Due to the volume of content on Facebook (two billion people adding even one post a day is a *lot* of posts) the chances of a true stranger seeing your post is low. Rather, the people in the "public" who will likely see your post are friends of your friends or other people whom you in some way interact with on Facebook — through a shared group, for example. If someone were to search you out and visit your Timeline, that person would be able to see any public posts you've made there.

Friends only posts

The second main option presented to you in the privacy menu is "Friends." Posts that are visible to friends are only visible to people you have added as friends. You already know that when you post something, it may appear in your friends' News Feeds; the same holds true when you set your privacy to Friends. Friends of friends will not be able to see your post, even if your friend comments on it. Someone searching you out and viewing your Timeline would not be able to see your post. This privacy option is why I recommend that you never accept friend requests from strangers. When you know everyone whom you are friends with, it is easy to know who can see your posts.

Friends except posts

Even though I recommend that you only accept friend requests from people you would willingly share all your posts with, sometimes that is just not possible. We all know what it's like to get a friend request from someone it's just not acceptable to reject (love you, Mom!). And sometimes our posts just are not meant for their eyes. Choosing this option opens a window where you can type in the names of friends you *don't* want to see your post.

Only Me posts

Posts that have this setting are visible to, you guessed it, only you. Frankly, I don't think I have ever used this setting. If I don't want *anyone* to see something, I don't put it on Facebook.

Privacy is a way of controlling who can see what, but the easiest way to measure it is not in counting the number of people who can see something. If you have a huge Friend List (and many people do) does the difference between something being available to 500 people or to 1,000 people or to 1,000,000,000 people matter? Well, maybe. The way I usually measure privacy is not numerical but emotional. Do you feel comfortable? Do you feel safe? These are the questions I think you should answer when you are choosing between privacy settings.

Whichever option you choose, the next time you go to post something, that same option will be selected. Facebook assumes that most of the time you are interested in sharing with the same people — either friends or everyone — so it doesn't force you to change your privacy each time you post.

Advanced sharing options

Often, people ask me about sharing content with a subset of their friends. This might be because they are only comfortable sharing with a small group of people, or because their Friend List includes people like their bosses or family members with whom they don't want to share everything. People also sometimes worry about being annoying to their friends. Parents on Facebook often get teased about adding too many photos of their babies, so a new mom or dad might want to share all those baby photos with a smaller group of people who *definitely* want to see them. There are three main ways to accomplish this: Friend Lists, groups, or custom privacy.

FRIEND LISTS

Friend Lists are a way of sorting friends into categories. These categories remain private to you; friends aren't notified when you add them to a friend list. Facebook also creates some lists for you automatically (you can edit those lists later, if you want). If you click on "More" and then "See All" in the privacy menu, you will see some of these lists appear: Close Friends, Family, <Current City>, and any other lists you have created. Selecting the list you want to share with means that only those friends will be able to see whatever it is you are posting. So if you want to post your thoughts about a ballot measure in your local elections, you could choose only to share that with friends in your city. Friend Lists are covered in Chapter 8.

GROUPS

Groups are a lot like lists when you use them to categorize your friends, except that groups provide a destination for all members to share content together. When you add friends to a group, Facebook notifies them of it and they must decide whether to stay in the group. Groups can be a really easy way to share content with a smaller circle — the dilemma of new parents with lots of photos of their babies can be relieved by creating a "Photos of Junior" group and inviting friends to join. Friends who would rather not see your baby photos all the time can leave the group, and people who stay in the group know what they are signing up for.

To share something with a group, navigate to that group's Home page from your left-side menu. Then use the Publisher there (it works the same as the Publisher at the top of your News Feed) to share your post. By default, friends in a given group are notified when you post something and may see that post in their News Feed. Groups are covered in greater detail in Chapter 10.

CUSTOM PRIVACY

Another option when you select More and then See All from the privacy menu is custom privacy. Custom privacy allows you to be incredibly specific in terms of choosing who can and cannot see your post. You can use it to specify that people in Seattle can see your post, but not Josh or David. Or that your friends can see it, but not people you went to high school with. I've seen people plan surprise parties this way: by posting a reminder about Phil's birthday and then reminding people that Phil can't see that post. I go over exactly how to use the Custom Privacy menu in Chapter 6.

REMEMBER

When you choose a new privacy option, that same choice will remain the next time you post something.

SB: THE POLITICS OF NEWS FEED

If you lived in the U.S. during the 2016 Presidential Election, chances are you heard a bit about Facebook and how it related to the election. There were two main parts of this: the proliferation of fake news headlines and the simple exhaustion many people felt (on both the right and the left) with what felt like constant political battles waged in comment threads between friends and strangers alike.

In response to the fake news issue, Facebook built a few tools for marking content as fake, or, as Facebook euphemistically puts it, "disputed." When people report content, Facebook has an option for reporting something because it is false. Things that get marked as false often enough may be reviewed by independent fact-checkers. If the fact-checkers find it to be false, that article or video or photo will then appear with a red warning badge next to it. Clicking that badge gives you more information about why it is considered disputed.

The difficulty of navigating a Facebook that seems full of political landmines is a little more complex. I, personally, really like to read articles that my friends share about politics, but hate discussing them via comments. Other people hate seeing these sorts of articles at all. Other people love to get into a good old-fashioned intellectual debate in the comments section. Still others love to get in a good old-fashioned *flame war*, where two people basically insult each other savagely and at length over any topic. My advice for dealing with politics on Facebook hopefully applies to everyone except the latter group, who I suspect aren't really looking for advice on this matter.

- **It's okay to opt out:** As I said, comment discussions are not really my jam, so I just don't do it. I don't really read all the comments on the articles I read. I read the articles, think my thoughts, and maybe talk about them with my family and friends. If you don't like these sorts of discussions, don't take part. If a discussion you don't like is taking place on something you posted, ask that people keep it civil or take it elsewhere. Or delete their posts. You, personally, are not obligated to broker peace between two disagreeing relatives or between yourself and a former classmate who has completely opposing views to you. If you like these discussions but are reaching the end of your rope, simply stop. Step away from the keyboard for a little while. Come back to it when you're ready. Or don't come back to it. That's okay too.

- **Keep it civil:** This is a big one. Remember that whatever you are saying is being read by real, live people with real feelings. It's easy to think of them as just that smiling little profile photo (and how dare they smile at you when you're being serious!) but they aren't that. They are a living, breathing person who has a mom who loves them and dreams for their life that have nothing to do with you. If you find yourself getting heated, ask yourself, "would I say this if they were sitting next to me? would I say this to a family member I disagreed with?" We are all capable of great compassion, and sometimes it's easy forget that when you are online.

- **Unfollow and Hide without regret:** Are you sick of seeing articles from certain news outlets? You can prevent posts from that source from showing up in your News Feed by clicking the little arrow in the top right corner of any post. You can then choose to hide a post or stop seeing stories from <PartisanNews.com>. If you know there are certain people whose posts set you off, unfollow them. They won't find out and you might find that you're seeing more of the things you like in News Feed. You can also hide comments for any reason—you don't agree, you find it annoying, or they confused its and it's and you cannot stand for such a thing. Hover over the comment you want to hide, click the ellipsis icon that appears in its upper right corner, and select Hide Comment from the menu that opens (sometimes comments appear with a small X in the upper right corner, which instantly hides the comment when clicked). Remember, this is your Facebook, so you get a big say in what you're looking at.

- **Report people and content freely. . .:** Facebook is a place where people can discuss contentious issues. However, it is not a place where people can be abusive or promote hate speech. If someone is being abusive (to you or to another user) or if they are promoting hate and violence towards another person or group of people, report them! You can report posts from the same Hide Post/Unfollow menu in the upper right corner of a post. If you want to report a comment, you must first hide it. After you do so, a link appears which you can click to report the comment. You will need to select a reason.

- **. . . but remember that "I don't agree" is not in the menu of options for reporting:** Alas, just because you report something doesn't mean it actually runs afoul of Facebook's nebulous rules. Items you report may or may not get taken down, and it should in no way be used to punish people with whom you disagree.

Chapter **5**

Timeline: The Story of You

One of the fun things about writing *Facebook For Dummies* has been noting what's important in my life based on the examples I use to explain certain concepts. When I wrote the first edition, I was just out of college and every example usually related to Ultimate Frisbee, whether it was posting photos (of a Frisbee game) or planning an event (like a Frisbee match). By the second edition, I'd been working a little bit longer and used examples related to some really fun travels I'd taken. The third edition was all about my wedding, the fourth about my time in grad school, the fifth about my new baby, the sixth about my second baby, and for this edition, well, turns out my two toddlers are still taking up a lot of space. As it turns out, your life can change a lot over the course of several years.

That moment of looking backward and seeing how far you've come is the idea behind the Facebook Timeline. Like many websites, Facebook wants you to establish a profile with the basic biographical information — where you're from, what you do, where you went to school. But in addition to that, Facebook also wants you to keep updating and posting and sharing and marking events that define you. Then it turns all that information into a virtual scrapbook that you and your friends can explore. That virtual scrapbook is your Timeline.

Although Facebook does a lot of the work, this is *your* Timeline, so all aspects of it can be edited, modified, and changed based on how you want to represent yourself and your history. This chapter covers all the ways you edit the information and appearance of your Timeline, as well as who can see what on your Timeline.

Scrolling Through Time

Figure 5-1 shows the top of a Timeline. The Timeline has a few different portions: the big cover photo and the smaller profile picture, the navigation tabs beneath the cover photo, the About (or Intro) box, the Share box, and the Timeline itself, extending from the present back and back and back to the day you were born.

FIGURE 5-1:
The top of a Timeline.

In terms of navigating the Timeline, the most important thing to know is that *you scroll down the page to go back in time.* As you scroll down, posts you and your friends have made and life events you have added keep on showing up. When you start scrolling down, a new menu appears at the top of the page (below the blue bar at the top). I call this the *Timeline navigator* (see Figure 5-2).

FIGURE 5-2:
Use the navigator to activate your nostalgia.

The Timeline navigator uses a series of drop-down menus to help you jump around in time. Click any of the buttons to view a drop-down menu of options (clicking your name will bring you back to the top of your Timeline):

>> **Timeline:** This drop-down menu lets you switch from the Timeline itself to the About section of your Timeline. I cover the About section in the "All About Me" section later in this chapter.

>> **Recent:** This drop-down menu lets you hop from year to year on your Timeline. As you go further back by year, an additional drop-down menu, All Posts, appears that lets you jump from month to month within a year.

First Impressions

If you're brand new to Facebook, your Timeline may seem a little empty compared to those of your friends. That's okay; your Timeline will fill up as you start to update your status, post links, and so on (see the upcoming "Telling Your Story" section). But before you do all that, you want to get the basics filled out so that people can find you, recognize you, and learn a little bit about you. This section covers the very first thing people see when they arrive on your Timeline: your cover photo and your profile picture.

These two photos at the top of your Timeline present the first impression to all visitors to your Timeline. The cover photo is the larger photo that serves as a background to your Timeline. People often choose visually striking photos or images that speak to who they are and what they love. To change your cover photo, follow these steps:

1. **Hover over your existing cover photo.**

A camera icon and the words Update Cover Photo appear in the upper-left corner of the existing cover.

2. **Click the camera icon.**

The Update Cover Photo menu appears with four options: Choose From My Photos, Upload Photo, Reposition, and Remove.

If you're using a Facebook Mobile app that syncs with your smartphone, you may also see an option to Take a New 360 Photo. Choosing this option lets you take a panoramic view of your surroundings with your phone's camera.

3. **Click Choose From My Photos to select a cover photo from photos you've already added to Facebook.**

The Choose from My Photos window appears, as shown in Figure 5-3. By default, it shows Recent Photos. You can get to a full list of your photos by clicking Photo Albums in the upper-right corner.

4. **Choose Upload Photo to select a cover photo from your computer.**

A window for navigating your computer's files appears.

5. **Select your cover photo from the options either on Facebook or on your hard drive.**

This brings you back to your Timeline, where you should see the new cover photo in place with the overlaid message, Drag to Reposition Cover.

TIP

Because the cover photo spans the width of your Timeline, you may occasionally find that when you try to add some photos as your cover, you get an error telling you that it isn't wide enough. Make sure your cover photo is at least 720 pixels wide to ensure that it will fit.

6. **Click and drag your cover photo to position it correctly within the frame of the screen.**

7. **Click Save Changes.**

Your new cover photo is now in place.

FIGURE 5-3:
Use the Choose from My Photos window to choose a cover photo.

TIP

If you don't like the way your cover photo is positioned, you can use the same Change Cover menu to either reposition or remove your cover photo. You can change your cover as often as you want.

Your profile picture is the smaller photo. This photo is what sticks with you all around Facebook, appearing wherever you comment or post something. For example, your friends may see your status post in their News Feeds, accompanied by your name and profile picture. Most people use some variation of a headshot for their profile picture. There are several ways to add a profile picture.

Add a profile picture that's already on Facebook

If you skip to Chapter 11, you'll see that Facebook is the number-one photo-sharing site on the web, which means there's a good chance someone has already added a photo of you to Facebook that you might like to use as a profile picture.

Use these steps to change your profile picture to one that is already on Facebook:

1. **Hover your mouse over your existing profile picture.**

   The Update Profile Picture button appears.

2. **Click the Update Profile Picture button.**

   The Update Profile Picture window (shown in Figure 5-4) appears. Across the top are three options: Upload Photo, Add Frame, and Edit Thumbnail (indicated by a pencil icon). The bottom part of this menu displays photos of you that are already on Facebook that you may want to choose as your profile picture.

3. **To choose from the photos of you on Facebook, browse the displayed photos.**

   This window displays several rows of photos. Each row shows a certain category of photos such as Your Photos (photos you've previously added to Facebook) and Photos of You (photos in which you've been tagged). You can see more photos in any category by clicking the See More link on the right side of any row of photos.

4. **Select the photo you want as your profile picture by clicking it.**

   This brings you to the photo cropping interface, as shown in Figure 5-5.

5. **Using the cropping functions, choose the portion of the photo you want as your profile picture.**

   Move the transparent box around the photo by clicking and dragging the photo. Zoom in and out using the slider on the bottom of the box. Zooming out will include more of the photo in the profile picture, zooming in will allow you to zero in on your own face.

TIP

In the lower-left corner of the cropping interface is a Make Temporary button. People often want to change their profile pictures just for a day or two—for example, changing your profile picture to a photo of your wedding on your anniversary—clicking this button allows you to choose a date for your picture to switch back to your normal profile picture.

6. **Click Save when you've finished.**

This step takes you back to your Timeline. The new profile picture should be visible.

FIGURE 5-4: Choose your profile picture here.

FIGURE 5-5: Crop profile picture to focus on just you.

Add a profile picture from your hard drive

If there aren't any photos of you on Facebook that would make suitable profile pictures, you can choose a photo from your computer's hard drive:

1. **Hover the mouse over your existing profile picture.**

   The Update Profile Picture button appears.

2. **Click the Update Profile Picture button.**

   The Update Profile Picture window appears (refer to Figure 5-4). Across the top are three options: Upload Photo, Add Frame, and Edit Thumbnail (indicated by a pencil icon). The bottom part of this menu displays photos that are already on Facebook that you may want to choose as your profile picture.

3. **Select Upload Photo.**

   An interface for navigating your computer's hard drive appears.

4. **Locate and click the desired photo.**

5. **Click Open or Choose.**

   This brings you to the photo cropping interface, shown in Figure 5-5.

6. **Using the cropping functions, choose the portion of the photo you want as your profile picture.**

7. **Move the transparent box around the photo by clicking and dragging the photo. Zoom in and out using the slider at the bottom of the interface. Zooming out will include more of the photo in the profile picture, zooming in will allow you to zero in on your own face.**

8. **Click Save when you've finished.**

   This step takes you back to your Timeline. The new profile picture should be visible.

Add a frame to your profile picture

Often people use their profile pictures as way to show solidarity with something that's happening in the world. This can run the gamut from expressing sympathy for victims of a natural disaster to supporting certain legislation, to rooting for your alma mater during football season. Frames are the easiest way to modify your profile picture for these reasons. Frames are just what they sound like, something that goes around your picture. Frames are created by outside developers, submitted to Facebook, and assuming they adhere to Facebook's guidelines and policies, available for you to add to your profile picture. To add a frame to your profile picture, follow these steps:

1. **Hover the mouse over your existing profile picture.**

The Update Profile Picture button appears.

2. **Click the Update Profile Picture button.**

The Update Profile Picture window (shown in Figure 5-4) appears. Across the top are three options: Upload Photo, Add Frame, and Edit Thumbnail (indicated by a pencil icon). The bottom part of this menu displays photos that are already on Facebook that you may want to choose as your profile picture.

3. **Select Add Frame.**

An interface for choosing frames, shown In Figure 5-6, appears. Facebook displays the most popular frames by default on the left side of the screen. You can use the search box at the top of the interface to look for something specific like a particular sports team.

4. **Click on any frame to see what it will look like on your profile picture**

Whenever you choose a frame, the profile picture on the right side of the interface shows you what that frame will look like on your picture. You can click and drag your profile picture to reposition it within the frame, as well as use the slider to zoom in and out on your picture.

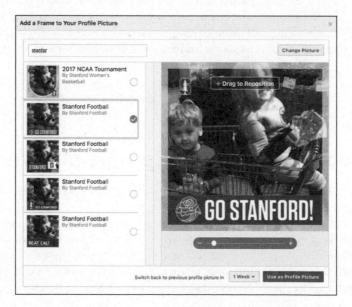

FIGURE 5-6:
Add a frame to make your profile picture say something

5. **When you're happy with your frame, click Use as Profile Picture.**

By default, Facebook has frames expire after one week, meaning that after a week your picture will go back to its frame-less state. You can change how long your frame will stick around using the drop-down menu next to the blue Use as Profile Picture button.

Much like your cover photo, you can change your profile picture as often as you choose. Every photo you select as your profile picture is automatically added to the Profile Pictures album.

REMEMBER

Your cover photo and profile picture are visible to anyone who searches for you and clicks on your name. Make sure you're comfortable with everyone seeing these images.

Telling Your Story

Getting back to the main focus of your Timeline, take a look at the stuff below the cover photo. Two columns run down the page:

>> The skinny column on the left side contains some biographical info, as well as sections about your friends and photos. I go over this in the Sections portion of this, well, section.

>> The wider right column is where posts and life events live. These posts might be something you've added to Facebook, like a status or a photo or something someone has added to Facebook about you, like a photo tag. These posts constitute your Timeline. As you scroll down your past, you can see what you were posting last week, last month, last year.

Whether you joined Facebook yesterday or five years ago, you can use Facebook to highlight important events in your life that are happening now or in years past. This section goes over the basics of sharing your story, from the ongoing process of status updates and photo posts to the posting of life events to the capability to curate your Timeline to highlight your favorite posts and events.

Posts

Posts are the type of sharing you'll be doing most often on Facebook. These are the bread and butter of sharing. People post as often as they like about an array of topics. And they post things from the Share box, also known as the Publisher. The Publisher is the text field at the top of your Timeline's right column, as shown in Figure 5-7.

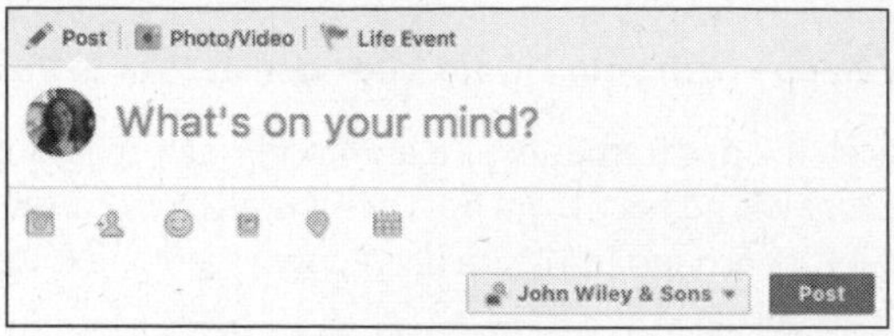

FIGURE 5-7:
The Publisher on
the Timeline.

The Publisher is what you use to post content — statuses, photos, places, links, and so on — to your Timeline. When you post content, you can also choose who can see it. Friends and subscribers then may see these posts in their News Feeds when they log in.

The Publisher on your Timeline is very similar to the Publisher at the top of your News Feed. Both are used to create posts. You can use either one to add a status, photo, video, or link. You can add tags, emotions, and location information to posts made in either Publisher. The main difference is that the Publisher on your Timeline also lets you create life events, and lets you change the date of your post to add content (like photo albums) to the proper point in your history.

Status

The most common type of post that you see people make from the Share box is a basic text update that answers the question, "What's on your mind?" On Facebook, people refer to this type of post as a *status update* or just as their *status.* Status updates are quick, short, and completely open to interpretation. People may update them with what they may be doing at that moment ("Eating a snack"), offer a random observation ("A cat in my backyard just caught a snake!"), or request info ("Planning a trip to India this summer. Anyone know where I should stay?"). It's very easy for friends to comment on statuses, so a provocative update can really get the conversation going. I comment on commenting in Chapter 4.

Status updates sound small and inconsequential, but when they're added together, they can tell a really big story for one person or for many people. For close friends, these statuses let you keep up-to-date on their daily lives and share a casual laugh over something that you might never hear about otherwise. As a collective, statuses are how news spreads quickly through Facebook. Because your posts go into your friends' News Feeds, a single update can have a big impact and is somewhat likely to be repeated in some way or another. For example, news of a minor earthquake in my area spread faster on Facebook than it did on news sites.

To update your status, follow these steps:

1. **Click in the What's on Your Mind field of the Share box.**

   This step expands the Share box.

2. **Type your comment/thought/status.**

3. **(Optional) Add any extra details you want to your post:**

- **Background Color**: If you want your status to appear on a colorful background instead of the usual black on white text box, choose from the colors displayed at the bottom of the Share box when you start to type.

- **Photo or Video (camera icon)**: You can add photos or videos from your computer's hard drive by clicking the camera icon and selecting the photos you want.

- **Tags (+ person icon)**: Tags are ways of marking people you're with when you're writing a status update. The tags link back to your friends' Timelines and notify them of your update.

  If you want to tag someone as part of a sentence as opposed to just noting that he's with you, add an @ symbol and begin typing the person's name. Facebook auto-completes as you type, and the tag appears as part of your status update: for example, <Eric> kicked my butt at Settlers of Catan.

- **Doing/Thinking/Feeling Information (lower smiley face icon)**: You can add details to your status about what you're reading, watching, listening to, feeling, doing, and so on. Click on this icon and select from the menu that opens up to choose what you are doing and append it to your post.

- **Photo Albums (photo album icon)**: If you're posting a photo, you can choose to add it to an already existing album by clicking this icon.

- **Location info or check-in (pin icon)**: You can click this pin and begin typing a city or place name, and Facebook tries to auto-complete the place where you are. A post with location info is often referred to as a *check-in*.

- **Emojis (smiley icon on the right side of the share box)**: If you want to add emojis to your post, click this icon to browse Facebook's selection and find the one that best fits your post.

4. **(Optional) Click the audience menu in the lower-right corner to change who can see this particular post.**

You can choose from the usual options: Public, Friends, Friends Except, or Custom . . . . Whatever you select will be saved for your next status post. In other words, if I post a link to Friends, the next time I go to update my status, Facebook assumes I also want to share that with Friends. I go over post privacy, including more advanced privacy options, in Chapter 6.

5. **Click Post.**

TIP

If that made you feel like updating your status requires way too much work, I want to remind you how many of those steps are optional. You can follow the abridged version of the preceding if you prefer:

1. **Click in the Share box.**
2. **Type your status.**
3. **Click Post.**

POSTS WITH LINKS

Frequently, people use their status updates to bring attention to something else on the Internet. It may be an article they found interesting, or an event, a photo album, or anything else they want to publicize. Usually, people add a comment to explain the link; other times, they use the link itself as their status, almost as though they're saying, "What I'm thinking about right now is this link."

Posts with links mean you can share something you like with a lot of friends without having to create an email list, call up someone to talk about it, or stand behind someone and say, "Read this." At the same time, you're almost more likely to get someone to strike up a conversation about your content because it's going out to more people, and you're reaching a greater number of people who may be interested in it.

To post a link, simply follow the instructions for updating a status and copy and paste the link you want into the field where you normally type a status. This automatically expands a preview of what your post will look like, including a preview of the content (as shown in Figure 5-8).

A preview usually contains a headline, a thumbnail photo, and teaser text. You can add your own thoughts about the link to the space above the preview.

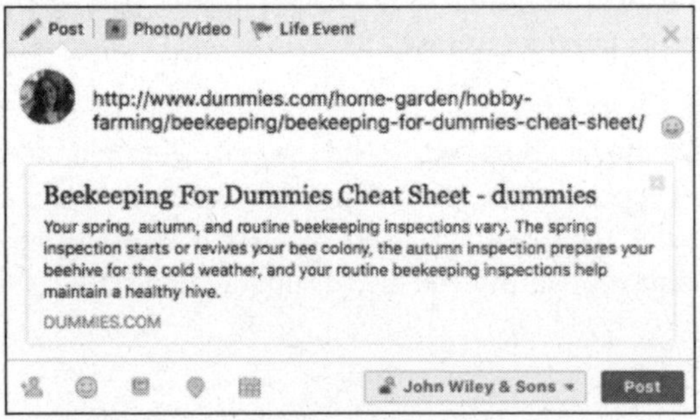

FIGURE 5-8: A preview of your post.

TIP

If you delete the URL text from the Share box, it doesn't actually remove the link from your post. In fact, deleting the link can make your post look cleaner and leave more room for your own thoughts about the link.

PHOTOS AND VIDEOS

Facebook is actually the Internet's number-one photo-sharing website. In other words, people love to share photos, and they post a lot of them on Facebook. In Figure 5-7, you can see that Photo/Video is one of the options at the top of the Publisher. You can also click the camera icon to add photos to a status update. Consider these facts a teaser trailer for Chapter 11, where we go over the entire Photo application, including adding photos and videos from the Publisher.

Life events

Part of what's nice about Facebook is the way it lets you connect with friends over the small stuff: a nice sunset on your walk home, a funny observation in the park (cats in strollers! Hilarious!). But Facebook is also awesome for letting you connect over the big stuff. Babies being born, houses being purchased, pets being adopted. The milestones, if you will. The Life Events section lets you make a note of that event on your Timeline.

Although it's not required, you may also feel an urge to fill out your history on your Timeline. If you're new to Facebook, you may want to expand your Timeline back past the day you joined. Life Events is a good way to think about what you want to add in your history.

To add a life event, follow these steps:

1. **Click the Life Event section in the Publisher.**

   A menu of various types of life events appears. The categories are listed here although when you click each one, you'll find many subcategories as well:

   - Work & Education
   - Family & Relationships
   - Home & Living
   - Health & Wellness
   - Travel & Experiences

Milestones can be big or small; if you check out the subcategories, you'll see things that range from getting your braces removed to learning a new hobby to having a baby. And you should feel free to make up your own. Lots of people use Life Events to represent small accomplishments in a humorous way. For example, one of my friends posted a life event to commemorate the day he successfully canceled his cable service.

2. Select the event you want to create from the menu.

This opens a pop-up window with specific text fields to fill out and space for photos to go along with the event. You can see an example in Figure 5-9.

3. Fill out the details you want to share.

You don't have to fill out all the fields, but it's pretty important to fill in the date of the event so that it goes to the right place on your Timeline.

4. Add a photo to illustrate the event.

Click Choose From Photos if there is already a photo on Facebook you want to use, or choose Upload Photos to add photos from your computer.

5. Use the Privacy menu to choose who can see this event in your Timeline.

You have the same basic options as you have all over Facebook. The most commonly used are Public and Friends.

6. Click Save.

The event is then added to your Timeline, with any photos you've added featured prominently.

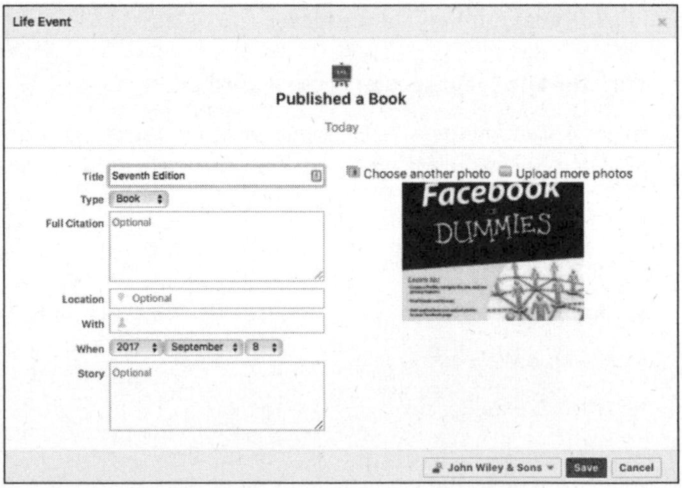

FIGURE 5-9:
Add a life event
from the recent
or distant past.

As you scroll down through your history, you may realize that you want to add an event or milestone. Don't worry about scrolling back up to the top of the page. The Timeline navigator should be following you as you scroll down, showing your name and the year you're looking at.

Editing posts

After you create a post, you may realize that you typed something wrong, or want to add more details to the post. You can edit almost every part of a post you created after the fact. Click the tiny grey down arrow in the upper-right corner of any post to reveal the Edit Post menu, shown in Figure 5-10 (in some browsers, this may be an ellipsis icon instead of a down arrow). This menu displays slightly different options depending on the type of post, but for the most part, the Edit Post menu has at least the following options:

>> **Save Post:** Saving a post adds it to your Saved Items, which you get to from the left-side menu of your Home page. I usually use Saved Items to keep track of other people's posts that I want to check out at a later time, not for saving my own posts.

>> **Edit Post:** Choosing to edit a post reopens the Share box so you can change any portion of the post, whether that's changing the wording of your status or removing a photo you had previously shared. Click Save to make your changes.

Once you've edited a post, you can view the history of that post by clicking View Edit History from the Edit Post Menu. Viewing the edit history lets you see all the changes you've made in the order you made them.

>> **Change Date:** Often you share items on Facebook after the date when they happened. For example, photos from a wedding might not be available to be shared until well after the wedding happened. You can change the date of a post so it shows up at the right spot on your Timeline. Click Save to make your changes.

>> **Turn off/on notifications for this post:** If you post something that a lot of people are responding to, you may find yourself inundated with notifications. You can turn notifications off for any given post if you are finding those notifications annoying. You can turn them on again from the same Edit Post menu.

>> **Show in tab:** This opens the post in a chat window at the bottom of your screen. This is another option that mostly gets used with posts that are getting a lot of attention. If you want to keep up on the discussion happening on something you (or someone else) posted, you can open that post in its own chat window and continue browsing Facebook at the same time.

>> **Hide from timeline:** Hiding a post is different from deleting it. When you hide a post, you keep that post from appearing on your Timeline, but the post still exists. So if, for example, you hide a particularly bad photo from your Timeline, the photo album still exists. Anyone with permission to see it could navigate to your Photos section and check it out. But it's not going to get called out on your Timeline. If you delete a post, it's gone forever; even you won't be able to find it on Facebook.

>> **Delete:** Deleting a post gets rid of it from Facebook for good. That includes any photos in the post and any comments on the post as well.

>> **Turn Off/On Translations**: If you are using Facebook in English and all of your friends are English speakers, you will not really need this option ever, and you certainly won't need it on your own posts. For people who are seeing posts in multiple languages, Facebook automatically translates posts into their main language. Selecting this option turns off the automatic translations on a post so people can see it in its original form.

FIGURE 5-10:
Edit or delete a post.

TIP

If you're looking to remove things like photos or videos that exist only on Facebook, keep in mind that once they're gone from Facebook they're gone forever. It might be more practical to change the audience that can see the photo album than to delete it entirely. Trust me; one hard-drive crash, and your photos are Facebook-only.

The left column

The right column of your Timeline features your posts and life events and updates every time you add something new. The left column of your Timeline is a bit more static and provides snapshots of three parts of your profile that people tend to look for when they visit a Timeline:

>> **Intro:** The Intro box shows a portion of the information you may have added to your About section (which I cover soon in the "All About Me" section). The part it does show includes the things that help identify you as you.

TIP

I think of it as "dinner party introduction." These pieces of info — where you work, where you live, where you're from, who your spouse is — are the sorts of things you might talk about the first time you meet someone.

The Intro box also includes featured photos. Featured photos are your most favorite photos. You can choose from photos you have added or that other people have added of you. To add featured photos, follow these steps:

1. **Click the Add Featured Photos link in the bottom of the Intro box.**

   The Edit Featured Photos box appears (see Figure 5-11).

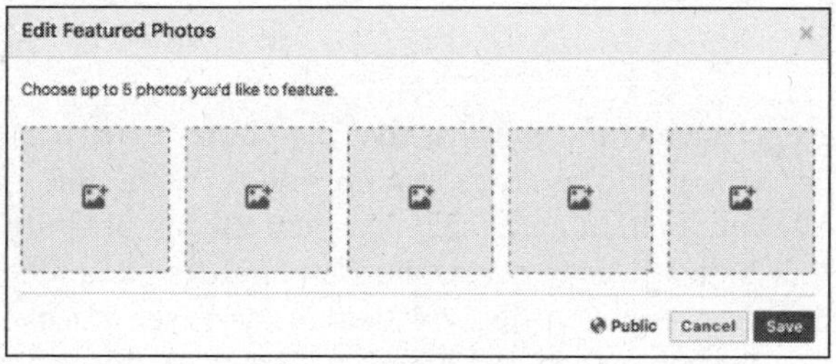

FIGURE 5-11: Add Featured Photos here.

2. **Click on any of the blank thumbnail images.**

   A box opens for browsing the photos of you on Facebook.

3. **Click on your desired photo to select it.**

   You return to the Edit Featured Photos box, which now displays that photo as one the thumbnails.

4. **Repeat steps 2-3 for the remaining four photos.**

   If you decide you don't want one of the photos you've chosen, hover your mouse over its thumbnail and click the X that appears in its upper-right corner.

5. **When you've chosen the photos you want, click Save.**

   Your photos now appear in your Intro box as Featured Photos.

WARNING

Featured photos, like your cover photo and profile picture, are *public*, meaning anyone who visits Facebook, or who Googles your name and clicks on your Facebook profile as a search result, can see them. Make sure they are photos you are comfortable with the world seeing.

» **Photos:** In addition to Featured Photos, the Photos box on the left side of your Timeline shows thumbnails of photos you've added or been tagged in, starting with the most recent one. Clicking on any photo thumbnail will open that photo up in the photo viewer. You can then click to page through all your photos.

>> **Friends:** The Friends box shows thumbnail photos of, you guessed it, your friends. Friends with new posts will appear at the top, followed by friends you have added most recently.

>> **Featured Albums:** If you are an avid photographer, you may want to feature certain albums on your profile in this section. Remember, albums you choose to feature are automatically made Public, so you shouldn't do this with any photos you aren't comfortable sharing far and wide.

All About Me

The Intro box gives you (and your friends) the dinner party basics: where you live, what you do, where you're from, whom you're with. But there's a lot more information about you that Facebook gives you the opportunity to share. Clicking the About link beneath your cover photo opens the expanded About section of your Timeline (see Figure 5-12). By default, you see an overview of all your information — from here you can choose different sections to edit.

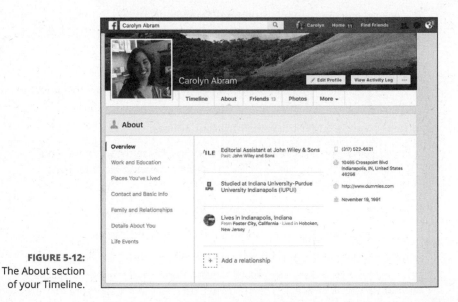

FIGURE 5-12:
The About section of your Timeline.

This page houses lots of information about you: Work and Education, Contact and Basic Information, Places You've Lived, Relationships and Family, Details About You, and Life Events. Much of this information won't change very much over time, so it needs to be edited only once or when something big happens, like you move to a new city. Click on any of the sections to edit or add to the information there.

You can also edit who can see it. Unlike the cover photo and profile picture, you choose who gets to see this information. By default, your information is public, meaning everyone can see it. I go over changing your privacy in more detail in Chapter 6.

Work and Education

Your work and education information is actually very important information to add to Facebook. This is the information that helps old friends find you for reunions, recommendations, or reminiscing. It is also what helps people identify you as you, as opposed to someone else with a similar name.

To add an employer, follow these steps:

1. **From the Work and Education section, click the Add a Workplace link.**

2. **Start typing the name of the company where you worked or currently work.**

    Facebook tries to find a match while you type. When that match is highlighted, or when you finish typing, press Enter.

3. **Enter details about your job in the fields that appear.**

    These include

    - *Position:* Enter your job title.

    - *City/Town:* Enter where you physically went (or go) to work.

    - *Description:* Provide a more detailed description of what it is you do.

    - *Time Period:* Enter the amount of time you worked at this job. If you select I Currently Work Here, it appears at the top of your Timeline.

4. **Select who you want to see this information using the privacy drop-down menu.**

    By default, this information is public. You can choose to only make it available to Friends, Only Me, or a custom set of people or friend list. These more advanced privacy options are covered in Chapter 6.

5. **Click the Save Changes button.**

    You can change any of the information about this job (or others) in the future by clicking the Options link next to the workplace you want to change and selecting Edit from the menu that opens.

TIP

If you're interested in using Facebook for professional networking, you can also add specific projects to your work history. For example, underneath my job at *Facebook For Dummies*, I could click Add a Project and fill out information about the most recent edition: who my editors are, how long the project took, and a description of what I'm doing.

Another option if you are job hunting on Facebook is to add a skill to the Professional Skills section. Simply Click the Add a Professional Skill link, type your skill into the box that appears, choose your privacy setting, and click Save Changes. Professional Skills can be whatever you think is relevant.

To add a college, follow these steps:

1. **From the Work and Education section, click the Add a College link.**

2. **Start typing the name of the college you attended (or attend).**

    Facebook tries to find a match while you type. When that match is highlighted, or when you finish typing, press Enter.

3. **Enter details of your school in the fields that appear.**

    These include

    - *Time Period:* Click the blue text Add Year to show when you started and finished your degree.

    - *Graduated:* You can check the graduated box to note that you actually received a degree (or uncheck it to denote you did not).

    - *Description:* Add details about your time at school that you think may be relevant.

    - *Concentrations:* List any majors or minors you had.

    - *Attended For:* Choose whether you attended as an undergraduate or a graduate student. If you select Graduate Student, you will have additional space to enter the type of degree you received.

4. **Select who you want to see this information using the privacy drop-down menu.**

    By default, this information is public. You can choose to make it available only to Friends, Friends Except. . . , Only Me, or a custom set of people or friend list. These more advanced privacy options are covered in Chapter 6.

5. **Click the Save Changes button.**

To add a high school, follow these steps:

1. **From the Work and Education Section, click the Add a High School link.**

2. **Start typing the name of the high school you attended (or attend).**

   Facebook tries to find a match while you type. When that match is highlighted, or when you finish typing, press Enter.

3. **Enter details of your school in the fields that appear.**

   These include

   - *Time Period:* Click the blue text Add Year to show when you started and finished your degree.

   - *Graduated:* Check this box if you graduated from this school.

   - *Description:* Add details about your time at school that you think may be relevant.

4. **Select who you want to see this information using the privacy drop-down menu.**

   By default, this information is public. You can choose to only make it available to Friends, Friends except Acquaintances, Only Me, or a custom set of people or friend list. These more advanced privacy options are covered in Chapter 6.

5. **Click Save Changes.**

   You can change any of the information you just entered in the future by clicking the Options link next to the school you entered and selecting Edit from the menu that opens.

Places You've Lived

This section allows you to add your hometown, current city, and any other place you've lived. If you haven't previously added your current city or hometown, click the Add Your Current City or Add Your Hometown links to do so. If you need to edit your current city, hover your mouse over the current city displayed, and click the Edit link that appears on the right side of the screen. As you type in your city, Facebook will auto-complete as you type. Simply select your city when you see it appear. Remember to click Save Changes when you've successfully entered your current city and hometown.

From this section of your About section, you can also create a life event to represent other places you have lived. To do this, click the Add a Place link under the Other Places Lived section. This automatically creates a life event about moving. You can then fill out all the fields related to moving (including when it happened) and even add photos from your move.

Contact and Basic Info

Your Contact and Basic Information is just what it sounds like: the very basics about you and how to get in touch with you. Contact information includes:

>> **Phone numbers:** You can add as many phone numbers as you have — home, mobile, and work.

>> **Address and Neighborhood:** You can choose to add this information in case anyone ever needs to mail you a present.

>> **Email address(es):** You can add as many email addresses as you want, and choose who can see those addresses.

>> **Website and Other Accounts:** You can add information about your account handle for other websites or services like Skype, Instagram, Twitter, and so on. You can also add a link to any personal websites you have.

>> **Facebook Username:** Facebook automatically creates a custom URL for your profile page when you join to make it easy to direct people to your Timeline. Usually usernames try to make use of your name, so a typical username might look something like: *www.facebook.com/carolyn.abram*.

You can add contact info you've never added by clicking the links to Add <Contact Info>. You can edit any existing contact information by hovering your mouse over the line of info you'd like to change and clicking the Edit button that appears. When you edit something, you can also edit *who* can see it by using the privacy drop-down menu. When you are done editing your information or privacy, remember to click the Save Changes button.

I know, it may seem a little scary to add your contact information to the Internet, and if you're not comfortable with it, that's okay. Facebook itself is a great way for people to reach you, so you shouldn't feel that it's required that you add other ways for people to contact you, as well.

That being said, it can be very useful for your friends to be able to find your number or address if needed, and there are privacy options (which are discussed in Chapter 6) that can help you feel more comfortable sharing some of this information.

Your Basic Information includes the following categories:

>> **Birth Date and Birth Year:** You entered your birthday when you registered for Facebook. Here, you can tweak the date (in case you messed up) as well as decide what people can see about your birthday. Some people don't like sharing their age, their birthday, or both. If you're one of these people, use this drop-down menu to select what you want to share.

Although you can change your birthday and year at will most of the time, Facebook's systems prevent you from changing your birthday too often and also prevents shifting to under 18 after you've been listed as over 18. If, through a legitimate mistake, this happened to you, contact Facebook's Help Team from the Help Center.

>> **Gender:** You entered your gender when you signed up for Facebook, and Facebook mirrors your selection here. If you're transgender or have a preference in how people refer to your gender, you can choose to edit your gender by selecting Custom from the drop-down menu and entering whatever word best describes you in the text box. You can also choose what pronoun should be used in News Feed stories and around Facebook.

>> **Interested In:** This field is primarily used by people to signal their sexual orientation. Some people feel that this section makes Facebook seem like a dating site, so if that doesn't sound like you, you don't have to fill it out.

>> **Languages:** Languages might seem a little less basic than, say, your city, but you can enter any languages you speak here.

>> **Religion:** You can choose to list your religious views and describe them.

>> **Political Views:** You can also choose to list your political views and further explain them with a description.

By default, your basic information (with the exception of your birthday) is public. Click Edit and then use the Privacy menu to change who can see any item of information.

Family and Relationships

The Relationship section and the Family section provide space for you to list your romantic and family relationships. These relationships provide a way of linking your Timeline to someone else's Timeline, and therefore require confirmation. In other words, if you list yourself as married, your spouse needs to confirm that fact before it appears on both Timelines.

You can add a relationship by following these steps:

1. **From the Family and Relationships section of the About section, click Add your relationship status.**

   An area for adding this information appears.

2. **Click the Relationship Status menu to reveal the different types of romantic relationships you can add.**

These include Single, In a Relationship, Engaged, Married, It's Complicated (a Facebook classic), Widowed, Separated, Divorced, In a Civil Union, In an Open Relationship, and In a Domestic Partnership.

3. **You can either stop here or choose to link to the person you're in this relationship with. Type the person's name into the box that appears.**

Facebook auto-completes as you type. Press Enter when you see your beloved's name highlighted. Once you've finished these steps, this person will receive a notification about being in a relationship with you.

4. **(Optional) Add your anniversary using the drop-down menus that appear.**

If you add your anniversary, your friends will see a small reminder on their Home pages on that date.

5. **Click Save Changes.**

If you ever need to change this information, hover over it and click the Edit link to reopen this interface.

TIP

For many couples, the act of changing from Single to In a Relationship on Facebook is a major relationship milestone. There's even a term for it: Facebook official. You may overhear someone saying, "It's official, but is it Facebook official?" Feel free to impress your friends with this knowledge of Facebook customs.

You can add a family relationship by following these steps:

1. **From the Family and Relationships section of the About section, click Add a Family Member.**

A menu for editing this information appears.

2. **Click in the text box for Family Member and start typing your family member's name into that box.**

Facebook tries to auto-complete as you type. When you see your sister's or mother's or whoever's name appear, click to select it.

3. **Select the type of relationship from the drop-down menu.**

Facebook offers a variety of family relationships ranging from the nuclear to the extended.

4. **Click Save Changes.**

Facebook sends a notification to that person.

Details About You

The Details About You section is a bit of a catch-all section for details that don't really fit anywhere else:

» **About You:** This section is a free form place for you to describe yourself, if you so choose.

» **Name Pronunciation:** If people are always mispronouncing your name, you can choose to add a phonetic spelling of it. This pronunciation will be available on your profile with an audio component that people can choose to play to learn the proper way to say your name. This information is always public and can be found by clicking the About section of a Timeline and navigating to the Details About <Name> section.

» **Other Names:** You can add nicknames, maiden names, or any other names people might use to search for you. This information is always public. Click the "Show at top of profile" box to display this name at the top of your profile next to your real name. This is especially helpful for maiden names.

» **Favorite Quotes:** If you have any quotations you live by, you can add them to this free form field.

Life Events

You can see a summary of all the life events that exist on your Timeline in this space. If you see big gaps in your history that you'd like to fill, you can click Add a Life Event. You then can select from the same categories and fill out the same forms that I talk about in the Telling Your Story section.

Sections

Sections are parts of your Timeline you and your friends can jump to in order to see compilations of, for example, places you've checked in or what books you've read. To view your sections, click on the More tab underneath your cover photo. Some common Sections you see listed here are listed below:

» **Likes:** The Likes section shows Pages that you have liked, starting with the most recent one. As you scroll back in time, this box shows Pages you liked at particular times. You can also click to view likes by category (such as Restaurants or Books).

>> **Check-ins:** The Check-ins section displays locations where you've checked in recently.

>> **Interests:** There are multiple interest boxes for things like Music, Movies, Books, and so on.

Adding to your Interest sections

Interest sections are a part of the Timeline that can be a really fun way to let your friends know the music, movies, television shows, books, and other things that really define you. Most of you have at least one book that's your favorite, and maybe another that you're reading right now and would really like to talk about with someone.

You can share both books you have read and your favorite books with your Facebook friends following these steps:

1. **Navigate to the expanded Books section of your Timeline by clicking the More link beneath your cover photo and selecting Books from the drop-down menu.**

   TIP

   Although I'm using Books as an example, the same applies to the other Interest sections.

   This takes you to the expanded Books section of your Timeline, shown in Figure 5-13. There are three subcategories of books that you can add to: Read, Want to Read, and Likes.

2. **Click into the section you want to be adding books to.**

   By default, you will be in the Read section.

3. **Type the name of the book you want to add into the search box.**

   Facebook will attempt to autocomplete as you type. When you see the book you want to add, click it or press Enter.

4. **Repeat Step 3 until you add every book you've read ever.**

   Or, you know, until you get bored.

5. **Click the Want to Read or Likes section to add books that are on your list or that you want to actively recommend to people.**

   TIP

   Adding books in those sections is exactly the same: Search for the ones you want to add and then click them to select them.

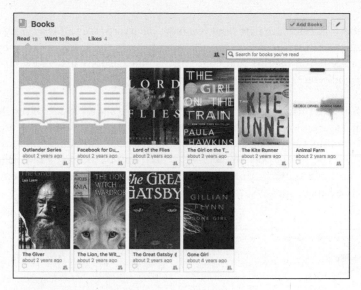

FIGURE 5-13:
An expanded
Books section on
your Timeline.

Editing sections

You can decide which sections are part of your Timeline. Click the More tab beneath the cover photo and select Manage Sections at the bottom of the menu that opens. This opens the Manage Sections box. You can check and uncheck your sections to decide which ones appear as part of your Timeline.

To edit the privacy of any individual section, navigate to that section (for example, select Movies from the More menu to go to the Movies section). Click the pencil icon in the upper-right corner of the section to open a menu of options.

» **Hide Section:** Select this if you want to hide the Movies section from appearing on your Timeline.

» **Activity Log:** Click this to be taken to Activity Log and see all activity related to movies that could appear in the Movies box. Activity Log gets a little more attention in Chapter 6.

» **Edit Privacy:** Click this to edit who can see all the movies you have liked on Facebook.

Your Friends and Your Timeline

Your Timeline is what your friends look at to get a sense of your life, and it's also where they leave public messages for you. In this way, your friends' posts become part of your history (just like in real life). Think about all the things you learn about a friend the first time you meet his parents, or all the funny stories you hear when your friend's significant other recounts the story of how they met. These are the types of insights that your friends may casually leave on your Timeline, making all your friends know you a little better.

When friends visit your Timeline, they'll also see a version of the Publisher (shown in Figure 5-14. This Publisher allows them to post some text or a photo to your Timeline. Check out the posts on your friends' Timelines. Chances are that you'll see a few "Hey, how are you, let's catch up" messages; a few "That was an awesome trip/dinner/drink" messages; and maybe a few statements that make so little sense, you're sure they must be inside jokes.

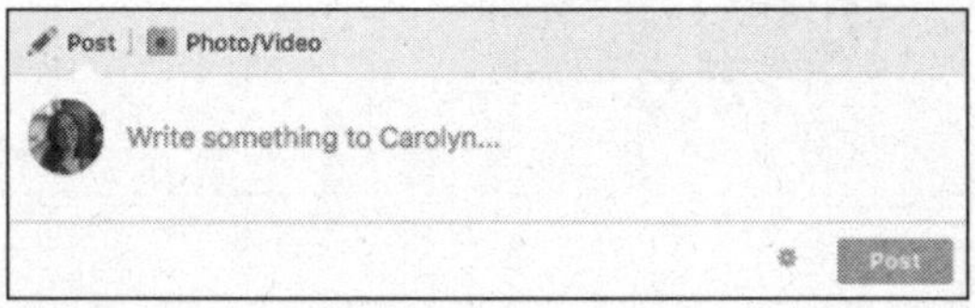

FIGURE 5-14: Leave a public message for a friend on his Timeline.

![Post | Photo/Video — Write something to Carolyn... — Post]

If you're on a friend's Timeline around his birthday, you're sure to see many "Happy Birthday" posts. There aren't many rules for using Facebook, but one tradition that has arisen over time is the "Happy Birthday" post. Because most people see notifications of their friends' birthdays on their Home pages, the quickest way to say "I'm thinking of you" on their special day is to write on their Timeline.

TIP

Although I think that the back and forth between friends is one of the delights of the Timeline, some people find it a little hard to let go. If you're someone who doesn't like the idea of a friend being able to write something personal on your Timeline, you can prevent friends from being able to post on it within your Settings page. You can also limit who can see the posts your friends leave. From the Settings page, go to the Timeline and Tagging section and look for the settings related to who can post on your Timeline and who can see what others post on your Timeline.

REMEMBER

The best way to get used to the Timeline is to start using it. Write on your friends' Timelines, post a status update or a link on your own, and see what sort of response you get from your friends. After all, that's what the Timeline is all about — sharing with your friends.

Chapter **6**

Privacy and Safety on Facebook

When people talk about privacy online — and on Facebook in particular — I like to remind them that there's a spectrum of privacy concerns. On one end of the spectrum are true horror stories of predators approaching minors, identity thefts, and the like. Hopefully (and most likely), you will never deal with these issues, although I do touch on them at the end of this chapter. On the other end of the spectrum are issues I usually categorize as "awkward social situations" — for example, posting a photo of your perfect beach day that your coworkers can see on a day when you called in "sick" (not that you would ever do something like that). You'll probably deal with issues at the awkward end of the spectrum most often. Somewhere in between are questions about encountering hate speech, strangers seeing your stuff, and security issues like spamming and phishing. All these privacy-related topics are legitimate, and all are ones you can learn how to deal with and control.

Regardless of where on the spectrum your question or problem falls, you should be able to use your privacy settings to make things better. I can't promise that you'll be able to prevent 100 percent of the situations that make you annoyed or uncomfortable or leave you with that sort of icky feeling, but I can tell you that you should be able to reduce how often you feel that way. The goal is to get as close to 100 percent as possible so you can feel as comfortable as possible sharing on Facebook.

Of course, there's also a spectrum of what "being comfortable" means to different people. That's why talking about privacy can get kind of confusing: There are a lot of options, and what makes me comfortable might not make you comfortable. This chapter is meant to be a guide to all the privacy options Facebook offers so that you can figure out the right combinations that make you comfortable sharing on Facebook.

REMEMBER

Your own common sense is going to be one of the best helpers in avoiding privacy problems. Facebook status updates aren't the right place to post Social Security numbers or bank passwords. Similarly, if you're thinking about sharing something that, if the wrong someone saw it, could lead to bad real-world consequences, maybe it's not meant to be shared on Facebook.

Know Your Audience

Before getting into specifics about all the privacy controls, you need to understand some basic parts of the Facebook vocabulary. These terms are related to how Facebook thinks about the people you may or may not want to share with. For most pieces of information, the privacy options are related to the audience who can see what you're sharing. The first two options in this list — Public and Friends — are the most basic settings that are shown by default whenever you go to change your privacy. Figure 6-1 shows an example of the menu used to change your audience for a post. Note that some of the settings covered in the following list aren't visible in Figure 6-1. To see all the options described, click the More link at the bottom of the Privacy menu.

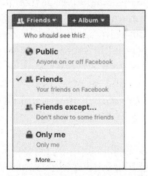

FIGURE 6-1:
The Audience options for your posts.

>> **Public or Everyone:** By setting the visibility of something you post or list to Public, you're saying that you don't care who, on the entire Internet, knows this information about you. Many people list their spouse on their Timeline, and, just as they'd shout this information from the treetops (and register it at

the county courthouse), they set the visibility to Public. This is a totally reasonable setting for innocuous pieces of information. In fact, some information is always available as Public Information that everyone can see. This includes your name, profile picture, cover photo, and gender.

Now, just because everyone *can* see something doesn't mean everyone *does* see everything. Your posts, information, friendships, and so on populate your Friends' News Feeds (assuming that your Friends can see this information), but never the News Feeds of people you're not Friends with (unless you allow followers to see your public posts). When I think about who will see the information I share as Public, I imagine someone like you searching for me by name and coming to my Timeline. Although (hopefully) that might be a lot of people, it isn't anywhere close to the number of people who use Facebook. By default, much of your Timeline and all your posts are publicly visible. This chapter covers how to change these settings if you want to.

» **Friends:** Any information for which you set visibility to Friends will be accessible only by your confirmed Facebook Friends. If you trust your Friends, this is a reasonably safe setting for most of your information. If you feel uncomfortable sharing your information with your Friends, you can use Custom Privacy, or you can rethink the people you allow to become your Friends.

TIP

Think of friending people as a privacy setting all on its own. When you add someone as a friend, ask yourself whether you're comfortable with that person seeing your posts.

» **Friends Except . . . :** Even though I always recommend adding friends only if you're comfortable with them seeing your posts, I have to acknowledge that sometimes you have not-quite-friends on your Friend List. These may be distant family members, professional contacts, old friends from way back when, or that super-friendly neighbor whom you maybe just wish wouldn't stop by quite so often. No matter who they are, you can exclude them from seeing your posts or other information by choosing the Friends Except setting. When you choose this setting, a pop-up window opens with options for choosing the friends you want to exclude. You can see this window in Figure 6-2. Your list of friends is ordered alphabetically by first name, or you can use the search box at the top of the box to search for a specific friend or Friend List. Select friends by clicking on their names.

REMEMBER

The names you select when using the Friends Except setting are the names of people who will *not* be able to see whatever it is you are posting.

» **Only Me:** This setting is basically a way of adding something to Facebook but then hiding it from being seen by other people. At first, this setting may not seem useful, but it can come in handy for those times when you want to work on something, such as a photo album, and hide it from view until you finish it.

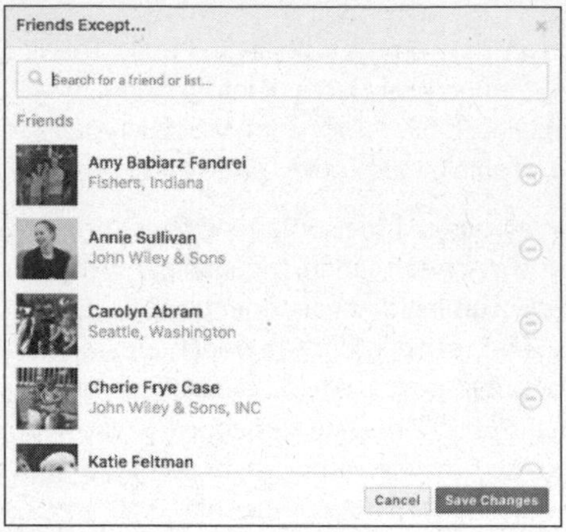

FIGURE 6-2: Choose the friends you *don't* want to see something using this box.

>> **Specific Friends:** This setting opens a pop-up window similar to the Friends Except setting. In this case, you are selecting the people or lists who *can* see something, as opposed to selecting who *can't* see it. If you have something you want only a few people to see, this is a good way to share with that smaller group of people.

>> **Custom:** If you have very specific needs, customized privacy settings may help you feel more comfortable sharing on Facebook. Anytime you select Custom from a privacy menu, you'll see the Custom Privacy window, shown in Figure 6-3. Customized privacy has two parts: those who *can* see something and those who *can't*.

In the top part of the Custom Privacy window, you enter the names of friends or Friend Lists that you want to see something. Simply type the name of the person or list into the text box to make something visible to them. Additionally, a checkbox allows you to choose whether the friends of any people you tag can see your post. Remember, tagging is a way of marking who is in a photo, who is with you when you check in someplace, or whom you want to mention in a post. For example, say that I'm going to spend a day at the park with one of my friends. I might post a status that says, "Taking advantage of the nice weather with **Marjorie.**" The name of my friend links back to her profile. By default, Marjorie's friends will be able to see this post, even if they aren't friends with me. If I deselect this box, Marjorie's friends will no longer be able to see that post.

The lower section of the Custom Privacy window controls who can't see something. Like the top part of the window, the Don't Share With section has a blank text box where you can type the name of people or Friend Lists. When you add their names to this box, they won't be able to see the content you post.

REMEMBER

Whatever customized audience you create for one post will be the audience next time you go to post something. Make sure you check the audience the next time you post!

>> **Lists:** Lists are ways to sort your friends into various categories. There are two types of lists: Smart Lists that Facebook creates on your behalf, and lists that you create for yourself. For example, Facebook creates the Family list based on information you enter about your family relationships. I've created a "Dummies" list to keep track of the various editors and co-authors I've had over the years. Often, you may want to share something with one list of people, in which case, you can choose the name of that list as your privacy setting.

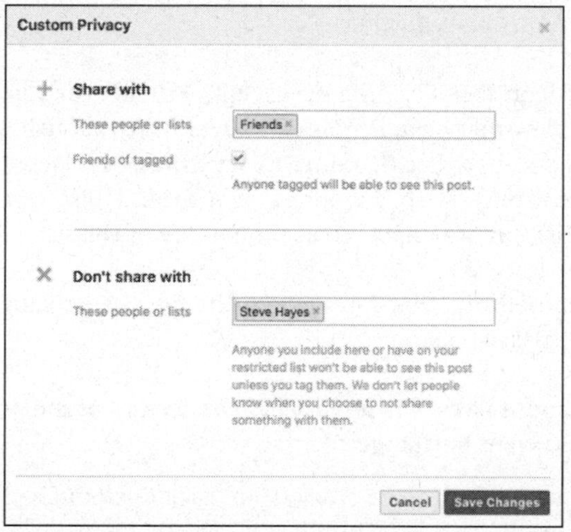

Custom Privacy   ✕

+ **Share with**

These people or lists   [Friends ✕   ]

Friends of tagged   ✓

                               Anyone tagged will be able to see this post.

✕ **Don't share with**

These people or lists   [Steve Hayes ✕   ]

                               Anyone you include here or have on your
                               restricted list won't be able to see this post
                               unless you tag them. We don't let people
                               know when you choose to not share
                               something with them.

                                              [Cancel] [Save Changes]

FIGURE 6-3:
The Custom
Privacy window.

Privacy on the Go

Setting your privacy settings on Facebook isn't a one-time thing. Because you are constantly adding new status updates, photos, and content to Facebook, constantly interacting with friends and reaching out to people, managing your privacy is an ongoing affair. To that end, one of the most common places you should know your privacy options is in the Publisher, also known as the Share box.

The *Publisher* is the blank text box that sits at the top of your Home page and under your cover photo on your Timeline. It's where you go to add status updates, photos, links, and more to Facebook. The part of the Publisher that's important for this chapter is the Privacy menu, in the lower-left corner of the Publisher. You can see this in Figure 6-1.

Whenever you're posting a status or other content, the *audience,* or group of people you've given permission to see it, is displayed within the Privacy button. The audience you see displayed is always the audience you last shared something with. In other words, if you shared something with the Public last time you posted a status, it displays Public the next time you go to post a status.

Click the Privacy button to reveal the drop-down menu. Click the setting you want before you post your status, link, or photo. Most of the time, I share my posts with Friends. As a result, I don't change this setting that often. But if you do share something publicly, remember to adjust the audience the next time you post something.

To see the full menu of options discussed in the "Know Your Audience" section, you will need to click the More link at the bottom of the menu, and then the See All link to expand the menu further.

WARNING

A post's privacy icon (Public, Friends Except, Friends, or Custom) is visible to anyone who can view that post. People can hover over that icon to get more information. Friend Lists appear as Custom Privacy unless the viewer is a member of a list you shared the post with. Members of a Friend List can see other people included on the list but are unable to see the name of the list.

After you post something, you can always change the privacy on it. From your Timeline, follow these steps:

1. **Hover your mouse over the privacy icon at the top of the post whose audience you want to change.**

Every post displays the icon for Public, Friends, or Custom.

2. **Click the button to reveal the Privacy menu.**

You'll see the usual options: Public, Friends, Friends Except, Only Me, and More. You need to click More to see choices like Specific Friends, Custom, or specific lists of friends.

3. **Click the audience you want.**

A change to Public, Friends, Friends Except, or a specific Friend List is automatically saved. Changing to Custom requires you to make selections within the Custom Privacy window again.

Privacy Shortcuts

There are so many settings related to privacy on Facebook that it can sometimes feel overwhelming. That's why I am such a fan of the Privacy Shortcuts menu, which helps direct you to the settings you'll want most often by asking the questions you'll ask most often:

>> Who can see my stuff?

>> Who can contact me?

>> How do I stop someone from bothering me?

To open the Privacy Shortcuts menu, open the Quick Help menu by clicking the question mark icon in the big blue bar at the top of any Facebook page. Then select Privacy Shortcuts from the menu that opens. The Privacy Shortcuts menu is shown in Figure 6-4. Click any of these three options to expand more privacy options.

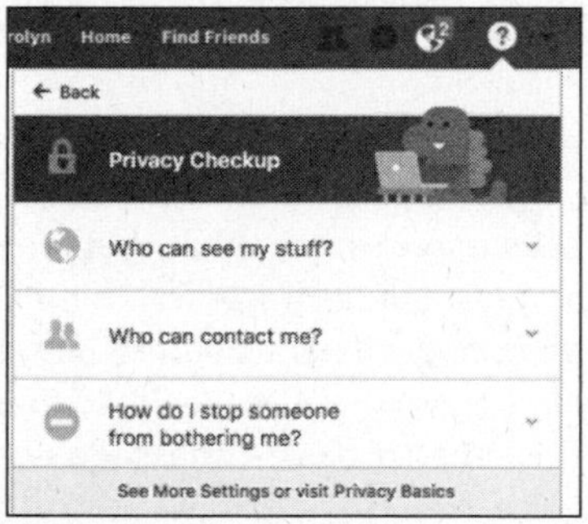

FIGURE 6-4:
You can find the answers to your most common privacy questions here.

Who can see my stuff?

You can adjust the privacy for each status or post you make, which means that over time you might find yourself asking, "Wait, who can see all of this? Who can see what I posted yesterday? Last week? What about if I post tomorrow?" Well, the answers can be found here. (The earlier "Privacy on the Go" section of this chapter covers the privacy options when you're sharing something.)

Facebook offers you one setting you can adjust here, named Who Can See My Future Posts. This is the exact same control that can be found in the Publisher. It's described this way to emphasize that whatever you select here will be the default going forward, until you change it again. Click the little arrow to change this setting. You will see the same options you see from the Publisher: Public, Friends, Friends Except, Only Me, and More.

Additionally, the Who Can See My Stuff section offers you two links to help you double-check and understand what people can see. The first is a link to Activity Log, which is a granular summary of everything you've done on Facebook and who can see that thing. It ranges from the status updates you write to the content you like or comment on. As you look through your Activity Log, you can change who can see it, or remove the content entirely. I go over how to navigate and edit your Activity Log in more depth in the "Privacy Tools" section later in this chapter.

Finally, the Who Can See My Stuff section offers you a link to another privacy tool, the View As tool. This tool allows you to look at your Timeline as though you are another person. I like to use this to double-check what people see when they search for me on Facebook — in my case, they mostly see my biographical information and none of my posts.

Who can contact me?

A common Facebook problem that sends people scurrying to their privacy settings is getting a Friend Request that they don't want to get. It might be from a spammer or just someone you don't know. This section is to help you control who can send you Friend Requests.

There are only two options for the Who Can Send Me Friend Requests setting: Everyone and Friends of Friends. Everyone means that everyone who searches for you or finds your Timeline can request you as a friend. Friends of Friends means someone must be friends with one of your friends before he's allowed to request you. As a personal anecdote, when I worked at Facebook, I received a lot of Friend Requests from people who wanted me to pass a message along to the CEO or something like that. I found this irritating, so I changed this setting to just Friends of Friends. When I moved to a new city, I realized the people I met were unable to add me as a friend. I changed my setting back to Everyone to make it easier for friends to find me.

How do I stop someone from bothering me?

Sadly, sometimes a friendship isn't really a friendship. If someone is bothering you, harassing you, bullying you, or in any way making your Facebook experience terrible, blocking might be the solution to the problem. Blocking is different than unfriending someone because someone who is not your friend might still wind up interacting with you on Facebook. For example, if you have mutual friends, you might wind up both commenting on the same post. Blocking someone means that as much as possible, neither of you will even know that the other person is on Facebook. You won't see each other's comments, even if that person is on the same person's photo. Blocked individuals won't be able to send you messages, add you as a friend, or view your Timeline (all things they would likely be able to do even if you unfriended them). While this may sound like a very serious tool, consider that perhaps one of the most common uses of it is blocking exes to prevent oneself from seeing how much fun they are having without you.

TIP

If you're the parent of a teen, this can be a very handy setting to know about. Unfortunately, bullying can sometimes spread to Facebook from the classroom, and blocking can be a useful tool in terms of keeping your child safer on Facebook.

Privacy Settings

In addition to the privacy shortcuts, there are several more granular privacy settings located within the Settings page. You can get to these settings from the Privacy Shortcuts menu (click the link on the bottom that says See More Settings).

The Privacy Settings and Tools section of the Settings page is shown in Figure 6-5. The left side of the Settings page is a menu of different settings you can adjust here. The settings that are relevant to privacy are in the second section: Privacy, Timeline and Tagging, and Blocking. Additionally, I go over the Apps and Ads settings sections because people commonly have questions about how their information is used in these locations.

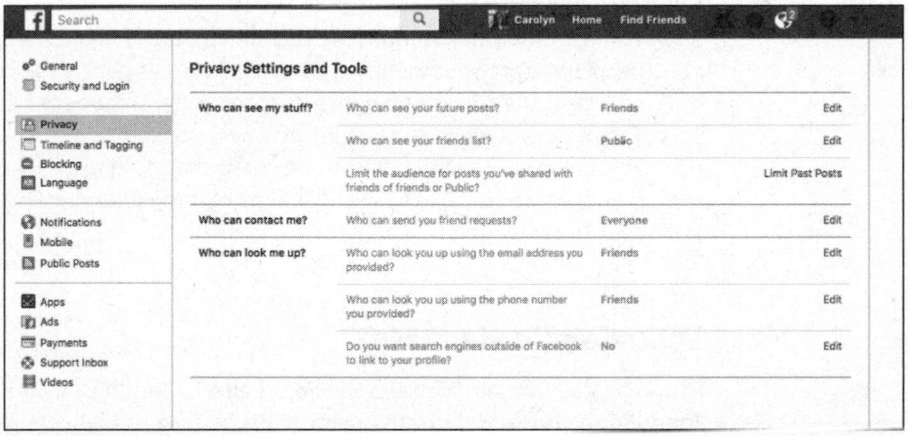

Search
Carolyn
Home
Find Friends
General
Security and Login
Privacy
Timeline and Tagging
Blocking
Language
Notifications
Mobile
Public Posts
Apps
Ads
Payments
Support Inbox
Videos
Privacy Settings and Tools
Who can see my stuff?
Who can see your future posts?
Friends
Edit
Who can see your friends list?
Public
Edit
Limit the audience for posts you've shared with friends of friends or Public?
Limit Past Posts
Who can contact me?
Who can send you friend requests?
Everyone
Edit
Who can look me up?
Who can look you up using the email address you provided?
Friends
Edit
Who can look you up using the phone number you provided?
Friends
Edit
Do you want search engines outside of Facebook to link to your profile?
No
Edit

FIGURE 6-5: Start here to set privacy options.

Privacy

The Privacy section of the Settings page is shown in Figure 6-5. It's broken into three sections: Who Can See My Stuff, Who Can Contact Me, and Who Can Look Me Up.

Who Can See My Stuff?

The Who Can See My Stuff section should look mostly familiar if you read the section on privacy shortcuts. There are three settings here, two of which are redundant with the Privacy Shortcuts menu.

>> **Who can see your future posts?** This setting shows you your current setting for when you create posts. This is who can see all your future posts (unless you change it). You can change this setting by clicking the Edit link on the right side of the page. A sample Publisher appears where you can select a new privacy setting.

>> **Limit the audience for posts you've shared with Friends of Friends or Public.** This setting is one you probably won't need too often, but it could come in handy occasionally. Remember, this setting is needed only if at any point, you shared posts with Everyone or with Friends of Friends. If you've shared only with Friends (or an even smaller subset of people), this setting won't change anything. Use it to change the privacy settings of all items that were previously public to be visible only to friends.

This setting might be useful if, for example, you're job hunting, and you don't want potential employers to find your public posts about the most recent election. Once you make this change, it can't be undone. In other words, those posts will always be visible only to Friends unless you go back and individually make them public.

To use this setting, click the Limit Past Posts link on the right side of the page; then click the Limit Old Posts button that appears.

>> **Who can see your friends list?** This setting shows who can see the list of people who are your friends. By default, this list is public. You can change this by clicking the Edit link on right side of the page. This opens further explanation of the setting as well as a Privacy menu for selecting who you want to be able to see your friends. Even if you change this setting to Only Me, your friends will still be able to see a list of mutual friends in the Friends box on your Timeline.

Who Can Contact Me?

The Who Can Contact Me section should also be familiar, as it is the same setting found in the privacy shortcuts menu. This setting lets you choose between allowing anyone on Facebook to send you a Friend Request or only allowing people who know your friends to send you a Friend Request. Click Edit and then use the Privacy menu to change your setting.

Who Can Look Me Up?

This section concerns how people can find you on Facebook. When you signed up for Facebook, you entered an email address and possibly a phone number. The first two settings ask if people who search by that information will be able to find you. If you're someone who has a slightly different name than your real name on your Timeline (for example, if I were to go by Carolyn EA on Facebook rather than my actual name, Carolyn Abram), I absolutely recommend leaving these settings set to Everyone. Limiting it limits your potential friends' ability to find you.

To change this setting for either your email address or phone number, click Edit on the right side of the page and use the Privacy menu to select whether Everyone, Friends of Friends, or only Friends can search for you by email or phone number.

The third setting here concerns search engine indexing. Search engines like Google or Bing use web crawlers to create indexes they can search to provide results to users. So when someone searches for your name on Google, by default, a link to your Facebook Timeline appears. If you deselect this setting, that will no longer be true.

To change this setting, click Edit on the right side of the page and deselect the check box labeled Allow Search Engines Outside of Facebook To Link To Your Profile. A pop-up window will ask if you're sure you want to turn off this feature. Click the Turn Off button to confirm.

REMEMBER

Even if you deselect the search engine indexing check box, people will still be able to search for you by name on Facebook itself. Apart from someone you have blocked, people will always be able to search for you and get to your Timeline from Facebook Search.

Timeline and tagging

The Timeline, as I describe in Chapter 5, is basically where you collect all your stuff on Facebook. That means photos, posts, posts Friends have left you, application activity, and so on. Your Timeline allows you to look through your history and represent yourself to your Friends.

Tags on Facebook are a way of labeling people in your content. For example, when uploading a photo, you can tag a specific friend in it. That tag becomes information that others can see as well as a link back to your Friend's Timeline. In addition, from your Friend's Timeline, people can get to that photo to see her smiling face. You can tag people and Pages in status updates, photos, notes, check-ins at various places, comments, and really any other type of post. And just like you can tag friends, friends can tag you in their photos and posts.

This section of the settings page allows you to control settings related to people interacting with you on your Timeline and tagging you in posts. For controlling the privacy on things *you* add to your Timeline (that is, your posts), you use the Privacy menu in the Publisher. The Timeline and Tagging Settings section is shown in Figure 6-6.

Who Can Add Things to My Timeline?

This section focuses on other people adding things like photos, posts, or tags to your Timeline.

REMEMBER

>> **Who can post on your Timeline?** In addition to being a place where you add posts, your Timeline is a place where your Friends can leave you messages or posts. If you don't want your Friends leaving these sorts of public messages (if you're using Facebook for professional or networking reasons, for example), you can set this to Only Me. To change this setting, click Edit on the right side of the setting and use the drop-down menu that appears to select Only Me.

By default, only Friends can post on your Timeline. Changing this setting means no one can post to your Timeline except you.

>> **Review posts Friends tag you in before they appear on your Timeline.** Timeline Review allows you to review the tags people have added of you before they are displayed on your Timeline. In other words, if I tag you in a photo, that photo won't appear on your Timeline until you log in to Facebook and approve the tag.

To change this setting, click Edit on the right side of the setting and use the drop-down menu that appears to toggle between Enabled and Disabled. By default, tags of you are automatically approved, and this setting is set to Disabled or Off.

Who Can See Things on My Timeline?

There's a difference between *adding* things to your Timeline, which the preceding settings control, and simply *looking* at your Timeline, which the settings in this section control. Three settings here concern what people see when they look at your profile.

>> **Review what other people see on your Timeline.** This isn't so much a setting as a link to the View As privacy tool (which I cover in detail in the "Privacy Tools" section later in this chapter). The View As tool allows you to look at your Timeline as though you're someone else, thus double-checking that your privacy settings are working.

>> **Who can see posts you've been tagged in on your Timeline?** After you've approved tags (or if you leave Timeline Review off), you can still decide who can see the content in which you're tagged on your Timeline. In other words, if your Friend tags you in a photo, you can control who sees that photo on *your* Timeline. The idea behind this setting is that, although you will never post anything embarrassing to your Timeline, a Friend might (accidentally, I hope) do so. Making sure that not everyone can see that post (except other, more understanding friends) cuts down on any awkwardness.

To change this setting, click the Edit link on the right side of the page and then use the drop-down menu that appears to choose who can see this information.

>> **Who can see what others post on your Timeline?** Another way to control the "embarrassing friend on your Timeline" problem is to limit who can see the posts your friends leave.

To change this setting, click the Edit link on the right side of the page and use the drop-down menu that appears to select who can see these posts.

How Can I Manage Tags People Add and Tagging Suggestions?

Although tagging has been mentioned in many of these Timeline settings, these settings refer to very specific use cases of tagging that you maybe never thought about before.

>> **Review tags people add to your own posts before the tags appear on Facebook.** This setting controls tags your friends add to content you've uploaded. For example, if I upload a photo of 20 people to Facebook and don't tag anyone in it, my friends might choose to add tags. This setting lets me choose to review the tags my friends add before the tag is visible to other people.

To change this setting, click Edit on the right side of the page; then use the drop-down menu that appears to select whether Tag Review is Enabled or Disabled. By default it is Disabled (Off).

>> **When you're tagged in a post, who do you want to add to the audience if they aren't already in it?** This setting sounds very complicated, so let's break it down with an example. Say that Claire has two friends: Jamie and Frank. Jamie and Frank are not friends with each other. Now, say that Frank adds a photo of Claire (meaning he has tagged her in it), and his privacy settings share that photo with his friends. Because Jamie and Frank aren't friends, Jamie cannot see that photo. If Claire allows her friends to be added to the audience of that photo, then Jamie *will* be able to see it. In other words, Claire can control whether Jamie can see a photo of her that Frank has added.

To change this setting, click Edit on the right side of the page and use the drop-down menu that appears to select who is added to the audience of a post you're tagged in. There are only three options for this setting: Friends, Only Me, and Custom. By default, this setting adds your friends to the audience of a post you're tagged in.

>> **Who sees tag suggestions when photos that look like you are uploaded?** Facebook employs some facial recognition software to help people tag photos. So if a Friend is uploading 50 photos and you appear in 30 of them, Facebook might recognize your face and suggest to your friend that you be tagged in those 30 photos. This is to save your friend time while he's adding photos, and to encourage people to add more tags to Facebook. You can choose not to appear in the suggestions Facebook gives your friends by disabling this setting.

To change this setting, click Edit on the right side of the page and use the drop-down menu that appears to select whether Friends or No One will see tag suggestions.

Blocking

Most of your privacy settings are preventive measures for making yourself comfortable on Facebook. Blocklists are usually more reactive. If someone does something on Facebook that bothers you, you may choose to block him or block certain actions he takes from affecting you. The Blocking section of the Settings page is shown in Figure 6-7. You can manage seven blocklists here: Restricted List, Block Users, Block Messages, Block App Invites, Block Event Invites, Block Apps, and Block Pages.

FIGURE 6-7:
Edit your
blocklists here.

Using the Restricted List

The Restricted List is a list you can create that accomplishes something like using the "Friends except" privacy option. Friends who have been added to your restricted list cannot see posts and other information that are visible only to Friends. They will still be able to see any public posts you have shared, and they'll see you interacting with people on Facebook. Think of it as one step below blocking someone.

To add someone to this list, click Edit List on the right side of the page. A pop-up window appears, as shown in Figure 6-8. If you've already added people to this list, they appear here, and you can remove them from the list by hovering over their pictures and clicking the X that appears in the right corner of the photos.

FIGURE 6-8:
Add people to the
Restricted List.

To add people to the list, follow these steps:

1. **Click the button in the top left of the box named On This List.**

   A menu of two options appears: Friends and On This List.

2. **Click Friends.**

   A grid appears showing all your friends listed alphabetically by first name.

3. **Select friends to add to the restricted list by clicking their pictures or by searching for them by name in the upper-right corner and then clicking their pictures.**

4. **When you're done, click the Finish button in the lower-right corner of the box.**

Blocking users

Blocking someone on Facebook is the strongest way to distance yourself from someone else on Facebook. For the most part, if you add someone to your Block List, he can't see any traces of you on Facebook. You won't show up in his News Feed; if he looks at a photo in which you're tagged, he may see you in the photo (that's unavoidable), but he won't see that your name has been tagged. When you write on other people's Timelines, your posts are hidden from him. Here are a few key things to remember about blocking:

>> **It's almost entirely reciprocal.** If you block someone, she is just as invisible to you as you are to her. So you can't access her Timeline, nor can you see anything about her anywhere on the site. The only difference is that if you blocked the relationship, you're the only one who can unblock it.

>> **People you block are not notified that you blocked them.** Nor are they notified if you unblock them. If they are savvy Facebook users, they may notice your suspicious absence, but Facebook never tells them that they have been blocked by you.

>> **You can block people who are your friends or who are not your friends.** If you are friends with someone and then you block her, Facebook also removes the friendship. If, at some point in the future, you unblock her, you will need to re-friend her.

WARNING

Blocking on Facebook doesn't necessarily extend to apps and games you use on Facebook and around the Internet. Contact the developers of the apps you use to learn how to block people within games and apps.

To add people to your blocklist, simply enter their names or email addresses into the boxes provided. Then click the Block button. Their names then appear in a list here. Click the Unblock link next to their names if you want to remove the block.

Blocking Messages

Blocking someone from sending you messages is very useful if someone is specifically bothering you through either the Facebook Messenger app or by sending you Facebook messages from their computers. Messages, in this case, includes chats, voice, and video calls from the Facebook Messenger app. If someone is bothering you in comments sections or on your Timeline, you need to fully block them to get them to leave you alone. But if messages are the only problem, then you have an easy solution here.

Note that you can only add friends to the messaging Block List. If you are being bothered by someone who is not a friend, you will need to report and/or block them entirely.

To add people to the Messages Block List, simply enter their name in the box provided and press Enter. Their name appears in a list, as shown in Figure 6-9. Click the Unblock link next to their name if you want to remove the block.

FIGURE 6-9:
View who you've blocked, and click to unblock

Block messages from	Type the name of a friend...
• Steve Hayes Unblock	
• Carolyn Abram Unblock	

Blocking App Invites

An *app* is a term used to describe pieces of software that use Facebook data, even when those apps weren't built by Facebook. As friends use apps and games, they may want you to join in on the fun and send you an invite to join them. This is all well and good until you find that certain people send you wayyyy too many invites. Rather than unfriend or block the overly friendly person who's sending you all those invitations, you can simply block invitations. This option still allows you to interact with your friend in every other way, but you won't receive application invites from him or her.

To block invites from a specific person, just type the person's name in the Block Invites From box and click Enter when you're done. That person's name then appears on the list below the text box. To remove the block, click Unblock next to that name.

Blocking Event Invites

As with App Invites, you may have friends who are big planners and love to invite all their friends to their events. These may be events that you have no chance of attending because they're taking place across the country, and your friend has chosen to invite all his friends without any regard for location. Again, your friend is cool; his endless unnecessary invitations are not. Instead of getting rid of your friend, you can get rid of the invitations by entering his name here.

To block event invites from specific people, just type their names into the Block Invites From box and click Enter when you're done. Their names then appear on the list below the text box. To remove the block, click Unblock next to their names.

Blocking Apps

Occasionally, an app behaves badly once you start using it. By "behave badly," I mean things like spamming your friends or using your information in ways that make you uncomfortable. If an app is doing so, you can block it to prevent it from contacting you through Facebook and getting updated Facebook information about you.

To block an app, type its name in the Block Apps text field and press Enter. The name of the app appears on the list below the text box. To remove the block, click Unblock next to its name.

Blocking Pages

Pages are basically Timelines for non-people (things like businesses, brands, famous people, pets, anything that isn't covered by the term "person"). Pages can often interact in many of the same ways as regular people on Facebook (for example, commenting on or liking your posts), which means you might find yourself in a situation where you need to block one. When you block a Page from interacting with you, it will no longer be able to interact with you or your posts, and you won't be able to interact with that Page via message or post. It also automatically includes un-liking and unfollowing the Page.

To block a Page, type its name into the Block Pages text field and press Enter. The name of the Page appears on the list below the text box. To remove the block, click Unblock next to its name.

Apps

An *app* is a term used to describe pieces of software that use Facebook data, even when those applications weren't built by Facebook. You may use apps as games, websites, and useful tools, all of which make use of the data you already share on Facebook. To make it easier to get people using these applications, they import the data from Facebook. Chapter 15 covers the specifics on using applications. For now, keep in mind that the apps you see on this page are those you chose to interact with. You won't see random applications appear here without you giving them some permissions first.

The App Settings section, shown in Figure 6-10, is where you go to edit how apps, games, and websites interact with your Timeline.

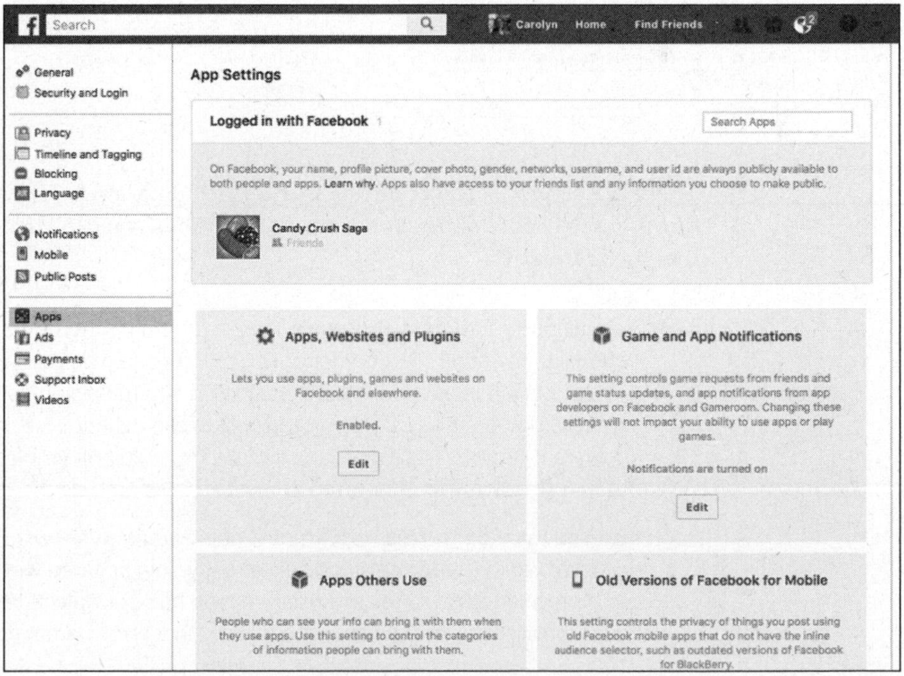

FIGURE 6-10: App settings.

Logged In with Facebook

The Logged In with Facebook section at the top of the App Settings page shows all the apps you've used, including websites where you've used Facebook to log in. Under each app's name in this list is the audience that can see that app on your Timeline. Click on the privacy icon or the pencil icon that appears when you hover your mouse over the app's name to open the Edit App menu.

Figure 6-11 shows the Edit App menu, where you can review and edit the information that the app can access as well as how the app can interact with your Facebook usage.

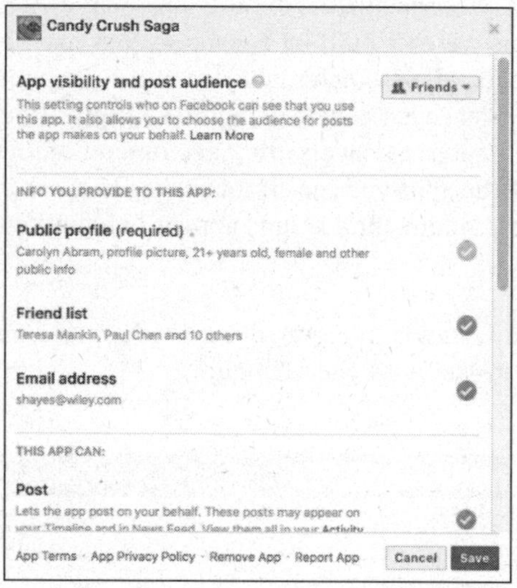

FIGURE 6-11:
Edit app settings
here.

There are several sections of this menu (including a few that you need to scroll down to see). Some of these sections have options you can change, and others are merely informative.

>> **App Visibility and post audience:** The Privacy menu here has the same options as any other Privacy menu. You can choose who can see both that you use a given app as well as any posts that app makes on your behalf. For example, I keep my Kickstarter app visible to friends because I like them to know what projects I'm supporting. I make my Hulu app visible to Only Me because I'm ashamed of how much reality television I watch.

>> **Info You Provide to This App:** This list of information shows what information from your Facebook account is currently being shared with the app in question. In addition to the information type (for example, Friend List or Education History) you can see examples of that information (for example,

Oliver, Felicity, John; Tufts and Phillips Academy). Apart from your Public Profile (which includes your name, profile picture, age, gender, and any other publicly available info), you can stop sharing other types of info with an app by unchecking the blue circle next to it in this menu.

» **This App Can:** This section lets you control whether an app can post to your Timeline on your behalf, and whether it can send you notifications. For the most part, apps only post to your Timeline when you have taken an action within the app (for example, completing a new level in Candy Crush Saga). If you don't want the app to do this anymore, uncheck the blue circle. If you are receiving too many notifications from an app, you can use the menu here to make that stop. Simply use the menu next to *Send you notifications* to switch from Yes to No.

» **Learn More:** This section provides links to learn more about different aspects of using apps. It also provides links to contact the developers of the app you are using. Remember, Facebook isn't always the company that has built an app, so if you are having trouble using that app or want your info deleted, you will need to contact the company who built the app, instead of contacting Facebook.

» **Links:** At the bottom of the Edit App menu, next to the Cancel and Save buttons, are a few links that may come in handy:

- **App Terms:** This link takes you to the app's Terms of Service.

- **App Privacy Policy:** This link takes you to the app's Privacy Policy.

- **Remove App:** If you want to sever all ties with an app, you can click this link to remove it entirely from your Facebook experience. It won't be able to access any of your info going forward.

- **Report App:** You can use this link to report an app for things like spamming, abusive behavior or content, or for using your information inappropriately.

Apps, Websites, and Plugins

This setting is like a big giant "kill" switch for using Apps, Websites, and Plugins with your Facebook account. If you are sure that there is no way you will ever want to use any sort of app under any circumstance, you can choose to disable Facebook Platform. If you do so, any apps you have used will be removed, and their posts will be deleted from your Timeline. You won't be able to log in to external websites with your Facebook credentials, and your friends won't be able to interact with you through their apps. If you're sure that this is what you want, click Edit to open the Turn Platform Off menu, then click the blue Disable Platform button.

Apps Others Use

Even if you don't use applications, your friends may. Just as your friends can add and tag photos of you even though you haven't added photos yourself, your friends may also pass on information about you to applications. You can restrict what applications can see by clicking Edit and using the check boxes pictured in Figure 6-12.

Apps Others Use

People on Facebook who can see your info can bring it with them when they use apps. This makes their experience better and more social. Use the settings below to control the categories of information that people can bring with them when they use apps, games and websites.

- ☑ Bio
- ☑ Birthday
- ☑ Family and relationships
- ☐ Interested in
- ☐ Religious and political views
- ☑ My website
- ☑ If I'm online

- ☑ Posts on my timeline
- ☑ Hometown
- ☑ Current city
- ☑ Education and work
- ☑ Activities, interests, things I like
- ☑ My app activity

If you don't want apps and websites to access other categories of information (like your friend list, gender or info you've made public), you can turn off all Platform apps. But remember, you will not be able to use any games or apps yourself.

Cancel Save

FIGURE 6-12:
What can your friends share with apps and games?

Game and App notifications

If you don't like receiving notifications from any apps, regardless of what type of app it is or what it does, you can turn off all notifications. Personally, I prefer to turn off notifications on an app by app basis, because I generally like to be notified when my friends take actions that may link back to my Timeline. When you turn off notifications, you are not limiting your ability to use an app, nor are you limiting your friends' ability to interact with you. All you are doing is muting the stream of notifications that may be bothering you.

To turn off notifications, click the Edit button in the center of the Game and App Notifications on the right half of the App Settings page. A pop-up box opens confirming that you want to turn off notifications.

Old Versions of Facebook for Mobile

If you've never used Facebook on a mobile phone or are certain you're using the most recent Facebook app on an iPhone or Android phone, this setting doesn't apply to you. But if you're using a version of Facebook for Mobile that doesn't allow you to change your privacy for each post you create, you can use this setting to control who sees posts you make from your phone. Click the Privacy menu at the bottom of this box to make your selection.

Ads

Facebook is free for you to use. Instead of charging its users money, Facebook pays the bills by selling ads. These ads are then shown to you. So, in a way, looking at ads is the way you pay for using Facebook.

Facebook chooses which ads to show you in many ways. The Ad Preferences page, shown in Figure 6-13, is what opens when you choose Ads from the left side of the Settings page. Here you can see some of the ways Facebook chooses which ads to show you. You can exert some influence on some aspects of the ads you see, but no matter what, you will still see ads.

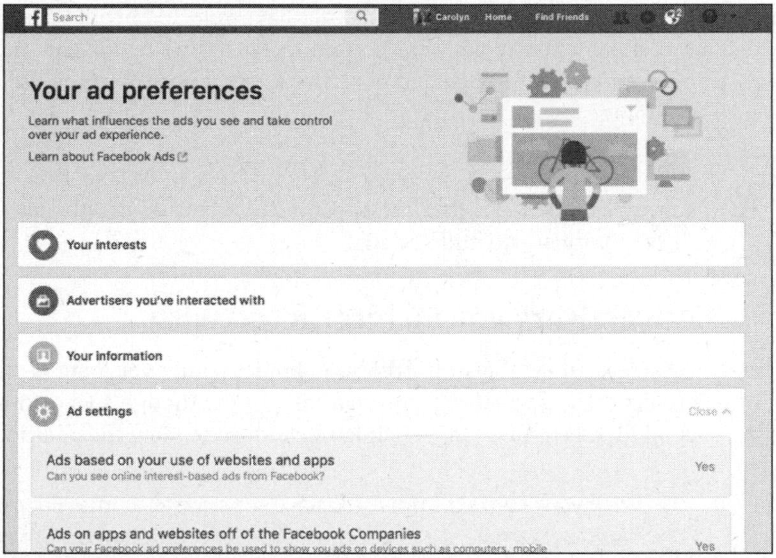

FIGURE 6-13: Learn more about why you see the ads you see here.

Note that advertisers never get any personally identifying information about you from Facebook. They only get *aggregated* data, or data that has been compiled about many users without specifically naming any one user. So an advertiser never sees that you, personally, clicked on that one ad for the new season of *Outlander* upwards of ten times. All they know is that their ad received a certain number of clicks from women in the 30–35 age range. Similarly, Facebook is not showing an advertiser a picture of you and saying, "this person lives in Seattle and likes coffee and has two children and is afraid of clowns." If an advertiser selects "coffee" as an interest for their desired audience, they are told how many people might see that ad.

The Ad Preferences page has five sections. Click on any of the top four sections to see more information and options. You can also click on the fifth section to open another page where you can learn more about how Facebook advertising works.

Your Interests

When advertisers create an ad on Facebook, they select an audience for their ads. Their audience might be selected based on age, gender, country, or some combination. They may also be selected based on interests. The Your Interests section displays the interest categories that you fall into. Some of these are Pages you have liked or things that you have listed on your Timeline's Interests sections. Other items are ones that Facebook has algorithmically decided to apply to you. For example, if you like a local coffee shop's Facebook Page, you may find that you now have "coffee" as an interest in this section.

Your interests are displayed as thumbnail images. You can click on any of these images to see a preview of the sorts of ads you might see because of that interest. In other words, you can see ads that have selected people like you as part of their audience. If you don't want certain interests to include you anymore, hover your mouse over that image and click the X that appears in the upper-right corner of the image.

REMEMBER

Even if you clicked X on every single interest in this section, *you will still see ads.* You will not see ads that are specifically aimed at people who like, for example, coffee, but you will still see ads.

Advertisers you've interacted with

This section displays information about the ads you may be seeing currently. It breaks these advertisers into five categories, though two or more categories may be hidden behind a "More" link. Click More to view the additional sections.

>> **With your contact info:** If you have separate accounts with certain companies (for example, if you get email promotions from a retailer), those companies can feed those email lists into Facebook and target their subscribers with ads. You can see advertisers who have targeted you based on your contact info here.

>> **Whose website or app you've used:** Facebook and many other websites use something called "cookies" to track users across different websites. Cookies allows ads to be shown to you based on the other websites and apps you have used. You can see advertisers who have used cookies to show you ads here.

>> **Whom you've visited:** If you use Facebook's app on your mobile phone and have location services enabled, Facebook may be able to serve you ads based on the physical stores you visit. If you have seen ads based on stores you have visited, those advertisers will appear in this space. This feature is very new so it's very likely this space will be blank at the moment.

>> **Whose ads you've clicked:** Anytime you have clicked on a Facebook ad that action gets recorded by Facebook's systems. You can see the advertisers whose ads you have clicked in the past here.

>> **Whom you've hidden:** When you hide advertisers, that fact is recorded and stored by Facebook's systems. You can view all the advertisers you have hidden here.

In any of these sections, you can choose to hide ads from any individual advertiser. Simply hover your mouse over the thumbnail image and click the X that appears in the upper-right corner. You will no longer see ads from that company.

Your information

This section has two components: About You and Your Categories. Your About You section displays the biographical information you've chosen to share on your profile. By default, Facebook is able to show you ads based on these fields. For example, a single person may see different ads than a married one. Employees of a certain company may see recruiting ads from a competitor. Click on the blue toggle next to any category to prevent Facebook from showing you ads based on that information. The toggle will slide from blue to gray to signify that it is no longer available.

The Your Categories section makes visible some of the inferences Facebook has made about you and the categories of ads that might apply to you. These range from the very specific—Parents with preschoolers 3–5 years—to the very broad—Arts, Entertainment, Sports, and Media. This is basically showing you all the buckets you fall into that advertisers might be choosing from. If any of these categories are ones you'd rather not be part of, hover over that category and click on the X to remove yourself from it.

I wouldn't recommend spending too much time worrying about which buckets you fall into unless you are getting a type of ad that is upsetting to you for personal reasons. For example, women who experience a miscarriage may find that they are still getting pregnancy-related ads and may be able to remove themselves from related categories here.

Ad settings

The first setting on this page is for Ads Based on Your Use of Websites and Apps. Facebook can choose to show you ads based on other websites you have visited. It calls these ads *online interest-based advertising.* You can choose to turn these ads off. Remember, this doesn't turn ads off, it simply means you won't see online interest-based ads.

The second setting, Ads on Apps and Websites off the Facebook Companies concerns whether your Facebook ad preferences can be used on third party sites or apps where you have connected your Facebook account. By default, your ad preferences can be ported over to any sites with your Facebook account the same way your profile picture and name can be used.

Ads with Your Social Actions concerns how your Facebook information may appear alongside ads on Facebook. Facebook differentiates its ads from other ads on the Internet by pointing out that their ads are "social." In other words, if my friend likes something, there's a good chance I will like it, too. So in its ads, whenever possible, Facebook includes social information. You can see an example of this in Figure 6-14.

FIGURE 6-14:
An ad with social information.

Personally, I'm comfortable with my friends seeing things that I've liked, or public events I've attended, or places I've checked in, being paired with an ad for that thing, event, or place. If you aren't comfortable with this, that's okay, too; you can prevent it from happening here.

To prevent your friends from seeing any information about you next to an advertisement, click Only My Friends on the right side of the section. Use the drop-down menu that appears (below all the text) to toggle between Only My Friends and No One.

REMEMBER

Even if you don't change this setting, only your Friends ever see information about you next to ads. If we're not Friends, you'll never see a notice that "Carolyn Abram likes this movie" next to an advertisement for a popular film.

Timeline Privacy

In addition to the content you post — which was covered earlier in the "Privacy on the Go" section — you can control the information that you've entered in the About and Interests sections of your Timeline.

All about privacy

This information, such as where you went to school or your relationship status, changes infrequently, if ever. You can edit the privacy for this content in the same place you edit the information itself. To get there, go to your Timeline, then click on the About tab at the bottom of your cover photo.

The About page has several sections, each representing a different information category. So, for example, all your work and education information appear in the Work and Education section. When you hover your mouse over any item, a privacy icon appears signifying who can see that piece of information. By default, most of this information is set to Public and visible to Everyone, although contact information is visible only to Friends by default.

Figure 6-15 shows me editing the privacy for a piece of information — in this case, my current city in the Living section of my About page. Clicking the privacy icon to the right of the field opens an interface for editing that information as well as changing who can see it. Use the privacy menu to change the privacy and click Save Changes when you're done. Rinse and repeat for any other pieces of information in the About section.

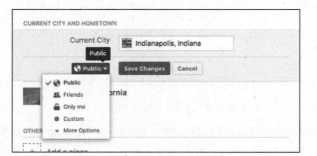

FIGURE 6-15: Edit privacy for every piece of information on your Timeline.

Timeline information is one of the places where the Only Me setting might come in handy. For example, lots of people don't like sharing their birthdays on Facebook, but Facebook requires you to enter a birthday when you sign up. By making it visible only to you, it effectively hides your birthday from everyone.

REMEMBER

Click Save Changes when you're done editing privacy settings. Otherwise, the new settings won't stick.

Interested in privacy

On your Timeline, interests are sorted into categories like Movies, Music, Books, and so on. For your TV Shows section, for example, you can add TV shows that you've watched, TV shows that you want to watch, and TV shows that you like. Each time you add a TV show to the list of shows you've watched or want to watch, you can also control who sees that you've added that show to that list. Figure 6-16 shows me editing who can see that I've watched the television show *Arrow*. I opened this Privacy menu by clicking the privacy icon beneath the image representing the show.

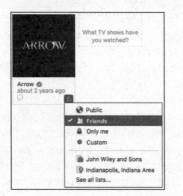

FIGURE 6-16:
Selecting who can see what I've watched.

Additionally, I can control who can see what TV shows I like. Unlike the Watched and Want to Watch sections, where I can edit this individually, I decide who can see *all* the shows I've liked. To edit who can see what you've liked, follow these steps:

1. **Make sure you're looking at the correct section on your screen.**

   In this case, I'm looking at the TV Shows section.

2. **Click the pencil icon button in the upper-right corner of the box.**

   A menu of options related to this section appears.

3. **Click Edit Privacy.**

   A pop-up window opens.

4. **In the section of the box labeled Likes, click the Privacy menu.**

   This opens the Privacy menu with familiar options: Public, Friends, Only Me, Custom, or More Options.

5. **Choose whom you want to see the TV shows you have liked.**

6. **Click Close to save the changes.**

Privacy Tools

Okay, that was a lot. A lot of settings, a lot of information. What if you don't want to worry about these small settings and who tagged what when? What if you just want to make sure that your Timeline looks the way you want to your friends and that people who aren't your friends can't see anything you don't want them to see? Well, the good news is that the View As tool allows you to do just that, and the Activity Log tool allows you to keep track of everything that's been happening recently and to make any needed adjustments without trying to figure out which setting, exactly, needs to be changed. You can also run a privacy checkup to make sure that your expectations of what your privacy is matches the reality.

View As

To get to the View As tool, open the Quick Help menu (the question mark icon) in the big blue bar on top of any page. Click the Privacy Shortcuts menu item. This opens the Privacy Shortcuts menu that was covered earlier in this chapter. Click on the "Who Can See My Stuff?" section to expand the menu of options, then click the View As link.

Clicking View As brings you to your Timeline. Except, it's probably not the way you usually see your Timeline. The black bar running across the top of the page lets you know that you're currently viewing your Timeline as someone who is not your friend (also known as *everyone* in the Public bucket of people). You can click through to the various sections of your Timeline. (Photos tends to be a section that people like to check, double-check, and triple-check.)

Note that no matter how much you've hidden your information and posts, everyone can see your cover photo and profile picture, gender, and current city. Anything else the public can see can be hidden, if you so choose.

In the black bar on top of this view of your Timeline, there's a white bold link labeled View as Specific Person. If you want to check on, for example, which acquaintances or people you've added to a list can see, click this link and enter a friend's name into the text box that appears. If you're surprised by what that friend can see, you can go change the privacy on any content you don't want her to see. (If you've forgotten how to change the privacy on a post, head back up to the "Privacy On the Go" section.)

Activity Log

As you've probably noticed, a lot happens on Facebook. You take all sorts of actions: liking, commenting, posting, and so on. And people take all sorts of actions that affect you: writing on your Timeline, tagging you in photos, and inviting you to join groups. If you want to know, line by line, everything that could possibly be seen about you by someone on Facebook, Activity Log is for you.

You can get to Activity Log from a few places. You can get there from the Privacy Shortcuts menu or from your own Timeline. On your Timeline, simply click the View Activity Log button, located at the bottom right corner of your cover photo. This takes you to Activity Log (see Figure 6-17).

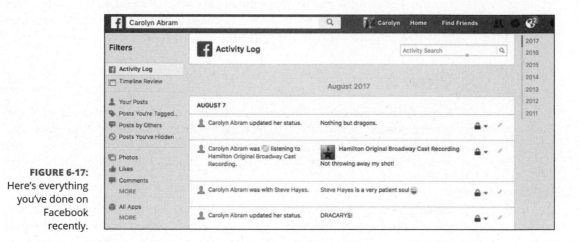

FIGURE 6-17: Here's everything you've done on Facebook recently.

When you're looking at Activity Log, notice that there's a menu on the left for viewing only certain types of posts. For example, you can choose to view all the posts you've been tagged in, or all the photo posts, or all the app-related posts.

When you're looking at an individual line item, you see several columns of information. First is an icon and sentence explaining what you did (or what a Friend did). This might be something like "Carolyn wrote on Dana's Timeline" or "Carolyn was tagged in Dana's photo." Then there is a preview of that post, photo, comment, or whatever it is related to. For example, if you commented on a photo, the preview will show you that photo and the comment that you made.

To the right of the preview is an icon representing who can see that item. Hover your mouse over the icon to see text explaining who can see it. This might be the usual privacy options, or it might be members of a group you belong to, or in the case of a post to a Friend's Timeline, it will be that person's friends. For posts that you create, you can change the audience by clicking the icon, which opens the Privacy menu.

However, you'll find you can't change the privacy on lots of content. For example, a comment on someone else's post isn't something you can change the audience for. If you realize a comment you made or something you liked is visible to more people than you'd want, your only option is to delete that content.

You can delete content using the final icon to the right side of each item in Activity Log. This little pencil icon can be found all over the site and generally indicates that you can edit something. When you hover over the icon here, it explains that the item is allowed on Timeline. This means that people may see that item — possibly as its own post, possibly as a summarized item in recent activity, possibly in an Interests section when they visit your Timeline. Clicking the Edit button reveals a menu of options for changing whether something appears on Timeline. For some items, such as likes or comments, the only option is to unlike the content or delete the comment. For others, like posts you've made or posts you've been tagged in, there are more options that allow you to hide something from the Timeline or edit it on your Timeline (these are the same options that appear when you go to edit or highlight something on your Timeline).

REMEMBER

When I say something is visible on Timeline, I also mean that your Friends might see that item in their News Feed.

Personally, I find Activity Log useful in that it helps me understand all the ways I participate on Facebook and all the things my friends might see about me and my life. But I've found that I don't change the privacy or the Timeline settings on items here all that often.

Privacy Checkup

Privacy Checkup is a tool Facebook built to make it easier for you to make sure that everything is on the up-and-up privacy-wise. Especially if you've been using Facebook for a long time, you can start to feel uncertain about who can see what. Privacy Checkup is designed to make it easy to become certain and feel comfortable sharing.

To use Privacy Checkup, open the Quick Help menu, and click on Privacy Checkup. This opens the Privacy Checkup window, which has three sections:

>> **Posts:** The first section concerns your posts, and lets you change the default setting for who can see the posts you make.

>> **Apps:** The second section shows your apps and lets you make choices about who can see the apps you use. In other words, the same things found in the Apps section of your settings page.

>> **Profile:** The third section shows some of the contact and basic information from your Timeline, and lets you double-check who can see each piece of information. You can edit your privacy for any of this information directly from the Privacy Checkup window.

One of the hardest moments to hear about from frustrated Facebook users is when they say, "But I thought no one could see that!" Privacy Checkup is a great way to make sure that what you think matches the reality of your privacy settings.

Remembering That It Takes a Village to Raise a Facebook

Another way in which you (and every member of Facebook) contribute to keeping Facebook a safe, clean place is in the reports that you submit about spam, harassment, inappropriate content, and fake Timelines. Almost every piece of content on Facebook can be reported. Sometimes you may need to click an Options link to find the report link.

Figure 6-18 shows an example of someone reporting an inappropriate photo.

The reporting options vary depending on what you're reporting (a group as opposed to a photo, for example). These reports are submitted to the Facebook Help Team. The team then investigates and takes down inappropriate photos, disables fake accounts, and generally strives to keep Facebook clean, safe, and inoffensive.

When you see content that you don't like — for example, an offensive group name, hate speech, or a vulgar Timeline — don't hesitate to report it. With the entire Facebook population working to keep Facebook free of badness, you hopefully prevent a lot of inappropriate content from disseminating too widely.

REMEMBER

After you report something, Facebook's Help Team evaluates it in terms of violating Facebook's Statement of Rights and Responsibilities. This means that pornography gets taken down, fake Timelines are disabled, and people who send spam may receive a warning or even have their account disabled. However, sometimes something that you report may be offensive to you but doesn't violate the

Statement of Rights and Responsibilities and, therefore, will remain on Facebook. Due to privacy restrictions, the Help Team may not always notify you about actions taken because of your support, but rest assured that the team handles every report. Facebook will correspond with you about reports you make in the Support Inbox, which you can find in the Quick Help menu.

Peeking Behind the Scenes

Facebook's part in keeping everyone safe requires a lot of manpower and technology power. The manpower involves responding to the reports that you and the rest of Facebook submit, as well as proactively going into Facebook and getting rid of content that violates the Statement of Rights and Responsibilities.

The technology power that I talk about is kept vague on purpose. I hope that you never think twice about the things that are happening behind the scenes to protect you from harassment, spam, and pornography. Moreover, I hope that you're never harassed or spammed, or accidentally happen upon a pornographic photo. But just so you know that Facebook is actively thinking about user safety and privacy, I talk about a few of the general areas where Facebook does a lot of preventive work.

Protecting minors

In general, people under the age of 18 have special visibility and privacy rules applied to them. For example, Tag Review, which is turned off by default for adults, is turned on, by default, for minors, thus meaning minors must actively approve tags from their friends.

Other proprietary systems are in place that are alerted if a person is interacting with the Timelines of minors in ways they shouldn't, as well as systems that get alerted when someone targets an ad to minors. Facebook tries to prevent whatever it can, but this is where some common sense on the part of teens (and their parents) can go a long way toward preventing bad situations.

REMEMBER

You must be at least 13 years old to join Facebook.

Preventing spam and viruses

Everyone can agree that spam is one of the worst parts of the Internet, all too often sliming its way through the cracks into email and websites — and always trying to slime its way into Facebook as well, sometimes in the form of messages to you, or Timeline posts, or groups, or events masking as something they're not to capture your precious attention.

When you report a piece of content on Facebook, "It's spam" is usually one of the reasons you can give for reporting it. These spam reports are incredibly helpful. Facebook also has a bunch of systems that keep track of the sort of behavior that spammers tend to do. The spam systems also keep track of those who message people too quickly, friend too many people, post a similar link in too many places, and do other such behaviors that tend to reek of spam. If you end up really taking to this Facebook thing, at some point you may get hit with a warning to slow down your messaging. Don't take it too personally, and just follow the instructions in the warning — this is the spam system at work.

Preventing phishing

Phishing is a term that refers to malicious websites attempting to gain sensitive information (like usernames and passwords to online accounts) by masquerading as the sites you use and trust. Phishing is usually part of spamming: A malicious site acquires someone's Facebook credentials and then messages all that user's friends with a link to a phishing site that looks like Facebook and asks them to log in. They do so, and now the bad guys have a bunch of new Facebook logins and passwords. It's a bad cycle. The worst part is that many of these Facebook users get locked out of their own accounts and are unable to stop the spam.

Just like spam and virus prevention, Facebook has a series of proprietary systems in place to try to break this cycle. If you do have the misfortune to get phished (and it can happen to the best of us), you may run into one of the systems that Facebook uses to help people take back their Timelines and protect themselves from phishing in the future.

The best way to protect yourself from phishing is to get used to the times and places Facebook asks for your password. If you just clicked a link within Facebook and suddenly there's a blue screen asking for your information, be suspicious! Similarly, remember that Facebook will never ask you to email it your password. If you receive an email asking for something like that, report it as spam immediately. Also, beware of attachments from friends that you must download or strange messages from friends who don't normally message you.

TIP

If you want to stay up-to-date with the latest scams on Facebook, or want more information about protecting yourself, you can like Facebook's Security Page at www.facebook.com/security. This provides you with ongoing information about safety and security on Facebook.

One Final Call to Use Your Common Sense

No one wants anything bad to happen to you because of something you do on Facebook. Facebook doesn't want that. You don't want that. I definitely don't want that. I hope that these explanations help to prevent anything bad from happening to you on Facebook. But no matter what, *you* need to take part in keeping yourself safe. To ensure your own safety on Facebook, you have to make an effort to be smart and safe online.

So what *is* your part? Your part is to be aware of what you're putting online and on Facebook. You need to be the one to choose whether displaying any given piece of information on Facebook is risky. If it's risky, you need to be the one to figure out the correct privacy settings for showing this information to the people you choose to see it — and not to the people you don't.

REMEMBER

Your part is equivalent to the part you play in your everyday life to keep yourself safe: You know which alleys not to walk down at night, when to buckle your seat-belt, when to lock the front door, and when to toss the moldy bread before making a sandwich. Now that you know all about Facebook's privacy settings, you also know when to use the various privacy options, and when to simply refrain from posting.

I'M HAVING A PRIVACY FREAK OUT; WHAT DO I DO?

I cannot tell you how many times I've gotten a frantic email from a family member or friend saying something like, "Oh my gosh, my friend just told me that his friend was able to see these photos that I thought only my friends could see and now I'm freaking out that everyone can see everything; do you know what to do?"

The first step is to take a deep breath.

After that, the next best thing to do is to go to the Privacy Shortcuts menu and click the View As tool.

That allows you to click around your Timeline as though you're someone who isn't your Friend. If you think that person is seeing too much, I recommend using the Limit the Audience for Past Posts setting on the Privacy section of the Settings page. This pretty much changes anything that used to be visible to more than just friends to be visible only to Friends. After you do that, usually you can begin the process of adjusting your settings so that, going forward, you won't have any more freak-outs.

Chapter **7**

Facebook on the Go

I had an existential argument with myself about this chapter as I sat down to write it. I wasn't sure it needed to exist. Not because you'll never use mobile features, but the opposite. Using Facebook on a mobile phone is so integral that it is virtually indistinguishable from using it on the computer.

In part, that's by design. Any actions you take on Facebook on the web are visible on Facebook on your phone and vice versa. You can start a comment thread on your phone and pick it up on your computer. You can post a photo from your computer and check on how many likes it received while you're on your phone at a coffee shop later. The Facebook app is designed to look and feel like Facebook, so that without even thinking about it, you'll likely be tapping on the link or button you need instinctively.

Personally, I use Facebook more from my phone than I do from my computer. It's when I'm out and about that I see things happening that I want to share. I take photos on my phone and want to get them out into Facebook-world immediately. When I'm out and about is also when I tend to have time to kill: waiting for a doctor's appointment to start, sitting on a bus, pacing back and forth with a screaming baby. These are the times when I most want to read about my friends, catch up on interesting links and articles, and generally know what's going on around me.

In this chapter, I make a foolish assumption: I assume that you have a mobile phone and know how to use its features. In addition, for the bulk of this chapter, I assume that you have an iPhone or Android phone where you can use apps, or at least browse the web from your mobile browser. If you have a mobile phone that can send and receive text messages but can't use apps or browse the web, skip over the bulk of this chapter to learn about Facebook Texts.

The Facebook App

The Facebook app exists for iPhones and Android phones, as well as special versions for Windows phones. I am an iPhone user, so the steps and figures in the upcoming section are based on my experiences using Facebook for iPhone. If you are an Android user, worry not; the functionality is largely the same, and many of the numbered steps will likely be very similar to what you see on your phone. The biggest differences will be in the locations of certain buttons or links.

Before you can get started with the Facebook app, you need to download the app to your mobile phone. For Android phones, that means doing so from Google Play, and for iPhone users, that means doing so from the App Store. The app is free to download and use. Once it has been downloaded, you will need to log in to your Facebook account (shown in Figure 7-1). You will only need to log in the first time you use the Facebook app; after that, your phone remembers your login info.

REMEMBER

Even after you download and log in to the Facebook app, you may need to additionally grant it access to things like your phone's camera roll, camera, contacts list, and so on to use all of Facebook's features on the app.

Layout and navigation

The bulk of the Facebook app's Home page (shown in Figure 7-2), much like the Home page on the web, is News Feed. You can use your finger to swipe News Feed up and down to browse your friends' posts (a bit more on News Feed in a little bit). A News Feed icon in the bottom menu ensures that you are always able to return to this Home page from wherever else you are on Facebook.

The other parts of Facebook you see in your web browser — the left-side menu, the Publisher, and the blue bar on top — are distributed between menus at the top and bottom of the screen.

FIGURE 7-1:
Log in to the
Facebook app for
iPhone.

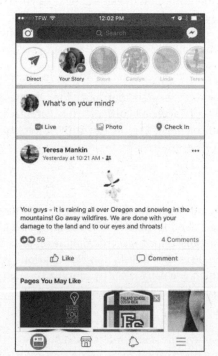

FIGURE 7-2:
Facebook for
iPhone home.

To navigate around Facebook using the app, simply tap on what you want to see more of. See a photo thumbnail that looks interesting? Tap it. You want to see a person's Timeline? Tap his face or name. You can navigate back from wherever you go by tapping the back arrow or X in the upper-left corner of whatever you wind up looking at. You can also tap on the News Feed icon in the bottom menu to go back to News Feed and your Home page. When you click a link in a post you will need to tap the back arrow to get back to News Feed, since the bottom menu may no longer be visible.

TIP

For Android users: Instead of menus at the top and bottom of the screen, the Facebook app for Android has two menu bars at the top of the screen, one blue and one white.

Search

The app does have a blue bar on top, but it has only three items. A Camera icon (more on that in the upcoming "Posting from the app" section), a Search box, and an icon that represents the Facebook Messenger app, which is where you can go to read and respond to all your Facebook messages. You can use the search box to find your friends and search for trending topics. When you tap into the search box, the keyboard interface appears, as well as recent searches and trending topics.

If you want to search for something that doesn't appear in your search history or as a trending topic, simply type your query and tap Search. Facebook auto-completes when you type, so the items you see beneath the search box will shift as you type. If you're just typing in a friend's name to get to their Timeline, simply tap on their face when you see it to go there.

REMEMBER

Facebook Search allows you to search not just for people but for places, Pages, posts, and other types of Facebook content. The search results page has an extra menu bar at the top of the page. Tap on any of the filters to see only results of that type.

Notifications

When you use Facebook on the web, the blue bar on top of the screen contains icons to represent incoming Friend Requests, Notifications, and Messages. On the mobile app, message notifications appear as a red bubble on top of that Messenger icon at the top of the screen. Friend Requests and Notifications get collapsed into the Notifications screen, which you can access by tapping the Bell icon at the bottom of the screen. When you have new notifications, a small red bubble appears above the Bell icon.

The Notification screen displays the same info that displays in the notifications menu on the site. Tap on any notification to go to the content it's referring to. For example, tapping on a birthday notification brings you to your friend's Timeline, where you can leave a Happy Birthday post. Tapping on a notification about people liking your status brings you to that status post.

Marketplace

Marketplace is an easy way to buy and sell items from your home to people on Facebook. Tap the Storefront icon at the bottom of the screen to browse items to buy or post one to sell. I go over the basics of using Marketplace in Chapter 12.

TIP

The icons you see in the bottom menu vary depending on what features you use and what features Facebook is promoting at any given time.

More

The More icon at the bottom of the screen, represented by three horizontal lines, is basically where all the links normally found on the left-side menu can be found. Tapping the More icon brings you to a menu, shown in Figure 7-3.

TIP

At time of writing, some iPhones show this menu as seen in Figure 7-3, with each option represented as a bubble, while others show this menu as a list, with each option getting a line in that menu. Regardless of how your menu looks, it works the same way. Tap the items as described below to explore Facebook's many features, regardless of whether they appear in bubbles or in a list.

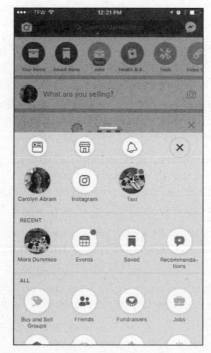

FIGURE 7-3:
More links.

On the website, the various sections and features of Facebook are represented by a list of links that can be clicked on. Here, each section and feature are represented by a bubble. Each bubble can be tapped to explore that part of Facebook. This menu is broken into a few sections: A top section for navigating to your own Timeline and any Pages you manage, a Recent section that displays links to groups, events, games, or sections you've visited most recently, and an All section where all the other links are (you may need to tap See All to view absolutely everything in this section). Here's a list of all the bubbles you may encounter, with a very brief description of where you'll go when you tap on any of them.

>> **<Your Name>:** This menu option takes you to your own Timeline. In general, Timelines are organized into the same format as Timelines on the regular site, with a few stylistic changes to make sure all the information can fit on the screen.

>> **<Pages>:** If you admin any Pages, they appear here. You can tap on them to view their Timelines.

>> **Friends:** The Friends section of the iPhone app should resemble your phone's contact list. You can scroll through your friends from A to Z or search for them from the Search box at the top of the list.

>> **Groups:** This lets you interact with any groups you are a part of. This way, you don't miss out on discussions when you're out and about.

>> **Events:** This lets you view any events you've RSVP'd to. This is incredibly useful when it turns out neither you nor your significant other remembers the exact street address of the dinner you're going to.

>> **Saved:** You can save links, articles, and videos for later viewing from your News Feed. When you decide you have time to look through these saved items, tap on this option.

>> **Feeds:** Tapping this brings you to a menu of options for viewing your News Feed. You can choose to see Most Recent posts, or choose to view only posts from certain groups of people like Family or only Close Friends.

>> **Explore Feed:** Unlike most of your Feeds, including News Feed, the Explore Feed shows you posts from people and Pages you aren't friends with and haven't liked or followed. Instead, the Explore Feed shows you some popular posts that people across Facebook are liking and talking about.

>> **Messenger:** Tapping this opens the Messenger app, which is used to message back and forth with friends. I cover this in greater detail in the Messenger section of this chapter.

>> **Recommendations:** This brings you to a page where you can solicit recommendations in your city (or another city), as well as view the recommendations your friends have asked for.

» **Pages:** View a list of the Pages you manage.

» **Buy and Sell Groups:** View buy/sell groups in your area and join ones you want to start selling your stuff or getting some good deals.

» **Fundraisers:** Facebook provides an easy way for you to ask your friend group to support a personal or charitable cause, called Fundraisers. Get started here.

» **Instant Games:** Choose from a list of games built by third-party developers that you can start playing with friends right away.

» **QR Code:** If you don't already have a QR code reader on your phone, you can use Facebook's to scan QR codes (they look sort of like a cross between a bar code and a fingerprint), which provide a direct link to a website or coupon on your phone.

» **Rewards:** Some of your local businesses may participate in some sort of Facebook Rewards program. This is where you go to display your own personal QR code, which the business can then scan to keep track of your rewards points. For example, a frozen yogurt shop may use this rewards system instead of a punch card system. I haven't personally seen many businesses using Facebook Rewards, but sometimes these sorts of features start very small and grow over time.

» **City Guides:** Using aggregated public data, Facebook has created city guides that you can explore about cities all over the world. If you're researching for an upcoming trip, you might find it useful to see Facebook's suggestions for attractions, restaurants, and "places the locals go." You can save places that sound good to you for later and then reference them once you arrive.

» **Apps:** This opens a menu of apps and features that you have used, including many of the built-in apps that Facebook has created such as Messenger or Jobs. Many of these links are redundant with other links on the More menu, so you don't need to worry too much about what's here.

» **Crisis Response:** Whenever there is a natural (or man-made) disaster, Facebook activates a few features that allow people affected to let people know that they are safe (this is called *Safety Check*, and I hope you never need to use it), offer or receive help from neighbors or any agencies reacting to the disaster, and fundraise for relief efforts. All these features can be found in the Crisis Response center.

» **Device Requests:** If you are connecting Facebook to another device such as a smart TV or smart home assistant, you will see requests for that connection here.

>> **Discover People:** If you are in a new city, you may want some help connecting with the people in your new community. Discover people shows you upcoming events and helps you find people you may know in your area.

>> **Find Wi-Fi:** Facebook can search for Wi-Fi networks near you that you can connect to. Using Facebook over wi-fi instead of your cellular data network usually makes it load a bit faster and lets you avoid extra data charges.

>> **Jobs:** I wouldn't recommend Facebook as your first stop when you are job hunting, but it is one of many sites you can check out that show you job listings based on location and industry. You can also post a job that you are looking to fill here.

>> **Local:** This highlights upcoming events in your area, local restaurants or attractions you might want to explore, and local businesses you might be interested in learning more about.

>> **Movies:** Learn more and check out showtimes for recent movie releases.

>> **Offers:** Sometimes you may see posts in your News Feed that include offers, like coupons, on goods and services. If you save those offers, you can later find them here.

>> **On This Day:** You need to have been using Facebook for over a year for this feature to become interesting, but once you hit that milestone you will be tickled by the memories that you can find here. Sometimes the memories of what you posted a year ago are big ones, but it's often the mundane ones—the random photo of my son in his Captain America costume from just two years ago—that strike a chord, and let you take a moment to savor your memories.

>> **Order Food:** Facebook has partnered with various food delivery services, like GrubHub or DoorDash, to let you order food from nearby restaurants and have it delivered to your door.

>> **Send or Request Money:** You can transfer money between yourself and Facebook friends provided both of you have debit cards. Go here to initiate a transfer.

>> **Sports:** If you're a sports fan (I admit, I have limited experience in this realm) you can get live updates on various matches that are being played at any point in time. You can browse for matches by league or subscribe to certain teams.

>> **Town Hall:** Virtually every politician—from your local city council member to your senator to the president—has a Facebook Page where they post updates, responses to news, and so on. Town Hall makes it easy for you to follow your representatives, send them feedback, and find information related to voting.

» **Weather:** Facebook provides access to a weather forecast based on the location of your phone. If you'd like, you can have weather updates sent to your News Feed so that you know what to wear in the morning as you blearily check your News Feed.

» **Settings and Privacy:** Get to your Account Settings, Privacy Shortcuts, Chat Settings, Payments Settings, News Feed Preferences, Activity Log, Edit Shortcuts, and Code Generator (for when you are logging in from an unfamiliar location). This is also where you go to log out of Facebook.

» **Help and Support:** If you ever have a question that I can't answer, tap on Help and Support to visit the Help Center, check out the community help pages, report a problem, or read Facebook's Terms and Policies.

WARNING

You might see slightly different or additional items in the More section. These may be links to other features or applications within Facebook. Facebook is tailored to you so what you see may be a bit different from what I see.

News Feed

Use your finger to scroll down News Feed and see what all your friends have to say. If new stories appear while you are reading News Feed, a "New Stories" bubble appears at the top of the screen. You can tap that bubble to speed all the way back to the top of News Feed without having to manually scroll all the way back up.

A News Feed story in the app looks like a News Feed story on the web. As a reminder, every post, regardless of what type of post it is, contains the following information:

» Name and profile picture of the person (or Page) who posted it.

» Time and date of posting. Usually Facebook tries to show you things that happened recently.

» Location information, if your friend chooses to share it.

» The content of the post, whether that's a status update, a photo, a life event, or a link to something else on the web.

» Info about the reactions this post has gotten so far and how many comments it's received.

» Links to Like/React, Comment, and Share (if available).

Tap on a photo to see it in the photo viewer. Tap a name to go to that person's Timeline or Page. Tap on the number of comments to read what's been said about a post. Tapping on a link will open the linked article or webpage within the Facebook app.

As you scroll down on your News Feed, you may notice that videos begin to play as you get to them, however the sound doesn't turn on automatically. You need to tap on these videos to play them with sound. Doing so will focus the screen on only that video. If you'd like to continue browsing Facebook while the video plays, tap the corner square icon in the top left of the screen. This moves the video to a corner of the screen, as shown in Figure 7-4. While the video plays, you can continue browsing Facebook.

FIGURE 7-4:
You can watch a video while you browse.

Reacting to Posts

If you like what you see, tap the Like button (Thumbs Up icon) at the bottom of every post to let your friend know, hey, I liked that. You can also tap and hold that button (in other words, just put your finger down on it without lifting it back up) to open the full menu of Facebook reactions: Like (thumbs up), Love (heart), Haha (laughing emoji), Wow (open-mouthed emoji), Sad (crying emoji), Mad (red and angry emoji). Figure 7-5 shows the many Facebook reaction icons.

No matter where you are on the Facebook app — it doesn't have to be News Feed — you can usually like something in this exact same way. Tap once to like, and tap and hold to have another reaction.

Commenting on Posts

If you have something to say in response to a friend's post, tap the Comment button (with a Word Bubble icon) to open a text box where you can type your comment, as shown in Figure 7-6.

FIGURE 7-6:
You got
something
to say?

Use your phone's keyboard to type in your comment. Tap on the Camera icon next to the comment box to add a photo to your comment. Similarly, tapping on the GIF icon or Smiley icon allows you to add GIFs and Stickers, respectively, to your comment. When you're done with your comment, tap the Paper Airplane icon to send it, adding it to any other comments that already are attached to the post. Your friend will be notified that you commented on their post.

Often people are speaking to each other in comments, and to get the attention of certain friends, people will often address a comment to them by typing the @ symbol and their friend's name. This *tags* your friend in the comment and notifies them that they have been tagged. This ensures that your friend will see your comment as soon as possible.

Post and News Feed options

At the top right corner of each post is a tiny More [. . .] link, signified by three dots. Tapping these dots opens a menu of options for that post, shown in Figure 7-7.

This menu has the following options:

>> **Save:** This adds the post to your Saved section, so you can easily get back to it later.

>> **Give Feedback on this post:** This is how you report offensive material, harassment, fake news, hate speech, or even suicidal behavior to Facebook.

Facebook's systems strive to remove offensive content, label fake news, and get help to people in need.

» **Hide Post:** If a post isn't technically something that needs to be reported, just something you don't want to see because it bothers you, you can hide that post. After you hide a post, it is immediately removed from your News Feed. In its place, you see an additional set of options. You can choose to see less altogether from the person who made the post. Depending on the type of post, you can also choose to see less from a source such as a certain app or news site. You can also undo your hiding of the post, or decide to report the post, after all.

TIP

Liking posts and hiding posts are sort of the yin and yang of adjusting what you see in News Feed. These actions tell Facebook the sorts of posts you like and the sorts of posts you don't, and the algorithm adjusts based on what you do so that over time, you see more and more interesting stories.

» **Unfollow or Snooze <Friend>:** Unfollowing a friend basically removes all their posts from your News Feed. If you aren't sure you're ready to fully commit to such an action, you can temporarily unfollow, or *snooze* them by tapping this option. Once you tap, you can select to snooze them for 24 hours, 7 days, 30 days, or Unfollow entirely.

» **Hide all from <Source>:** Often people are sharing from specific websites or using certain apps. If you realize that there are sources whose posts you just don't like, you can choose to hide all posts from that source.

» **Turn on notifications for this post:** If you are interested in the discussion happening on a certain post, you can choose to turn notifications on for that post. You'll then receive a notification whenever there is a new comment or reaction to the post. Whenever you comment on a post, you receive notifications (when someone comments after you or reacts to your comment) by default.

Viewing Facebook Stories

At the very top of News Feed in the Facebook app, you may see a section labeled "Stories." *Facebook Stories* are a way for people to share snippets of their day without adding them to their Timelines. The photos and other content within a person's story disappear after 24 hours. This can be a fun way to share a ton of photos of a cool hike, or some other activity, without it taking over your friends' feeds. I talk more about sharing a story later in this chapter, but for now let's just focus on checking out your friends' stories.

First, it's important to note that your ability to view stories depends on whether your friends are creating Facebook Stories. When you look at the stories section, you should see a series of bubbles, as shown in Figure 7-8. A faded-out bubble means that that friend doesn't have a story available for you to look at. A fully saturated bubble with a tinier bubble of your friend's profile picture indicates that you can tap to see their story.

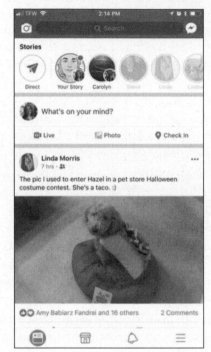

FIGURE 7-8:
Stories can be found at the top of your News Feed.

Tapping a story opens it, filling your whole screen. Stories are often composed of a series of photos or videos, sometimes with text or other visual effects superimposed over them. Stories play like a slideshow. At the top of the screen, a series of thin white lines indicates how many slides the story contains, as well as how far along you are in the story. As you're watching, tap on any of the emojis at the bottom of the screen to react to what you're seeing. You can also comment on anything you see by tapping into the text box at the bottom of the screen. If you get bored of the story you're watching, tap the X at the upper-right corner of the screen.

Posting from the app

Much like on the website, you can post content from the top of your News Feed. Tap on the What's on Your Mind? box to open the mobile Publisher, shown in Figure 7-9.

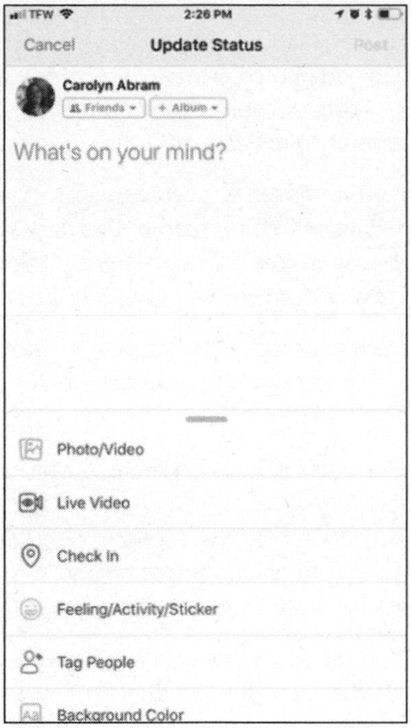

FIGURE 7-9: iPhone status updates start here.

The mobile Publisher has all the same options as the Publisher on the web, the main difference being the location of some of these items. Follow these steps to post a simple status update:

1. **Tap in the "What's on your mind?" field.**

This opens a keyboard for typing.

2. **Type what you want to say.**

3. **Tap Post in the upper-right corner of the screen.**

Your status is posted to your Timeline and shared with friends via News Feed.

That's the simple status post. Just three steps. Of course, there are a bunch of other options you can add or adjust every time you post.

» **Privacy/audience:** The box beneath your name displays who the audience for that post is set to (usually Public or Friends). Tap on that box to open a menu for choosing a new audience.

» **Background color:** As you type, background color options appear just above the keyboard. Tap the one you want to see what it will look like behind your text.

TIP

» **Photo/video:** Tap the Photo icon (it looks like two playing cards, one has an image of a mountain on it) to add photos or videos from your phone's camera roll to your post. The "Photo Posts" section covers a ton of options available with the photos and videos you add to Facebook.

If you want to add photos you've chosen to post to an existing album, tap the gray box that says +Album, right below your name. This displays a list of your existing albums. You can choose to create a new album of the photos you've just selected, or add them to an album you've previously created.

» **Live Video:** Live Video is a way to broadcast whatever you are looking at or doing Live on your phone. I talk about this option more in the upcoming Live Video section.

» **Check in:** By default, if you've enabled location services when you first added the Facebook app, Facebook will include some general location info, like your city and state, whenever you post something. A *Check in* is a way for you to select a more specific location like a restaurant, attraction, or even your own home. The upcoming "Check ins" section covers more about location sharing.

» **Feeling/activity/sticker:** You can add emojis, stickers, or activity info to your post. Tap to open a menu that lets you choose whether you want to share feelings (search through and select smiley face emojis), stickers (search through and choose from your sticker packs), or activities (search through and add specific things you might be doing, listening to, watching, eating, and so on).

» **Tag people:** Tagging people is a way to link them to your post. You might tag a friend because they are with you, or because something you are posting would be of interest to them. You can add tags by tapping Tag People or by typing their name when you are writing your status update. Facebook automatically displays a menu of friends when you start typing a friend's name.

» **Life event:** Add a life event from the Publisher by tapping this option. You can choose from various categories such as Travel or Firsts. Then add details as prompted to let the world know.

» **Sell something:** Tap to create a quick post including the name/description of the item you are selling, and a price. You will probably want to add a photo of the item as well.

» **Ask for recommendations:** Let's imagine you are out with your phone and you are hungry, but don't know where you want to eat. You can quickly solicit recommendations from friends. Tap to choose a location, then describe what it is you're looking for in the text of your post.

>> **Slideshow:** Tap to create a slideshow of photos as a post. More about slideshows in the upcoming Photo Posts section.

>> **360 photos:** Using your phone's camera, you can take a 360-degree photo of the area around you and share it on Facebook.

>> **Poll:** Tap to create a poll that can quickly aggregate answers to a question from your friends. Polls can be used for answering questions serious or whimsical. For more details on polls, check out Chapter 10, as polls are a feature of groups as well.

>> **Support nonprofit:** This feature makes it easy to solicit donations for any cause that's near and dear to your heart. Tap to select from a menu of nonprofits you can choose to start a fundraiser for.

>> **Answer a Question:** This feature prompts you to answer a question presented to you by Facebook and then post the answer to your friends. Questions are usually about personal trivia such as "I sleep facing. . ." or "The TV series that I'm watching right now is. . ."

Photo posts

Given that so many photos live on phones these days, chances are you may want to use Facebook to share them. Sharing photos can be incredibly easy, but there are also a lot of advanced options. First, let's go over the basic photo sharing post:

1. **Tap the Photo button in the center of the Publisher.**

Your phone's camera roll appears.

Facebook may group certain photos together for you in case you want to use them in a slideshow.

2. **Tap on the photos you want to select.**

Facebook highlights selected photos in blue and counts how many photos you have selected (shown in Figure 7-10).

Tap photos in the order you want them to appear.

3. **Tap Done in the upper-right corner.**

Publisher opens and displays the photos you have added.

4. **Tap Post in the upper-right corner.**

News Feed appears, and you can see your new post being added as a new story.

FIGURE 7-10:
Share photos
from your
phone's camera
roll.

Those are the basics. Just a few taps and you've shared a moment of your life with your friends. Now, if you want to be a bit more advanced about it, including a few photo editing options, read on:

1. **Tap the Photo button in the publisher at the top of News Feed.**

   This brings up your phone's camera roll, which you can use to select photos.

2. **Tap on the photos you want to select.**

   Facebook highlights selected photos in blue and counts how many photos you have selected (shown in Figure 7-10).

3. **Tap Done in the upper-right corner.**

   This brings you back to the Publisher, with the photos you have added now displayed.

4. **Tap on the photo you want to edit.**

   This expands the photo. You can scroll down using your finger to get to each individual photo for editing.

5. **Tap on the Edit button in the upper-left corner of the photo.**

   To remove a photo at this point, click the X in the upper-right corner of the photo you want to remove. You don't have to edit any of your photos, or you can edit all of them. You can see a few of the editing options in play in Figure 7-11. You can edit photos in any of the following ways:

- **Filters**: Filters are ways to change the overall color or tone of the photo. For example, you can convert a photo to black-and-white.

- **Tag**: Tags are ways to mark who is in a photo. Tap on a face to open a tagging box. This highlights the face in question and opens a text box where you can type in the name of that person. Facebook auto-completes as you type; tap on the correct name when you see it appear.

- **Crop**: You can crop photos by using your fingers to move the proposed border of a photo. You can also find a button here to rotate a photo (no sideways photos for you!) and to automatically crop a photo into a square instead of a rectangle.

- **Text**: You can add a caption beneath a photo in Step 7, or you can add text that gets displayed on top of the photo. Tap to type the text you want to add, and tap Done in the upper-right corner. You can then use your finger to drag the text to where you want it in the photo. Tap again on the text to edit it or change the color of it by dragging your finger up and down the color palette on the right side of the screen.

- **Stickers**: You can add a sticker to the top of a photo. You can select from a basic set of stickers that Facebook provides or download various "sticker packs" such as mustache shapes or holiday-related stickers. After you select the sticker you want, you can use your finger to drag it to where you want on the photo.

- **Doodle**: You can doodle a little drawing on the top of any photo. When you select doodle, a small color chart appears on the right side of the screen. Put your finger down on the color you want to select, and wait for a small dot in that color to appear to the left of your finger. Drag your finger up and down to change color, and to the left or right to change the thickness of your line. Once you are at the right color and thickness, release your finger. Then you can draw your doodle, using your finger, on top of your photo. Use the buttons at the bottom of the screen to undo your most recent line or reset the whole doodle.

6. **Tap Done in the upper-right of the page when you are done editing.**

   Repeat Steps 5 and 6 as needed for each photo you are sharing.

7. **Add photo captions.**

   If you are only adding one photo, that means tapping into the Say Something About This Photo field and writing a comment. If you are sharing more than one photo, tap beneath each photo where it says Add a Caption.

8. Tap the Album button to add a photo to an existing album or create a new album.

Tapping the Album icon brings you to a menu of your previously created albums. Tap on the one you'd like to add to, or tap to create a new album. When you have named your album, you return to the mobile Publisher, and the name of the album is displayed at the top of the screen.

9. If you are posting three or more photos, choose whether you want to display them as a collage or a slideshow.

By default, most photo posts are collages, meaning that when your friends see them in News Feed, they see thumbnail images of the photos you're sharing and a number to tell them how many more photos there are. Tap where it says 'collage' to open a menu for choosing either slideshow or collage. There are so many slideshow options that I've dedicated the next section to it.

10. Tap the Location icon to add location info.

As with any other post, you can add location info so that people can know where a photo was taken.

11. Double-check who can see your photos at the top of the post.

At the top of every post is information about privacy. At the top of the Publisher a gray box is prefilled with your most recent privacy choice. You can change the privacy for this post by tapping and selecting new privacy options from the menu that opens.

12. Tap Upload or Post in the upper-right corner.

This brings you back to News Feed, where you can see the News Feed story that has been created about your new photos.

Slideshows

As I mentioned in Step 9 of the photo posts section, one option you have when posting at least three photos is creating a slideshow. You can also start a slideshow from scratch by opening the Publisher and tapping Slideshow from the menu at the bottom of the screen.

WARNING

Some users might not yet see the option for creating slideshows appear in their publishers.

Once you have your photos selected, creating a slideshow brings up a preview of it. You can get a sense of this in Figure 7-12.

FIGURE 7-11:
Make your
photos awesome.

FIGURE 7-12:
Make a
slideshow.

Along the bottom of the preview screen are options for editing your slideshow. From left to right the sections are:

>> **Library**: Browse your phone's photo library for the photos you want included in the slideshow.

>> **Themes:** Themes range from heroic, which plays intense super hero music and transitions your photos as if they are panels in a comic book, to classical, which plays classical music and does straightforward transitions. Tap on any of the themes to watch (and listen to) your slideshow play with that theme. Facebook displays some of its themes along the bottom of the screen; use your finger to slide along the options and tap on the one you want. You can also tap on Categories to get a full list of themes you can browse through.

>> **Edit:** Edit allows you to scroll through the photos in your slideshow and remove any ones you realize you don't want.

>> **More [. . .]:** Tap More to add a title to your slideshow and to tag people in it.

When you're done with your slideshow, click Done in the upper-right corner. It will save the slideshow, and then you will need to tap Post to post it to your Timeline and share it with your friends.

Taking Photos to Share

In modern life, the *selfie*, or picture you take of yourself with your phone's camera, is pretty much the most basic way of documenting your life. Here I am in line at the DMV. Here I am on the bus. Here I am at Machu Picchu. Facebook makes it easy for you to take and share photos, including selfies. It also provides cool effects that can give your selfies a bit more pizzazz.

To understand the various options available to you, let's take a closer look at the phone screen when you're using the camera through Facebook, which you can see in Figure 7-13. You can get here by tapping the Camera icon in the big blue bar at top of the app, or by swiping right while using Facebook (in other words, put your finger on the left side of the screen and drag it across to the right side of the screen).

At the top of the screen are three options: Live, Normal, and Text. Use your finger to swipe between them. Live is where you would go to start broadcasting a live video (which I discuss a bit more in the next section), Normal is what I'm about to cover—it's how you take and share photos, and Text is where you go to write a status update.

FIGURE 7-13:
Selfie!

Beneath the Live/Normal/Text options is the camera screen, which has six buttons distributed at the top and bottom of the screen. Some of these should look familiar from using your camera on your phone:

>> **Take photo:** The big circle in the center of the screen is what you tap to take a photo. Hold this button to record a video.

>> **Flip camera direction:** The Camera icon in the upper right corner has a little circle of arrows inside. This indicates that you can tap it to switch from selfie mode to regular camera mode, where you take photos of what's ahead of you.

>> **Flash on/off:** Tap the Flash On/Off icon (it looks like a tiny bolt of lightning) to turn your camera's flash on and off. When it's off, the lightning appears next to a little X.

>> **Options [. . .]:** Click the ellipsis icon to adjust settings such as whether photos you take on Facebook get saved to your phone's camera roll. You can also double check your privacy settings on posts.

>> **View camera roll:** Tap the little images in the lower-right corner to view recent photos you've taken, regardless of whether they were taken while you were using Facebook.

The icon that may look unfamiliar to you is the Photo Filters icon (it looks like a magic wand), which opens Facebook's various photo filter options at the bottom of the screen. You can apply most filters either before or after you take a photo. Facebook has a huge variety of filters, some of which are shown in Figure 7-14.

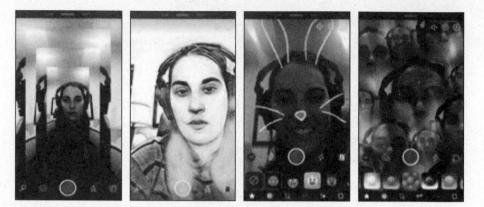

FIGURE 7-14: Funny faces.

Here are some examples of what you can do.

>> **Change your photo's mood:** Many photo filters add certain colors or effects that can change your photo's mood. For example, a black-and-white photo tends to look more poetic. A sepia-toned one looks aged and historic. Browse the color effects by scrolling through the options that appear on the bottom of the screen. Tap on each one to see what it does to your photo.

>> **Add a mask:** Mask filters are specifically for selfies. When applying a mask filter, your camera will display a box in the middle of the screen that says, "Find a Face!" Once it locates your face it will apply a filter over your face that ranges from animal faces to giving you a hat to enlarging your eyes. Many of these filters have added sound effects or effects that will happen if you open your mouth, such as breathing fire or eating carrots.

TIP

If you have a small child in your life that you are looking to impress, try entertaining them by letting them see themselves with various masks. As my two-year-old likes to say: "Do funny faces! Do funny faces!" Don't share any photos of them without their parents' permission, though!

>> **Add an artistic effect:** These filters range from altering your photo to look like a pencil drawing to repeating the image in many colors like a Warhol painting.

>> **Add a frame:** Frames are images that appear around the edges of your photo. If you can imagine doodling with a gel pen over the edges of a photo in a scrapbook, you can get a good idea of what a frame is.

After you've taken your photo by pressing the big center button, the photo then is displayed on the screen. If you decide you don't like it after all, click the X button in the upper-left corner of the screen. You can add a sticker, text, or doodle by tapping their respective icons at the top of the screen.

Meanwhile, at the bottom of the screen, you can continue to experiment with various photo effects, save the photo to your phone's camera roll, or add the photo to your Facebook story, which is a compilation of tidbits you share that expire and are deleted from Facebook in 24 hours.

If you're happy with your photo, you can share it by tapping the arrow or Next button on the right side of the screen. This opens a menu for sharing. You can choose to add it to your story, post it to your profile like a normal photo post, or post it directly to specific friends.

Posting something to specific friends basically gives that friend (or friends) the chance to see that image for only 24 hours. It can be fun to exchange images that expire or go away with friends.

After you choose how you want to share your image, tap the blue button at the lower-right corner of the screen (it has a paper airplane in it). Voilà! Your photo has been posted to Facebook.

Live Video

Live Video is a feature that lets any user broadcast video from their phone live. To get started with Live Video, follow these steps:

1. **Tap the Live button in the Publisher at the top of your News Feed.**

This opens the camera on your phone, but you are still within Facebook. This screen has a lot of options, many of which are explained in the above Selfies section. You can use most of the same photo filters and masks in your Live Videos that you used for you selfies and other photos you took.

2. **Check on your audience.**

By default, this is usually set to Public or Friends. Tap on the audience selector beneath your name to change who will be able to see the video.

3. **Decide on whether you want this video to be available on your Timeline when you stop recording.**

By default, Live Videos are included in the Facebook Stories that your friends see for 24 hours. They also appear by default as video posts on your Timeline. If you don't want your broadcast to show up on your Timeline once it's over, tap on the

Post, Story box under your name. This opens a menu Live Settings. Uncheck the Post option to keep your broadcast from appearing on your Timeline.

4. **Tap the red Start Live Video button to start broadcasting.**

Often a question I get asked about Live Video is "What should I be sharing?" and the answer is, whatever you want. Maybe you want to broadcast the concert you're watching, or give a brief glimpse of the waterfall you just hiked to, or feel that people should share in your toddler's tantrum. Celebrities and other Pages often use Live Video to give a behind-the-scenes peek to their fans or followers. Plenty of News Stories have been based on Live broadcasts. Just because you aren't a celebrity doesn't mean that you can't share a behind-the-scenes peek of your own life.

TIP

You can add a donation button to your Live Video or choose to only broadcast audio by tapping the ellipsis icon to the right of the Start Live Video button.

Facebook Stories

Facebook Stories are a way to share several tidbits of your day with your Facebook friends without creating a permanent Facebook post that will live in perpetuity on your Timeline. You can add many things to your story at once or add things to it as your day progresses. I find that it can be a fun way to document whatever's happening to me in a given day but not worry about the quality of the photo I'm sharing, or feel the need to provide the perfect clever caption to whatever's happening.

You can add photos to your story whenever you are taking photos directly with Facebook's camera feature. Your story can include one photo or hundreds of photos. Feel free to experiment with what you choose to share, since whatever you do will be gone the next day.

Friends who are using Facebook during the days you share stories can view your stories, comment on them, and react to them. You'll receive notifications about these responses alongside the rest of your notifications.

Check Ins

Whenever you post something to Facebook, you can add location information, also known as a *check-in* to your post. This is true on the website as well as when you are using the Facebook app on your phone. When you are using the app, Facebook expects that you are going to be more likely to want to check in someplace, so it makes it easy to check in from the app.

When you check in, you see a list of locations based on the location information shared by your phone (you may have to grant Facebook permission to access this information). These might be restaurants or parks or buildings. When you select a location by tapping on it, you *check in* to that location. Checking in basically means actively telling Facebook that you're there. Facebook won't share your specific location unless you check in (it does frequently include general location information like the name of the city you are in).

You can tag friends in your check-ins or add photos or a few words about what's going on. After you check in, your friends can see where you are in their News Feeds. If they're out and about and using Facebook on their phones, they can see if they are near you by tapping Nearby from the More menu.

Checking in leads to all sorts of nice serendipitous encounters. When I was in Boston once, I checked in to a few different restaurants. An old friend I hadn't seen in ten years sent me a message asking how much longer I'd be in town. I didn't even know she had moved to Boston. We had brunch the next day.

Checking out Timelines

Like News Feed, Timeline in the Facebook app should look familiar, if a bit narrower than you're used to. Figure 7-15 shows a friend's mobile Timeline. A cover photo sits across the top of the screen, with a profile picture in the center. You can see some info on your connection (friends) and some basic biographical info about them.

FIGURE 7-15:
A friend's Timeline in the Facebook app.

On your own Timeline, you'll see links beneath your profile picture to post, edit the About section of your Timeline, view your Activity log, and More. Tapping More gives you options to change your profile and cover photos or go to your privacy shortcuts. Underneath these links is your biographical information like where you work, live, and where you went to school.

Use your finger to scroll down the page. As you do, you'll pass by featured photos, the mobile Publisher, thumbnails of recent photos, as well as a preview of your friends. Beneath that are your actual posts. Most recent posts appear first, and you can keep scrolling back to the very beginning, if you so choose.

When you view posts, you can tap on the tiny down arrow or ellipsis in the upper-right corner of the post to see options related to that post (see Figure 7-16). Depending on the type of post you will see different options, but in general, this is where you can go to hide a post from your Timeline, edit the content of a post, change the privacy settings on a post, and more.

FIGURE 7-16:
Post options.

Profile Videos

One mobile-only feature you can add from the Facebook app is a profile video. Profile videos are meant to be like a profile picture just, you know, in motion. Profile videos are up to seven seconds long and play on a loop when people are looking at your Timeline from their phone. A still image from the video will then appear as your profile picture in thumbnails around the site. Follow these steps to record a profile video:

1. **From your Timeline, tap the Edit link at the bottom of your existing profile picture.**

   A menu appears for changing your profile picture and profile video: Add Frame, Take a New Profile Video, Select Profile Video, Select Profile Picture, View Profile Picture.

2. **Tap Take a New Profile Video.**

   This opens your phone's camera interface. (You may have to tap to allow Facebook access to your camera.)

3. **Center your face in the screen as indicated by the oval outline.**

4. **Tap the red button to begin recording.**

   Remember, you have a maximum of seven seconds to work with. Do whatever comes naturally.

5. **Tap the red button again to stop recording.**

   A preview of your new profile video appears.

6. **Use the options at the bottom of the screen to trim your video, add sound, or choose a cover image from the video to be your new profile picture.**

   To record a new video, tap the back arrow in the upper-left corner.

7. **Tap Use when you're ready.**

   This brings you back to your Timeline, where you can see your profile video in its natural habitat.

REMEMBER

Profile videos are visible to anyone who visits your Timeline, just like your profile picture and cover photo. Thumbnails from your profile video appear in News Feed and anywhere else on Facebook you might see a profile picture.

Using Groups

You can use Facebook groups to communicate with a group of friends about anything in the world. Groups are covered in detail in Chapter 10, as is the Facebook app that's *only* for groups (named, aptly enough, Groups). However, you can access and interact with any groups you belong to through the Facebook app.

1. **From the Facebook app, tap the More icon at the bottom of the screen.**

   This brings you to the menu of apps and favorites you might want to visit from your phone.

TIP

For Android users: Often your groups appear listed on this page, instead of on a separate Groups page, in which case you can skip to Step 3.

2. **Tap Groups.**

   This brings you to the Groups page, shown in Figure 7-17. Each group is represented by a circle that you can tap on to visit. This page is broken into a few sections: Favorites, Recently Viewed, and Create New Group.

3. **Tap on the group you want to go to.**

   This brings you to your group's Mobile Home page.

FIGURE 7-17:
The Groups home on your phone.

Unsurprisingly, your group's home looks a lot like its home on the website (shown in Figure 7-18). You see the cover photo on top; links to Add Members, Search, and get Info; Publisher; and any recent posts displayed in the group's Timeline.

Tap into the mobile Publisher (the Write Something box) to post something to the group. You can post links, articles, text, or photos, and it will be available to all members of that group.

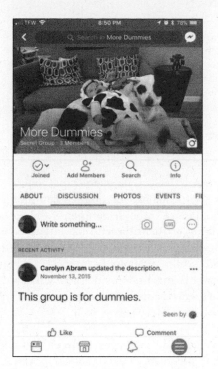

FIGURE 7-18:
A group on your
phone.

TIP

Just as you can on the website, you can search within a group's posts for information. Tap the Search icon (beneath the cover photo) to bring up a search interface. You can then enter a search term (or terms) into the Search box in the blue bar on top. The search results you see come only from the group you are currently viewing.

Events

I'm not going to pretend that Facebook Events is the feature you use most when you are out and about. But I will say that when you want to view an event on the Facebook app, it's because you *really* need to see that event. You either need an address, or a start-time, or a number to call, and the only place you know for sure you can find it is from that event's page. To get to an event, follow these steps:

1. **From the Facebook app, tap the More icon at the bottom of the screen.**

   A menu of apps and favorites appears that you might want to visit from your phone.

2. **Tap Events.**

   The Events page opens. This page shows you upcoming events that you have been invited to, as well as upcoming public events that are popular in your area, and upcoming birthdays.

3. **Tap on the event you are looking for.**

Tapping the event brings you to that event's page, where you can see information about the event and its guests, as well as publish a post to the event.

Facebook Messenger

The Facebook app is designed to let you do everything you can do on Facebook from your phone. One big part of using Facebook is communicating with your friends. Communication can happen through comments and posts, but a big piece of talking to friends is talking to them directly using Facebook messages (the details of using Facebook messages are covered in Chapter 9). Because getting in touch directly with a friend is sometimes more important when you're out and about than, say, checking out his latest photos, Facebook has built a separate app for messages. If you use the Facebook app and ever try to send a message, you will be asked to add the Facebook Messenger app as well.

Messenger handles all the chats and messages between you and your Facebook friends when you are on your phone. As a stand-alone app, you can easily get to it and use it to communicate on the go, without getting distracted by the rest of Facebook. My husband and I use Messenger as our chief means of communication during the day while we're at work. It's just as immediate as texting but doesn't incur any additional texting charges on our phones, and it's easy to switch from a chat on the computer screen to a chat in Messenger without losing any of what we were talking about. Messenger has all the same functionality as sending Facebook messages: You can message one person or multiple people, send photos, videos, stickers, and GIFs, and conversations are easily grouped in one place.

REMEMBER

The Messenger app described and shown in this section is being used on an iPhone. There might be a few slight differences between it and the Android version.

Navigating Messenger

Opening the Messenger app brings you to your recent messages, shown in Figure 7-19.

The bulk of the page is taken up by your messages, organized by conversation, with the most recent one at the top. Each conversation shows the profile picture of the friend (or friends) you are conversing with. Any conversations that have unread messages appear in **bold.** Each conversation has a time or date next to it reflecting the last time anyone on that thread sent a message. Use your finger to scroll down to older conversations. Tap on any conversation to open it up and view its contents or add to the conversation.

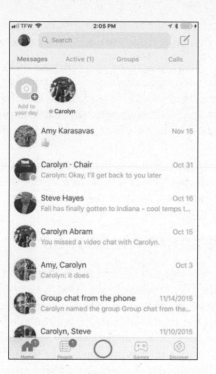

FIGURE 7-19:
Your Messenger
Inbox.

Above the conversations are little bubbles showing friends that are currently online or who have shared a "My Day" story that you can browse. My Day is a version of Facebook Stories that lives in Messenger instead of the main Facebook app.

At the top of the screen is a search bar that lets you search for people and groups you might want to message. You can swipe between viewing Messages, Active friends, Groups, and Calls. Tap on the paper and pencil icon in the upper-right corner to open a new message. Tap on your own face in the upper-left corner to open your settings.

REMEMBER

When you use Facebook messages, new messages simply get added to any previously sent messages, sort of like your text messages on your phone. They don't get sorted by subject matter or date, only by who is talking to one another.

At the bottom of the screen are five icons.

» **Home:** Tapping this at any point brings you back to your recent messages.

» **People (bullet list icon):** Tapping this brings you to a list of your friends who also use Messenger. You can also view your message requests, find contacts from your phone's contact list, or invite people to use Messenger.

» **Take a photo:** The central circle icon is meant to look like the camera shutter button. Tapping it opens a camera interface where you can take photos to send to friends or add to the My Day feature.

>> **Games:** Browse games that you can play with your friends, often within Messenger.

>> **Discover:** Browse the various chatbots that you can message back and forth with. Chatbots use automated messaging to get you helpful info if you ask for it. For example, I just messaged wikiHow to ask how to clean dirt out of Velcro. When you message with Pages in this way they will be able to see your public information (name, profile picture, etc.), but not your whole profile.

TIP

For Android Users: The locations of the menus in the Messenger Inbox are swapped. Search, Phone, and New Message are at the bottom of the screen, and Recent, Groups, People, and Settings are at the top of the screen.

Viewing and sending Messages

Figure 7-20 shows how a message thread or conversation looks inside the Messenger app. It looks a lot like a text message thread, with each message contained in a speech bubble. Your messages appear on the right side, in blue bubbles, messages from other friends appear on the left side, in gray bubbles. The most recent message is at the bottom of the screen and you can use your finger to scroll up to view older messages. Your entire history of messaging with this friend can be found here. It doesn't matter whether you were messaging from phones or computers; you can go back to the beginning of it all.

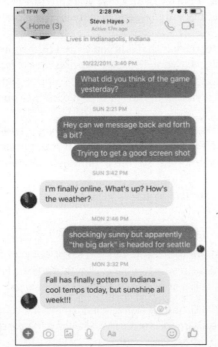

FIGURE 7-20:
A message thread between friends.

At the top of the screen you can tap ‹ Home to go back to your recent messages, and tap either the phone icon or video player icon to start a phone or video chat, respectively.

At the bottom of the screen is a space for typing your message. Use the keyboard to enter your message and then tap the Send button (it looks like a paper plane) on the lower right of the text you've entered.

Next to the text box you may notice a series of icons that show off the variety of content you can append to a message:

>> **More [+] icon:** Tap this More icon to see apps that can integrate into Messenger, such as Payments, Games, apps for making plans or sending music, and more.

>> **Camera icon:** Tap the camera icon to open your phone's camera and take a photo or video to send to your friend. You may have to authorize Facebook Messenger to access your camera the first time you do this. You can use any of Messenger's filters, which I talk about in the upcoming "Video Calls" section, to add a little flair to your photos.

>> **Photos icon:** Tap the photos icon to attach photos that already exist in your camera roll. You can browse through your camera roll using your finger, then tap the photo you want to send. You can choose to edit a photo or send it immediately. Editing options are adding a text overlay or adding a doodle to it. Remember to tap Send (in the upper-right corner) when you're done editing. You can learn more about photo editing in Chapter 11.

>> **Microphone icon:** Tap this icon to record an audio message to send to your friend. Tap and hold the microphone icon to start recording, then let go when you're done recording. Keep in mind that you won't be given a chance to review your recording; it just gets sent as soon as you're done.

>> **Aa icon:** By default, when you open a message, you land in a text box where you can type your message. If you ever tap on some of the other icons but want to get back to regular old words on a screen, tap the Aa icon.

>> **Smiley icon:** Tap the smiley face icon to add stickers, GIFs, or emojis to your message. There are thousands (perhaps more) of sticker options you can add. Simply tap to select one. If you want to search more widely, look for the magnifying glass icon at the bottom of the screen (after you have tapped the Smiley icon). This is the search icon and it allows you to browse through stickers by category.

A GIF is a file format that has over time come to describe short (really short, often only a second or two) looped videos. GIFs are used to capture emotions or sentiments that can be hard to express in words (or easy to express in words, but more fun to describe in a short motion). For example, you might choose to tell someone that something she said is exciting, or you might choose to send a GIF of a unicorn shooting a rainbow out of its horn. You can browse through GIFs by tapping the GIF icon and tapping on the GIF you want to send to your friend.

Like stickers, emojis are small drawings, often smiley faces but truly representing anything and everything, that you can send in place of messages. After you tap to add emojis, you can browse through the various categories. Tap on the one you want to send to add it to your message.

>> **Like icon:** Tap this to send your friend a Like, which appears as a "thumbs up" in the message thread.

Video Calls

One of the best parts of using Messenger is the ability to easily start voice and video calls with your friends. You don't need to be using the same type of phone, or even both need to be on a phone (one of you can be on your computer). To start a video call, open a conversation with the friend you want to call, and tap the video camera icon in the upper-right corner of the screen.

While you're talking to your friend, you have the option to add photo effects and filters to your video. Tap the Photo Effects icon (it looks like a magic wand) to open all the photo effects, which you can scroll through from side to side to browse. Effects fall into a few general categories:

>> **Masks:** Masks are fun to use because they adapt to your face as you move around and speak. They range from sunglasses and hats to ones that transform your face into a fox's face.

>> **Frames:** Frames are doodles or other effects such as twinkling stars or hearts that appear over your face as you're speaking to your friend.

>> **Color Effects:** Change the color balance on your camera so you appear as shades of blue in a red background, or in black and white. Or choose an effect where you look, for example, like you're on an old television screen.

You can take a photo of a moment within the conversation by tapping the Camera icon at the bottom of the screen. A screenshot will be taken and automatically saved to your phone's camera roll.

Tap the Smiley icon to send reactions across the screen as you're speaking. So if you're listening to a friend describe her bad day, you can tap the angry face. She'll then see an angry face shoot across the screen. You can see an example of some photo effects, as well as what the reaction options are, in Figure 7-21.

FIGURE 7-21:
Make your video calls more fun with photo effects.

You can video chat with more than one friend at a time, provided they all have access to Messenger on their phone or a webcam on their computers.

My Day

My Day is the equivalent of the Facebook Stories feature found in the Facebook app. Basically it allows you to share tidbits of your day (usually photos and videos) with your friends who use Messenger. Photos and other things you post expire in 24 hours and don't leave a permanent record behind.

From the Messenger Home screen (where you see a list of your conversations) tap the Camera icon toward the top of the page—this particular Camera icon says Add to Your Day underneath it. Tapping this icon opens the camera interface. You can scroll back and forth through various photo effects—masks, frames, and color effects alike—when you find one you like, tap on it, then tap on the center circle button to take your photo. You can hold the center button to record a video.

After you take your photo or video, you can choose to add stickers, text, or doodles to it using the icons at the top of the screen. You can choose to abandon that photo by tapping the back arrow or X in the upper-left corner. Save it to your phone's camera roll by tapping the Save icon in the bottom left. But assuming you took a photo because you want to share it, tap the arrow button in the bottom-right to decide who will see it.

By default, Facebook assumes you want to both add it to your day and save it on your camera roll. You can also choose to send that photo or video as a message to specific friends by tapping their names from the displayed list. Once you're confident with who you're sharing with, tap the send button in the bottom right.

Sharing things using the My Day feature is a way to share things from your day without inserting it into people's News Feeds. People using Messenger must click on your day to see the photos you share. In other words, you won't be annoying people unless they are choosing to be annoyed by you. People also like the way that sharing something that disappears means they don't have to share something perfect. It's just a quick way to pass the time and mark what happened to you today, in all its banal glory.

The Facebook Family of Mobile Apps

In addition to the basic Facebook app and the Messenger app, Facebook has other stand-alone apps to enhance very specific portions of the Facebook experience.

Moments

The Moments app is a great app for people who take a lot of photos on their phones, but only want to share them with a small number of people. Like, only the people who are in them. It provides an easy way to sync photos from an event with other people who were there. Instead of publishing photos to Facebook, as you might do from the Facebook app itself, Moments lets you send photos from your phone to other Facebook users. You get the benefit of Facebook's photo tools, such as facial recognition, but you don't have to create big albums or share your photos more widely if you aren't comfortable doing so.

Instagram

Instagram is a social media app used for sharing photos with friends and followers. Instagram also happens to be owned by Facebook, so it's worthwhile to point out that if mobile photography is your thing, you might find Instagram to be just what you were looking for. Some people use only Facebook, others use only Instagram to share photos online. Some people use both, and some people sync their accounts so that whatever they share on Instagram goes straight into Facebook's News Feed in addition. Check out the sidebar in Chapter 11 to learn a little more about Instagram.

Facebook on Your Mobile Browser

Viewing a web page from your phone can be extremely difficult because the information that is normally spread across the width of a monitor must be packed into one tiny column on your phone. Facebook is no exception to this, which is why the very first tip in this section is: Never go to www.facebook.com on your mobile phone. You'll regret it.

But fear not, you still have a way to carry almost all the joys of Facebook right in your purse or pocket. On your mobile phone, open your browser application and navigate to m.facebook.com — a site Facebook designed specifically to work on a teeny-tiny screen.

The first time you arrive at m.facebook.com, you're asked to log in. After that, you never (or rarely) have to reenter your log-in info unless you explicitly log out from your session, so be sure you trust anyone to whom you lend your phone.

WARNING

If you plan to use the Facebook Mobile site frequently, I recommend you have an unlimited data plan that allows you to spend as much time on the mobile web as you like for a fixed rate. The Facebook Mobile site is nearly as comprehensive and rich as the computer version. You can spend hours there — and if you're paying per minute, spend your life savings, too.

Mobile Home

After you log in, you see the mobile version of the Facebook Home page, shown in Figure 7-22. The design of the mobile site closely resembles the design of the regular website, with some minor differences. Some differences exist simply because of less space; the mobile site must cut to the chase while allowing you to get more information on a particular topic.

TIP

To follow along with this section, you can navigate to m.facebook.com on your web browser. Just imagine what you see on about one-tenth of the screen.

In this section, I detail what you see on the Mobile Home page; I cover the other pages in the following sections.

Friend Requests   Notifications

Newsfeed   Messages   Search   More

FIGURE 7-22:
Facebook Mobile
Home.

From m.facebook.com you'll see these items in your Mobile Home page:

> **» Blue bar on top of the page:**
>
> Much like on the regular website, the blue bar contains many of the links you will need most often for navigating Facebook:
>
> - **News Feed:** Tap the News Feed icon (it looks like a little newspaper) in the blue bar on top at any time to see or refresh your News Feed. News Feed itself takes up the bulk of your Mobile Home page.
>
> - **Friend Requests, Messages, and Notifications:** The three icons across the top of your screen are used throughout the Facebook experience: Friend Requests, Messages, and Notifications. New or unread actions are marked by a red flag in each category, just like when you log in to your Facebook account from a PC. Tap any of these icons to review that category.
>
> - **Search:** Tap the magnifying glass icon to open a search page where you can search for friends, Pages, posts, and trending topics.
>
> - **More:** The More icon has three horizontal lines. Tap it to open a menu with links to the things usually found in your left sidebar: your profile, Events, Groups, favorites, Apps, and so forth.

- >> **Publisher:** Facebook makes it easy to update your status, share photos, and check in so you can spread the news the moment you're doing something you want people to know about. The Publisher on your phone has the same privacy options; just tap or select the People icon on the left side of the Publisher to change who can see your post.

- >> **News Feed:** News Feed itself takes up most of the space on the Mobile Home page. Scroll down to keep seeing stories from your friends. Just like on the regular site, you can like, comment on, or share your friends' posts.

Mobile Timelines

Timelines on Facebook resemble Timelines on the regular site, except there is only one column of stuff instead of two. As you scroll down a mobile Timeline, here's what you'll see:

- >> **Profile picture and cover photo:** Just a smaller version of the profile picture and cover photo you see on the regular site.

- >> **Action buttons:** If you are looking at a friend's Timeline, you see blue links indicating that you are friends and are following that person. If you aren't yet friends with that person, you see links to Add Friend or Message her. Buttons labeled About, Photos, and Friends let you jump to those sections of your friend's Timeline.

- >> **Publisher:** Use the mobile Publisher to leave a post on a friend's Timeline or share a photo there. Remember, things you post on a Timeline are visible to your friend's friends.

- >> **Photos and Friends:** Before you start seeing your friend's posts on her Timeline, you can see thumbnails of recent photos she has added or been tagged in, as well as a preview of her friend list.

- >> **Timeline:** As on the regular site, the star of the show is your friend's Timeline, where you can see her most recent posts, whether that's a status update or a photo. You can also see how many people liked or commented on her posts, and you can add to those counts yourself by doing the same.

Mobile Inbox

The Mobile Inbox functions the same as the Inbox on the regular site, but in a more compact view. In the Mobile Inbox, your most recent messages appear first. You can see the name and profile picture of the people on a given thread, as well as a preview of the most recent message sent.

Tap on a message preview to open it. When you open a mobile thread, as with regular Facebook, the newest message is at the bottom with the Reply box beneath it. You can access a drop-down menu with action links by selecting the Take Action icon in the upper-right corner (below the blue bar, it looks like an envelope with an arrow coming out of it). You can choose from Mark Read/Unread, Delete, Delete Selected, Archive, Block Messages, or Report Spam or Abuse. The Mark as Unread option is particularly handy because often you read a message on your mobile phone, but don't have time or energy to type a response right then. Marking it as Unread reminds you to respond when you return to your computer.

Facebook Texts

Much of this chapter assumes you have a smartphone, or at least one with some capacity to use a browser. However, if you don't have a phone like that, you can still use Facebook via text message. To get started with Facebook Texts, you first need to enter and confirm your phone number in the Settings page from your web browser:

1. **Choose Settings from the Account menu (down arrow) in the upper-right corner of the big blue bar on top.**

2. **Click the Mobile tab on the left side of the page.**

3. **Click the green Add a Phone button.**

   You may be prompted to reenter your Facebook password. When that's all squared away, the Confirm Your Number dialog box appears.

4. **Choose your country and your mobile carrier.**

TIP

   If your carrier isn't listed, you may be out of luck using Facebook Texts from your mobile phone.

5. **Click Next.**

   This brings you to Step 6, which you must do from your phone.

6. **From your phone, text the letter F to 32665 (FBOOK).**

   FBOOK texts you back a confirmation code to enter from your computer.

   This can take a few minutes, so be patient.

7. **Enter your confirmation code into the empty text box.**

8. **If you see the Share My Phone Number with My Friends check box, choose whether you want your phone number added to your Timeline.**

   I find it very useful when friends share their mobile numbers on Facebook because it allows me to use Facebook as a virtual phone book. If you're not comfortable with that, simply deselect the check box. If you don't see this check box, skip to Step 10.

9. **If you see the Allow Friends to Text Me from Facebook check box, select whether you want friends to be able to text you from Facebook.**

Again, I find this useful, so I leave this check box selected. If you don't want people to be able to text you through Facebook, simply deselect the check box. If you don't see this check box, skip to Step 10.

10. **Click Next.**

This confirms your phone.

After your phone is confirmed, Facebook Texts are the most basic way to use Facebook on your phone. You don't need a camera on your phone or a smartphone to use Facebook Texts. Using just a simple Short Message Service (SMS) or text message, you can update your status to let people know where you are and what you're up to. You can also choose to receive text message notifications for things like Friend Requests as well as comments people have made on your posts.

Here are the various actions you can take on Facebook via SMS; all messages get sent to 32665 (FBOOK):

>> **Update your status:** Type any sort of phrase into a text message. Your status will appear on your Timeline and in your friends' News Feeds.

>> **Get a one-time password for accessing Facebook:** Text the letters OTP. One time passwords allow you to access Facebook from a new computer without accidentally letting your password be saved and giving someone else access to your account. Just remember to log out when you're done!

>> **Stop getting texts.** Text the word stop.

>> **Restart getting texts.** Text the word start.

Mobile settings

Once you've started using Facebook Texts, there are a number of settings you can adjust to better suit your texting lifestyle. You can get to these settings on the regular Facebook website by clicking the Account menu (the down arrow on the right side of the big blue bar on top), selecting Settings from the menu that opens, and then selecting Mobile on the left side of the page that opens.

>> **Text Messaging:** Decide which phone number you want your texts to be sent to. You need to change this setting only if you have more than one mobile phone number listed for your account.

>> **Mobile PIN:** Creating a mobile PIN is a security precaution you can take to keep someone from accessing any part of your Facebook account by spoofing your phone number or borrowing your phone. If you choose to create a PIN, you will need to start all texts to Facebook with that PIN.

>> **Daily Text Limit:** The Daily Text Limit allows you to modify the number of text messages you receive per day.

WARNING

If you have a mobile plan for which you're charged per text message (and you're exceedingly popular), use the settings that limit the number of messages Facebook sends you per day. Otherwise, you may have to shell out some big bucks in text message fees.

Remember to click Save Changes after updating this setting.

>> **Time of Day:** You can choose to only get texts from Facebook at certain times of the day, so that your phone doesn't bother you when you're sleeping (or while you're at work, perhaps).

Mobile notifications

Just when you thought you were done with Facebook Texts settings, I introduce a whole 'nother bunch of settings to further fine-tune your Facebook Texts experience. To get started, head to the Notifications tab of the Settings page and click Edit next to the Text Message section.

From this section, you can change the following settings:

>> **Turn text notifications on or off.** Fairly self-explanatory, although it's worth noting that even if you turn off these notifications, you can continue to use the SMS commands I describe earlier in this section to update your status, add a new friend, and so on.

>> **Decide which actions are text-worthy.** Choose up to three categories to be notified about via text: be notified when someone comments on your posts or status updates, when you receive a Friend Request or have a Friend Request you sent confirmed, and whether to receive texts about everything else, which encompasses actions like being tagged in a photo or receiving an Inbox message.

>> **Receive text notifications from friends only.** This check box controls whether you want to receive a text only when you receive an Inbox message from a friend. This means that if, for example, a non-friend sends a message to your Inbox, you will not be notified by text.

3

Connecting with Friends on Facebook

IN THIS PART . . .

Finding and adding friends

Sending messages

Managing your inbox

Creating groups

Sharing with groups

Chapter **8**

Finding Facebook Friends

undreds of sayings abound about friendship and friends, and most can be boiled down into one catch-all adage: friends, good; no friends, bad. This is true in life and also true on Facebook. Without your friends on Facebook, you find yourself at some point looking at a blank screen and asking, "Okay, now what?" With friends, you find yourself at some point looking at photos of a high school reunion and asking, "How did that last hour go by so quickly?"

Most of Facebook's functionality is built around the premise that you have a certain amount of information that you want your friends to see (and maybe some information that you don't want *all* your friends to see, but that's what privacy settings are for). So, if you don't have friends who are seeing your posts, what's the point in sharing them? Messages aren't that useful unless you send them to someone. Photos are made for viewing, but if the access is limited to friends, well, you need to find some friends.

On Facebook, the bulk of friendships are *reciprocal,* which means if you add someone as a friend, he has to confirm the friendship before it appears on both of your Timelines. If someone adds you as a friend, you can choose between Confirm and Delete Request. If you confirm the friend, *Congrats!* You have a new friend! And if you don't, the other person won't be informed.

If you're low on friends at the moment, don't feel as though you're the last kid picked for the team in middle-school dodge ball. There are many ways to find your friends on Facebook. If your friends haven't joined Facebook, invite them to join and get them to be your friends on Facebook as well as in real life.

What Is a Facebook Friend?

Good question. In many ways, a *Facebook Friend* is the same as a real-life friend (although, as the saying goes, "You're not real friends unless you're Facebook friends"). These are the people you hang out with, keep in touch with, care about, and want to publicly acknowledge as friends. These aren't people you meet on Facebook. Rather, they're the people you call on the phone; stop and catch up with if you cross paths at the grocery store; or invite over for parties, dinners, and other social gatherings.

In real life, there are many shades of friendship — think of the differences between acquaintances, a friend from work, an activity buddy, and best friends. Facebook gives you a few tools for negotiating these levels of friendship, which I cover in the "Managing How You Interact with Friends" section of this chapter. But by default, most friendships are lumped into a blanket category of "friend."

Here are the basics of what it means to be friends with someone on Facebook, though you'll notice that each of them comes with a few caveats on how it can be adjusted by either person in the friendship.

>> *They can see all the stuff on your Timeline (like your posts and other information) that you have set to be visible to Friends.*

Remember, this is what happens by default. You can control which friends can see which posts more specifically by learning about your privacy options (which you can do in Chapter 6), and about Friend Lists, which I go over later in this chapter.

>> *They see new posts you create in their News Feeds on their Home pages.*

Again, the information your friends see in their News Feed depends on the audience you've chosen to share each post with. It may also depend on your friends' News Feed settings.

>> *You can see their posts and other information on their Timelines.*

This, of course, depends on their own privacy settings, but in general, you'll be able to see more as a friend than you did before you became friends.

» *You see new posts from them in your News Feed on your Home page.*

This depends on your friend's sharing settings, but more importantly, you can control whose posts you see in your News Feed by managing your own News Feed settings and preferences. See Chapter 4 for more information on News Feed settings.

» *You'll be listed as friends on one another's Timeline.*

This is a small detail, but it's important in understanding the difference between becoming friends with someone and simply following someone. Lots of people, especially public figures or people who have a business of some sort, allow you to subscribe to their posts without becoming friends. In these cases, you see their posts in your News Feed, but they won't see your posts unless they choose to subscribe to you.

Adding Friends

Over time, Facebook has created some unique lingo. One of the most important Facebook terms is the verb "to friend." *Friending* is the act of adding someone as a friend. You may overhear people use this casually in conversation: "You won't believe who finally friended me!" And now, you too, will be friending people.

Sending Friend Requests

Now that you know what a friend is, it's time to send some requests, and maybe even accept some pending ones. For the purposes of this example, I searched for the Timeline of Amy Karasavas using the search box in the blue bar on top. I cover using Search to find friends later in this chapter, so for now just remember that as you type, Facebook tries to auto-complete what you're looking for, meaning search results will appear below the search box as you type, as shown in Figure 8-1.

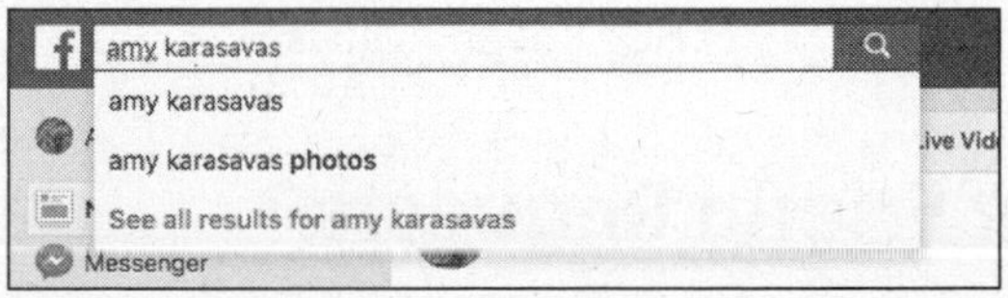

FIGURE 8-1:
The search results for Amy Karasavas.

Click the name of the person you think you want to add. You will see a page with search results for that person's name. When you locate the correct person, click the gray Add Friend button to the right of their search result to send your friend request. Another option is to click the person's name to go to her Timeline. Within her cover photo, toward the bottom, is a gray Add Friend button. Click this button to send your request. There may also be a green Add Friend button below her cover photo that you can click to send a request. You can see both buttons in Figure 8-2. No matter which method you use, when she accepts the request, you'll become friends.

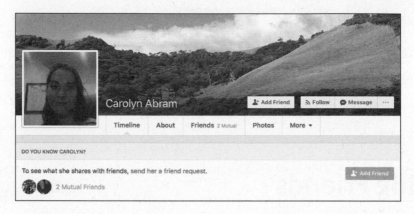

If you decide after the request is sent that you in fact did not want to send it, navigate back to her Timeline and locate the Friend Request Sent button (previously the Add Friend button). Click it to open a menu and choose Cancel Request from the menu. Click Cancel Request again in the pop-up window and presto, it's like the request never happened.

TIP

Depending on people's settings, you might not see an Add Friend button. If you can't send a friend request, you can usually send the person a message or follow her public posts without becoming friends first.

REMEMBER

You won't be friends with someone until she confirms your Friend Request. After she confirms, you're notified by a red flag appearing above the Friend Requests icon in the blue bar on top.

So what does your potential friend see after you send a request? That is a brilliant segue into the next topic, accepting Friend Requests.

Accepting Friend Requests

When you receive a new request, a little red flag appears over the Friend Requests icon in the blue bar on top of each page. You may also be notified in your email or on your phone. Figure 8-3 shows an example. The number in the red flag indicates how many Friend Requests are waiting for you.

FIGURE 8-3:
Someone wants
to be your friend!

Clicking this icon opens the Friend Requests menu, as shown in Figure 8-4.

FIGURE 8-4:
Click Confirm or
Delete Request.

To accept the Friend Request, click the Confirm button. You now have a friend. To reject the request, click Delete Request. When you click Delete Request, you will have the option to mark that request as Spam if you suspect it's from a fake profile.

TIP

Some people worry about clicking that Delete Request button. If you're not sure what you want to do, you can always leave the request untouched. But never hesitate to click Delete Request for someone you really just don't want to be friends with. Facebook won't notify her that you ignored her request.

Choose your friends wisely

Generally, you send Friend Requests to and confirm Friend Requests only from people you actually know. If you don't know them — *random Friend Requests* — click Delete Request. Accepting a Friend Request from unknown people has a tendency to ruin the Facebook experience — it puts random content in your News Feed, exposes your own content to people you don't know, and is generally a bad practice. Remember the lecture you got about choosing good friends when you were in high school? It's every bit as true now.

If there are people you don't know personally but find interesting (such as a celebrity or public figure), you may be able to subscribe to their posts without becoming friends with them (more on that in the "Following" section near the end of this chapter). If that's not a possibility, you could add them as friends and then add them to your Acquaintances or Restricted Friend List, if you use these lists to control your privacy.

It's quality, not quantity

Another common misconception about Facebook is that it's all about the race to get the most friends. This is very, very wrong. Between the News Feed and privacy implications of friendship, aim to keep your Friend List to the people you actually care about. Now, the number of people you care about — including the people you care about the most and those you care about least — may be large or small. It doesn't matter how big or small your list is as long as the people you care about most are on it. In fact, one of the reasons for the Friend List management tools that I cover in this chapter is because, over time, people's Friend Lists tend to bloat.

As you change jobs or cities or start a new hobby, you add more and more friends, but that doesn't displace the fact that you care about friends from your past. The Friend List management tools aim to help you keep track of the people you care about most, and not get distracted by the more distant friends.

TIP

If looking at the number of Friends in the Friends box on your Timeline gets you down, you can always choose to hide that number from other people in your privacy settings. See Chapter 6 for details.

Finding Your Friends on Facebook

How do you get to the people you want to be your friends? Facebook is big, and if you're looking for your friend John, you may need to provide some more detail. Facebook has a couple of tools that show you people you may know and want as your friends, as well as a search-by-name functionality for finding specific people.

Import your friends

If you're someone who uses email to communicate with your friends and family, an easy list of people you'd probably want to add as Facebook friends already exists — your email address book. Facebook has a tool, which I refer to as *Friend Finder*, that matches email addresses from your email address book to people's Timelines on Facebook. Because each email address can be associated with only one Facebook account, you can count on such matches finding the right people.

With your permission, when you import your address book, Facebook also invites people who don't have a Facebook account but whose email addresses match those in your address book to join Facebook. Sending invites this way causes Friend Requests to automatically be sent to those people. If they join based on an invite you send, they find a Friend Request from you waiting when they join.

To add your email contacts, you need to give Facebook your email address and email password. Facebook doesn't store this information. It just uses the information to retrieve your contacts list that one time.

Chances are that you came across the opportunity to add your personal contacts when you first set up your account. The following steps make several assumptions — namely, that you use web-based email (Hotmail, Yahoo! Mail, and so on), that you haven't already imported your contacts, and that the address book for the email has a bunch of your friends in it.

Here's how to add your email contacts to your Friend List:

1. **Click the Friends icon on the blue bar on top.**

   The Friend Request menu opens.

2. **At the top-right corner of the menu, click the Find Friends link.**

   Figure 8-5 shows the Add Personal Contacts section of the Find Friends page. It's usually on the right side of the page.

Add Personal Contacts

Choose how you communicate with friends. See how it works, manage imported contacts, or give feedback.

amykarasavas

Find Friends

3. **Select the email or instant message service you use by clicking its icon.**

   Some examples are Outlook.com, Hotmail, Gmail, AOL, or Yahoo! Mail.

4. **Enter your email address in the Your Email field.**

5. **Enter your email password (not your Facebook password) in the Email Password box and then click Find Friends.**

TIP

These instructions are meant for first-time users of the Friend Finder. If you've used it before, or if you're currently logged in to your webmail client, you may see some fields prefilled or additional pop-up prompts asking you for your permission to send information to Facebook. Don't worry if what you see on the screen doesn't match the figures here at the beginning.

If Facebook finds matches with the emails in your address book, you see a list of people Facebook thinks you might know.

6. **Click the check box to the right of anyone's name and photo to add him as a friend.**

   Everyone you select receives a Friend Request from you.

After you click either Add as Friends or Skip, you land on the Invite Friends portion of Friend Finder. Here you find a list of contact names and email addresses. These emails or phone numbers are those that don't have matches on Facebook.

7. **(Optional) Invite people to join Facebook and become your friends.**

   Any of your contacts who have not yet joined Facebook can be invited to join. If they do join, when they sign up they will receive a friend request from you. By default, all the contacts on your list are selected. You can:

   - *Invite all these contacts:* Make sure the Select All/None box is checked and click Send Invites.

   - *Invite none of these contacts:* Make sure the Select All/None box is unchecked and click Skip.

   - *Invite some of these contacts:* Uncheck the Select All/None box and then use the check boxes to the left of their email addresses to choose which ones you want to invite to join Facebook. Selected check box = invite sent; deselected check box = no invite sent.

   After you make your selections, click Send Invites or Invite to Join. If you don't want to send any invitations, click Skip.

After taking these steps, I hope you manage to send at least a few Friend Requests. Don't be shy about adding people you know and want to keep up with; it's not considered rude to add people as your friends. Your friends need to confirm your requests before you officially become friends on Facebook, so you may not be able to see your friends' Timelines until those confirmations happen.

If the whole experience yielded nothing — no friends you wanted to add, no contacts you wanted to invite — you have a few options. You can go through these steps again with different email addresses. You should probably use any email address that you use for personal emails (from where you email your friends and family). If that's not the problem, you have more ways to find friends.

People you may know

After you have a friend or two, Facebook can start making pretty good guesses about other people who may be your friends. Facebook primarily does this by looking at people with whom you have friends or networks in common. In the People You May Know box, you see a list of people Facebook thinks you may know and, therefore, may want as friends. People You May Know boxes appear all over the site — on the Find Friends page, on your Home page, and sometimes on your Timeline. Usually the boxes include a list of names, profile pictures, and some sort of info like how many mutual friends you have or where the other person attended school. These little tidbits are meant to provide context about how you might know that person.

Anytime you find yourself looking at the People You May Know list and you do, in fact, know someone on the list, simply add that person as a friend by clicking the Add Friend button. If you're not sure, you can click a name or picture to go to that person's Timeline and gather more evidence about if and how you know that person. Then you can decide whether to add that person as a friend. If you're sure you don't know someone, or if you do know someone but are sure you don't want that person as your Facebook friend, mouse over the person's picture and click the X that appears in the upper-right corner. After you do that, she stops appearing in your People You May Know list. As you remove people from the list, more pop up to take their places. This fun can last for hours.

Find classmates, co-workers, neighbors, and mutual friends

Especially when you are just getting started on Facebook, it can be helpful to look for large groups of people you might want to become friends with. A common assumption is that you are likely to be friends with your friends' friends, as well as with people you've gone to school with and worked with over the years. To find these people, use the Search for Friends box, located beneath the Add Personal Contacts box on the right side of the Find Friends page.

The Search for Friends box, shown in Figure 8-6, lets you isolate potential friends along a variety of criteria. You can mix and match these criteria or just use one at a time.

>> **Name:** You can search for an individual by entering their name into the Search for Someone box.

>> **Mutual Friend:** You can browse for friends by looking at your existing friends' friends. Facebook displays the names of three friends, and you can view their friends by selecting the check box next to their name. You can also enter a friend's name into the Enter Another Name box in order to add him to this list. One good way to home in on the people you most likely want to be friends with is to select at least two names from your Mutual Friend List. If two (or three, or four . . .) of your friends are friends with the same person, the chances are even greater that you want that person to be your friend.

>> **Hometown:** If you've previously listed your hometown on your Timeline, you can select it here to view people with the same hometown. If you haven't, or if you have another city you consider a hometown, you can enter a city name

into the Enter Another City box to view potential friends from the old stomping grounds.

>> **Current City:** If you've previously listed your current city on your Timeline, you can select it here to view other people who live there. If you haven't, or if you have another place you consider to be where you *really* live, you can enter a city name into the Enter Another City box to view potential friends from the current stomping grounds.

>> **High School:** If you've previously listed any high schools you attended on your Timeline, you can select them here to view other people who went there. You can also use the Enter a High School box to enter a high school name and look for people who went there.

>> **College or University:** Any colleges you listed as having attended appear here. Select any of them to see people who went there as well, or enter a college name into the text box to search for people who went there.

>> **Employer:** Any employers you've listed on your Timeline appear here. Click the check boxes to select or use the text field to search for a different employer.

>> **Graduate School:** If you've listed a graduate school you attended on your profile, you can click here to select it. You can also enter any school's name into the text field to see people who went there.

Search for Friends

Find friends from different parts of your life

Name

Search for someone

Mutual Friend
☐ Amy Babiarz Fandrei
☐ Katie Purdum Mohr
☐ Lindsay Sandman Lefevere

Enter another name

Hometown
☐ Foster City, California

Enter another city

Current City
☐ Indianapolis, Indiana

Enter another city

High School

Enter a high school

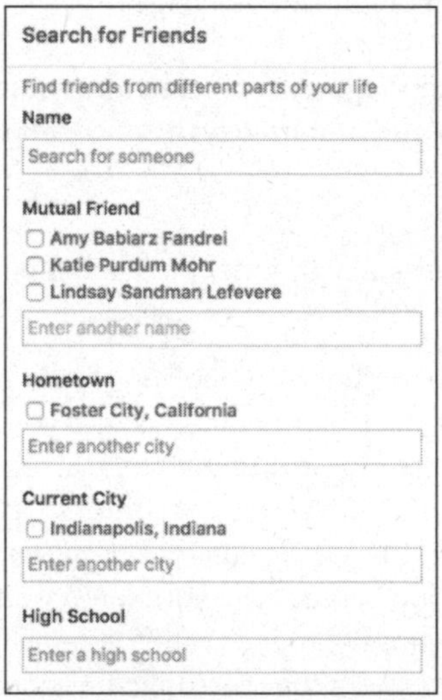

FIGURE 8-6: Use the check boxes to find your friends.

REMEMBER

When you select more than one check box, it actually shows you *fewer* people because now Facebook is looking for people who both worked at Mom's Pizza *and* went to Hamilton High School. To find more people, select only one check box at a time.

Find what you're looking for: Search

When you're just starting on Facebook, you want to find everyone you know as quickly as possible and build out your Friend List. After you build it, though, what if you find other people who may want to be your friends? Facebook Search offers you the capability to seek out certain friends by name.

WARNING

The search box in the blue bar on top lets you search a whole lot of things on Facebook: Pages, Groups, Events, even things your friends have posted. But most of the time, you use it to search for people. It may be people you're already friends with and you just want to go to their Timelines. Sometimes it will be people you aren't friends with yet but whom you want to reach out to.

Basic Search can be a little confusing because Facebook autocompletes the names that you type and assumes you're trying to get to your friends' Timelines. If you're the type of person who is used to pressing the Enter key to begin a search, this can lead you to friends' Timelines when you meant to search for someone *else* named Waldo.

You'll wind up using Search two basic ways. The first way is if the name of the person you're looking for (or at least someone with the same name) appears in the autocomplete menu. You can accomplish that sort of search following these steps:

1. Begin typing the name you're looking for in the search box.

Pay attention to the people who appear in the autocomplete menu. Facebook displays first your friends and then friends of friends. There's a good chance that you may find the person you're looking for in this menu.

2. If you see the name in the autocomplete menu, use your mouse or arrow keys to highlight the person you're looking for.

3. Click the name or press Enter.

This brings you to the person's Timeline, where you can verify that you know the person and add him as a friend.

If you don't see the person you're looking for, don't despair; you can get more results by typing the person's full name into the search box and selecting "See all results for <person's name> at the bottom of the auto-complete menu. This brings you to a search results page, where you can see all matches for the name you just searched for.

TIP

If you know you have the right name but there are too many search results, try going to the Find Friends page and using the Name field in the Search for Friends box. When you get the results, you will then be able to add more details like where that person is from or where they went to school to help you find your friend.

Managing How You Interact with Friends

After you do all the work of finding and adding your friends, at some point, you may find that things are feeling a little out of control. Chances are you may be seeing posts from someone you find uninteresting; you might not be sure who, exactly, can see your own posts anymore; or you may just want to tidy up your Friend List. At this point, it's a good idea to get acquainted with the way Facebook automatically helps you end the madness, as well as some of the specific actions you can take.

Friend Lists

Friend Lists are subsets of your master list of friends. Friend Lists are a way of organizing your friends into lists to make your Facebook experience even easier and more personalized to you and your types of friends. Organizing your friends into lists allows you to share different types of information with different sets of friends. For example, your best friends may get to see your party photos while your family may get to see your wedding photos. This is a custom privacy setting you can use all over Facebook.

Pre-fab lists

Facebook creates three lists for you when you join that you can choose to add people to:

>> **Close Friends:** You can add your best friends to your Close Friends list. Adding them to this list signifies to Facebook that you want to see a lot more of them in your News Feed. You can then select this list as a custom privacy setting when you are posting something to Facebook.

>> **Acquaintances:** The opposite of the Close Friends list. This list is meant to be a place where you can cordon off the people you don't know as well. They may be perfectly nice people, but they aren't necessarily the people you want to share everything with. Anyone you add to this list won't appear as often in your News Feed.

>> **Restricted:** This list is for people you want to add as friends but don't want to see posts that are visible to friends. In other words, people on this list only see posts that you choose to make public.

By default, these lists will be empty. In other words, Facebook creates lists that get special treatment for certain parts of Facebook, but it's up to you to let Facebook know who belongs on any of them. To learn how to add and remove people from these lists, you can skip ahead to the "Managing lists" section.

Smart Lists

Smart Lists are the lists that Facebook both creates and populates on your behalf. These lists are created automatically based on shared characteristics of your friends. Here are some common Smart Lists:

- » **Family:** Based on information you've entered about your family, they may show up on this Smart List.

- » ***<Your High School>*:** If you've caught up with a lot of old friends on Facebook, a Smart List might be created so you can post photos from the reunion or share memories just with them.

- » ***<Your college/university/workplace>*:** Similar to a high school list, depending on the information your friends have listed on their profiles, additional Smart Lists may be created for these groups. For example, I have Smart Lists for Boston University (where I was an undergraduate) and Facebook (where I used to work).

- » ***<Your current/former city> area*:** Depending on the info you and your friends have listed on their profiles, Facebook creates a list of people who live in or near your current city.

TIP

You can change the radius on a location-based list. Click Friend Lists from the Explore section of the left-side menu on your Home page and select the list you'd like to adjust. From that list's page, click the Manage List button and then select Edit Radius from the menu that opens. You will be able to change the radius of who is included from as small as 5 miles to as large as 200 miles.

Facebook is smart, but it's not perfect. Although these lists will be mostly accurate, you may find that you have to edit them. The accuracy of the lists may also depend on how you want to use your lists. For example, you may want your Family list to make it easy to share with just your immediate family and, therefore, need to remove the more distant members. Or you want it to be a giant family reunion all the time, in which case, you need to add some of the third and fourth cousins once removed to the mix.

Creating your own Friend Lists

Smart Lists can help you figure out whom you want to share your own posts with. But sometimes you may want a specific list that Facebook can't figure out. This might be a sub-sub-group, like all the people who belong to your book club. In these cases, you can create your own list.

To create a Friend List, follow these steps:

1. **From the Home page, click on Friend Lists under the Explore section of the left-side menu.**

   This brings you the Friend Lists page, which displays every list of your friends, both Smart Lists and lists you've created yourself.

2. **Click the Create List button at the top of the page.**

   The Create New List window appears, as shown in Figure 8-7.

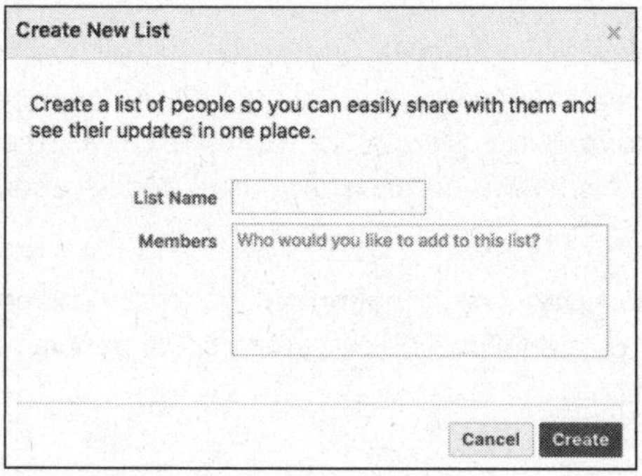

FIGURE 8-7:
Creating a
Friend List.

3. **In the List Name box, type the name of your list.**

   Maybe something like Study Group for your Calculus class.

4. **Add friends who belong on this list by typing their names in the Members box.**

   Facebook autocompletes as you type. Press Enter when you highlight the correct friend's name.

5. **Click Create.**

   Now, wherever Friend Lists appear on Facebook, including where you set privacy for posts, you have access to the new list you just created.

REMEMBER

Friend Lists you create are private, so even if the list you're messaging is known in your mind as *Annoying Co-Workers*, all that your annoying co-workers see is a list of names. Members of Smart Lists are able to see the name of a list they've been added to.

Managing lists

Regardless of the type of list, adding and removing people from a list follows the same steps:

1. **Click Friend Lists in the left-side menu.**

The Friend Lists page appears.

2. **Click on the list you want to manage.**

For example, clicking on Close Friends opens the Close Friends page. If you already have friends on this list, you will see a feed of stories only from friends on this list. If you don't have any friends on this list yet, you'll see a big blank space where a feed would normally appear. On the right side of the page is an On This List box, shown in Figure 8-8.

FIGURE 8-8:
Adding people
to a list.

3. **To add people to a list, enter their names in the text box in the On This List section.**

Facebook autocompletes as you type. Select your friends' names when you see them.

To remove people from a list (starting from the list's page), follow these steps.

1. **Click the Manage List button in the upper-right corner of the list's page.**

2. **Choose Edit List from the menu.**

A pop-up window displays the names and pictures of all members of the list.

3. **Hover over the person you want to remove.**

A small X appears in the upper-right corner of the person's picture.

4. **Click the X.**

5. **Repeat Steps 3 and 4 for each person you want to remove.**

6. **Click the Finish button when you're done.**

Updating lists on the go

After you create and start using your lists, you can continuously add people to them at the same time you add them as friends.

When you're the one sending a Friend Request, follow these steps to also add the person to a particular Friend List:

1. **From his Timeline, after you've added him as a friend, click the Friend Request Sent button.**

   A menu appears asking you if you want to add that person to any of your Friend Lists. By default, your most commonly used lists will appear at the top.

2. **Click the list you want to add your friend to.**

   You may need to select Add to Another List to see your full menu of lists.

If you're the one receiving the Friend Request, you can follow these steps to add someone to a list as you accept the request:

1. **From the Friend Request menu, click Confirm.**

   This adds the person as a friend. The blue Confirm button changes to a gray Friends button.

2. **Click the Friends button that appears.**

   A drop-down menu with options related to becoming this person's friend appears.

3. **If you don't see the list you want, click Add to Another List.**

   You can check off as many lists as you want. For example, if someone is a member of your family and they also live in your current town, you may want them on both lists.

   If you realize you don't currently have a fitting list for this person, click +New List at the bottom of the menu and create a list right on the spot.

TIP

If at any point you remember, *Hey, I meant to add So-and-So to the Book Club list*, simply visit that person's Timeline and click the button that says Friends at the lower right of the cover photo. The menu covered in the preceding steps appears, which you can use to add So-and-So to the right list.

Deleting lists

You can delete lists you create that you no longer use (for example, a list of ex-coworkers). To do so, follow these steps:

1. **Click Friend Lists from the Explore section of the left-side menu of your Home page.**

2. **Hover your mouse over the list you want to delete and click the gear icon that appears in the upper-right corner.**

3. **Choose Delete List from the drop-down menu that appears.**

4. **A pop-up window confirms that you want to delete the list and reminds you that past posts available to this list will remain visible to those people.**

5. **Click Delete List to confirm.**

REMEMBER

You can't delete Smart Lists, but you can archive them by following the preceding steps and clicking Archive List. This way, the list no longer appears in your privacy settings menu. You won't be able to archive or delete a Pre-Fab list, but you can remove all of the people you added to that list so it's empty.

Groups

Groups are, in many ways, a more public version of Friend Lists. Instead of your friends not knowing which list they're on, friends are always notified when they're added to a group. Depending on the group's privacy settings, they may be able to add their friends to the group if they think the information shared there is relevant to them. Groups are extremely useful for sharing information that only a specific group of people might care about. For example, a funny video from a family gathering that perhaps only members of your crazy family will understand is a good candidate to be shared in a family group. We cover Groups in great detail in Chapter 10.

News Feed options

In addition to News Feed views, you can use News Feed options to help you control which friends' posts you see when you log in to Facebook. For example, if one of your friends changes her profile picture back and forth between two photos all week long, it might start to clutter up your News Feed. Chapter 4 covers controlling your News Feed and which posts you see from which people in great detail.

Following

Following is a way of saying you really really want to see someone's posts. On some social media sites, following is the primary way of interacting with other people. On Facebook, following is baked into friending someone or liking a Page. However, you can follow someone you are not friends with. In fact, by default when you add a friend, you follow them, even before they've accepted your friend request. The catch here is that following someone without becoming their friend means you only see their public posts in your News Feed.

Certain people (often public figures) allow people to follow their public posts without requesting friendship. Following someone is as easy as — actually, it's easier than — adding someone as a friend. Navigate to that person's Timeline and click the Follow button at the bottom right of their cover photo. To unfollow her, click that same button (it now says Following) to open a menu of options. Select the Unfollow option (the last item on the menu).

If you're someone who plans on posting lots of public updates or are a public figure (locally or nationally), you can allow people to follow you instead of becoming your friend (they'll also be able to add you as a friend, but you won't have to accept their requests for them to see your posts). Follow these steps to allow people to follow you:

1. **Click the Account Menu (down arrow) in the upper-right corner of the blue bar on top.**

   A menu of options appears.

2. **Select the Settings option.**

   The Settings page appears, which has a menu running down the left-hand side.

3. **Select Public Posts from the left menu.**

   The Public Posts Settings page appears.

4. **Use the privacy menu in the Who Can Follow Me section to determine who can follow you.**

   You can toggle between Public and Friends. If you choose Public, congrats! People can now follow your public posts. Once you opt into this feature, more settings appear on the page. These settings allow you to specify how followers can find and interact with your Timeline. This is also where you can connect a Twitter account so your tweets will also be imported to Facebook.

Unfriending

It happens to everyone: After a while, you start to feel like a few people are cluttering up Facebook for you. Maybe you feel like you have too many friends, or maybe you and a friend have drifted apart. Don't worry; Facebook friendships are not set in stone. You can *unfriend* just like you friend people.

To unfriend someone, do the following:

1. **Go to the person's Timeline.**

2. **Click the Friends button.**

   A menu appears that is for assigning people to Friend Lists. The last item in this list is Unfriend.

3. **Click the Unfriend link.**

Take a moment of silence. Okay, that was long enough.

TIP

People aren't notified when you unfriend them, but people who care about you (that is, family, close friends) have a tendency to notice on their own that, hey, you're not in their list of friends anymore. This can sometimes lead to awkwardness, so it might be worth using your privacy settings to further limit these people's knowledge of your life *before* you unfriend them.

Lots of people go through periodic friend-cleaning. For example, after changing jobs or moving, you may notice that you want to keep in touch with some people from that chapter in your life; others, you just don't. Unfriend away.

Chapter **9**

Just between You and Me: Facebook Messages

C hances are that you're someone who communicates with other people online. You may use email all the time or use instant messaging programs like iMessage or Skype. If you have a smartphone, you probably check email and text messages on it as well. Facebook has similar functionality and integrates into all these programs. In other words, Facebook Messages stitches together email, texting, and instant messaging with a Facebook twist.

One special component of Facebook's messaging system as opposed to other systems is that you no longer have to remember email addresses, screen names, or handles. You just have to remember people's names. The other benefit is that your entire contact history with specific people is saved in one place. I refer to this ongoing conversation as a *conversation* or *thread*.

If this sounds confusing to you, think of it as mirroring the fact that usually you don't simply stop speaking to someone in real life. You may have asked a friend about getting lunch next week, but then you pick up the conversation again a week later to figure out where you want to go for lunch, or to let her know that you're running 30 minutes late. Even after the lunch is over, chances are one of you will want to meet up again soon.

Instead of splitting all of these up into discreet emails, texts, or phone calls, Facebook thinks of your communication as one long, ongoing discussion that lasts the entirety of your friendship.

Sending a Message

Figure 9-1 shows the basic New Message chat window. I opened this by clicking the Messages shortcut in the big blue bar on top (it looks like a word bubble with a horizontal lightning bolt inside it) and clicking the New Message link from the menu. A New Message chat window opens from the bottom of the page. This interface, with the message window floating over Facebook in the background, is designed to look like an instant messaging service. Remember, on Facebook there's no real distinction between chats (instant messages) and messages. Everything gets saved to your message history. Anytime you click on a Message button or link from a friend's Timeline or Timeline preview, a new message window opens, with that friend's name pre-filled in the To: field.

FIGURE 9-1:
The New Message chat window.

The New Message chat window has only two fields for you to fill out: a To: field and a message box where you type the text of your message. Unlike emails, this chat window has no spaces for CC, BCC, or a subject line.

To address your message, simply start typing the name of the person you're messaging into the To: field. Facebook autocompletes as you type, and you'll see that it tries to fill in the names of friends as well as friends of friends. In other words, it assumes you are messaging someone you know somehow. When you see the name you want, highlight it and click or press Enter. You can type more than one name if you want to have a conversation with more than one person at the same time.

This isn't the only way to open a message window to a friend. Clicking the Message button on a friend's Timeline or preview opens a chat window. Clicking their name in the Chat menu opens a chat window (more on that in the Chat Menu section). Regardless of how you got here, messaging works the same way.

After you enter a friend's name, you can click in the Type a Message field to start typing your message. Enter your message in the message box. There are no rules around what goes here. Messages can be long or short, fat or skinny, silly or serious — whatever you have to say. Press Enter to send your message (or Shift + Enter to create a paragraph break). If you have an existing message thread already started with that person, you see that your new message simply gets added to the bottom of the conversation.

As you and your friend message back and forth to each other, you can continue to use Facebook — scroll up and down in your News Feed, browse photos, check out a Timeline. Regardless of where you go on Facebook's site, your chat windows will remain open at the bottom of the screen. They won't close unless you close them or close Facebook.

You can react to specific messages that your friend has sent by hovering your mouse over the text and clicking the gray Smiley icon that appears next to it. This opens a menu of the usual Facebook reactions: love, laugh, surprise, cry, angry, thumbs up, and thumbs down.

Figure 9-2 shows a chat window between friends. It is designed to look somewhat like the text message interface on your phone. A profile picture of your friend is shown on the left side of the chat window, next to the white speech bubble that contains her message. Your own messages appear in blue anchored to the right side of the chat window. You can scroll up to see older messages.

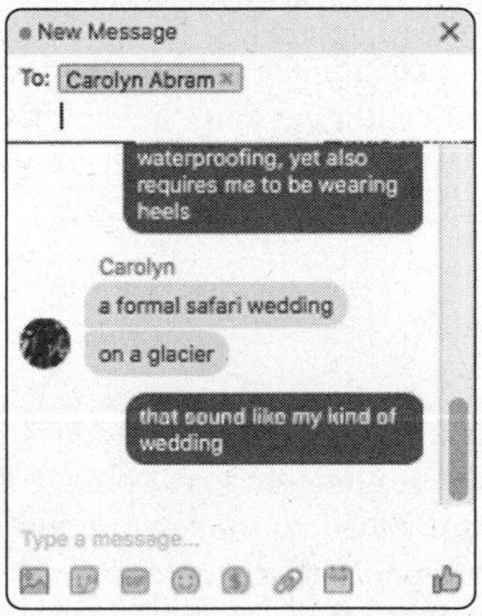

FIGURE 9-2:
A conversation between friends.

Group Messages

You can message more than one person at a time. Doing so creates a new conversation among all the people you message. Everyone can see and reply to the message. So if you send a message to Mike, Jenny, and Steve, a new conversation is created. When you're looking at that conversation, you can see all the messages that have been sent by all the people involved. As you're reading, you can see who said what by looking at the names and profile pictures identifying each message. Each message is separated and has a timestamp so that you can see when it was sent.

The main thing to remember about group conversations is that you cannot reply individually to members of the conversation. When you reply, all members of the conversation see your reply. If you are in multiple conversations with some of the same people, double check to make sure you're in the right conversation before hitting reply!

Group messages have some specific options, like removing yourself from a conversation and naming a conversation, that are covered in the Message Options section.

Sending links

If you want to add a link to a website or article to a message, you can copy and paste it into the message box. Facebook then generates a preview of the article so that your friend has more info before clicking the link. You can remove this preview by clicking the X in the upper-right corner of the preview. If you ever choose to share a link from another website (many news sites have links to share articles, for example) you can select to share it in a private message and accomplish the same thing: sending the link and a preview to a friend, as well as explaining why you are sending it.

TIP

Much like when you create a post, you can make your messages a little less messy by only sending the preview without sending a long, unwieldy URL. Once you can see the preview, simply delete the actual URL from your message. Your friend will be able to click through on the preview alone.

Sending photos

To add photos to your message, click the picture icon (it looks like a framed picture of a mountain) at the bottom of the chat window. Doing so opens an interface for navigating your computer's hard drive, so make sure you know where your photo is saved. If you want to share a photo that is already on Facebook, the easiest way to share it is to navigate to that photo, click the share link at the bottom of the photo, and choose to share it in a private message.

REMEMBER

If you're sharing a photo that is on Facebook, privacy rules may sometimes prevent your friend from being able to see it.

Sending stickers

Stickers on Facebook are a lot like the stickers you might have once used to adorn a school notebook or a letter from summer camp, except, you know, digital. There are virtually infinite sticker options you can send to friends, from smiley faces to ones related to various holidays to ones created by specific artists.

Clicking on the square Smiley icon at the bottom of a chat window opens the Search Stickers menu, shown in Figure 9-3.

FIGURE 9-3:
Selecting stickers.

You can browse through the various categories of stickers here. Click a category name to see stickers in that category, then scroll down to see the full collection. As soon as you click on a sticker, it is sent to your friend.

Along the top of the Search Stickers menu are recently used sticker collections you have used. You can also click on the plus sign here to go to the sticker store. In the sticker store you can browse through sticker options and choose to add them to your personal collections. After you have added a sticker collection (by clicking the green Free button), close the sticker store by clicking the X in the upper-right corner. Then, when you reopen the Search Stickers menu, you'll see your new sticker pack along the top of the menu.

Sending GIFs

A *GIF* is a file format that supports animated images. But when people talk about GIFs, they are usually referring to how GIFs are used on the Internet: as ways to share a clip, usually on a loop, that captures a moment, emotion, or thought. So, for example, if someone tells you something that exasperates you, you could send a GIF of a famous person rolling his eyes to communicate that you are, in fact, rolling your eyes as well.

You can click on the GIF icon at the bottom of the chat menu to browse through GIFs that you can send to a friend. By default, Facebook shows you trending GIFs (in other words, GIFs that other people have been sending). You can search for the type of GIF you are looking for using the Search box at the top of the GIF menu. As soon as you click on a GIF it is sent to your friend.

Sending Emojis

Emojis are small digital images that express an emotion or idea. The most common emojis are the yellow smiley (or frowny or crying) faces. You can select from a multitude of emojis on Facebook, ranging from the usual smileys to specific foods, locations, or modes of transportation.

To choose an emoji, click the round Smiley icon in the bottom of the chat window. This opens a menu for browsing emoji. Click on the one you want to add to any text you have written. Unlike stickers and GIFs, emojis get added within your text, so you will need to press Enter to send them.

Sending payments

You can use Facebook to send money to friends. It requires both you and your friends to enter debit card info into Facebook, which it stores securely in its systems. Facebook does not charge a fee to send payments between friends.

If you've never sent money before, follow these steps the first time you want to send money to a friend:

1. **Tap the $ icon in the bottom of a chat window with your friend.**

   A payment interface appears, shown in Figure 9-4.

2. **Type the amount of money you want to send into the payment field.**

3. **(Optional) Type in the reason for the payment in the "What is this payment for?" field.**

4. **Click the Next button.**

   A window opens for entering your debit card info for making the payment.

5. **Enter your debit card info into the relevant fields.**

6. Click the Pay button.

The money has been sent to your friend. He will need to enter a debit card into Facebook to receive the money.

FIGURE 9-4:
Sending money to friends.

REMEMBER

Payments only work with debit cards. Using debit cards allows you to pay directly from your bank account and allows your friend to put money directly in her bank account. Make sure that when you enter your card info, it is for a debit card, not a credit card.

WARNING

Once you send money, you can't cancel the payment. Be sure that you are okay with the money leaving your account before you click the Pay button.

TIP

If you'd like to add extra security around payments, check out the Payments section of the Settings page.

Sending attachments

Much as it does in many email programs, an icon shaped like a paperclip signifies attaching files to a message. Clicking the attachment icon opens an interface for searching and selecting files from your computer's hard drive. You can attach photos, videos, documents, and so on.

Playing games

Games are more fun with friends. That's pretty much true in real life, and it's true online. Facebook is one way for people to connect with real-life friends to play games online. Click the Games icon (it's shaped like a video game controller) to open a menu of games that you can choose to play against (or with) the friend you are messaging. These games usually have not been built by Facebook, so by using them you are technically sharing some basic information (like your name and friend list) with third-party developers. You can learn more about using your Facebook information with third party applications in Chapter 15. Click the Play button next to the game you want to play. Once you've played a round, your friend will be sent a challenge.

TIP

Many games are optimized for mobile phones, so they might look a little weird if you're playing them on your desktop or laptop computer. Try playing from your phone sometime!

Taking photos to send

The Camera icon at the bottom of the chat window opens an interface for taking photos with your computer's built-in webcam (or, if you're using Messenger on your phone, it connects to your phone's camera). You may need to approve the use of your webcam or install a driver to your computer to access this feature.

When you look at a preview of yourself on the screen, click the green Take Photo button to take your photo. If you like it, click the blue Send button to send it to your friend.

The Facebook Like

The last icon you see in the composer section of the chat window is a thumbs-up icon, also known as the Like icon. You can click this icon to send a thumbs-up icon to your friend at any time.

Message Options

Chances are if you send a message, pretty soon you'll get a reply. Depending on your settings and whether you're logged in to Facebook, when you receive a new message, you see either a new chat window open (like you're receiving an IM) or a little red flag on your Home page over the Messages icon in the big blue bar on top. Click the flag to open the Inbox preview; then click the message preview to open the conversation in a chat window at the bottom of your screen.

At the top of each chat window is a blue bar displaying the name (or names) of the person you're chatting with and several icons.

Add friends

The plus sign icon allows you to add more friends to a conversation you are having with a friend. Click this to open a text field where you can enter a friend's name. Remember to click the Done button when you have finished adding names. This opens a new conversation among all of you and will appear as a separate conversation in your Recent Messages.

Start video/voice call

Assuming your computer is up to the task, you can click on the video camera icon or the phone icon to start a video or voice call, respectively, with your friend (or with multiple friends).

The first time you use either of these features, you may have to set up video calling, which may include installing Flash or another driver to your computer's hard drive.

When you initiate a video call, a pop-up window opens on your screen. Your friend will see something similar appear on her screen asking if she wants to accept a video or voice call. If she wants to take the call, she simply clicks accept and the two of you will be able to speak face to face (or voice to voice).

TIP

Video and voice calls can also be made from smartphones using the Facebook Messenger app. You can learn more about Facebook's suite of apps for phones in Chapter 7.

REMEMBER

Video calls assume both people have webcams either built-in or installed in their computers. If you don't have a webcam, you won't be able to make video calls.

Options

Click the gear icon to view a full menu of options related to your conversation. Some of these options only appear in conversations with one friend (I've added a 1-1 note to those) and some only appear for group conversations. Most, however, appear for one-on-one and group threads alike:

>> **Open in Messenger:** Selecting this option opens Messenger, the Facebook equivalent of your Inbox. Here you will be able to view the entire conversation and search it. More details about Messenger/Inbox can be found in the next section.

>> **Add Files:** Just like clicking the paperclip icon at the bottom of a chat window when you're sending a message from the Inbox, you can select this option to search your computer for files you want to share.

>> **Add Friends to Chat**: If you're discussing something with a friend and think that you need the opinion of someone else, you can add her to the chat, which opens a new group chat window.

>> **Turn off Chat for *<Friend>* (1-1):** Friends may be more likely to chat with you when they see that you're online. If any friend is popping up a little too often, you can turn off chat for that individual person. From that point on, she will no longer see you in the Chat menu.

>> **Edit Conversation Name (group):** You may want to give conversations amongst friends a helpful nickname like "Vacation Planning" or "Dummies." Select this option and a small text field appears at the top of the chat window. Enter the new name of your conversation there and press Enter.

>> **Edit Participants (group):** Everyone within a group message has the same ability to add and remove participants from the message. Removing someone does not prevent someone from being re-added by another member of the conversation, nor does it stop that person from starting a new thread with all the same people. However, if there is a legitimate need to remove someone from a conversation, click this option and select their name from the list of names that appears.

>> **Edit Nicknames:** Often most helpful in group message threads, nicknames allow you to make sure everyone in the conversation knows who is speaking, especially if people use a variant of their name as their Facebook name. Clicking this option opens a pop-up window with a list of every participant's name. Click on the name you want to add a nickname for, type in the nickname you want to use, and click Save. Keep in mind that all members of the conversation will see this nickname, so be nice!

>> **Change Color:** If you have multiple conversations happening at once, you might find it convenient to change the color of the word bubbles within the conversation. Once you click this option, a pop-up window opens with color options. Click the color you like to select it. Facebook will change the color for all participants in the thread.

>> **Mute Conversation:** Muting a conversation allows you to stop receiving notifications (such as a flashing chat bar or a red bubble in the big blue bar on top) for a particular conversation. Selecting this option allows you to choose how long you want a conversation to be muted for. It can be as short as thirty minutes or as long as forever. I've found muting particularly helpful with group conversations, where I want to be able to view the thread when it's convenient to me, but don't want to be distracted by a million people replying all at once.

>> **Delete Conversation:** Deleting a conversation is permanent. It deletes the entire history of your messages with a friend. Keep in mind that deleting it only deletes it for you. Your friend (or friends) will still be able to see the message history.

>> **Leave Conversation (group):** Another option for a group conversation you don't want to be a part of is simply to leave the conversation. Leaving a conversation posts a small notice to the rest of the members that you have left.

>> **Start Plan:** When you are messaging back and forth with friends, you may notice that whenever you use certain time-based words like "tonight" or "Wednesday" Facebook displays a little link prompting you to "Start Plan." Clicking that link, or this option in the menu, allows you to create a quick event with info like date, time, and place, as shown in Figure 9-5. All members of the thread can then see the plan, RSVP, and change the plan if needed. Facebook will automatically send everyone in the group message a reminder about the plan about an hour before it begins.

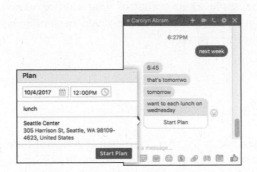

FIGURE 9-5:
Let's make a plan.

>> **Ignore Messages (1-1):** Ignoring messages is a variant on muting messages from a particular friend. If you choose this option, Facebook will begin to treat the messages from that friend as if they are messages from a stranger. They'll show up in the Message Requests section of your Inbox instead of the main section of your Inbox. Your friend won't be told that you've ignored their messages.

>> **Block Messages (1-1):** You can prevent someone from sending you messages entirely by choosing to block messages from her. If people are harassing you on Facebook, you might also consider blocking them entirely or reporting them for harassment.

>> **Report:** If you're getting odd messages from a friend promoting something he wouldn't normally promote, there's a chance his account was *phished,* meaning someone who shouldn't have gained access to it. Report the spam messages to protect yourself, your friend, and other users from having the same thing happen to them. You can also report messages for being harassing or hateful. If you are reporting those actions, you may also want to consider blocking the person sending the hateful content to you.

>> **Create Group (group):** *Groups* are a Facebook feature that allows, well, groups of people to congregate and share information around a specific topic.

If you come to realize that a group of people you are often messaging together would benefit from a space on Facebook to share posts with one another, use this option to create that group. You can learn more about what to do with groups in Chapter 10.

>> **Create Event (group):** *Events* are a Facebook feature that allows you to plan and create an event and invite your friends. If you want, you can use this option to create an event with members of a certain group conversation as the guest list. You can learn more about events in Chapter 13.

X

Clicking the X in the upper-right corner of your chat window closes the chat. Remember, everything you've said remains saved in your message history, so never worry about closing a window.

The Chat Menu

The Chat menu is like a buddy list that you may use for instant messaging. You can always see a minimized version of the Chat menu in the lower-right corner of Facebook. It is a tiny bar that says Chat (*n*), where *n* is the number of friends currently online. Click the bar to open the Chat menu, shown in Figure 9-6.

By default, the top Contacts section of the Chat menu displays the friends you messaged with most recently. A green dot next to their names means they are currently on Facebook and will likely see a message you send them pop up right away. A timestamp such as 20h or 2d indicates how long it's been since they've been on Facebook. Rest assured that any messages you send to them will be delivered. Often people receive notifications in email or on their phone when they get a new Facebook message, so just because they haven't been active very recently doesn't mean they won't get your message soon.

Beneath the friends you message most often are the rest of your friends, as well as any existing group conversations you might want to participate in. Scroll down to browse your friends.

At the bottom of the Chat menu is a Search bar. To quickly find the friend with whom you want to chat, or to see if that friend is even online, start typing that friend's name in the Search box at the bottom of the Chat menu. As you type, the list of online friends narrows to only those with names that match what you've typed. After you see the friend you were looking for, click their name to start chatting.

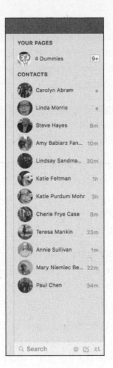

FIGURE 9-6:
The Chat menu.

When the Chat menu is expanded, three icons appear at the bottom of it. There is a New Message icon depicted as a pencil and paper icon. There is a Create New Group icon that looks like the outline of two people with a plus sign. The Settings icon is shaped like a gear; it offers the following options for adjusting your Chat experience:

>> **Chat Sounds:** If Chat Sounds is on (signified by a checkmark next to this option), you will hear a sound every time you receive a new chat.

>> **Emoji:** You can select the default skin color of the emojis that you send to friends. Facebook tries to represent a variety of skin tones, so you can choose whichever most suits you. By default, this emoji is a bright yellow.

>> **Block Settings:** Selecting this option brings you to the Blocking section of the Settings page. There you can block people who may be bothering you through messages from messaging you, or from interacting with you at all on Facebook.

>> **Advanced Settings:** Selecting this option reveals a pop-up window of options. These options help you control who can and cannot see you as online and available in Chat. Three options are available here:

   • **Turn Off Chat for Only Some Contacts:** If there are just a few friends or friend lists you don't want to know when you're online, enter their names into the box below this option, and they won't be able to chat with you. Instead, messages from them will go straight to the Inbox.

- **Turn Off Chat for All Contacts Except:** This is the option if you really don't want to talk to anyone except your nearest and dearest via Chat. When you select this option, you then enter the names of people or Friend Lists that will be able to see that you're online.

- **Turn Off Chat for All Contacts:** This option means no one will see that you're online or be able to send you instant messages via Chat. Instead, messages sent to you will go to the Inbox.

» **Collapse All Chat Tabs:** When you collapse Chat tabs, they don't go away completely. Instead, along the bottom of the screen, next to the Chat menu, you will see a header bar for each chat you have closed. The header bar displays the name of the person you are chatting with. Click on any of these headers to open that conversation back up again.

» **Close All Chat Tabs:** If you are simultaneously chatting with lots of different people and want to close all the Chat windows you have open, select this option. All your Chat tabs will close (but don't worry, none of your conversations will be lost).

» **Hide Sidebar:** If you don't want to see the Chat menu open on the right side of the page, you can choose to hide it by selecting this option. Once you do so, you will see a collapsed Chat menu header in the bottom right corner of the page. Click that to reopen the Chat menu.

» **Hide Pages:** If you are a Page admin, you may not want to see your Pages listed on your Chat menu. Use this option to hide them.

» **Hide Groups:** When you hide groups from Chat you'll no longer see previews of your group conversations in the chat menu.

» **Turn Off Chat:** This is the same as the "Turn Off Chat" option found in the Advanced settings. Lots of people like to use Chat sometimes but not at other times (for example, I sometimes turn Chat off when I'm working from home). This option lets you easily toggle Chat on and off.

» **Turn Off Video/Voice Calls:** If you are okay chatting by typing, but don't want to receive any voice or video calls, use this option to toggle video and voice calls on and off.

» **Turn Off Post Tabs:** When you create a new post, such as a status update or a shared photo, Facebook automatically creates a tab within chat for that post. That way you can respond to any comments and see any reactions to it as you continue to navigate Facebook. If you don't like having your post stay open as you use Facebook, you can turn off that feature here.

REMEMBER

Turning off Chat simply means messages won't pop up, unbidden, at the bottom of your screen. Messages will still be delivered to your Inbox and you will be able to read and respond to them there.

TIP Depending on the width of your screen, your Chat menu may already be expanded as an additional column to the right of your right column. When it is expanded in this way it may display your games and Pages in addition to the contact lists described above.

Messenger Inbox

After you're comfortable sending and receiving messages to and from your friends, it's time to find out about *Messenger*, which is what Facebook calls your message Inbox, where all your messages are collected for easy viewing at any time. Messenger is also the name of the mobile app you can download and use on your phone to communicate with Facebook friends. You can learn more about the Messenger app in Chapter 7.

Messenger is organized a bit differently from traditional email inboxes. Most significantly, messages you receive from people you aren't friends with and are unlikely to know are separated from the conversations you're having with friends.

To understand how this works, look at how Messenger is organized on the page. First, navigate to Messenger from your Home page by clicking the Messages icon in the big blue bar on top (it looks like a word bubble with a horizontal lightning bolt inside). This opens a preview of your most recent messages. Click on See All in Messenger at the bottom of the preview to go to Messenger. Figure 9-7 offers a snapshot of a sample Messenger Inbox.

The main portion of this page, the center area, is where conversations appear. As you click different conversations, which are listed on the left, the contents of that conversation — messages, photos, links, and files — appear in the main portion of the screen.

The left side of the page displays your conversations. Each conversation gets its own line in the Inbox. Like your email inbox, these conversations are organized from most recent near the top to older ones toward the bottom of the page. As you scroll down, Facebook will continue to load your conversation history.

Figure 9-8 shows a close-up of two conversation previews. The top one is a group message, the bottom one is a one-on-one conversation with a single friend. Your friends' names are listed, and their profile pictures are displayed in this preview. On the right side of each is the conversation's timestamp. And below the name of the person or people you're talking to is a snippet of what was most recently said. Messages that you haven't read yet will appear in **bold**.

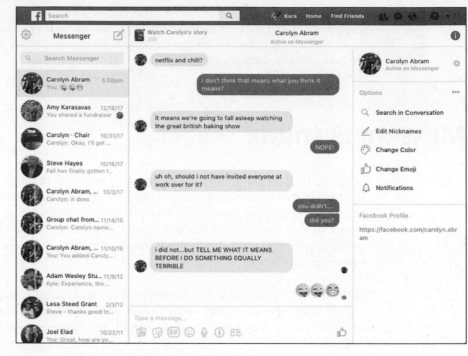

FIGURE 9-7:
Welcome to Facebook Messages.

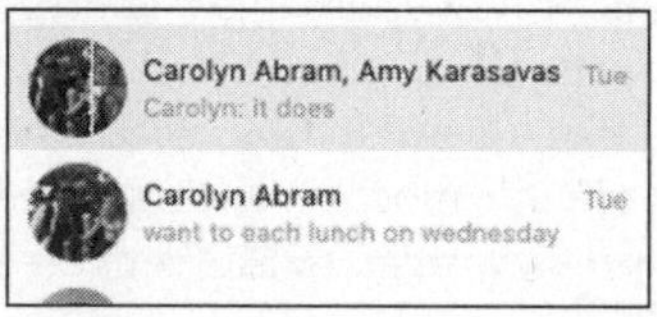

FIGURE 9-8:
Conversation previews in the Messages Inbox.

When you hover your mouse over a conversation, a gear icon appears right below the time stamp. Clicking this icon opens a menu with options for that conversation:

>> **Mute:** Muting a conversation means you won't receive notifications about incoming messages for a certain amount of time that you choose.

>> **Leave Group (Group messages only):** If you are part of a group conversation and don't want to be, you can choose to leave the group. Once you leave you won't receive any future messages within that conversation.

>> **Archive:** Archiving a conversation removes it from this main Messenger landing page. You will still be able to find it if you search for it.

>> **Delete:** Deleting a conversation removes it and all its contents from your Inbox. Keep in mind that deleting a conversation only deletes it for *you*. The other person or people involved in it will still be able to view it in their own inboxes.

- » **Mark as Unread:** Much like email, you can mark a conversation as "unread" if you'd like to return to it later.

- » **Mark as Spam:** If you receive spam or junk mail, mark it as spam. This reports it as spam back to Facebook and removes it from your Messenger Inbox.

- » **Report Spam or Abuse:** If you'd like to report any sort of abuse that's happening via Messenger — phishing attempts, harassment, pornographic or hateful content, or anything else — you can send a report to Facebook to be handled by its Help team. Just because you report something doesn't necessarily mean Facebook will agree with you that what you submit qualifies as abuse, but I believe it's always better to report something than not.

- » **Ignore Messages (1-1 messages only):** If one friend is bothering you with too many messages, you can choose to ignore those messages. You won't be notified any time they message you and their conversation with you will be moved to the Connection Requests section of Messenger.

- » **Block Messages (1-1 messages only):** An even more stringent way to prevent someone from messaging you is to block messages from them. You won't see any of the messages they send you or calls they make to you.

Connection requests

Whenever you get a message from someone you aren't friends with yet, these go to a section of your Inbox labeled Connection Requests. When you get a new one, you'll see a bold preview in your list of messages, which you can click to view the message. You can also view your history of connection requests by clicking the gear icon in the upper-left corner of the Messenger Inbox and selecting Connection Requests from the menu that opens.

You can choose to Accept or Decline connection requests from people. Often a connection request is a person you know simply verifying that you know each other. Once you accept the request, you can write back, and that conversation then appears in the main section of your Messenger Inbox. If you choose to decline a connection request, that person is not notified, but the message from them will be permanently deleted from Messenger. You can also choose to leave connection requests in a sort of limbo, where you neither respond, accept, nor decline the request. It will just hang around in the connection requests section of your Inbox gathering dust until you are ready to do something with it.

Conversations in the Inbox

The center portion of the Messenger Inbox is dedicated to whichever conversation you have selected to look at. The most important thing to notice is that all the content here is the same content you would see in a chat window. Facebook doesn't care where you wrote a message from, all of it goes into your message history. The most recent message is on the bottom of the page. Scroll up to see older messages. This should look like the same conversation in a chat window, just a bit bigger.

At the bottom of your conversation, below the most recent message, is the message composer. The message composer is similar to the one you use in the chat window. Simply type your response and press Enter to send. You can click the icons for sending photos, stickers, gifs, emojis, money, photos from your webcam, or likes.

One additional option you have from the composer is a microphone icon for recording voice messages to send to friends. Click the microphone icon then click the big red Record button to start recording your message. Click it again when you're done to send it. You won't have a chance to review your recording before it gets sent.

To the right of your conversation is info about the person (or people) you are talking to, as well as options related to that conversation. There is also a space where photos you have shared recently in the conversation are displayed. Some of the options, like Edit Nicknames and Change Color are the same as the options available to you when you're using a chat window while browsing Facebook. The new options are:

>> **Search in Conversation:** Because Facebook messages aren't broken into discreet emails with unique subjects, trying to scroll through a long message thread to find information like where you guys were supposed to meet or the name of so-and-so's new boyfriend can be challenging. You can use search to try and find this type of information. Clicking Search in Conversation opens a search box at the top of the message thread. Simply type in the term you are searching for and press Enter. Facebook displays any results highlighted with the messages that were sent immediately before and after that term was used. Use the arrows next to the search box to flip to the next occurrence of that term. When you're done using Search, click the Done button to the right of the search box to return to the entire conversation.

>> **Change Emoji:** Use this to choose an emoji to be the default emoji in the bottom right of the chat window. It will replace the Like emoji that is currently there. Everyone in the conversation will see that you've chosen a new emoji and be able to send it with just one click whenever they want.

>> **Notifications:** You can choose whether you receive notifications when you get a new message within a given conversation. You can also choose whether you get notifications when someone reacts (that is, likes or clicks another reaction icon) to something you said.

Settings

Once you are in the Messenger Inbox, you can go to other sections of the Inbox and access your settings by clicking the gear icon in the upper-left corner. This opens a menu with the following options:

>> **Settings**: Open a pop-up window to access a few settings and links that may be helpful to you as you use Messenger. You can toggle your online status on and off, enable and disable sounds, and enable and disable desktop notifications that appear even if Facebook isn't open in your browser. You will also find links to manage your Payments and Blocking settings. This is yet another place where you can choose your emoji's skin color.

>> **Active Contacts**: View a list of all your friends who are currently active on Facebook.

>> **Connection Requests**: View all your connection requests that you have not responded to yet.

GROUP CONVERSATIONS

A Facebook group is a way for a group of people to connect and share in the same place on Facebook. Creating and using groups is covered in detail in Chapter 10. But it bears mentioning here that one of the useful features of Groups is the capability to start message threads and chats with the members of your group.

To start a group chat, follow these steps:

1. **Navigate to the group's page on Facebook.**

2. **Beneath the cover photo, click the More [. . .] button.**

   This opens a menu of options.

3. **Select Send Message from the menu.**

   A window opens that allows you to select from the group's members.

4. **Select the group members you want to be part of the chat.**

   Click the faces of all the people you want included in the message thread. If you want everyone included, click Select All at the bottom of the window.

5. **Click the Start Chat button.**

   A chat window opens at the bottom of the screen. Use it as you would any chat window.

>> **Archived Threads**: View conversations you have archived.

>> **Unread Threads**: View only conversations with unread messages.

>> **Help**: Go to the Facebook Help Center.

>> **Report a problem**: If something is behaving wonkily, report it to Facebook so they know there's something wrong.

Messaging on the Go

Facebook integrates its messaging system seamlessly with its smartphone apps. It even has an app just for messaging: Facebook Messenger. Regardless of where you are looking at a message — on your phone, in a chat window, in the Inbox, you will see roughly the same thing, with only slight adjustments to account for the amount of space on the screen the message can take up.

The Facebook Messenger app is pretty simple. It displays the contents of your Inbox: a list of conversations from most recent at the top to oldest at the bottom. You can tap any conversation to open it and read it. When you're looking at a conversation, tap into the text box at the bottom of the screen to open a keyboard for typing a new message.

To start a new conversation, when you're looking at your Inbox, tap the new message icon (it looks like a pencil inside a box) in the upper-right corner of the screen. This opens a New Message screen, where you can enter the names of the people you want to message and the message itself. This should feel eerily similar both to sending a text message and to sending a message on Facebook.

If you're using an app like Facebook Messenger on your phone, you will likely be notified on your phone each time you get a new message. You can adjust these settings from the app itself. If you want to know more about using Facebook from your mobile phone, check out Chapter 7.

Chapter **10**

Sharing with Facebook Groups

By now, you've probably individually found and linked yourself to your friends. Hopefully, you've also started sharing with them by posting statuses and photos and links, and you're seeing your News Feed fill up with much of the same. All that is great, but as you share certain things, you may find yourself thinking, "Really, only people from work will care about this article" . . . or . . . "Really, only the people in my parent support group will find this funny." Now, you could elect to change your audience when you post. But you also want those people to talk about it with you. *Groups* are a way to truly interact with a group of people, almost as though you were sitting in the same room.

Groups can be large or small. They may have very active participants or have many people who just sit back and watch for relevant info. Some groups may involve ongoing forums; others may exist only to achieve a goal (for example, planning a big event), and the conversations will peter out over time. Groups can be open to anyone in the world to join, or they can be more private affairs that require invites to join. This chapter covers how to use the features of groups, as well as the many options that come with using, creating, and managing groups.

Evaluating a Group

When someone adds you to a group, a notification is sent to your Facebook Home page. The next time you log in, you'll see a little red flag over the notifications icon (the globe icon in the big blue bar on top). When you click it, it will tell you what the group is and who added you; then you can go check out the group and make sure you want to be a part of it.

Although your notification may explain that you were invited to join the group, these invitations work by adding you to the group until you decide to leave it. It's sort of like saying "RSVP regrets only" on an invitation to a party.

When looking at a group, you'll find a lot to pore over, as you can see by the sample group shown in Figure 10-1. Groups are designed to look a bit like a Timeline — the cover photo, the Publisher, and the recent posts from group members in the center of the page should all look familiar to you. Other parts of the group are unique, such as the members and description box on the right side of the page.

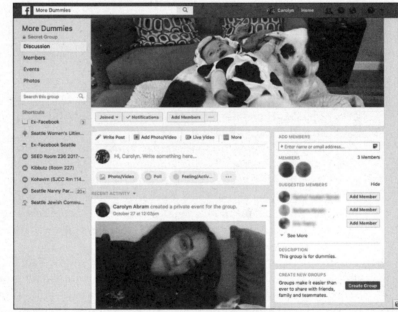

FIGURE 10-1:
Checking out
a group.

When you first visit a group, before doing anything else, make sure you want to be a part of that group. Although I'd like to think I'd join any group that would have me, I don't want to join groups that advocate for causes I don't believe in or that are just about something that's not interesting to me.

The first thing I look at when I get added to a group is the privacy settings. In Figure 10-1, the privacy of the group is listed on the left-hand menu, beneath the group's name. Facebook Groups have three privacy options:

>> **Public:** Open groups are publicly visible and available for anyone to join. In other words, anyone who uses Facebook will be able to see the posts and the members of that group.

>> **Closed:** Closed groups are only partially visible. Anyone on Facebook can see the name of the group and its members but won't be able to see the posts until becoming a member of the group. People are added to closed groups by other members, or they can request to join it.

>> **Secret:** Secret groups are the most private groups. No one other than those who have been added to it can see that it exists, who its members are, and the posts that have been made. If you're invited to join a secret group and you choose to leave it, you won't be able to add yourself again later, because you won't be able to find it.

Once I know who can see that I joined a group and any posts I make, I go on to look at the group name and who added me. Usually that's enough for me to know if I belong there or not. For example, if a friend from my parenting group adds me to a November/December Parents group, I know I want in. When a more distant friend adds me to the I Love Puppies group, I may do a bit more research to see if I want to be a member.

If I'm unsure about wanting to be part of a group, I also check out the group's description. Often group admins will create a description letting people know the purpose of the group, and any general rules for being a member. For example, a group about hiking in Seattle might say something like "A place to share tips for local hiking and backpacking, as far north as Canada and as far south as Oregon." If what I really want is info about hiking in California, I know to be on my way. The description can be found on the right side of the page, under the Add Members section.

I also like to check out the recent posts in the center of the page under the Recent Activity heading. These posts are ones that group members have shared directly with this group. In other words, say that I post a funny photo of my husband mowing the lawn with the baby on his back. If I post it from my Timeline or from my Home page, all my friends will see it. It won't appear in the Recent Activity section of any of my groups. If I post it to my New Moms group, only group members will see it, and it will appear in the group's Recent Activity section.

Looking at the recent posts tells me a lot about what to expect from a group in the future. Are posts relevant to the group or not? Is there a lot of discussion or not?

Am I interested in the posts I'm seeing? These are the sorts of things I think about when I decide whether to stay in a group.

Finally, one thing to ponder as you check out a group is the size of the group itself. Facebook groups might be enormous, or very tiny. You might be interacting with a handful of people you know or thousands of people you've never met and will never meet. Facebook itself has slightly different features for big and small groups that pop up from time to time—whether that's the tools for managing large groups or the fact that in smaller groups, you can see how many people have seen any particular post. Make sure you're comfortable sharing with the number of people in the group that you want to join.

After you acquaint yourself with the group, you can decide whether you want to remain a member or leave the group. If you decide you want to leave, follow these steps:

1. **Click the Joined button at the bottom of the cover photo.**

   When you click the Joined button, a drop-down menu appears.

2. **Select Leave Group from the drop-down menu.**

   A pop-up window opens, asking if you are sure that you want to leave the group.

3. **Decide whether you want to prevent members of the group from adding you again by selecting or deselecting the Prevent Other Members From Adding You Back To This Group check box.**

   You can check this box, which means you'll never be able to be added to the group again; or if you think maybe in the future you might want to be part of the group, leave it deselected.

4. **Click Leave Group.**

Often, however, you'll usually decide to stay in the group, which actually brings you to the point of sharing and communicating with fellow group members.

TIP

If you're considering leaving a group because you're being inundated by notifications about new posts, you can instead just turn off notifications from that group. From the group, click the Notifications button at the bottom of the cover photo. You can then select whether you want notifications about All Posts, Highlights (as determined by Facebook's algorithms), Friends' Posts, or None (Off).

You can get back to any particular group from your Home page by clicking its name in the left-side menu. Groups you look at frequently should be in the Short-cuts section. You may have to click the See More link to see a full list of your groups. Click the name of the group you want to visit.

Sharing with a Group

The whole point of creating or joining a group is to enable communication, so get started communicating! Ways that you can get involved include posting to the group, commenting on others' posts, chatting with group members, and creating files or events.

Using the Publisher

Posting to the group works the same way as posting from a Timeline or the News Feed, by using the Publisher. There is a Publisher at the top of the Recent Activity section of the group. This Publisher works the same as the Publisher in News Feed, with a few extra options that I go over in this chapter.

REMEMBER

The important thing to remember is that when you share something from a group, you're sharing it only with the members of that group. And if you're a member of a group, you also need to remember that you may not be friends with everyone in the group. In a big group, you may be sharing with many people who typically couldn't see the things you post.

Although the Publisher works almost the same way across Facebook, all the options are briefly explained here within the context of groups.

Writing a post

Posts are basically like status updates that you share only with the members of a group (unless the group is open, in which case anyone can see your post). You might post an update just to say "Hi" or to start a discussion with group members. To write a post, follow these steps:

1. **Click in the Publisher (where it says Write Something at the top of the group page).**

2. **Type whatever you want to say in the box.**

   For the Dummies group, this might be something like "What do people think of the new group?" or "Does anyone know how I can start group chat?" You can also post a link to a relevant article or website in this space. You can see a post in progress in Figure 10-2.

3. **(Optional) Add photos, tags, activity, or location information to the post.**

   Click the appropriate icon at the bottom of the Publisher to add any additional information or content.

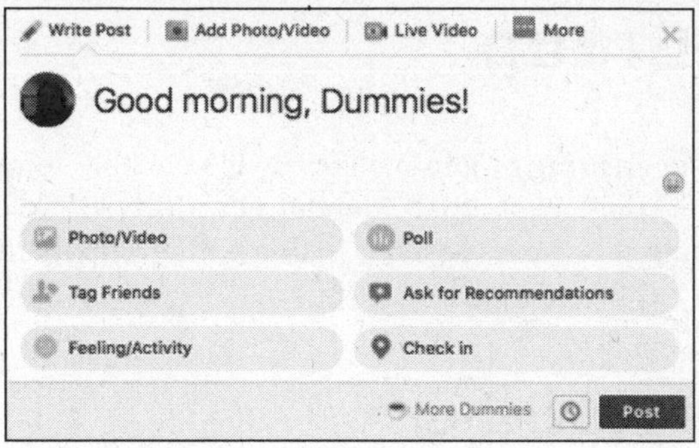

Good morning, Dummies!

Write Post | Add Photo/Video | Live Video | More ✕

Photo/Video   Poll

Tag Friends   Ask for Recommendations

Feeling/Activity   Check in

More Dummies   Post

FIGURE 10-2:
What's on
your mind?

4. **Click Post.**

Your post appears in the group, and group members can see it in their notifications and News Feeds.

> **TIP** If you want to share a link, usually some sort of article, video, or other online content that you want the group to see, simply type or paste the complete link to whatever you want to share, along with your thoughts or opinions, in the Publisher.

Creating a poll

One of the added features of Groups is the Create Poll feature. Polls allow group members to gather information in a more efficient way than simply using a post and then sorting through the comments for the answers. Members can vote on polls from the Recent Activity section of the group. To ask a question and poll your group, follow these steps:

1. **Click Poll in the Publisher.**

You may need to click into the Publisher and click the Poll option in the bottom section.

2. **Type your question in the Ask Something box.**

You can see a poll being created in Figure 10-3.

3. **Type your first option into the first Add an Option section.**

4. **Add more options until you're finished.**

Facebook keeps adding more boxes as you fill up these first few, so just stop when you're ready.

5. **Click on Poll Options at the bottom of the Publisher to choose whether people can add more options and if they can select more than one option.**

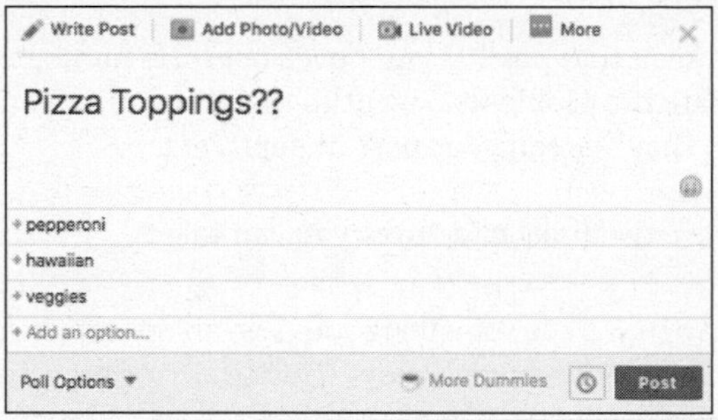

FIGURE 10-3:
You've got
questions?
Facebook has
answers.

The Allow Anyone to Add Options check box controls whether people can add more answers to a poll. If you only add two options, Dog or Cat, for example, group members may be able to add Hedgehog if they want. Depending on how big your group is, this choice may or may not be significant. You can also choose, via check box, whether people have to make one selection or can choose multiple answers from the poll.

6. **Click Post.**

   The question then appears in the group and in members' notifications and News Feeds. They will be able to vote, like, or comment on the question.

Sell something

One other option in the Publisher that you may not have encountered previously is the Sell Something option. This option allows you to create a classified listing with information about the item you are selling, how much you want to sell it for, and so on. Once you've posted your item for sale, members of the group can respond to it via comments or via private message.

You can create a post like this in any type of group, but you should be aware that there is a specific type of group called a "Buy/Sell" group that centers on this type of person-to-person selling. You can learn more about buying and selling on Facebook in Chapter 12.

Reading and commenting on posts

After you create a post or see a post that someone else has created, that's when things really get interesting, because members of the group can start talking about it. On Facebook, that means commenting, liking, and following posts.

One unique feature of posts to Facebook Groups is that — in smaller Facebook groups, at least—you can see who has read those posts. At the bottom of each post, look for a check mark icon. Next to it, Facebook displays the number of people who have seen that post. If you hover over the number, you will see a list of names. These are the people who went to the group after you posted. It doesn't necessarily mean they've read your post in depth yet.

Below each post are two links of actions you can take:

>> **Comment:** When you see something you have an opinion on, click Comment below the post and let everyone know. (This action means you'll be notified about all subsequent posts.) Often, you'll see a blank comment box already open beneath a post, just inviting you to chime in.

>> **Like/React:** When you like anything on Facebook, the person who created that content is notified that you like it. It's an easy and quick way to say, "Good job!" when you don't have an active comment to make. Hover over the Like button to choose from a more specific reaction: Like, Love, Haha, Wow, Sad, Angry.

Depending on your notification settings, you may be following all posts in a group, only ones from friends, or none. When you comment on a post or vote on a question, you automatically start following that post. Following a post means you'll be notified every time there's a new comment on that post, which can be awesome if you're actively talking about something with group members, or kind of annoying if there are too many people commenting. If that happens and the notifications are bothering you, you can always unfollow a post by taking these steps:

1. **Click the More [. . .] icon in the upper-right corner of the post you want to unfollow**

    This opens a menu of options.

2. **Click Turn Off Notifications For This Post.**

TIP

Just as you can unfollow a post you previously commented on, you can choose to follow a post you haven't commented on. If you want to read what others have to say, but don't have anything to add at this time, follow the preceding steps for the post you want to follow. Instead of the Turn Off option, you will see a Turn On option. Select that option to be notified every time a group member adds a new comment on that post.

You can also use the More [. . .] menu to open a post in a *tab*, or chat window, at the bottom of the screen. This lets you keep up with the discussion happening around that post while continuing to browse Facebook.

Events

Your group may be based around an activity, so Facebook makes it easy for people to plan events for group members, whether it's a game of pick-up or a family reunion. To create an event, follow these steps:

1. **From your group's page, click the Events link on the left side of the page.**

The group's Event Calendar appears. This calendar displays any upcoming group events.

2. **Click the Create Event button.**

The Create Event pop-up window appears (see Figure 10-4). These fields are like the ones you see when planning events, as in Chapter 13.

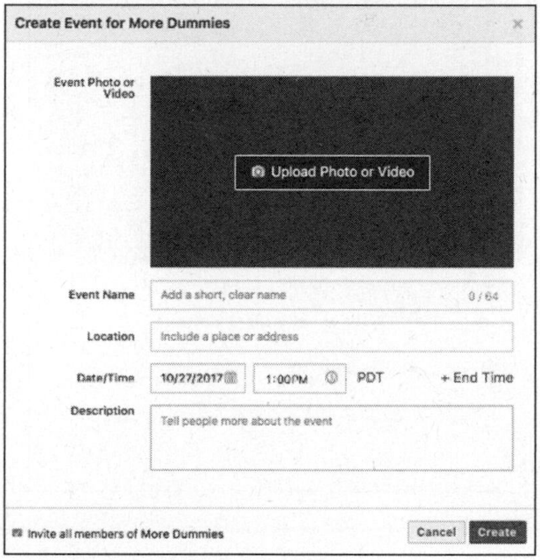

FIGURE 10-4:
Creating an event for group members.

3. **Fill out the event details.**

Event details include the event's photo, name, location, date, and time.

By default, a check box at the bottom of the screen notes that all members of that group will be invited.

4. **Decide whether you want to invite all group members by selecting or not selecting the Invite All Members check box.**

Regardless of what you choose, all members will be able to view the event and RSVP. However, if you leave the Invite All Members box selected, when group members are notified about the event, they will be told that you were the one who invited them.

5. **Click Create.**

   The event's page appears. Here you can add an event photo and keep track of RSVPs. (I cover this type of event maintenance in detail in Chapter 12.) As the event creator, you're automatically listed as attending. The post appears in the group's recent posts and in members' News Feeds.

To RSVP to a group event, follow these steps:

1. **Click the event's name in the Recent Activity section of the group.**

   The Event Home page appears (see Figure 10-5). This page shows you more information about the event, including who has already RSVP'd.

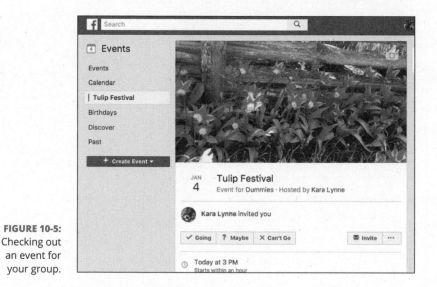

2. **Choose Going, Maybe, or Can't Go.**

   All these options are big buttons towards the top of the page, underneath all the event info. To find out more about how to interact with the event as it draws near, check out Chapter 13.

Files and docs

Other features that are particularly helpful to groups representing real-world projects are files and docs. These are ways to create and share files among group members. *Docs* are more like wikis in that they can be edited by all members of the groups. *Files* are more like a file-sharing system that allows people to upload and retrieve files from user to user.

Docs

Docs are sort of a cross between a wiki and a blog post. The way you create them and the way they look mimics the look and feel of a blog post, with a cover photo on top of the doc and the title and text beneath that. You can choose to simply publish a doc to your group or you can choose to make it so that all members of the group can edit it as well.

To create a document that all group members can see and edit, go to the Files section of the group (by clicking Files on the left side of the page or choosing Create Doc from the Publisher) and click the Create Doc button. This brings you to the New Doc page, where you can enter a title and body text. Some basic formatting options are available by clicking the paragraph icon, as shown in Figure 10-6. After you enter your text, click the Save or Publish buttons. *Saving* your work saves it as a draft (no other group members will be able to see it yet). *Publishing* it makes it visible to all members of your group.

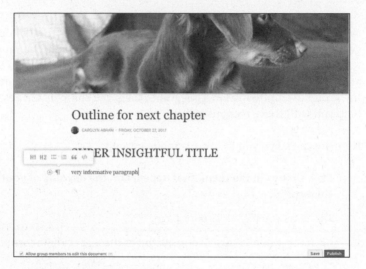

FIGURE 10-6:
What's up, doc?

By default, all group members can edit it. If you don't want them to do this, uncheck the "Allow. . ." checkbox at the bottom left of the Doc creation window. Assuming you leave it checked, any member of the group can view it, comment on it as though it were any other post, and click Edit Doc in the upper-right corner of the doc to change it. You can always find docs that have been created by clicking the Files tab. Click on the title of the document you want to change from the list of documents displayed on the screen and then click the Edit Doc button when you are looking at that doc. You can also leave comments on docs to let group members know what you liked or didn't like about them.

Files

Like docs, files are shared among group members, but unlike docs, they cannot be edited within Facebook. Instead, members upload, download, and then reupload files they want changed. Or they simply upload files they want to share, and other group members are then able to download the files to their own computers.

From the Files tab, click the Upload File button to add files from your computer. To download files that others have added, click More [. . .] icon and select Download from the menu that opens.

REMEMBER

Depending on the settings of the group you belong to you may not be able to add files without the approval of a group admin.

Creating Your Own Groups

Now that you understand how to use groups, you may find an occasion to create your own group. As a group's creator, you're by default the *group administrator*, which means that you write the group's information, control its Privacy settings, and generally keep it running smoothly. You can also promote other members of the group to administrator. This grants them the same privileges so that they can help you with these responsibilities.

Here are the steps you follow to create a group:

1. **Click Groups in the menu that appears on the left side of your Home page.**

   This takes you to your Groups page.

2. **Click the green Create Group button in the upper-right corner of the page.**

   The Create New Group window appears (see Figure 10-7).

3. **Enter a group name into the Name your group field.**

   Choose something descriptive, if possible, so that when you add people to it, they'll know what they're getting into.

4. **Type the names of people you want to add to the group.**

   At this time, you can add only friends as members. Facebook tries to autocomplete your friends' names as you type. When you see the name you want, press Enter to select it. You can add as many — or as few — friends as you like. If you forget someone, you can always add him later. Click the blue sticky note icon on the right of the Add some people field to add a personal note about your group that people will see when they get your invitation to join.

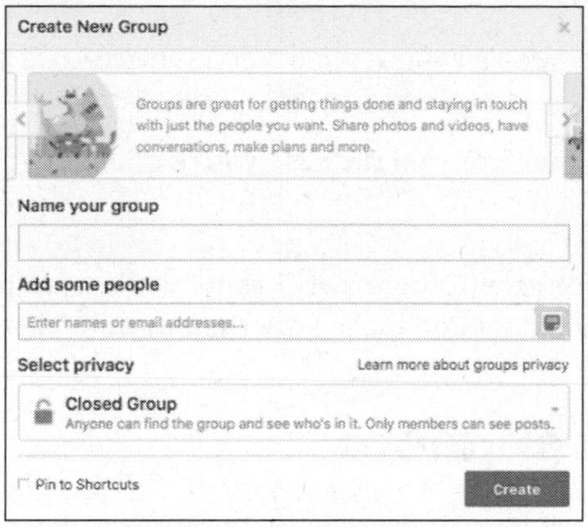

Create New Group

Groups are great for getting things done and staying in touch with just the people you want. Share photos and videos, have conversations, make plans and more.

Name your group

Add some people

Enter names or email addresses...

Select privacy   Learn more about groups privacy

🔒 **Closed Group**
Anyone can find the group and see who's in it. Only members can see posts.

☐ Pin to Shortcuts   **Create**

FIGURE 10-7:
The Create New
Group window.

5. **Choose the privacy level for your group.**

   Groups have three privacy options:

   - *Public:* Public groups are entirely available to the public. Anyone can join simply by clicking a Join button; anyone can see all the content the group posts. This type of group is best for a very public organization that wants to make it easy for people to join and contribute.

   - *Closed:* By default, your group is set to Closed. This means that anyone can see the list of members, but only members can see the content posted to the group by its members. People can request to join the group, but admins (like you) need to approve those requests before the requesters can see group info.

   - *Secret:* Secret groups are virtually invisible on the site to people who haven't been added to the group. No one except members can see the member list and the content posted.

   ⚠️
   WARNING

   People who have been added to the group can also add their friends, so if you're protecting state secrets, you might want to find a more secure method. I recommend carrier pigeons.

6. **Choose whether you want to pin your group to your shortcuts section.**

   You will always be able to get to this group through search or from the groups page, but if you think you'll be using it a lot it makes sense to pin it to the shortcuts section of your left-side menu. Check the Pin to Shortcuts box to pin it.

7. **Click Create.**

   The window changes to the icon selection window.

8. **Choose an icon from the options and click the OK button.**

Facebook tries to provide an option for lots of common group types. If you can't find anything that represents your group, click Skip.

9. **After you choose your icon and click OK, you're taken to your group's Home page.**

After you've set up your group, there's still some work to do to help friends and potential members evaluate it and make sure they want to join.

Adding a cover photo

If your group does not yet have a cover photo, the space where the cover photo will be should have two buttons: Upload Photo and Choose Photo. Click Choose Photo to choose a photo from either photos that you have added to Facebook or photos that have been shared within your group (if your group is brand new, you likely won't have any photos in the latter category). You can browse any photos you have added to Facebook. Click on the photo you want to use to select it. This brings you back to your group, where you can click and drag the cover photo to reposition it. Click the blue Save Changes button in the bottom right corner of the photo when you are done.

You can also choose to upload a photo from your computer's hard drive. Simply click the green Upload Photo button, navigate to the photo you want to use, and click Open or Choose. You then return to the group, where you can click and drag the cover photo to reposition it. Click the blue Save Changes button in the bottom right corner of the photo when you are done.

You can change your group's cover photo at any time by hovering your mouse over the cover photo and clicking the Change Group Photo button that appears in the upper right corner of the cover photo. You can then choose where you want to select a photo from (group photos, your photos, or uploaded from your computer).

Adding a description

Remember, when people are deciding whether to join a group, they need to know what that group's purpose is. One way to let them know is to create a group description. To add a group description, look over on the right side of the group for the Members and Description box. Click on the Add a Description link, then type your group's description into the box that opens.

This is a good place to outline why the group exists, and maybe some do's and don'ts for the group. For example, you might want a group for discussing parenting challenges, but you might want to request parents not post photos of their children's potty training successes. You may want teammates to coordinate travel to a Frisbee game but not smack talk the other team. Be descriptive and honest. And click the blue Save button when you're done.

You can edit your group's description at any time by clicking the blue Edit link next to the Description section.

Adding tags

Tags are a way that groups get sorted into various categories and can be found (and find their way to) potential members. Facebook often recommends groups to users based on their interests, so if you're creating a group for people interested in Ultimate Frisbee, add tags that would help people who play Frisbee find you— discs, ultimate, AUDL, team sports, and so on.

Group Dynamics

Now that you know how to create, share, and navigate your way through a group, it's time to look at some of the long-term things to keep in mind as you join groups.

Controlling notifications

Sometimes, especially in larger groups, you may find yourself a bit overwhelmed by all the notifications. To control them, you just need to get comfortable with the Notifications Settings menu, which you access by clicking the Notifications button from a group's Home page. Clicking Notifications (it's below the cover photo) reveals a drop-down menu with four options, as shown in Figure 10-8.

>> **All Posts:** Because comment threads can often become very long and rambling, this option allows you to see when a new post is created, but not see comments on those posts unless you follow the post.

>> **Highlights:** This option means you'll get notifications for posts that have lots of likes and comments, and for friends' posts.

>> **Friends' Posts:** In especially large groups, you might not be official Facebook friends with everyone in the group, so a good way to filter down to the material you're most likely to care about is to pay attention only to the things your friends post.

>> **Off:** Some people may want to read the posts only when they choose to look at the group and not receive any notifications from this group. Selecting Off gives you that silence.

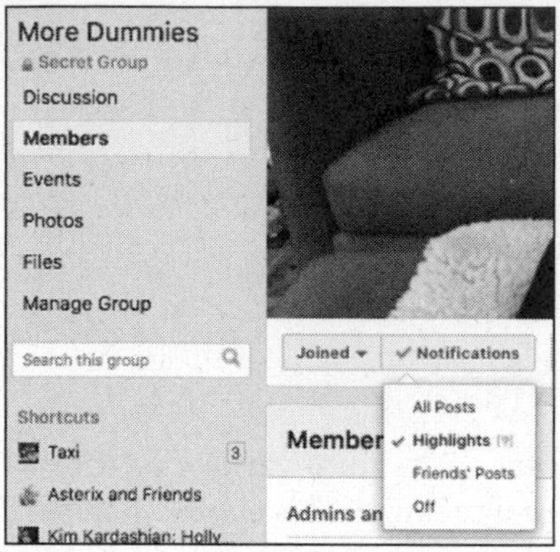

FIGURE 10-8:
Controlling
notifications.

If you're being inundated by email notifications but still want the notifications to appear on Facebook, you can change your email notification settings from the Account Settings page. To adjust this setting, follow these steps:

1. **Click the upside-down triangle icon in the blue bar at the top of any page.**

A drop-down menu appears.

2. **Select Settings.**

The Settings page appears. You can choose different types of settings from the menu on the left side of the page.

3. **Click Notifications on the left side of the page.**

This opens all notifications settings.

4. **Click Edit to the right of the Email option.**

This expands to three options for email notifications: All Notifications, Important Notifications, and Only Notifications about Your Account, Security, and Privacy.

5. **Select either Important Notifications, or Only Notifications about Your Account, Security, and Privacy.**

This step limits how many email notifications you receive from Facebook.

If, after you change this setting, you're still getting emails about activity happening in a group, scroll to the bottom of one of the offending emails and click the Unsubscribe link. You will be asked to confirm that you want to unsubscribe from that type of email. After you confirm, you'll no longer see emails about groups.

Limiting notifications doesn't mean you won't see posts from that group in your News Feed. If you don't want to see group posts in your News Feed, you need to unfollow that group:

6. **From the group's Home page, click the Joined button under the left corner of the cover photo.**

   A tiny menu appears. The menu has two options: Unfollow Group and Leave Group.

7. **Choose Unfollow Group.**

   You will no longer see News Feed stories about things that happen in the group.

Searching a group

If your group is particularly active — meaning that lots of people are constantly posting content and commenting on things — you may have trouble finding something that was posted in the past. Each group has a menu on its left side with links to things like Members, Events, Photos, and Files. At the bottom of this menu is a search box. Click into it to search posts by keyword. For example, you could search for reviews of specific hikes in the PNW Hikers Group by entering the name of a trail or park.

Adding friends to a group

In most groups, most members can add more members at any time. This is a fast and easy way for groups to get all the right people in it even if the original creator isn't friends with everyone in the group. For example, if I'm friends with someone creating a group for our neighborhood association, but he isn't friends with my husband, I can easily add my husband to the group instead of the group admin searching for my husband, adding him as a friend, and then adding him to the group. You can add friends to a group via Facebook or email. Simply look for the box on the right side of the group page that says Add Members. Choose this option to display photos of current members and display some of your friends' names. Click Add Member next to any of your friends to invite them to join. You can also enter friends' names or email addresses into the box at the top of this section. Facebook auto-completes as you type. When you've highlighted the friend you want or finished typing out the email address of a friend, hit enter to invite them.

Being a group administrator

If you're the creator of a group, you're automatically its *admin*, or administrator. Additionally, you can be added as an admin of someone else's group. After you have members in your group, being an admin means that you have a few extra features available to you, such as scheduling and pinning posts. You also have a suite of settings available to you to make your group the sort of group you want it to be.

Scheduling posts

Often group admins find they want to post something at certain times. If you're the admin of your college's alumni group, you might want to post the link to sign up for reunions as soon as it goes live. Or, if your group is about sharing inspirational quotes, you might know that you need to post an inspirational post every morning at the same time, so group members wake up to a new quote in their News Feed. Scheduling posts allows you to create a post and choose a time in the future when it will be published.

1. **Create a post following the same steps detailed in the Writing a Post section.**

Simply follow all the instructions but don't press post.

2. **Click the Clock button to the left of the Post button.**

This opens a window for scheduling the date and time of your post.

3. **Use the date selector to choose a date for your post.**

Clicking on the date opens a calendar, which you can use to choose a date in the future.

4. **Choose a time for your post.**

Click on the hour, minutes, and am/pm spot, then use the up and down arrow keys to change the time.

5. **Click the Schedule Button.**

This immediately adds the post to the schedule.

You can view all the posts you have scheduled from the Manage Group section of your Group's page.

Pinning posts

If you have a large group that has a lot of activity, especially a lot of people joining over time, you may find that similar posts happen all the time. If there are posts that you think need top billing, admins can "pin" posts to the top of the page. Pinned posts appear before more recent posts. One group I belong to, for example, is entirely made up of people who no longer work for Facebook. A pinned post at the top of the discussion section details commonly needed contact addresses and forms that people need to fill out right when they leave the company.

To pin a post, follow these steps:

1. **On the post you want to pin, click the tiny upside-down arrow or More [. . .] icon in the upper-right corner of the post.**

   A menu of options related to the post appears, including options to save it and report it.

2. **Select Pin Post.**

   The post then appears as a pinned post at the top of the page.

Pinned posts don't have to be just for new members, and they don't have to last forever. To unpin a post once it's outlived its usefulness, follow the steps above, and choose unpin post to remove it from the top of the page.

Edit Settings

The Edit Group Settings page and the Manage Group page are the two places you'll be going most to keep track of what's happening in your group. The Edit Group Settings page is shown in Figure 10-9. You get to this page by clicking the More [. . .] button on the right side of your group's page. This expands a drop-down menu with several options. Select Edit Group Settings from the menu, which takes you to the Edit Group Settings page.

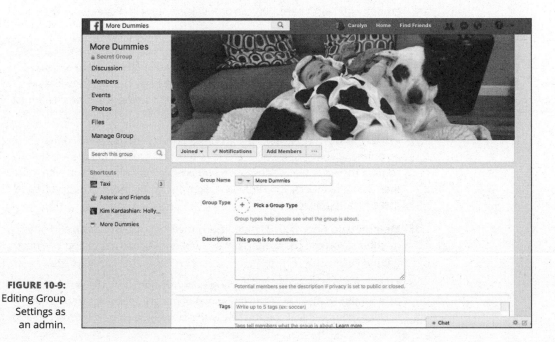

FIGURE 10-9: Editing Group Settings as an admin.

The Edit Group Settings page allows you to revisit some of the decisions you made when you were first creating your group, as well as adjust some settings that tend to be relevant only for people who are admins of large, open groups.

>> **Name:** Edit the group name here (but I don't recommend pulling the rug out from underneath people by, say, changing a group name from Yankees Fans to Red Sox Fans).

>> **Icon:** You can change your icon at any time from here.

>> **Group Type:** You can choose a group type here to provide more context to members. Keep in mind that a Buy, Sell, Trade group has additional features.

>> **Description:** The description of your group appears in the About section of the group the first-time members visit your group page. So this is a good place to set expectations for what the group is for and how you expect to use it.

>> **Tags:** Tags are another way to let people know what your group is about. Tags can be any sort of keyword such as "television" or "hiking."

>> **Locations:** Many groups are locally focused — Hikers of Seattle, Gamers of San Diego, you get the idea — you can add locations by listing as many of them as you want here.

>> **Linked Pages:** Many businesses might have Facebook Pages and Facebook groups to promote the community aspect of their business. If you want Page followers to be able to find the group more easily and vice versa, you can link groups with Pages here. You can only link groups with Pages you own or admin.

>> **Web and Email Address:** If you want, you can create a group email address and web address. Group addresses appear as something like groupname@ groups.facebook.com and web addresses appear as something like www. facebook.com/groups/groupname. Emails sent to the group email address are added as posts to the group wall.

>> **Privacy:** The privacy level of the group can change here. Again, I don't recommend changing a secret group to an open group if people are sharing content they may feel is sensitive. If you are the admin of a group with more than 5,000 members, you can only make your group more closed, you can't make it more public.

>> **Membership Approval:** By default, any member of a group can add other members. You can change this option by requiring admins to approve new members.

>> **Membership Requests:** Often group admins want a way to vet new members, simply to make sure the intentions of the group stay intact and the existing members feel comfortable with new people coming in. You can add

up to three questions that new members will be asked to answer here. That way when you are approving membership requests, you know a bit more than just a name and profile picture.

>> **Posting Permissions:** By default, all members of a group can post to it. But if you're the admin of a large group, you may want to change this setting so that only administrators can post. Keep in mind that this can really limit discussion.

>> **Post Approval:** Similarly, if you want to make sure the content of a group is appropriate and relevant, you can choose to have admins approve posts before all group members see them.

Click Save when you're done editing your group's information; otherwise, all your hard work will be lost.

Managing a Group

You can get to the Manage Group page, shown in Figure 10-10, by clicking the Manage Group option on the left side of your group's page.

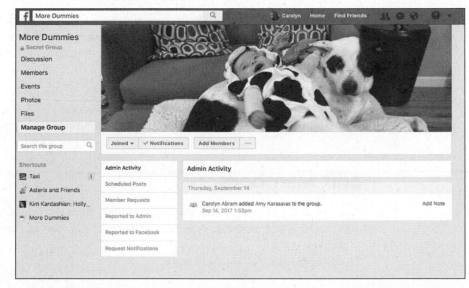

FIGURE 10-10:
Manage your group here.

The Manage groups page is an easy place to keep track of what's been happening in your group lately. I will say that although admins of smaller groups may find parts of this useful, most of it is geared more towards groups with hundreds if not thousands of members, who have multiple admins and moderators. So if you just have a group of twenty people from your kid's new classroom, you might not find yourself here as much.

- **Admin Activity:** View recent actions taken by all admins, including adding new members, creating new posts, and so on. Click on the Add Note link to the right of any entry to leave a note for other admins letting them know why you did something or asking a question about it.

- **Scheduled Posts:** View all upcoming posts in a list. Click on the More [. . .] icon to view a menu for each post. Use this menu to reschedule, edit, or delete posts.

- **Member Requests:** View all new requests to join a group. You can sort these requests in a variety of ways (by when the requests were made, by location, by gender, and so on). You can approve or reject requests individually or use the Approve All or Decline All buttons to approve or decline in bulk.

- **Reported to Admin:** Admins and moderators may be asked by other members to review problematic content or members of the group. Facebook also uses some automated systems to automatically report content that it thinks is likely to be problematic, offensive, or need to be taken down later. You can view all reports here and act on them (Ignore it, Delete it, Delete it and block the offensive poster, which blocks the poster from rejoining the group). If this turns out to be a lot more work than you'd like, you may want to consider adding more admins and moderators to share the workload.

- **Reported to Facebook:** When content is reported directly to Facebook (as opposed to being reported to the admins), the admins are automatically notified of that report. You can find the reports that have been made to Facebook here.

- **Request Notifications:** By default, you will see a notification in your usual Facebook notifications list when a new person asks to join your group. You can opt to only see requests when you are looking at the group instead.

Edit Members

As an admin, you can remove and ban members from the group, as well as create other admins and moderators to help shoulder the burden of admin-hood.

To edit members, follow these steps:

1. **From the left menu on your group's page, click the Members tab.**

The Members section of the group appears, the bulk of which is taken up by images of group members. If you are an admin, below each group member's name is the More [. . .] icon.

2. **Click the gear icon below the name of the person you want to remove or make an admin or moderator.**

   A menu, shown in Figure 10-11, appears.

3. **Choose whether you'd like to make a member an Admin, a Moderator, Remove them from a group entirely, or Mute them.**

   Making someone an admin means they will have all the same powers as you to add new admins, edit the groups privacy (and other) settings, and so on. Moderators have the same abilities to review requests to join, reported posts, and schedule posts, but they cannot add more admins or edit the group's settings.

   When someone is already an admin, you can remove her admin status by choosing Remove as Admin from this same menu.

If you choose to remove someone from the group a window appears with options for deleting that member's posts, as well as blocking them permanently and blocking them from any other groups you manage. Hopefully you never need to use these options because people in your groups won't be jerks, but unfortunately that's just not always true.

Reporting offensive groups and posts

If you stumble upon an offensive group in your travels, you should report it to Facebook so that the company can take appropriate actions. To report a group, follow these steps:

1. **Click the More [. . .] icon under the group's cover photo and then select the Report Group link.**

   A form appears in a pop-up window.

2. **Fill out the report by choosing a reason for the report.**

3. **Click Submit to Facebook for Review.**

   Facebook attempts to remove groups that

- Contain pornographic material or inappropriate nudity.

- Attack an individual or group.

- Advocate violence.

- Serve as advertisements or is otherwise deemed to be spam by Facebook.

REMEMBER

Many groups on Facebook take strong stands on controversial issues, such as abortion or gun control. In an effort to remain neutral and promote debate, Facebook won't remove a group because you disagree with its statements.

To report offensive content within a group, such as a post written by a group member, follow these steps:

1. **Click the More [. . .] icon at the upper-right corner of the post.**

   This opens a menu of options for that post.

2. **Choose to report that post to the admins or report it to Facebook.**

   Reports to admins won't notify Facebook, but reports to Facebook will notify the admins. You will need to verify that you want to report a post, and reports to Facebook will request more information about why you are reporting something.

Depending on the nature of your group, reporting content to your admins might have the same effect as reporting it to Facebook. However, admins may be either more lenient or harsher than Facebook. Some Facebook groups have strict "be kind" policies, so a post reported to Facebook might be permitted to remain, whereas the admins or moderators may deem it too mean for the group. As with most reporting questions, I advocate for reporting the things that concern you rather than not.

4

What to Do on Facebook

IN THIS PART . . .

Creating photo albums

Sharing photos and videos with friends

Creating and managing events

Buying and selling items using Marketplace and Groups

Fundraising for a good cause

Interacting with Pages

Using games, websites, and apps with Facebook

Creating Pages for promotion

Chapter **11**

Filling Facebook with Photos and Videos

acebook Photos is the leading photo-sharing application on the web. This may sound surprising because entire sites are dedicated to storing, displaying, and sharing photos, whereas Photos is just one piece of the Facebook puzzle. But the fact that *all* your friends are likely on Facebook and using Photos makes it a one-stop shop for tracking all the photos of you, all the photos you've taken, and all the photos of your friends.

Additionally, Facebook Photos allows you to add and share videos. Though less common, videos are pretty similar to photos. If you let them languish on your hard drive or on your mobile phone, nobody gets to enjoy them. Nobody gets to tell you how cute the photos of your baby are. No one lets you know that she likes your wedding video. When you share photos and videos, they can become even more cherished, even more valuable as keepsakes.

Viewing Photos from Friends

Just by opening up Facebook and looking at News Feed, you'll find yourself looking at lots of people's photos. You'll see photos a few different ways: in your News Feed, in the photo viewer, and in an album format.

Photos in News Feed

Figure 11-1 shows an example of how a single photo appears in News Feed. The photo takes up most of the screen. Running across the top is the name of the person who posted it and any description she wrote about it. There is also info about when the photo was added and possibly where it was added (for example: Indianapolis, Indiana). Underneath the photo are links to Like and Comment on the photo. You may sometimes see a link to Share the photo. Beneath those links is the count of how many likes and reactions the photo has already received, and any comments people have already made. You may even see a blank comment box, waiting for you to add your two cents.

FIGURE 11-1:
Looking at a friend's photo in News Feed.

Clicking the photo expands the photo viewer, which is covered in the following section.

Figure 11-2 shows an example of a photo album preview in News Feed. It's similar to the single photo, but previews additional photos from the album. The name of the album appears at the top of the post and tells you how many photos are in the album. Clicking any of the photos expands the photo viewer, and clicking the album title brings you to an album view.

FIGURE 11-2:
Looking at a
friend's album in
News Feed.

Photo viewer

The photo viewer is an overlay on top of Facebook that allows you to quickly browse photos and leave likes and comments. Clicking a small version of a photo almost anywhere on Facebook expands the photo viewer and fades the rest of the screen to black, as shown in Figure 11-3. The left side of the viewer is where the photo appears, and the right side is where comments, likes, and info about the photo appear.

REMEMBER

When I mention liking something, I am referring to all of the reaction options Facebook provides. There are times when a like isn't specific enough – perhaps you prefer to love your friend's engagement photo or want to express astonishment at a photo of breathtaking views.

When you hover your mouse over the photo, more options show up in white on the photo. On either side is an arrow that allows you to navigate through a photo album. Clicking anywhere on the photo will also advance the album forward. The following information appears at the bottom of the viewer:

>> ***<Album Name>:*** The album's name is usually one your friend has created, like "Summer in February!" or a descriptive name generated by Facebook, such as "Mobile Uploads." You may also see the album name at the top of the photo.

>> **Photo count:** The number of the photo you're on in the album (for example, 5 of 8) is also displayed.

>> **Tag Photo:** Clicking this allows you to add *tags* or labels for those in the photo. I cover tags in the upcoming section, "Editing and Tagging Photos."

>> **Options:** Clicking this reveals a menu of options for things like downloading the photo to your computer, reporting the photo, or entering a full-screen view.

>> **Share:** Clicking this lets you post the photo to your own Timeline. Privacy settings determine whether share is available on a photo.

>> **Send or Send In Messenger:** Clicking this option lets you send a message to a friend with the photo attached. Keep in mind that sometimes you may be able to see photos your friend cannot see. Privacy settings apply to send as well – you may not see this option on every photo.

>> **Like:** Same as with the Like link that appears on the right side of the viewer, selecting this option lets the person who added the photo know that you like the photo.

TIP

You can also use the left and right arrow keys on your keyboard to scroll through an album.

The album view

The album view is the grid of thumbnail photos that you see when you click the name of an album. Most screens can fit about 8 to 12 photos in this view, and as you scroll down the page, more and more photos appear until you reach the end of the album. Sometimes if people add a really large album, you may want to skim the album view to identify the parts of the album that interest you. Clicking on any one photo brings up the photo viewer.

At the top of the album view is the name of the album and any general info your friend has added about the album. Beneath the last row of photos, you can see who has liked the album or commented on it. Figure 11-4 shows an example album view.

FIGURE 11-4:
An album view of photos.

Commenting on an album is different than commenting on a single photo. Leave a comment on an album to comment on the collection: "Looks like a great trip!" "Can't wait till we see the place ourselves." Comment on a single photo when you have something to say about that photo in particular: "Did you use a fish-eye lens to get this shot?" or "OMG I was at this exact spot a year ago!"

Viewing photos on your mobile device

Chances are that if you have a smartphone or a tablet computer like an iPad, you'll wind up looking at photos using the Facebook app. Looking at photos on these devices isn't too different from looking at them on a computer screen. Tapping a photo in News Feed expands the photo and fades the rest of the screen to black. At the top of the screen are icons for closing the photo and returning to News Feed (X), tagging the photo (tag icon), and more options (. . . icon). At the bottom of the screen are buttons you can tap to like, comment on, or share the photo. Tapping the count of likes or comments expands a screen where you can scroll through the comments people have made on the photo.

When someone has added multiple photos in one post, you see a preview of those photos in your mobile News Feed. When you tap on any of the photos, you are taken to an album view, where you can scroll up and down to browse through all the photos that have been added. Tap on the back arrow in the upper left corner to return to News Feed. Tap on any photo to view it in the photo viewer, and then swipe left and right to navigate through the album. The two-finger method of zooming in and out also works on Facebook Photos.

Viewing tagged photos and videos of yourself

When I say *photos and videos of yourself,* I'm referring to photos and videos in which you're *tagged.* Tags are ways of marking who is in a photo — the online equivalent of writing the names of everyone appearing on the back of a photo print. Tags are part of what make Facebook Photos so useful. Even if you don't add lots of photos, other people can add photos of you. Photos you've been tagged in might be scattered across your friends' Timelines, so Facebook collects all these photos in the Photos section of your Timeline. You can get there by clicking the Photos tab underneath your cover photo.

The Photos section defaults to showing Photos of You. You can also view photos you've added (Your Photos) or albums you've added (Albums). The Photos of You section shows the most recently tagged photos at the top of the page. As you scroll down, you see older and older photos of yourself. This is a great place to take a trip down memory lane, and also to make sure that you're aware of all the photos of you that are out there.

If you've been tagged in a photo and you don't like that tag, you can always remove the tag by clicking Options from the photo viewer and choosing Remove Tag. Then that photo will no longer be linked to your Timeline, and it won't appear in the Photos of You section of your Timeline either.

If there's a photo or video you don't want on Facebook at all, even after you've removed the tag, get in touch with your friend and ask him to remove it. If you think it's offensive or abusive in any way, you can also report the photo and ask Facebook to remove it.

Adding Photos to Facebook

Facebook is a great place to keep your photos and videos because it's the place where most of your friends will be able to see them. Whether that's a single photo you snapped on your phone or a big album detailing the latest family vacation, photos are most fun when you can share them and talk about them with your friends.

Facebook distinguishes between uploading photos and creating a photo album. Albums are often created to document a particular event or period of time, whereas uploads happen on an ongoing basis. Because photo uploads tend to happen more frequently, I go over all the ways of uploading photos before going into Album creation.

Uploading photos

If you have a few photos you want to quickly share, follow these steps to get them out to your friends:

1. **Click Photo/Video at the bottom of the Publisher on your Home page.**

   A window appears allowing you to browse your computer's hard drive and select the photo you want (see Figure 11-5).

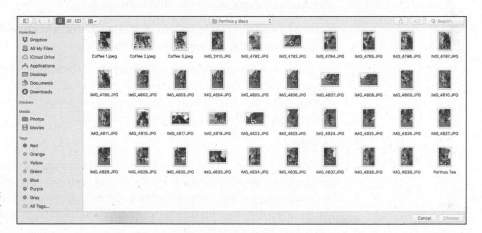

FIGURE 11-5:
Choose your
favorite photos.

2. **Click the photo(s) you want to share.**

3. **Click Open or Choose (the wording may depend on your browser and operating system).**

   Clicking Open or Choose brings you back to Facebook. A thumbnail of that photo appears inside the Publisher (shown in Figure 11-6).

WARNING

   Sometimes Facebook may be a little slow to add your photo. A progress bar or circle may appear instead of thumbnails. You won't be able to post your photo until the photo has been added.

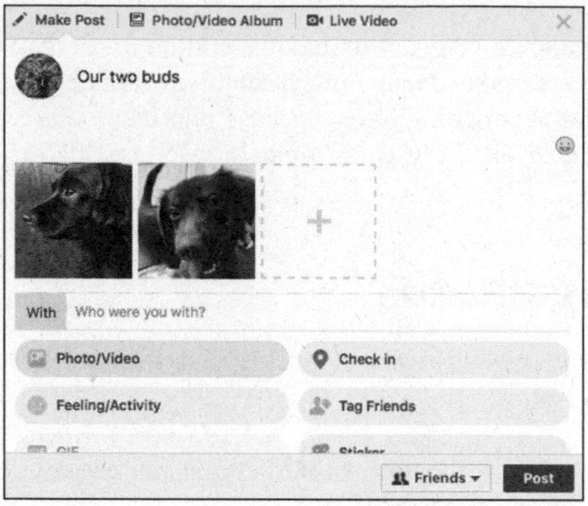

FIGURE 11-6:
Share your photos with your friends.

4. **Click in the Publisher (where you see Say Something About This Photo) and type any explanation you think is necessary.**

5. **(Optional) Add tags, location info, and change the privacy of those photos from the options at the bottom of the Publisher.**

If you've never changed your Privacy settings, by default, everyone on Facebook can see your photos if they navigate to your Timeline. I usually like sharing my photos with Friends. Of course, you can always choose custom groups of people who can and cannot see the photo.

6. **Click Post.**

Clicking Post officially shares the photo to Facebook. People will be able to see the photos on your Timeline and in their News Feeds (provided they're allowed by your Privacy settings to see the photo). By default, this photo is added to an album called Timeline Photos, which is basically a collection of all the photos you've ever added individually.

Editing photos as you add them

Uploading photos is meant to be pretty easy. In essence you click on the photos you want to share and then you click post. Voilà, shared photos. However, Facebook offers a whole bunch of cool photo-editing options that you can choose to use as you add your photos. To get to these options, hover your mouse over any of the thumbnail previews of the photos you have chosen to add (do this *before* you click Post). When you hover over the thumbnail, three icons appear. Click the X icon to remove the selected photo from the post. Click the tag icon to tag people in that photo. Click the paintbrush icon to open a photo viewer with editing options (shown in Figure 11-7).

FIGURE 11-7:
Photo editing
options.

WARNING

This is one of those places where what you see on-screen might be different than what's pictured in the figures in this book. Don't worry, the editing options are the same, just some of the locations (left versus right, top versus bottom) might be different.

FILTERS

Filters allow you to change the color balance of the photo you have chosen. Changing the color balance has a tendency to change the mood of the photo, so a silly photo can become more romantic if it is now black and white, or a photo might appear more retro if it has a vintage filter.

TAG

You can tag people in a photo by clicking on their face and then typing their name into the text box that opens. Facebook auto-completes as you type; hit Enter to select their name when you see it highlighted. Tagging friends will notify them that they have been tagged in a photo and may allow their friends to view that photo as well.

CROP

Cropping the photo involves changing the borders of the photo. After you click Crop, guidelines appear that you can move to crop the photo. Grayed-out areas don't appear. You can also choose to keep the Original photo size or make it Square. Since many photos appear as thumbnails (such as in album previews), changing to square can make them fit more nicely into those square boxes.

When you crop a photo, you can also choose to rotate it. No need to make people tilt their heads at their computer screens in order to see your photo properly. Click Rotate to rotate the photo 90 degrees. Click it as many times as you need to get it to the proper orientation.

ADD TEXT

Unlike a caption, which tends to describe a photo, text on a photo is a way of editing the photo itself to say something. Text appears overlaid on top of the photo. Click on Add Text to open a text box, and then start typing to add your text.

You can change the color of the text using the color palette on the left side of the screen. Simply drag the circle over the color palette until the text changes to the color you want, then release it. Use the Left and Centered buttons to decide whether your text should be centered in the text box or left-justified. Use the Font drop-down menu to choose a font for your text.

Click and drag the text box to move it to where you want it to appear on the photo. Click on the blue two-way arrow to change the size and orientation of the text. Drag it out to make it bigger and in to make it smaller, and drag it up or down to spin the text on its axis. Click the X at the upper-left corner of the text box to delete the text entirely.

Once you're happy with what the text says and how it appears on the photo, click on another portion of the photo to remove the text box, leaving just the text behind. Click on the text again to bring back the text box and the relevant editing options. You can add more than one text box to a photo.

ADD STICKER

Stickers are pretty much exactly what they sound like: digital drawings you can stick on top of your photos. Click on Add Sticker to browse through the sticker store for the sticker you want. When you click on the sticker you want, it appears in the center of your photo with a circle around it. Hover your mouse cursor over it until the cursor turns into a four-way arrow, and then click and drag it to your desired location on your photo. Click the blue two-way arrow to rotate the sticker and change its size (drag out to make it bigger, in to make it smaller). Click the X to delete the sticker. When your sticker is the proper size, orientation, and location, simply click another part of the photo to remove the circular frame from the sticker. Click the sticker again if you want to change something about it. You can add as many stickers as you want to a photo.

SHRINK OR ENLARGE

At the bottom of every photo-editing screen is a slider with an image of a small mountain on the left side and a larger version of the same image on the right side. Click and drag the blue circle in the middle of the slider to adjust the size of your photo. Dragging to the left shrinks the photo and dragging to the right enlarges it.

When you finish editing your photo, click the blue Save button. This brings you back to the Publisher, where your edited photo now appears as a thumbnail.

You can repeat the editing process for each photo you are adding, but keep in mind that these advanced editing options are entirely optional. Well, if your photo is upside down I strongly recommend rotating it to the proper orientation, but everything else is totally up to you.

Adding photos from your iPhone

Lots of photos you see on Facebook are added when people are nowhere near a computer. Instead, they're the photos of things that happen while you're out and about. Things that are beautiful (spring blossoms!), or weird (how did this person lose only one high heel?), or just emblematic of your day (another cute photo of the dog).

If you add the Facebook app to most smartphones, you can send photos from your phone right to Facebook. We go over how to add a photo from the Publisher of the iPhone app in Chapter 7. You can also add a photo from your iPhone's camera roll.

To add a photo from your iPhone's camera roll, follow these steps:

1. **From your photo gallery, tap the photo you want to share; then tap the Send icon at the bottom left of the photo.**

   A menu of options appears, including things like email or text messages. If you previously installed the Facebook app, you should see the Facebook icon among the other options.

2. **Tap the Facebook icon.**

   A Facebook Publisher appears, as shown in Figure 11-8.

FIGURE 11-8:
Don't let your photos go unshared!

3. **(Optional) Click Say Something and use the keyboard to type any explanation the photo needs.**

4. **(Optional) Tap the Album icon to add the photo to an existing album on Facebook.**

   By default, Facebook adds your photo to a Mobile Uploads album.

5. **(Optional) Tap on any of the icons at the bottom of the photo to add tags, activity info, or location info, respectively.**

6. **(Optional) Tap the To: field at the top of the Publisher to edit who can see that photo.**

   Remember, by default, the audience you shared your last post with will be the people who can see this post.

7. **Tap Post in the upper-right corner of the Facebook window.**

   The photo is added to your Timeline as part of the Mobile Uploads album, and it may appear in your friends' News Feeds.

TIP

The mobile Facebook app allows you to create 360-degree photos. Click inside the Publisher and choose 360 Photo from the list of actions that appear. Follow the prompts to slowly move in a circle while continuously photographing your surroundings from your phone's camera. When you've posted the image, your friends will see that it's a 360 photo. If they click on it, they'll be able to drag their mouse cursor left or right to see the static panorama as you captured it.

Creating an album

Whereas a single photo can share a moment, an album can truly tell a story and spark conversations with your friends. To create an album, follow these steps:

1. **From the Publisher, click Photo/Video Album in the top menu.**

   This opens the same interface for exploring your hard drive that you used to upload a single photo.

2. **Select multiple photos by pressing the Shift or Command button and clicking the files you want.**

TIP

   If you use a program like iPhoto to organize your photos, create an album there first; then navigate to it and select all those photos to add to Facebook. You'll save yourself some time trying to figure out whether you want to use IMG0234 or IMG0235.

3. **When you're done, click Open.**

The Create Album window appears, shown in Figure 11-9. The progress bar fills with blue as your photos are uploaded. You can always add more photos by clicking the Add Photos/Videos button at the top of the Create Album window.

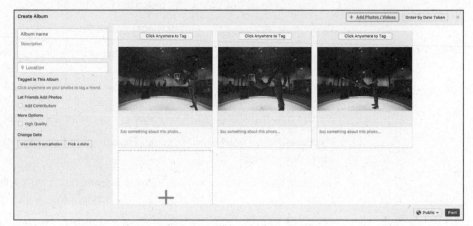

FIGURE 11-9:
Create your album here.

4. **Edit the Album info and options.**

The left side of the screen contains all the relevant album info:

- **Album Name:** Enter your album title here. Usually something descriptive does the trick: "Hawaii" or "Halloween."

- **Description:** Click here to add context to your album. You might talk about why you took these photos, or anything else you think people might want to know about your album: "Snaps from Jill's Birthday Party!"

- **Location:** Click here to add information about where these photos were taken. Location information may be added automatically, as Facebook pulls location info from your computer and from your photos. Any locations you enter get added as tags the album has.

- **Tagged in This Album:** As you add tags to your photos (more on that in Step 8), your friends' names will appear here.

- **Let Friends Add Photos:** Often photo albums center on an event where many people took photos. You can create a shared album to allow multiple friends to add photos to the album. If you check this box, a text field appears where you can enter the names of people you want to share the album with. The name of anyone you tag will automatically appear here, but you can remove their tag by clicking the X next to their name.

- **High Quality:** High-resolution photos obviously look a bit better, but they also take longer to upload. Unless you're a pro photographer or using a truly professional-level camera, standard quality is usually sufficient.

- **Change Date:** By default, your album will be dated from the date you upload it. If you want, you can use the date the photos were taken as the date of the album, or you can pick a date for the album.

5. **Choose who can see the album by using the Privacy menu.**

   The Privacy menu reflects the privacy setting from the last time you posted something. If you last posted something publicly, for example, the Privacy menu displays the globe icon and says "Public." As usual, the basic options are Public, Friends, Only Me, or a Custom set of people. If you are uploading a shared album, the options will be Public or Friends of Contributors.

6. **(Optional) After your photos finish uploading, add descriptions to individual photos.**

   The thumbnail of each photo has a blank space beneath it. Click in that space to add a caption or description of that individual photo.

TIP

Hover the mouse cursor over any preview and click on the rotation icon that appears in the upper left corner to rotate the photo.

7. **(Optional) Click and drag photos to reorder them in your album.**

8. **(Optional) Click friends' faces to tag them. Type the name of the friend in the box that appears.**

   The tagging box is shown in Figure 11-10. You don't have to tag friends in your album. However, tagging is highly recommended. It allows your friends to learn about your photos more quickly and share in discussing them with you.

   Facebook's facial recognition may automatically add tags of people it recognizes. This allows you to make sure your friend is tagged in many photos without having to enter his name a zillion times. You can remove any incorrect tags by clicking the X next to the person's name underneath the photo in question. You can remove all tags for a particular friend by clicking the X next to his name in the Tagged in This Album section on the left side of the Create Album window.

9. **Click Post.**

   Whew! That was a bit of a marathon. If you need a break or a drink of water, feel free to indulge. Then, when you're ready, jump to the "Editing and Tagging Photos" section to find out how to edit your album and the photos in it.

FIGURE 11-10:
Who is it?

Editing and Tagging Photos

After uploading a photo, you can still make changes to the way it appears on Facebook. If you added a whole album, you may want to add more photos or rearrange the order of the pictures. For any photo you added from a phone or just quickly from your computer, you may want to add tags, date, or location information. Doing all of this is relatively easy using the following common editing "tasks."

Editing albums

Editing an album usually consists of editing the album's information or settings. You may also want to edit specific photos within an album. For those types of edits, hop on down to the "Editing a photo" section.

Editing album name, location, description, and privacy

First, let's navigate to the album view by choosing Photos from the Explore section of the left-side menu on your Home page. Click the blue text that says Albums and then choose the album you want to edit. Look above the top row of photos for an Edit button and click it to bring up an Edit Album screen (see Figure 11-11). It should look familiar — it's pretty much the same screen you saw when you created the album.

The fields at the top are the same as when you created the album: album name, description (Say Something), location (Where Were These Taken), contributors, and a Privacy menu. Remember to click Save when you finish editing this information.

FIGURE 11-11:
Editing your
album's info.

Deleting an album

While you're looking at the Edit Album screen, look for a button in the upper-right that says Delete Album. If you ever decide, in retrospect, that adding a particular album was a poor choice, you can click this button to remove the whole thing.

WARNING

If you delete your photo album, all the photos in it will be gone forever, so make sure you want to get rid of it completely before you delete it.

Reordering photos in the album

Chances are that if you added your photos in bulk, they don't appear exactly in the right order. And it's awkward when the photos of the sunset appear first, and the photos of your awesome day of adventure come afterward. To reorder photos from the album view, follow these steps:

1. **Hover the mouse pointer over the photo you want to move.**

2. **Click and hold the photo.**

3. **While holding the mouse button down, drag the photo thumbnail to its correct place in the album.**

   The other photos shift positions as you move your chosen photo (as shown in Figure 11-12).

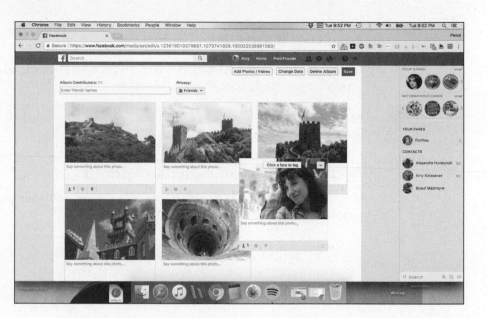

FIGURE 11-12:
Making your
album tell a story
in the right order.

4. **When the photo is in the spot you want, release the mouse button.**

5. **Repeat with the next photo until your whole album is organized correctly.**

Facebook automatically saves the new order of your album, but it never hurts to click the Save button anyway.

Adding more photos

After you create a photo album, you can add more photos later. Sometimes, depending on how organized the photos on your hard drive are, you may want to add photos in batches anyhow. To add more photos, follow these steps:

1. **From the Edit Album screen, click the Add Photos/Videos button.**

   This opens the interface for exploring your computer's hard drive.

2. **Select the photos you want to add.**

3. **Click Open or Choose.**

   The upload process begins and you go to the Create Album window. You can tag your photos, add captions, and rotate them as needed.

4. **Click the Post button after the upload is complete.**

Editing a photo

In addition to the actions you can take on an entire album, you can also take actions on individual photos within an album.

For all of these possible photo edits, I assume you're already looking at the photo you want to edit in the photo viewer.

Adding a tag to an individual photo

If you skipped adding tags earlier, you can always add your tags to individual photos.

1. **Hover your mouse over a friend's face.**

   The tagging box appears, as shown in Figure 11-13.

FIGURE 11-13:
Tagging a friend in a photo.

2. **Enter the name of the person you want to tag in the text box.**

   Facebook tries to auto-complete your friend's name as you type.

3. **Repeat Steps 1 and 2 until everyone in the photo is tagged.**

   Or stop after you tag a few people. You can always come back to this later.

Rotating a photo

Lots of times, photos wind up being sideways. It's a result of turning your camera to take a vertical shot as opposed to a horizontal one. You don't have to settle for this.

1. **Click Options in the bottom right corner of the photo.**

2. **Choose Rotate Left or Rotate Right from the menu that appears.**

3. **Keep clicking Rotate Left or Rotate Right until your photo is at the correct orientation.**

Adding or changing a description or date for an individual photo

Just like you can add a description to the album as a whole, you can add descriptions or captions to individual photos:

1. **Click the Edit button on the right side of the photo viewer.**

2. **Enter your description in the text box.**

3. **(Optional) Add any tags to indicate who was with you when the photo was taken.**

4. **(Optional) Add location information about where this photo was taken.**

   Facebook tries to autocomplete your location information as you type.

5. **Use the date selector to change the date when the photo was taken.**

6. **When you're finished, click Done Editing.**

Album covers

From the Edit Album view, Facebook lets you designate a photo to act as your album cover. The cover is the first photo people see when they click on your album. To choose an album cover:

1. **Hover your mouse over the top right corner of the photo until you see a gray arrow.**

2. **Click the arrow.**

   A menu of options appears.

3. **Choose Make Album Cover.**

Moving photos

Sometimes you realize a photo you added to an album is better suited to a different album. There's a quick and easy way to transfer that photo, also from the Edit Album view:

1. **Hover your mouse over the top right corner of the photo until you see a gray arrow.**

2. **Click the arrow.**

   A menu of options appears.

3. **Choose Move to Other Album.**

   A pop-up window appears with a drop-down menu of all your photo albums.

4. **Choose the album you want to move the photo to.**

5. **Click Move Photo.**

Deleting a photo

Maybe you realized that all 20 group shots from the high school reunion don't have to go in the album, or that one photo has a whole bunch of crossed eyes. From the Edit Album view, you can remove photos entirely from Facebook:

1. **Hover your mouse over the top right corner of the photo until you see a gray arrow.**

2. **Click the arrow.**

   A menu of options appears.

3. **Choose Delete This Photo.**

   A pop-up window appears asking if you are sure.

4. **Click OK.**

   You're taken back to the album view, now with one less photo.

Automatic albums

Most of the time when you're creating a photo album, you decide what to title it and which photos go into it. There are a few exceptions to this rule. Facebook assembles certain types of photos into albums on your behalf. Most importantly, every time you change your profile picture or cover photo, Facebook adds it to the Profile Pictures or Cover Photos albums, respectively. Facebook creates albums of all your profile pictures and cover photos automatically.

You can access this album by clicking your current profile picture or cover photo from your Timeline. This takes you to the photo viewer, where you can click through your historical record of profile pictures. Even though your current Profile and Cover photos are always Public, you can edit past photos to change the audience, add tags, location, a description, or delete a photo simply by clicking the Edit button to the right of the photo. Make sure to click Done Editing to save your changes.

You can turn any photo from this album back into your profile picture by navigating to the Options menu at the bottom of the photo and selecting Make Profile Picture.

Similarly, single photos that you add to your Timeline are collected into the Time-line Photos album. Photos that you add from your phone are added to a Mobile Uploads album. Videos are collected into a Videos album.

Working with Video

Too often, videos wither away on hard drives or cameras or on mobile phones. The files are big, and they can be difficult to share or email. Facebook seeks to make sharing videos easier. So film away and let everyone see what you've been up to.

Viewing videos

You'll mostly encounter videos in your News Feed with a big fat Play button in the center (see Figure 11-14). If you pause in your scrolling to look at the video, it will begin playing, but without sound. If you aren't interested in the video, keep scroll-ing. If you are, hover your mouse over the bottom of the video and click on the muted sound icon (it's a megaphone with a white X next to it). This will turn the sound on for the video.

FIGURE 11-14:
A video on
Facebook.

Videos play inline in your News Feed. While the video is playing, you can hover your mouse over it to see the progress bar, change the volume, switch the video to HD, or expand it to full screen.

TIP

If you want to keep scrolling and watch a video at the same time — you can! Just click the Continue watching while you use Facebook button (looks like a square with the top left corner filled in) to move the video to the top left of your Home page and out of the News Feed. The video automatically follows as you scroll down.

WARNING

If you like a lot of Pages, you may see more videos in your News Feed. For example, I follow a Page that posts nothing but videos of unlikely animal friends all day long. Some of these videos play for 15 or 30 seconds before being interrupted by a video advertisement. Just kick back and enjoy the brief ad. The video you're watching will return right after the ad finishes.

Adding a video from your computer

Uploading a video to Facebook includes going out into the world, recording something, and then moving it from your camera onto your computer. I'm going to assume you've already done that part and are now back in front of your computer. Now, to upload a video to Facebook, follow these steps:

1. **Choose Photo/Video in the Publisher at the top of your Home page or Timeline.**

   This expands a window that allows you to navigate your computer's hard drive.

2. **Select a video file from your computer.**

   This brings you back to Facebook, where your video is appended to your post.

3. **(Optional) Type any explanation or comment into the Say Something About This Video box.**

4. **(Optional) Select who can see this video using the Privacy menu.**

   As usual, your basic options are Public, Friends, Only Me, and Custom.

5. **(Optional) Use the icons at the bottom of the Publisher to add tags, activity or location information.**

6. **Click Post.**

   A blue progress bar appears at the bottom of the post. Uploading a video can sometimes take a while, so be patient. If you click to Post and are notified that your video is processing, it means you need to wait a little while until your video is ready. You can use Facebook in the meantime and wait for a notification that your video is uploaded.

Adding a video from the Facebook app

Much like photos, many of the videos you want to share most are ones you take when you're out and about: someone attempting to park a car in a spot that's too small, your dog chasing a tennis ball, the bride and groom cutting the cake. More and more often, you may find yourself using your phone to record these videos.

You could move the video from your phone to your computer and then add it to Facebook, or you could skip the middleman and share it directly from your phone using the Facebook app:

1. **Tap the Photo option at the top of your mobile News Feed.**

   Your Photo and Video roll from your phone appears.

2. **Tap the video you want to add.**

3. **Tap Done in the upper-right corner.**

   A preview of your video appears in the mobile Publisher. You can play it here to make sure you want to share it.

4. **(Optional) Tap the Say Something space above the video to add a caption or description of the video.**

5. **(Optional) Use the icons on the bottom of the Publisher to add tags, activity, or location info to your post.**

6. **Double-check your privacy by seeing who can see the video in the To: field at the top of the Publisher.**

   Remember, by default the video will be shared with the same group of people you last shared a post with.

7. **Tap Post in the upper-right corner of the screen.**

   The video is then added to Facebook. Your friends will be able to see it on your Timeline and in their News Feeds (depending on your privacy settings, of course).

Live Video

There may be instances when something you're witnessing should be shared with your friends in real-time. Maybe there's a deer on your lawn or a particularly nasty storm you're caught in. This is where Live Video comes into play. To create a live video, click the Live Video button at the top of your Publisher and follow the prompts to give Facebook access to the camera on your computer or mobile phone. Adjust privacy settings as necessary then start shooting by clicking the blue Go Live button. You know a video is live because of the red button and word Live in the upper–left corner of the video. If your friends miss the live version, they'll be able to catch the video on your Timeline or in their News Feeds at a later point.

Discovering Privacy

While privacy is covered in detail in Chapter 6, it's worth going over a few settings again now that you understand what it is you're choosing to show or not show to people.

Photo and video privacy

Each time you create an album, post a photo, or add a video to Facebook, you can use the Privacy menu to select who can see it. These options are as follows:

>> **Public:** This setting means that anyone can see the album. It doesn't necessarily mean that everyone *will* see the album, though. Facebook doesn't generally display your content to people who aren't your friends. But if, for example, someone you didn't know searched for you and went to your Timeline, she would be able to see that album.

>> **Friends:** Only confirmed friends can see the photos or videos when you have this setting.

>> **Only Me:** Only you will be able to see that photo or video.

>> **Custom:** Custom privacy settings can be as closed or as open as you want. You may decide that you want to share an album only with the people who were at a particular event, which you can do with a custom setting.

TIP

Another way to control who sees an album or video is to share it using Facebook Groups. So, for example, a video of your kids playing might be of interest only to people in your family. If you have a group for your family, you can share it from the Publisher within the group, and then only people in the group will be able to see it.

WARNING

If you're brand new to Facebook and have never changed a single privacy setting, by default, all posts you add — including photos and videos — are visible publicly. If you aren't comfortable with this, remember to adjust your Privacy settings accordingly when you add new photos and video.

Privacy settings for photos and videos of yourself

The beauty of creating albums on Facebook is that it builds a giant cross-listed spreadsheet of information about your photos — who is in which photos, where those photos were taken, and so on. You're cross-listed in photos that you own and in photos that you don't own. However, you may want more control over these tags and who can see them. To control this, click Settings from the Account menu (down arrow) in the big blue bar. Click the Timeline and Tagging section on the left side of the page.

The following settings can help you further control who can see photos and videos of you:

>> **Review posts friends tag you in before they appear on your Timeline?** Turning this option from Off to On means you get to make sure you want to be tagged in photos (and other posts) before anyone can see that you've been tagged.

In other words, say that I tag my friend Carolyn in a photo.

- If this option is *Off,* as soon as I tag her, the photo is added to her Timeline and (usually) her friends will be able to see that she's been tagged in their News Feeds.

- If this setting is *On,* she has to approve the tag before it appears on her Timeline and in her friends' News Feeds. The photo itself still gets shared and is visible on my Timeline and in my friends' News Feeds.

>> **Who can see posts you've been tagged in on your Timeline?** Regardless of whether or not you choose to review tags before they appear on your Timeline, you can control who can see posts where you've been tagged. So, for example, if you set this to "Friends" and you get tagged in a photo, even though it has been added to your Timeline, a non-friend visiting your Timeline would not see it displayed there.

>> **When you're tagged in a post, whom do you want to add to the audience if they aren't already in it?** Another way to limit who can see that you've been tagged in a post is to change this setting from Friends to Only Me or Custom.

By default, if I tag Carolyn in a photo, her friend Stephanie, whom I'm not friends with, will be able to see the photo. If Carolyn changes this setting to Only Me, then when I tag Carolyn, Stephanie will not be able to see that photo.

WHAT'S THE DEAL WITH INSTAGRAM?

As you scroll through your News Feed you may see photo posts that have the word *Instagram* next to their timestamp information. At this point, you've probably heard of Instagram and wondered if it was for you. Aren't you already putting all of your photos on Facebook? Do you need another website to keep track of? Instagram is owned by Facebook, but provides a more focused service to its over 500 million daily users. The site is only for photos and short video posts (as of the time of this writing). Many people use both websites, but favor Instagram for their photo posts, which they can always share to their Facebook Timeline at the same time they post to their Instagram account. If you tend to enjoy visual posts more than text posts in your News Feed, I recommend signing up for an Instagram account as well. You can follow your Facebook friends in Instagram to see their posts, but it does not need to be a reciprocal relationship. You can also follow celebrities, brands, and strangers to see what they post. As a personal example, I adopted one of my dogs after I saw a photo of him on an animal rescue's Instagram feed and reached out to the organization to inquire about him.

Chapter **12**

Buying, Selling, and Fundraising

Have you ever tried to get a friend to take an old sofa off your hands? Or asked them to spread the word about a spare room you have for rent? Have you ever run a marathon (or, in my case, a "fun run") for charity? These types of social interactions have, of course, always happened on Facebook as well as in the real world, so after a while Facebook built out a few features to make these types of interactions easier and more streamlined. In addition, Facebook can help be the middleman between you and your local community so that you can reach a larger group of people than you would by just reaching out to your friends.

Marketplace and the Buy/Sell groups are going to be your first stops for local buying and selling. Think of it as a better way to do a yard sale. Marketplace is run by Facebook, and Buy and Sell groups are a type of group managed by local members of the group. Depending on where you live, one or the other might be more helpful to you. Marketplace covers virtually every type of thing you might want to sell, while Buy/Sell groups often have a specific focus on what type of item people who join will be posting. For example, you might join a Buy/Sell group specifically for childcare posts, or one specifically for buying and selling bike gear.

Fundraising is a way for you to solicit donations. It's a very flexible system that allows you to fundraise both on behalf of an established charity or on behalf of yourself or another person (for example, a school trip, a memorial fund after someone's death, and so on). For the purposes of this chapter, I'm assuming that you are going to be fundraising for a noble cause, whether or not it's attached to a 501(c)(3).

Getting the Most Out of Marketplace

Marketplace is Facebook's central location for browsing, buying, and selling used items. It offers tools for searching and filtering in on your searches, as well as easy ways to keep track of items that you've listed for sale.

Browsing and buying in Marketplace

To check out Marketplace, click on the Marketplace link in the left-side menu on your Home page (it has a little storefront icon). This brings you to Marketplace, shown in Figure 12-1.

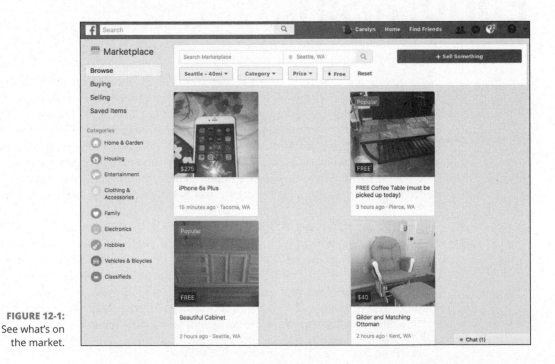

FIGURE 12-1:
See what's on
the market.

Marketplace has its own left-hand menu and search functionality across the top of the page. The bulk of the page is taken up with the listings. Each listing has a photo, title, and info about how recently and where it was posted.

The left-hand menu has links to different sections: Browse (where you start), Buying, Selling, and Saved Items. You can also click on any of the categories listed on the left side of the page to check out that specific category of item. Often, when you click on a category, you'll be able to see further subcategories. For example, when you click on the Family Category, you find that you can in fact drill down on any of the following smaller categories: Toys & Games, Baby & Kids, Pet Supplies, and Health & Beauty.

If there's something in particular you're looking for, use the search box at the top of the page to search for it by name or keyword. You can also change the city you are searching in (Facebook will autocomplete a city as you type in the name of your desired location). Use the drop-down menu to change the radius of your search. You can search as locally as within two miles of your city or town, or as far as 100 miles away. By default, Facebook sets the radius at forty miles.

You can also use the drop-down menus to filter by category and price (you can set a range). There is also a button you can press to just see items that have been listed for free. If you find that you have added so many restrictions that you no longer see any results, click the blue Reset link to undo all the filters you have set.

As you are browsing, you may notice some tags on top of various images. Some may note that an item is popular, that it is sold pending pick-up, or that it is free. Whenever you see an item that interests you, click on it to open a larger image of it and view more. You can see a sample listing in Figure 12-2.

FIGURE 12-2: Checking out an item in Marketplace.

When you view an item's listing, you can click through the various photos of the item (if there are multiple photos of it). To the right of the photos you can view a more detailed description of the item, as well as a map indicating the general area it's being sold from, and how many people have viewed the item. You can also view the seller's name and click through to view their public profile. This is one of those places where your sense of whether a profile is real comes into play. You don't want to start messaging back and forth with a fake or scammy account, so paying attention to when they joined and whether their profile seems fishy is important. Facebook suggests you never include your email, phone number, or financial information in the first message to a seller, and that is sound advice.

You can take several actions from the item's listing. You can mark that you are interested in the item, or save the item so you can go back to it later. You can also click to share the item with an interested friend. Most prominently, if you're ready to go beyond just looking at an item, click the big blue Message Seller button to start a thread with the seller.

Clicking the Message Seller button opens a message window with a blank text box, shown in Figure 12-3. You can write any questions you have about the item here, or you can choose to use one of the pre-filled text questions listed below. These commonly used phrases, like "I'm interested in this item," can be added to the body of your message with a simple click. After you finish your message, click the Send Message button to send it. This opens a chat window between you and the sender. If you don't hear back right away or you leave your computer, you can always find this item and a record of the conversation in the Buying section of Marketplace (click Buying in the left-hand menu of Marketplace).

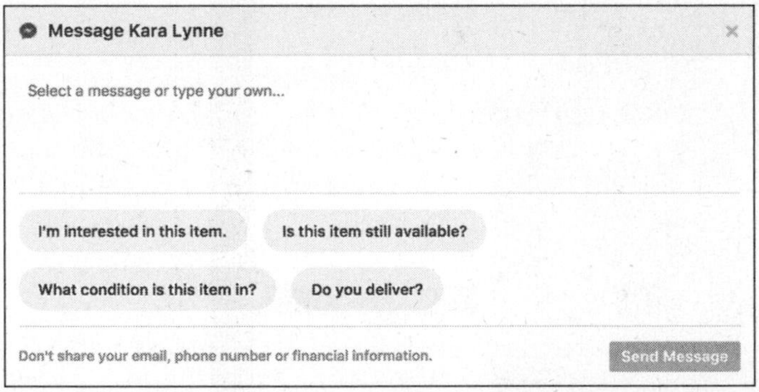

💬 Message Kara Lynne   ✕

Select a message or type your own...

I'm interested in this item.	Is this item still available?
What condition is this item in?	Do you deliver?

Don't share your email, phone number or financial information.   Send Message

---

FIGURE 12-3:
Write to the
seller here.

TIP

People often refer to messages between buyers and sellers as direct messages (*DMs*) or private messages (*PMs*). You might see this term pop up in descriptions like "DM me for pricing" or "PM me for more info."

Often the process of buying something can require a bit of a back-and-forth between you and the seller: you need to agree on a price and method of payment, coordinate a time and location for picking it up or getting it delivered, and then actually go and get the item. The seller might also be managing many incoming messages or people who are interested in the item as well, so try to have patience with each other.

TIP

If you are looking for something specific, such as a brand of clothing. When you search for something, look at the top of the results for a grey "Follow" button. Click this button to receive notifications any time something that fits your search terms is posted to Marketplace.

Selling your stuff on Marketplace

If you're trying to create a listing for something you want to sell, you can easily do so by going to Marketplace and following these steps:

1. **Click the blue Sell Something button in the upper-right corner of the page.**

   This opens the Sell Something box, shown in Figure 12-4.

2. **Enter the item's info into the appropriate space.**

   - **What are you selling?** This will be the title of your item in Marketplace so best to make it short and descriptive: IKEA Table and Chairs, Bundle of 3T clothing, Vintage iPad — whatever makes sense for the item your selling.

   - **Add price:** Decide how much you think your item is worth and add a price. If you aren't sure what price to choose, try searching for similar items already in Marketplace and see what other people are asking for it.

   - **Change location:** By default, location gets set to your current location. If you want to have this listed in a different location, click the X next to the current location to delete it. Type in your preferred location into the now-empty Add Location field. Depending on where you live, you can often type in a specific neighborhood, not just the main city where you are selling something.

   - **Select a category:** Click the Select a Category field to open a menu of categories for you to choose from.

   - **Describe your item (optional):** You don't have to fill any additional description out, but adding details about the item you're selling can be helpful. You can describe the condition it's in, include its measurements, and make any notes about use or care.

3. **Add photos of your item by clicking the gray Add Photo box at the bottom of the Sell Something box.**

   This opens an interface for selecting photos from your computer's hard drive. After you add your photos, you can edit them by hovering your mouse over the thumbnail of the photo you want to edit and clicking the paintbrush icon in the lower-right corner of that thumbnail. Click the X icon to remove that photo entirely.

4. **When you're done, click Post.**

   Your listing immediately goes into Marketplace, where everyone can see it and respond.

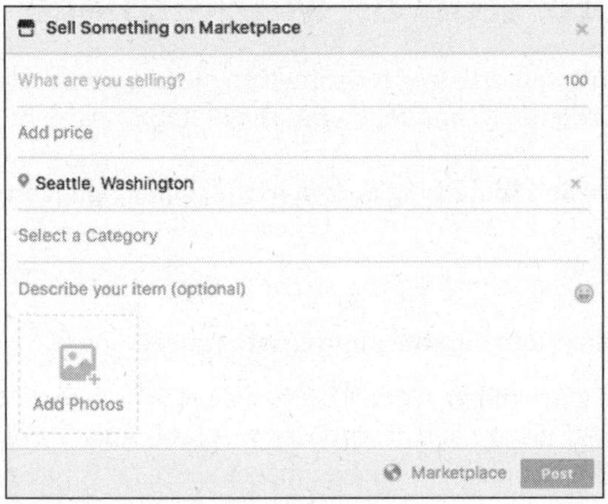

FIGURE 12-4:
Create a listing here.

Sell Something on Marketplace

What are you selling?   100

Add price

Seattle, Washington   ×

Select a Category

Describe your item (optional)

Add Photos

Marketplace   Post

You can keep track of your listings by going to the Selling section of Marketplace (click Selling in the left-hand menu). Here, you can see all the items you have listed for sale. When you sell something, click the blue Mark as Sold button to take it off the Marketplace. Click the Manage button to open a menu where you can either delete the listing entirely or edit it.

REMEMBER

All posts to Marketplace are public, which means everyone on Facebook can see them. Don't post any personally identifying information, such as your address, phone number, or credit card number.

Using Marketplace on your phone

Marketplace is easy to browse and use on your phone. To get to it (assuming you are using the Facebook app on an iPhone or Android), tap on the Marketplace icon at the bottom of the Home page (it looks like a little storefront) to start browsing through Marketplace. Use your finger to scroll up and down and browse. Tap on any listings you find interesting to learn more. You can quickly tap the blue "I'm Interested" or "Make Offer" button to let the seller know you're interested without having to compose a more in-depth message. You may also see other buttons like "Check out on Website" or "Add to Cart" from established businesses (as opposed to another individual).

Creating a new listing on your phone is very convenient because you can easily take a picture of the item you are selling without having to search your hard drive or transfer photos from your phone to your computer:

1. **Tap on the Publisher in Marketplace that says, "What are you listing?"**

   This opens a menu of categories for your listing.

2. **Choose from Item for Sale, Vehicles for Sale, Housing for Rent/Sale, Jobs.**

   All categories except Jobs opens an interface for navigating your phone's camera roll.

3. **Tap on a photo to select it or tap the camera icon in the upper-left corner to open your phone's camera.**

4. **Point and shoot!**

5. **When you've taken a photo you're happy with and edited it to your heart's content, click Use in the upper-right corner.**

   This returns you to your phone's camera roll. You can take more pictures by returning to the camera or choose existing photos from your phone's camera roll.

6. **After you select the photos you want, click Next in the upper-right corner.**

   This opens the New Item interface.

7. **Enter your item's info (title, price, category, location, and so on) into the fields of the New Item interface.**

   There are some additional options here that are not on your computer. You can choose to offer shipping for the item, or if you are selling one item in multiple colors or styles, you can add that information by clicking the blue Add More Options link.

8. **Decide whether you want to share this item on your profile in addition to on Marketplace, and in any Buy/Sell groups you may be a member of.**

   By default, your items only get listed in Marketplace. Tap on the other options to select them as well.

BUYING AND SELLING SAFELY

While Facebook tries to take some of the guesswork out of buying and selling your used items online, the fact remains that you will be interacting with someone you don't know. Here are a few basic safety tips to keep in mind:

- **Watch out for scammers:** If something sounds too good to be true, it probably is. Don't let people upend your common sense. There is no reason someone selling something or buying something from you will ever need your passwords, credit card numbers, or anything like that. You should never transfer money to someone until you have the item in your hands and have checked to make sure it is as advertised.

- **Use cash or person-to-person payment methods:** You can use Facebook to make payments (if both people are using debit cards), or other apps where the money immediately gets moved from one account to another. Checks can be faked or bounced. Cash is probably your best bet.

- **Try to meet in neutral locations:** If possible when arranging to sell someone something, try to meet in a neutral, public location. This makes both people feel safer about, you know, meeting someone from the internet. Let someone know where you'll be and who it is you are going to meet.

- **Give out your address judiciously:** Of course, a neutral location might not be possible, or worthwhile to you, especially if you're selling something small. So don't give out your full address to someone until they've committed to coming to pick up your item. And if something about them sets off your Spidey sense, don't force yourself to meet them!

9. **Tap Post.**

   Your listing is added to Marketplace.

Don't let the number of steps here fool you. I once listened to someone describe the process of listing multiple items to Facebook as something that was easily accomplished with a tasty beverage in one hand and their phone in the other.

Belonging to Buy/Sell Groups

In addition to Marketplace, many people use Buy/Sell Groups to buy and sell used items. You can use both (and, in fact, Facebook makes it easy to post Marketplace listings to Buy/Sell groups you belong to and vice versa). Usually people tend to use Buy/Sell groups for the following reasons:

» **Groups require membership**: Because members of a group must actively join that group, this acts as a bit of a filter on both the number of people who will see your listing and the type of buyer/seller you are interacting with. Not to say that the Buy and Sell safety tips don't apply, it just means that you are sharing listings with a particularly interested group of people.

» **Groups can get quite specific:** I live in a city divided by neighborhoods. Even though, as the crow flies, it isn't far to pick up an item in Downtown, I'd rather pick up something in my own ten-block radius. Buy/Sell groups often limit themselves to certain neighborhoods, so I can accomplish just that. They also can be for very specific categories of items, such as outdoor gear, children's gear, and housing. This can make your browsing more targeted.

» **Groups often have a trade element:** In addition to selling more locally and in a more community-based way, many Buy/Sell groups offer an option to trade items. If you are short on cash or hoping to get rid of a few of your own possessions, the barter system might be what you're looking for. Beyond this, keep an eye out for local "Buy Nothing" groups, built around the minimalist notion that we don't need to buy anything new, ever. In those groups, members can create requests for items and other members, if they are able, fulfill those requests.

The mechanics of using Buy/Sell groups are very similar to any other group—you use the Publisher, comment on posts you're interested in, and message other people in the group. If you need a refresher on how groups work, I recommend checking out Chapter 10.

You can look for Buy and Sell groups near you by clicking the Buy and Sell Groups link in the left-side menu. This brings you to a Buy and Sell Groups home page, which displays a few of the local groups you might be interested in. Click the Join Group button next to any of the groups that look appealing to you.

Browsing and buying in a Buy/Sell group

As shown in Figure 12-5, a Buy/Sell group looks pretty much like most other groups. The main differences are that the Publisher defaults to Sell Something instead of prompting you to start a discussion. Under the Publisher is a preview of items that are currently for sale. Scroll down on the page to view the most recent listings. These listings should look familiar to you—they're just posts, albeit with titles and fields for prices. Some posts will have comment threads where people ask questions about the item's condition, pick up locations, or other related topics.

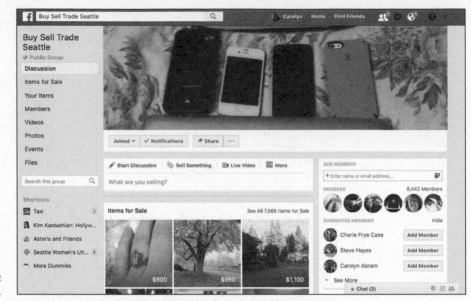

FIGURE 12-5:
Buy/Sell Groups.

In general, people don't use comment threads to perform the final negotiations for buying and picking up an item. Instead, when they're ready to make an offer, most people message the seller directly (and there is a handy Message Seller button in the lower-right corner of the post).

If you are really on the hunt for something, you can try using the search bar in the left menu to search for that item within the group's posts. You can also click on the Items for Sale link in the left-hand menu to view a condensed list of all the items currently for sale within the group.

Selling items in a Buy/Sell group

If you want to list something for sale in a Buy/Sell group, click in the Publisher. This is the little text box near the top of the group (under the cover photo). When you click in it, the Sell Something box opens (see Figure 12-6).

Does this look familiar? It should—it's literally the same box you saw in Figure 12-4. You'll need to fill out the following fields:

>> **What are you Selling**: Your answer to this question becomes the title of your post, so be descriptive.

>> **Price:** Let people know how much you are looking for them to pay for the item.

>> **Location:** Facebook may automatically fill in your zip code. Delete this info to use a different zip code.

>> **Description:** Add any details about your item that may be relevant—condition, measurements, and so on.

>> **Photos:** Add any photos of the item you are selling. In general, I've found that more than one photo is usually helpful to people.

At the bottom of the Sell Something box, next to the blue Post button, is a menu for deciding whether you want to add your listing to Marketplace in addition to whichever group you are about to post to. By default, Facebook assumes you will want to list it in both places. If you only want to list it in the group, click this menu and deselect Marketplace. If you are a member of more than one Buy/Sell group, you also have the option here to create a listing that gets posted to those groups as well.

When you've added all the info you need to your listing, click the blue Post button. You'll be notified about any comments on the listing, as well as any incoming messages from people who are interested in buying it.

Using Buy/Sell groups on your phone

Much like using Marketplace, using Buy/Sell groups on your phone — particularly for selling items — can be even easier because you can take pictures directly from your phone and include them in your listing. As someone who has made many a listing in my day, I can attest to the fact that if you are sitting at your computer trying to create a listing, you will inevitably need to make about ten trips back to the garage to check your measurements, take a new photo, and so on. Make your life easier and create the listing from where the item is.

To navigate to the Buy/Sell group you are interested in using for your sale, type its name into the search bar at the top of the app. You can also tap on the More button in the bottom right corner of the app to view a menu of all the shortcuts, features, and destinations you can go to within Facebook. You can click on your desired Buy/Sell group there, or tap on Buy and Sell Groups to view a preview of *all* items listed in *all* the Buy/Sell groups you are a member of.

Fundraising for Causes

For as long as there's been a Facebook people have found ways to use it to drum up support for a cause. Virtually every feature has been co-opted at one point or another for causes both serious and silly. People changed their profile pictures to a photo of their school mascot long before Facebook made it easy to put a temporary frame around your profile pic. Anyone who has participated in a fundraising effort like Team in Training has often reached out to their Facebook network for donations and support. In this way, fundraising on Facebook is nothing new, but the tools now available make it much easier to get support from your friends for any sort of cause.

Donating to a fundraiser

You might learn about fundraisers from an invite or see that one of your friends has created or donated to a fundraiser in your News Feed. You can see a sample post in Figure 12-7.

FIGURE 12-7: Your friend is raising money!

Much like any other post you might see in your News Feed, these posts have like buttons, a space for comments, and a share button. In addition, they also have a Donate button in the lower right corner of the post, which you can click to initiate a donation.

If you want more info about the fundraiser, you click on the fundraiser's cover photo or title to go to the fundraiser's page. There you can read the full story about the fundraiser — why your friend has started it, what exactly your money will be accomplishing, and so on. If they are raising money for a nonprofit, it usually makes sense to double-check to see if what your friend says the money is for is the same thing the nonprofit says the money will be for.

Clicking Donate on either your friend's post or the fundraiser's page opens the donation window shown in Figure 12-8. In the top part of this window, choose the amount you wish to donate and decide who can see that you've donated. By default, the fact that donations are made is public, though the amount of any donation is kept between you and the person organizing the fundraiser (and the eventual recipient of the donation). You can also choose to keep your donation only visible to friends, or only visible to yourself, though again, the organizer and recipient will always be able to see that you have donated.

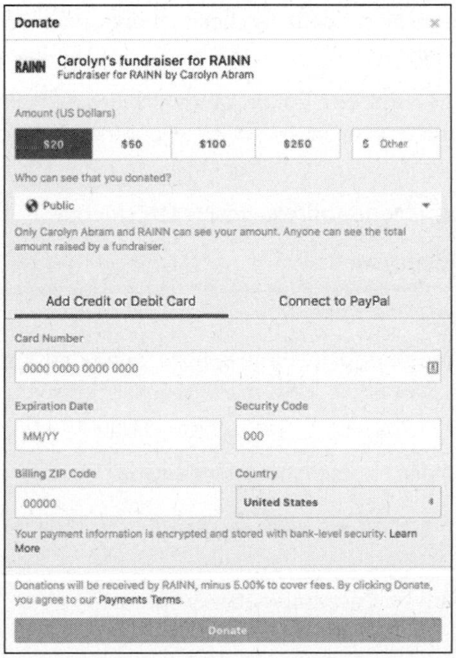

FIGURE 12-8:
Donate here.

In the bottom part of the donation window, enter your credit card information or log in to your PayPal account. After you enter all the info needed, click the blue Donate button.

Even if you don't donate to a fundraiser, you can show your support by leaving a post on the fundraiser's page. Much like writing a post on a friend's Timeline, this is something that many people will see, so if you're wanting to offer support to someone more privately, consider sending a message instead.

Creating your own fundraiser

You can start a fundraiser for any reason at any time. Often current events will inspire people to create fundraisers — whether that's linking to a big charity like the Red Cross after a natural disaster or donating to a memorial fund after the death of a friend or loved one. Another common time for creating a fundraiser is around one's birthday. Since Facebook promotes your birthday to your friends, it's a time when you know a lot of people will be visiting your Timeline and leaving a message, so there's a good chance they'll see your call to give as well.

To get started with your fundraiser, follow these steps:

1. **Navigate to the Fundraisers page by clicking Fundraisers in the Explore section of the left-side menu.**

   This brings you to the Fundraisers page, which includes more information about fundraisers and a list of any fundraisers your friends are currently running.

2. **Click the green Raise Money button on the left sidebar.**

   This opens a Raise Money window.

3. **Click the blue Get Started button.**

   The Raise Money window displays three options for fundraising: Friend, Nonprofit, or Yourself. After you have made your selection, you go to the "Basics" Section of creating a fundraiser, shown in Figure 12-9.

   - **Friend:** You will need to enter your friend's name.

   - **Nonprofit:** You will need to search through a list of nonprofits to find the one you want.

   - **Yourself:** You name will get automatically entered.

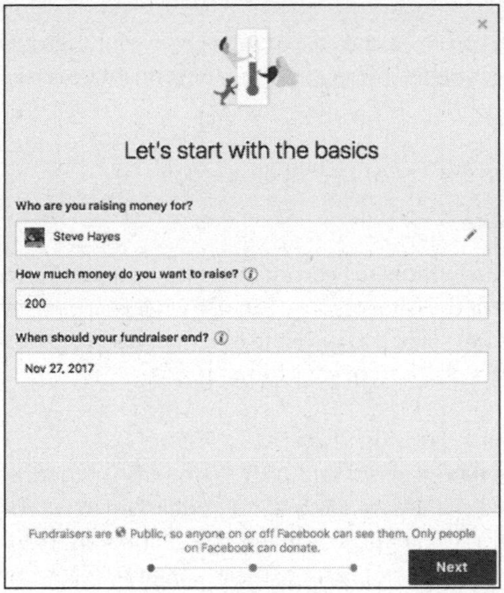

FIGURE 12-9:
Create your
fundraiser here.

4. **Double check that the correct name or organization is listed in the "Who are you raising money for?" section.**

5. **Set a fundraising target.**

   It's usually better to set a slightly lower target and then increase it later once it's been hit.

6. **Pick an end date for your fundraiser.**

   Having an end date helps your friends know how long they have to donate and lets you issue reminders like "only three days left!"

7. **Click Next.**

   This brings you to the Tell Your Story section of the process.

8. **(For Personal/Friend Fundraising Only) Select a category for your fundraiser.**

   Categories include things like medical, education, sports, and so on.

9. **Double-check (or create) a title for your fundraiser.**

   Titles should be brief and descriptive: "John Smith Memorial Fund," "Help Tyler Pay for College," "Carolyn's Fundraiser for RAINN."

10. **Tell your story.**

    Use as much space as you need to explain why you are creating the fundraiser and what the money will go towards. This is a great place to anticipate any questions your friends may have about the fundraiser: explain why you are fundraising, why you were moved to donate, how your friend will be receiving the money and any other information you think might be relevant.

11. **Click Next.**

This brings you to the Pick a Cover Photo section.

12. **Pick a cover photo.**

Facebook recommends default cover photos for your fundraiser depending on the organization or the category. You can use what Facebook recommends or click Edit in the lower-right corner of the cover preview to choose a different option or choose a photo from your computer.

13. **Click Create.**

This brings you to your Fundraiser's page. In the case of fundraisers for nonprofits, your fundraiser is automatically published to Facebook (and, keep in mind, all fundraisers are public). In the case of fundraisers for individuals, Facebook reviews such fundraisers to make sure they follow their standards.

WARNING

If you are creating a personal fundraiser, you must be at least 18 years old.

Facebook prompts you here to invite friends and post about your fundraiser. I go over these aspects in the next section, "Promoting and managing your fundraiser."

Promoting and managing your fundraiser

After you create your fundraiser, it's important to spread the word about it so people know about it. You can do this in two ways: you can invite people to support your fundraiser, and you can post about your fundraiser on your Timeline.

INVITING FRIENDS TO SUPPORT YOUR FUNDRAISER

To invite friends to view and support your fundraiser, follow these steps:

1. **From your fundraiser's page, click the blue Invite button (underneath the cover photo and title).**

This opens a window with a list of your friends.

2. **Click the blue Invite button next to any friend's name to invite them to view your fundraiser and (hopefully) donate.**

You can use the search box at the top of the window to search for specific friends.

3. **When you're done inviting friends, click Done.**

Friends you've invited will receive a notification letting them know about the fundraiser.

Sometimes people wonder about which friends to invite to a fundraiser. On the one hand, if you're fundraising for a cause you believe in, you should reach out far and wide; on the other hand, sometimes people can feel like it's rude to ask their friends for money constantly. I don't have a perfect answer for this question, other than to recommend that you invite the same people you would reach out to via direct email or phone call for a fundraising effort. I'd leave out any coworkers (especially if you're their boss!) or people who might feel awkward declining to donate.

CREATING POSTS ABOUT YOUR FUNDRAISER

Facebook will prompt you to create a post about your fundraiser after you've created it. If you choose not to do it then, you can create a post for it at any time by clicking the Share button on the fundraiser's page. This opens a window for creating a post. It should look familiar because it's the same as the Publisher you normally use to create your posts, but the information about your fundraiser gets pre-filled. Add any text you want to include about why you're creating the fundraiser or why you want people to donate to the text box above the fundraiser's cover photo, and then click Post.

Remember, fundraisers are public, so even if you only share your post with friends, those friends will be able to share the fundraiser with their own friends if they are so inclined.

GETTING THE MONEY WHERE IT NEEDS TO BE

If you are running a fundraiser for an established nonprofit, Facebook automatically links up with their online payment systems to route donations to that organization. However, if you are creating a fundraiser for yourself or for a friend, you will need to make sure that the money goes to the right place. Facebook uses Stripe, a credit card processing company, to run these transactions. You will need to know the account number and routing info for the account where you would like the money deposited. To set up the payment options, follow these steps:

1. **From the Fundraiser, click the More button (below the blue Invite button).**

   This opens a menu of options.

2. **Select Setup Payments.**

   This opens a window for linking a checking account to the fundraiser.

3. **Enter the routing number for the bank.**

4. **Enter the checking account number.**

5. **Click Save.**

UNFOLLOWING, EDITING, ENDING, AND DELETING A FUNDRAISER

From the fundraiser's page, clicking the More [. . .] button (located underneath the cover photo and title) opens a menu with several options.

>> **Unfollow:** Once you donate to a fundraiser, you may see updates from that fundraiser in your News Feed. If you'd rather not see those updates, you can unfollow the fundraiser by selecting this option.

>> **Edit:** Often as fundraisers you've created go on, you find that you want to edit some detail of it. For example, you may decide to add a FAQ section to the story or increase the amount of money you want to raise. Selecting Edit from the More menu opens the Edit fundraiser window where you can change most of the fields you filled out when you were creating the fundraiser. Remember to click the Save button if you make any changes.

>> **End:** If you choose to end your fundraiser, for whatever reason, the fundraiser will still exist as a page on Facebook, and you can still post updates there and view any info there. This may not be significant for all fundraisers, but sometimes, the families of people who might have had a memorial fundraiser, for example, take comfort in being able to go back and view the messages people have left for them after a loved one's death.

>> **Delete:** When you delete a fundraiser, all info about it, including any messages people have left, will be deleted from Facebook. Nonprofits that are associated with it will still receive any donations that have been made so far.

Chapter **13**

Scheduling Your Life with Events

I n the real world, just because all your friends are on Facebook doesn't mean that it's the only place you interact with them. In fact, the people you interact with most on Facebook may be the same ones you see at PTA meetings or at a book club or have over for barbecues. Facebook Events can help you bridge the divide between all the things that happen online and all the things you want to have happen when you're not anywhere close to your computer.

Facebook Events work well for the same reason lots of other Facebook features work: Your friends are here on Facebook. You can invite them to events, keep track of RSVPs, and use Facebook to send updates or coordinate participants in an event to help out. Facebook's Event Calendar also helps you keep track of upcoming events and your friends' birthdays.

You're Invited!

The first way you'll most likely find out about an event is through a notification. When a friend invites you to an event, a small red flag appears over the notifications icon in the big blue bar on top. Click the icon to open your notifications menu; then click the invitation to be taken to the event. You can also see event invites on the right side of your Home page, above trending topics.

A sample event appears in Figure 13-1. The event photo appears at the top of the page, much like the cover photo does on your Timeline. Beneath the event photo is the event's name, host (which can be a person, group, or Page), and privacy info.

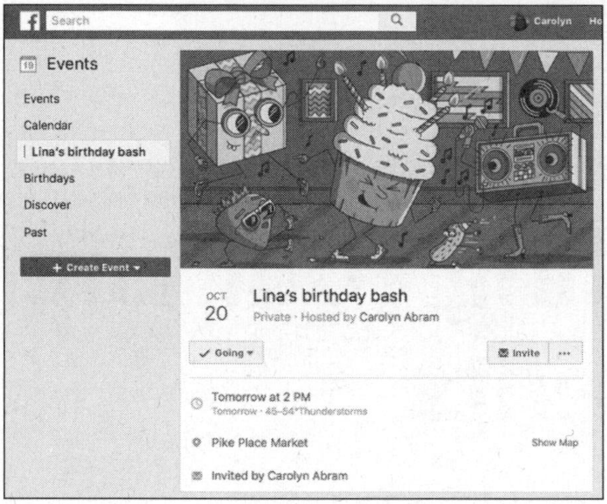

FIGURE 13-1:
An event on
Facebook.

Events have two possible privacy settings:

>> **Public:** Public events are just what they sound like — open to the public. Anyone can see the event with or without an invitation, view the guest list and posts, and join the event herself.

>> **Private:** Only people who have been invited are able to see the event and join it. Depending on the event creator's settings, invitees may be able to add more friends to the event as well.

The most important info about any event is in the center of the page: where, when, and what. There's a spot here for the date and time of the event, the location, and any info the event creator wants to share with guests. If the creator put in a specific address or location, you'll see a weather forecast. Click the Show Map link to open a map showing where, exactly, the party will be.

To RSVP to an event, look below the event photo where you can see who invited you to an event alongside three buttons: Going, Maybe, and Can't Go. Click on the appropriate button so your host can get an accurate head count. You can see other people's RSVPs so far beneath all the event's basic information.

Below the event info and RSVP box is the Posts section of the event (see Figure 13-2). The Posts section is where people can post messages and communicate with other guests (and potential guests) of that event. Event hosts use this section to post important updates — for example, a reminder to bring a sweater in case the weather is cold, or to let people know at which section of the park they'll be meeting. Depending on the event, the posts may be from people just saying how excited they are or from people coordinating rides or the food they'll bring to a potluck.

TIP

Certain kinds of events—those created by a group or a Page—have two tabs: an About tab with info about the event and a Discussions tab where all the posts are. If hosts have opted to only let admins post, then you won't see a publisher there. Even if you can post, your post may need to be reviewed by admins before it appears to the other guests. This is particularly likely for large public events.

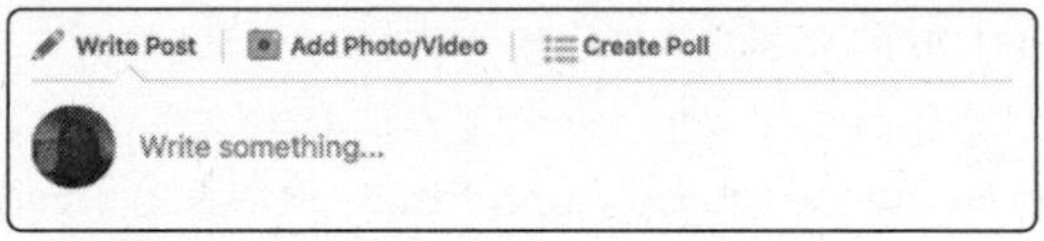

FIGURE 13-2:
Post here to communicate with other guests.

> ✏ Write Post | ▣ Add Photo/Video | ☰ Create Poll
>
> Write something...

To post to an event, follow these steps:

1. **Click in the Publisher (where it reads *Write Something*).**

This is the same way you update your status or post to a group, except in this case your post will be shared with people who can view the event.

2. **Type your message in the Publisher.**

3. **(Optional) Add photos, tags, activity, or location information by clicking their respective icons at the bottom of the Share box.**

4. **Click Post.**

Your message is posted to the Posts section of the event. Depending on settings, guests may be notified about it or see a News Feed story about it.

One feature of events is the ability to create a poll that all members of the event can respond to. This can make some of the planning that goes into certain kinds of events a little bit easier. Want to know how many people will eat pizza if you order it? If anyone has any food allergies you should know about? You can easily create a poll to ask them.

1. **Click the Create Poll tab at the top of the Publisher.**

The Write Something box becomes an Ask Something box.

2. **Enter your question in the Ask Something box.**

3. **Enter possible answers to the question in the Add an Option sections.**

   Although three sections are visible, you can add almost as many options as you can think of. To expand more option sections, add your first two options, then click into the third space. Another space expands below. As you keep clicking to add more options, more spaces will appear below you.

4. **After you add all the options you want, click Post.**

   Everyone who is invited to the event can then respond. Keep in mind that some events are public, in which case an unlimited number of people can respond.

While creating your Poll, click on the Poll Options button at the bottom of the Publisher to decide on two options:

>> **Allow anyone to add options:** By default, if poll participants don't see an answer that applies to them, they can create a new answer option. You can turn this option off if you'd rather they be forced to choose one of the options you provided.

>> **Allow people to choose multiple options:** By default, polls allow people to choose as many options as they like. If you'd rather people choose only one option, uncheck this box.

Public Events

Most of the time, you'll view an event because you were invited. But occasionally, especially for large-scale public events, you may see an event in your News Feed. These events look the same and have the same components as smaller, private events, but instead of the options for RSVP'ing being Going, Maybe, or Not Going, the options for public events are Interested or Going. When you are viewing the event, you can click the Going button to RSVP to the event, or the Interested button to see reminders about the event and receive updates from the event. In other words, "Interested" is the equivalent of subscribing or following someone. When you list that you are interested in or going to a public event, that may create a News Feed story that your friends could see.

Viewing Events

From your Home page, you can see reminders about upcoming events (including friends' birthdays) on the right side of the page. You can also view a complete Event Calendar by going to the Events page. To get there, click Events in the Explore section of the left-side menu. The Events page is shown in Figure 13-3. It lists your Upcoming Events (ones that you have been invited to, RSVP'd yes to, and said you are interested in). Beneath your upcoming events are public events that are happening in your area soon. On the right side of the page are search tools for finding events.

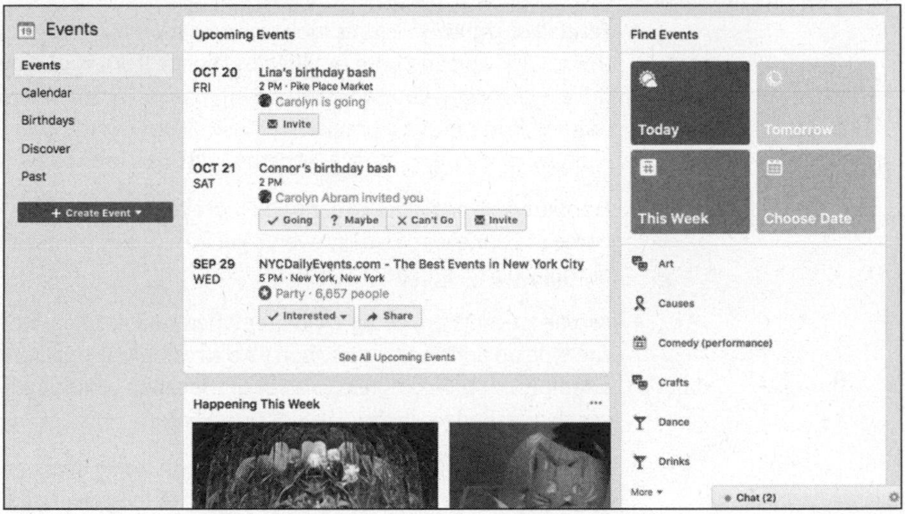

FIGURE 13-3:
Keep track of your busy social life.

On the left side of the page is a menu of options related to Events. You can click

>> **Calendar** to see a calendar of upcoming events listed by date.

>> **Birthdays** to see when your friends' birthdays are (assuming they share them).

>> **Discover** to check out events in your area you may be interested in.

>> **Past** to check out events you've been to in the past.

Creating Your Own Events

Eventually, the time may come when you want to organize an event. It might be a party or a barbecue or a book club or any other gathering of your friends. No matter what the context, follow these steps to create your own event:

1. **Click Events in the left-side menu of your Home page.**

2. **Click the Blue Create Event button at the bottom of the left-hand menu.**

   This opens the Event Privacy menu. You must choose whether you want your event to be private or public.

3. **Choose to create either a Public or Private Event.**

The Create New Event window appears, as shown in Figure 13-4.

4. **Fill out your event's info.**

You can fill out a number of fields:

- *Event Photo or Video:* Events look nice with a pretty picture to go along with them. Click Upload Photo or Video to choose from your computer's hard drive. Alternately, you can choose from one of Facebook's many pre-fab themes. You can see a preview of these themes in the Create Event window, or click the Choose a Theme button to browse by category.

- *Event Name:* Don't fill out your name here (a common mistake); this is the name of your event. Usually events get descriptive names like "Carolyn's birthday party" or "Labor Day in the park."

- *Location:* Events are generally better when people know where to go. You can type an address or a location (like a restaurant or a park). Facebook attempts to auto-complete to a specific location while you type. When you see the desired location, click it or press Enter.

- *Date/Time:* By default, Facebook assumes you're an impromptu party planner, so the date in the box is today. Click the calendar icon to change the date. Next to the date box is a box for the event's time. Type in the time your event begins. Click +End Time to also add an end date and time.

- *Description (optional):* This is the info guests will read about when they see the event, so provide any info that helps people understand what they're going to. For example, a bookstore event might list the readers who will be in attendance, or a party at a bar might let you know if there's going to be a cover charge to get in.

5. **Decide whether guests can invite friends.**

If you'd like for friends to be able to spread the word about your event, make sure the Guests Can Invite Friends box is checked. If your event is strictly invite-only, uncheck it.

6. **Click the Create button to create your event.**

TIP

If you are creating a private event, the button will read "Create Private Event."

You're taken to your event's page. Even though your event is created, you still need to make a few finishing touches, such as oh, I don't know, maybe inviting some people.

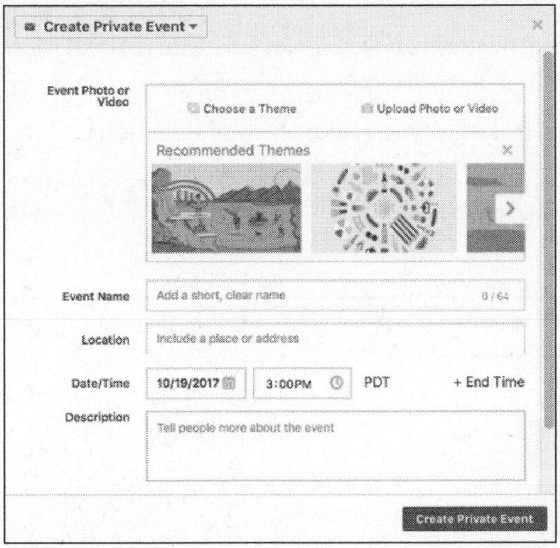

FIGURE 13-4:
Create your event here.

Inviting guests

Trust me, your party just won't be the same unless some people show up, and the number one way to get people to show up is to invite them. Inviting people to your event isn't a one-shot deal. You can follow these steps at any time to invite people to your event:

1. **From your event's page, click the Invite button in the upper right portion of the page (right under the event photo).**

   The Invite Friends menu appears. You can choose to invite Facebook friends, or Invite by Text or Email. Clicking either option opens the Invite window, shown in Figure 13-5. The only difference is whether you see Facebook friends right away, or search for them first.

2. **If you chose Invite Facebook Friends, click a friend's name or face to select her.**

   Because you may have a lot of friends, you can use the search box at the top to search for people by name. You can also use the categories on the left side of the window to filter down to certain friends. For example, you may be able to look at friends who live near you, or friends who are in a group with you. After you've selected a friend, they appear on the right side of the window under the heading "Selected."

3. **If you chose Invite via text or email, type a phone number or email address into the search bar at the top of the window.**

   Facebook will try to match you to a Facebook profile linked to that phone number or email address. If they match, tap on your friend's face to select them. If there is no match, or you're not sure, you can just choose to send the invite directly to that email or phone.

4. **Click Send Invites after you make all your selections.**

At this point, your guests receive the notification of a new invitation and will probably start to RSVP.

FIGURE 13-5: Inviting guests to your event.

Managing Your Event

After you set up your event and people start to RSVP, you may need to manage some things. You might need to provide more info or change the location to accommodate more people. If it's a large public event, you may need to do some moderation of the people posting. Here are some common management issues you might face and how to deal with them.

Editing your event's info

Need to update the event time or add info about a dress code? You can do so at any time by clicking the Edit button below the Event's cover photo on the right side of the page. This opens the Edit Event Info box, which looks exactly like the Create New Event box. You can change the name of the event, the date and time, add more event details, or change the location. You can also add more hosts to the event (by default, as the creator of an event, you're already its host). Hosts have the same capabilities you have in terms of editing the event.

REMEMBER

Click Save when you're done editing.

Canceling the event

If your life has gone a bit awry and ruined your event plans, not to worry — it's easy to cancel your event:

1. **From your event's page, click the Edit button.**

   The Edit Event Info window appears.

2. **Click Cancel Event in the lower-left corner of the window.**

   A window appears asking whether you're sure you want to cancel the event. You have two options here:

   - *Cancel Event:* Canceling an Event tells people that the event has been canceled but leaves the Event as a central place on Facebook where guests can communicate with each other.

   - *Delete Event:* Deleting an event tells people that it has been canceled and removes anything that's been posted to the event from Facebook. This is the option to choose if your goal is to act like your idea for that "Death"-themed fortieth birthday party never happened.

3. **(Optional) Write a quick explanation of why you're canceling in the Add a Post box.**

4. **Click Confirm.**

   The event is immediately canceled, and notifications will be sent to guests letting them know.

Messaging your event's guests

The most common way of communicating with your guests is simply to post something to the Posts section of the event. Much like posting something to your Timeline, you can simply click in the Write Something box and start typing.

In addition, you can start a group message thread with members of your event:

1. **Click Message Guests link, located under the RSVPs section.**

   A window for messaging guests appears. This window separates guests by their RSVP status. This can be useful for sending reminders to people who haven't RSVP'd or who haven't committed to attending yet.

2. **Click friends' faces to add them to the recipient list.**

   When a friend has been selected, a blue check box appears to the right of their name.

3. **Type your message into the Send a Message to Guests box at the bottom of the window.**

4. **Decide whether you want to send the message as a group message.**

   If you do not check the Send As Group Message box any message you send will appear as an individual message in each friend's Inbox. If you do check this box, a group message thread will be created and everyone on the list will be able to respond to each other. In other words, think of this as the difference between allowing people to reply only to you, or allowing people to reply-all on an email thread.

5. **Click Send.**

   Facebook sends your message to your guest list.

Removing guests

Although removing guests isn't something that happens often, if you're hosting a large event (say, a big public fundraising effort for a charity you head), you may find that certain guests are undesirable, especially in the Posts section of the event. You can remove any posts that are inappropriate (as well as reporting spam or abuse should that happen). If there's one bad egg, you can remove him from the event.

To remove a person from the event, follow these steps:

1. **In the RSVP box, click See All.**

   The Guest box opens.

2. **Click the X next to the name of the person you'd like to remove from the event.**

   A confirmation box appears.

3. **Click Confirm to confirm you really do want to remove this person from your event.**

   The person won't be told he was removed from the event; he'll just stop receiving notifications about the event. If your event also has a real-world component, you may want to compose a polite but firm message to that person letting them know they are no longer invited.

Chapter **14**

Creating a Page for Promotion

P icture your town or city. There's the park or school, the houses where people live, the offices where they go to work, and the stores they shop in. When you drive around town, you see all sorts of activities happening — whether people are walking their dogs, grabbing a cup of coffee, or working out. The world we live in is composed of people, the stuff they do, and the stuff that they need or want. People have real connections to all this stuff: the shops, the brands, the bands, the stars, the activities, the passions, and the restaurants and bars — things that are important. Facebook is about people and their real-world connections, including the connections that aren't just friends. On Facebook, all of these non-friend entities are represented as *Pages*.

REMEMBER

"Page" is a pretty common word on the Internet, so I always capitalize the *P* in Pages when talking about Facebook Pages.

There are two main types of Pages: *Community Pages,* which are collectively updated and managed by its fans, and *Official Pages,* which are updated and managed by authorized representatives of any business entity. People who manage a Page are known as administrators, or *admins.*

This chapter is all about understanding the world of Facebook Pages. If you just want to know what these things are that you've been liking and that have been showing up in your News Feed, check out the next section, "Getting to Know Pages." If you're looking to represent your business, brand, band, or anything else on Facebook, continue to the "Creating a Facebook Page" section.

Getting to Know Pages

You can do many of the same things with Pages that you can do with friends — write on their Timelines, tag them in status updates, and so on. The main difference is that instead of friending Pages, you like them.

When you like a Page, your information and access to your Timeline isn't shared with the Page and its admins, although any posts you make to a Page are public.

Anatomy of an Official Page

Official Pages are meant to be like Timelines, but they're intended for organizations. So if you've already read Chapter 4, most of the following will sound familiar. Figure 14-1 shows a sample Facebook Page from *For Dummies*.

FIGURE 14-1:
The *For Dummies* Facebook Page.

Here's the anatomy of an Official Page, across the top from left to right:

>> **Profile picture and cover photo:** Just like you and your friends, Pages use one photo to represent them across the site. Usually, it's a logo or an official press photo. Pages also have a cover photo, often an image that more broadly represents the organization's brand. A blue check mark to the right of a Page name indicates that it is a *verified Page*, meaning that Facebook has confirmed this Page is indeed managed by the company it represents.

>> **Like button:** The Like button is located under the Page's cover photo. To become a fan, click this button. (See the "Connecting and interacting with Pages" section for more on this topic). If you've already liked a Page, hover your mouse cursor over this button to open a menu where you can unlike the Page.

>> **Follow button:** When you like a Page, you automatically follow it and receive its posts in your News Feed. Hover your mouse over this button and click Unfollow if you want to like the Page but skip seeing its posts in your News Feed. However, you may want to follow a Page without liking it when you're interested in the content the Page produces, but don't want to be associated with "liking" that content. Like implies approval and not everyone is comfortable giving that approval to every entity they interact with.

>> **Share button:** Click this button to share the Page on your Timeline, in a group or event, or in a private message.

>> **Options (. . .):** Clicking the . . . icon opens a drop-down menu from which you can save, report, invite friends to like the Page, or block the Page. You can also use this menu to suggest edits to the Page admins or like the Page as one of your Pages (more on that in the "Using Facebook as Your Page" section).

>> **About, Photos, Posts, More:** On the left side of the Page, below the profile photo are tabs you can click to see specific content a Page has added, such as photos or events.

>> **Community:** On the right side of the Page is information about how many people have liked the Page, as well as a link to Invite your friends to like this Page. There may also be additional information here about which of your friends already like the Page.

>> **About:** Under the Community section is information about how long it usually takes the Page Admin to reply to messages, links to any external websites, and the type of Page it is (ex: Public Figure).

>> **Timeline (and Publisher):** The Timeline is the heart of a Page — it's where the admins post updates and where fans can leave posts and comments. Pages may or may not have a Publisher here, although most choose to let their fans interact as though they were friends (the Publisher on Pages has fewer

options than on your Timeline — usually just Status and Photo/Video). Scroll down to see posts the Page has added.

>> **Message button:** Click the gray Message button to say something directly (and more privately) to the admins of the Page you're looking at. Not all Pages have enabled the ability to get messages, so this button may be absent from some Pages.

Community Pages

Community Pages, or Pages that don't officially represent something or someone, tend to cover a wider range of things, from basic activities to political statements. Often, the object represented by these pages is something that simply can't be owned by a corporation or individual — things like "Cheese" or "I Love Dogs." Community Pages exist so that pretty much everything in the world has a way to be represented on Facebook. You can see the I Love Dogs Community Page in Figure 14-2.

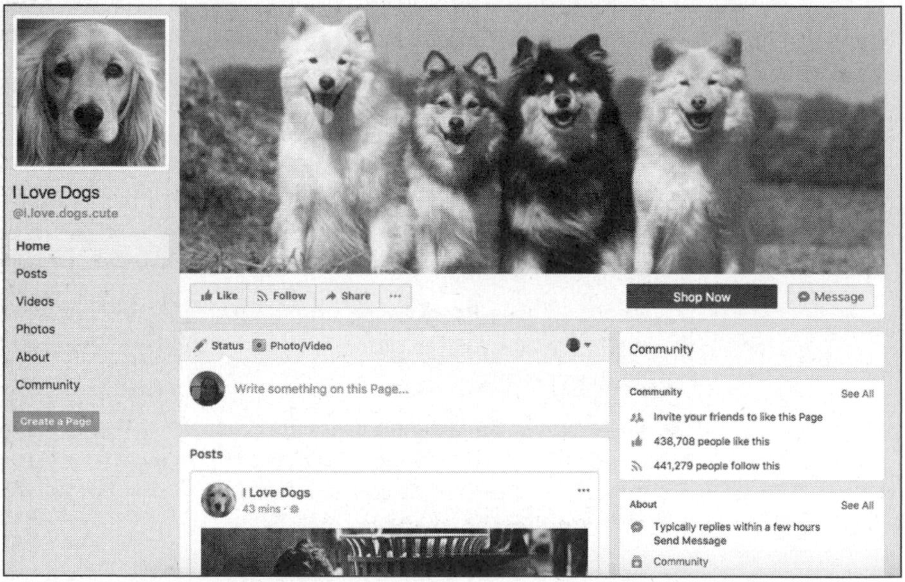

I Love Dogs
@I.love.dogs.cute

Home
Posts
Videos
Photos
About
Community

Create a Page

👍 Like   🔔 Follow   ➤ Share   ⋯   Shop Now   ⊙ Message

✏ Status 📷 Photo/Video   Community

Write something on this Page...   Community   See All
                                          👥 Invite your friends to like this Page
Posts   👍 438,708 people like this
                                          🔔 441,279 people follow this

🐶 I Love Dogs   About   See All
   43 mins · ⊙   ⊙ Typically replies within a few hours
                                             Send Message
                                          🏠 Community

FIGURE 14-2:
Ode to man's
best friend.

Community Pages look exactly like Official Pages. The Like, Follow, Share, and Options buttons are all in the same place. The main difference is that you'll see the word "Community" in a box on the right side, which helps you identify what type of Page it is.

Connecting and interacting with Pages

Wherever you go on Facebook, and in many places across the entire Internet, you'll see links and buttons prompting you to like something. You can like photos, statuses, comments, articles, websites, videos . . . if it's online, you can probably like it.

You can also like Pages. When you like a Page, it accomplishes a few things:

>> **Gives you a News Feed subscription.** After you like a Page, you may start seeing its posts in your News Feed. If you don't like what you see, you can remove that Page from your News Feed. To do so, go to the Page and hover over the Following button. From the drop-down menu, click Unfollow the Page. You will no longer see stories from this Page in your News Feed, but you will continue to like the Page.

>> **Find other Pages you like.** When you like a Page, Facebook may begin suggesting other Pages for you to like in a Pages You May Like box under a Page's cover photo. This is a great way to find Pages with useful and interesting content. For example, after I liked the Page for a local coffee shop, I saw the Page for a local hairdresser and liked that Page as well.

>> **Displays the Page you liked on your own Timeline.** Keep in mind that when you like a Page, it appears in the Likes section of your Timeline, and may appear as a News Feed story to your friends.

So what does this all mean for you? Basically, when you like something, you start a relationship with it that can be as interactive or as hands-off as you want. Frequently, people like a lot of Pages simply as a signifier or badge on their Timelines. However, just because you like *This is Us* doesn't mean you want to read episode recaps or watch interviews with the cast. And that's fine. On the other hand, if you like seeing those sorts of things, or interacting with other fans on the show's Page, you can do that as well. It's a pretty flexible system.

Creating a Facebook Page

A Facebook Page isn't equivalent to an account. Rather, it's an entity on Facebook that can be managed by many people with their own distinct accounts. The rest of this chapter takes you through all the steps of Page creation, administration, and maintenance.

Do I need a Page?

So, you want to represent something on Facebook, but you aren't sure of the best way to do so. The answer depends on what it is you want to represent and what you're trying to accomplish on Facebook. Facebook Pages, at their most basic level, are for anything that's not an individual person and can even be useful for individuals who are celebrities or who have a public presence beyond their friends and family. That includes small businesses, big businesses, bands, pets, charities, products, and much more.

Pages are best at promotion and distribution. If what you want is discussion and collaboration, groups might be a better fit for you. For example, if you are organizing a neighborhood fun run, you might create a Page to represent the event itself, post training schedules and weather updates there, and generally let people know what's going on. At the same time, you and other organizers might choose to create a group where you can discuss logistics. The Page is a public presence for everyone and the group is for the people running the show.

So whether you have a small consulting business, are fundraising for a local organization, or are a member of a performance troupe, creating a Facebook Page can work for you. You *do* need to be an authorized representative of any larger entity (for example, you shouldn't create a Page for a local congressperson unless you're working for her). But assuming that part is all squared away, you're ready to find out how to create and manage a Page.

Creating your Page

Before you get started, I recommend you read the Facebook Pages Terms at www. facebook.com/terms_pages.php. The terms clarify some of the expectations for owning a Page and who can create a Page for a business. One thing to note: you must have a personal Facebook account to create a Page and act as its admin. Your personal account will not be public information, so unless you broadcast the fact, your fans won't know which Facebook account is managing the Page.

There are also a few notes about who can see your content when you create a Page and age restrictions on your Page. I cover these topics throughout this chapter, but the terms provide a nice summary. If you violate these terms, your Page may be disabled, which could negatively impact your business. On the same note, if you use a personal Timeline to do the work of a Page (as I describe here), your Facebook account will almost certainly be disabled for violating the Statement of Rights and Responsibilities (which you can read at www.facebook.com/terms.php).

REMEMBER

Pages can have multiple admins. If you plan to have other people managing the Page you're creating, they can do so from their own accounts. There's no reason to share the email address or password with anyone. So use your real email address and birth date; don't create a fake persona just for the Page. Your information won't be revealed to anyone else, and it makes your future interactions on Facebook much easier. To create your own Page, follow these steps:

1. **Log in to Facebook with your username and password.**

2. **Navigate to the Account menu (down arrow), located at the right corner of the blue bar, and choose Create Page from the drop-down menu.**

   The Create a Page page appears, as shown in Figure 14-3.

3. **Click the category your Page falls under.**

   You can choose from the following:

   - Local Business or Place
   - Company, Organization, or Institution
   - Brand or Product
   - Artist, Band, or Public Figure
   - Entertainment
   - Cause or Community

   When you choose your category, a registry field appears.

4. **Choose your subcategory from the Choose a category menu.**

   Depending on the category you choose, there may not be sub-categories. For the purposes of these steps, I chose Artist, Band, or Public Figure.

5. **Enter the name of your Page into the Name text box.**

   Use the exact name of your business, just as you need to use your real name on your Facebook account. For example, if you are creating a Page to represent Anthony's Pizza, that should be the name of your Page, not *Anthony's Pizza Official Facebook Page.*

6. **Click Get Started.**

   Remember, when you click Get Started you are agreeing to the Facebook Page Terms.

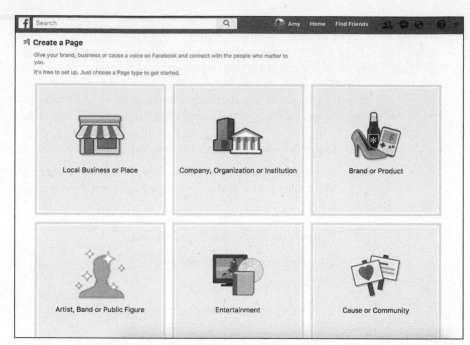

FIGURE 14-3:
What kind
of Page do
you need?

Getting started

In this section, I go over some of the things Facebook prompts you to do in order to set up your Page, as shown in Figure 14-4. Remember, this example is categorized as an Artist, Band, or Public Figure, so your own Page may look slightly different.

Step 1: Add a cover photo

You want to make a good first impression with your Page, and one of the easiest ways to do that is to choose a striking cover photo. To add it, click the Add a Cover button (to the right of the profile picture on your Page). You can select to Choose from Photos/Videos or Upload Photo/Video. Keep in mind that "Choose from Photos/Videos" means choose from the Page's photos or videos, so if you haven't added this kind of content yet, you'll want to upload something. When you're sure the image is positioned properly, click the blue Save Changes button.

TIP

A video may help you say more about your business than a photo. Cover photo videos are short videos meant to catch the eye of anyone looking at your Page. Videos must be 20-90 seconds long and a minimum of 820 x 312 pixels.

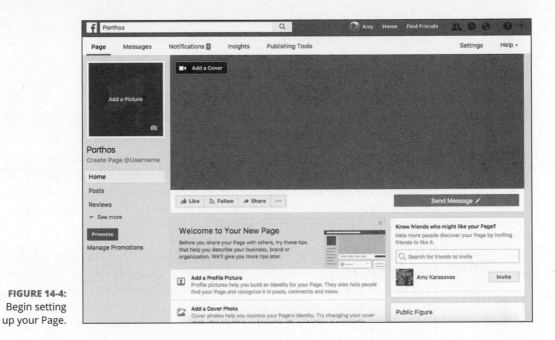

FIGURE 14-4:
Begin setting
up your Page.

Step 2: Add a profile picture

The second step is to get your Page's profile picture in place. You have two options for selecting an image:

>> **Click Take Photo** to open your webcam and take a photo. When the webcam interface appears, get ready to pose and click the blue Take Photo button.

>> **Click Upload Photo** to select an image from your computer's hard drive. Click Open or Choose to select the photo and upload it.

When the photo is successfully uploaded, it replaces the default profile picture on the left side of the Page.

TIP

Profile pictures are 170 x 170 pixels, and anything larger will be cropped to fit in a square. You want your picture to be as close to square as possible to prevent it getting cropped oddly. Also keep in mind that your profile picture is cropped as a circle when displayed in ads or News Feed posts.

TIP

You can edit your profile picture with filters, stickers, and text the same way you do for the profile photo on your personal Timeline. See Chapter 11 for details.

Step 3: Tell everyone about yourself

Add a short description of yourself or your business, organization, band, or whatever your Page is about, and a link to any other websites that represent you. This can be anything from a Twitter feed to your personal website.

Step 4: Create a unique address

Click Create Page @Username under the profile picture to choose a unique moniker for your Page. This also gives your Page a vanity URL that's easy to direct people to. If a local coffee shop decides to pick @seattlecoffeeshop as their username, their URL will be `http://facebook.com/seattlecoffeeshop`. See Figure 14-5 for the username interface.

WARNING

Your personal account must be verified before you can choose a username for your Page. If you aren't yet verified, head to `http://www.facebook.com/username`. You will be prompted to verify your account by having Facebook send a text to your mobile phone. Enter the code you receive in the text and you're good to go.

Step 5: Like yourself

Now that your Page is up and running, you can be the first person to like it! Just click the Like button to become your first fan.

Step 6: Invite your friends

One of the first steps in starting your Facebook account was to get some friends. This is even more important for Pages: Without likes, your updates and information won't reach anyone. A good way to start getting likes is to suggest your Page to your own friends. Look for the Know Friends Who Might Like Your Page box on the right side of your Page. Enter the names of your friends in the text box and click the Invite button next to their name when it appears. Your friends receive a notification that you invited them to like this Page.

Step 7: Add a button

There are plenty of things you can still do to customize your Page at this point, but one I highly recommend is adding a large button under your cover photo with a call to action. The default button is Send Message and for many Pages this is the action you want visitors to take. However, for service-based or retail businesses, a Book Services or Make a Purchase button can really come in handy. Hover over the Send Messages button and choose Edit Button from the drop-down menu. Click the Other Options button and browse the available button choices. Remember to click Save Changes when you've finished.

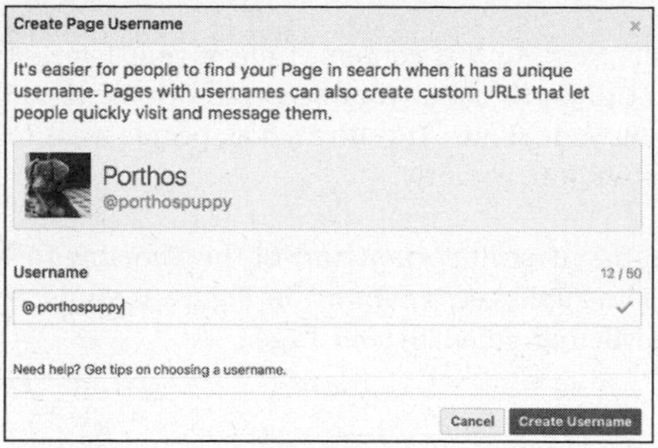

FIGURE 14-5:
Choose wisely.

Step 8: Pin to shortcuts

My final piece of advice is to make your life easier and place your Page in a prominent position on your Home page's left-side menu where you can access it with one click. Go to the ellipsis [. . .] icon under the cover photo and choose Pin to Shortcuts from the drop-down menu.

Sharing as a Page

After completing the previous steps, you'll be looking at a fairly empty Page Timeline. You can add a bunch of content immediately, or, like your personal Timeline, choose to fill it up over time. Your Page will be visible on Facebook right away, so if you are going to create it, be ready to start using it on a regular basis so that it remains active and interesting to people.

The Publisher

If you have a personal Timeline, your Page's Timeline will feel very familiar; it's the virtual scrapbook of posts you've added to Facebook. Your Page also needs a virtual scrapbook.

If you're a Page, the same things are true: People are going to want to hear from you and learn about you, and the place they go to do so is your Timeline. Any content you post to your Timeline also shows up in your fans' News Feeds. In other words, it's a very important place to represent yourself honestly and engagingly through continual updates.

REMEMBER

When I talk about "you" in this context, I mean your Page. So if you're a coffee shop, people want to know about your seasonal drinks. If you're a band, people want to know about your shows. If you're a dog, people want to know what sort of trouble you've gotten into recently.

As a Page admin, the most important part of the Timeline for you to understand is the *Publisher.* The Publisher, as shown in Figure 14-6, is where you and your fans create the posts that populate your Page.

FIGURE 14-6: Use the Publisher to send posts out to fans.

> ✎ Status ◉ Photo/Video ▣ Live Video ▦ Event, Products +   ③ ▾
>
> 👤 Write something...

The most basic post you can make is a *status update,* a short message letting people know what's going on, what you're up to, thinking about, and so on. Just like status updates from your personal Timeline, updates from your Page can be done quickly and easily, or with more options.

The basic steps:

1. **Click in the Publisher (where it reads Write Something at the top of the Timeline).**

2. **Type your update.**

3. **Click the blue Publish button.**

   The post now appears in your Timeline and will potentially appear in the News Feeds of people who have liked your Page.

ADD PHOTOS TO YOUR POST

Facebook offers some cool options to add albums or scrolling photo displays to your Page (covered in the later "Photos and videos" section). However, if you simply want to post a quick photo — for example, a company posting a photo from its holiday party, you can do so in Step 2 by clicking the camera icon at the bottom of the Publisher.

This opens an interface for exploring your computer's hard drive. Click on the photo (or photos) you want to add and click Choose or Open. Once you do so, you return to the Publisher, and the photo you selected appears as a thumbnail at the bottom of the post.

WARNING

The Publisher on a Page, though very similar to the Publisher on your Timeline, doesn't have all the same photo-editing options that your personal Timeline does. Make any edits such as rotation or adding filters before you add the photo here.

Click the X in the upper right corner of the thumbnail to remove a photo from a post, or click Publish when you're ready to share.

ADD FEELING OR ACTIVITY INFO TO YOUR POST

You can add information about what you (not you personally, but you the Page) are doing by clicking the smiley face icon at the bottom of the Publisher. Doing so opens a menu of various activities, and you can choose from any number of emotions your Page might be feeling or activities your Page might be doing. When you choose to add activity info, that info gets appended to the beginning of your post along with an emoji (or icon) representing that activity or feeling. You can see what this looks like in Figure 14-7.

FIGURE 14-7:
A day in a
dog's life.

ADD LOCATION INFO TO YOUR POST

You can add information about where you are when you post something by clicking the location pin icon at the bottom of the Publisher. This opens a text box where you can type in where you are (or where you were). Facebook attempts to auto-complete as you type; when you see the place you're looking for, click on it.

Location info gets appended to the beginning of your post. You can see an example of this in Figure 14-7.

REMEMBER

The icons at the bottom of the Publisher change depending on what type of Page you have. For example, the Page of a public figure might include an option to encourage people to contact their government representatives.

SCHEDULE OR BACKDATE YOUR POST

Many Pages find it useful to coordinate their posts with events or real-world happenings. You might not want to promote your holiday sale until a certain time or date, or you might want a specific post to appear on Thanksgiving, but not want to be sitting at your computer at either of these times. You can schedule posts to appear in the future by clicking the tiny down arrow to the right of the Publish button in the Publisher. Doing so opens a drop-down menu with three options: Schedule, Backdate, and Save Draft.

When you select Schedule, a window opens that allows you to choose when your post will appear. You can also choose to Stop News Feed Distribution for your post by choosing a date for the post to end. An end date doesn't mean your post will be deleted, but it does mean it will stop appearing in people's News Feeds. This can be really useful if you are promoting a limited-time offer or if you just want to make sure that your Page doesn't ever seem "stale" in News Feed.

When you select Backdate, a window opens that allows you to choose a date for your post. Posts that you backdate will appear further back on your Timeline, but could still appear in News Feed as a new post unless you check the Hide from News Feed box.

SAVE YOUR POST AS A DRAFT

You can save a post you are working on as a draft and return to it later. At any point while you are working on a post, click the down arrow next to the Publish button to open an options menu. Select Save Draft.

Drafts appear in a small box below the Publisher (only you and other admins can see this box). Click on the link to See Draft. This brings you to the Publishing Tools tab of your Page (more on that in the "Managing a Page" section). From there, you can click on the draft you want to work on, which opens the post in a new window. You can click on the Edit button to change the content of the post and save the new draft. When you decide it's ready for publication, click the down arrow on the right side of the Edit button and choose Publish. You will be asked to confirm that you want to publish the post.

BOOST YOUR POST

Boosting your post is a form of paid promotion. In other words, it's a Facebook specific form of advertising. Clicking on Boost Post opens an interface for selecting a target audience and setting an ad budget.

Photos and videos

In addition to adding photos or videos to your posts by clicking the camera icon in the Publisher, Facebook offers a few options for displaying photos. You can see these options by clicking Photo/Video at the top of the Publisher.

UPLOAD PHOTOS/VIDEO

Choosing to Upload Photos or Video basically functions the same as clicking the camera icon in the Publisher. This opens an interface for navigating your computer's hard drive. Select the photos or video you want to post and click Choose or Open. That brings you back to the Publisher where you can preview your photos or videos and write a little something to go with the post.

CREATE PHOTO ALBUM

Creating a photo album is a way to organize lots of photos. So a band might create an album of photos from shows, or an album of photos of merchandise, or an album of photos of the band on the road. Or all three. Selecting Create Photo Album opens an interface for choosing photos from your computer. Choose as many photos as you want and then click Choose or Open. This brings you to the Create Album window, shown in Figure 14-8.

FIGURE 14-8:
Create a photo album for your Page.

Creating photo albums is covered in detail in Chapter 11. So if this looks overwhelming to you, hop over there for a tutorial. As a brief refresher, from here you can:

>> Create an Album Title and Description

>> Add location info about where the photos were taken

- » Decide whether the photos should appear in High Quality

- » Decide if the Album should appear in News Feed or not

- » Pick a date for the album (or use the date information from the photos)

- » Tag people in the photos

- » Add captions to photos

- » Rotate individual photos

- » Add more photos

After you edit your album to your heart's content, click the blue Post button to post it to your Page.

CREATE A PHOTO CAROUSEL

Photo carousels are built using photos from an external website. So if you already have a band web page, you can reuse the photos that live there by simply entering your web address into the Destination URL box that appears when you click to Create a Photo Carousel. Doing so imports a selection of photos from your site. When you click Publish, the post appears as photos people can rotate through. Clicking on any photo takes them to your website.

CREATE SLIDESHOW

Slideshows allow you to choose 3–10 photos from your computer's hard drive. After you select these photos (the same way you would choose photos for a post or an album), Facebook automatically generates a slide show that plays as a video from your Page's Timeline. Add style to your slideshow by choosing a fade transition between each photo.

CREATE A CANVAS

Canvas is a special tool that allows you to combine photos and videos that load automatically in a full screen view from a post or mobile ad for your Page. The goal of a canvas post is to tell a complete story. A coffee shop might post a canvas following Arabica beans from harvest to cup.

Events

If you ever host an event for your business, you'll get a ton of value from using Facebook Events. Stores create events for their big sales, comedians create events for their shows, and clubs create events for their theme nights. To create an event, click Event, Products + in the Publisher, then click Create an Event. The Create New Event window appears. Fill in the Event info and click Publish. Head over to the event's page to invite your friends. Events you create for your Page are Public by default, meaning anyone can see and join the event.

If you haven't used Facebook Events before, see Chapter 13 to learn about creating and managing your own events.

Milestones

Much like on your personal Timeline, adding milestones is something you can do for your Page to acknowledge big moments in your history. If you're a charity you might want to create milestones for the date you were founded, or the day you reached a certain fundraising goal. You can add milestones on an ongoing basis as well as create as many past milestones as you want. Clicking on Event, Products + in the Publisher and then Add a milestone to your Page opens the Create Milestone window, shown in Figure 14-9.

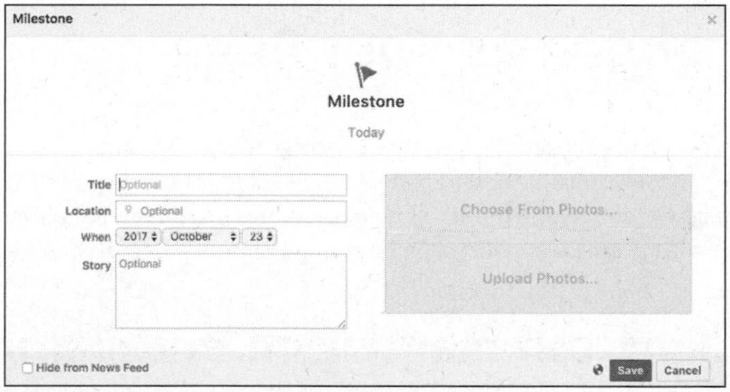

![Milestone creation window with fields for Title, Location, When (2017, October, 23), and Story, plus options to Choose From Photos or Upload Photos, a Hide from News Feed checkbox, and Save and Cancel buttons.]

FIGURE 14-9:
Add an important event to your Page's Timeline.

When you add milestones to your personal Timeline, Facebook asks you to choose the type of milestone so it can assign a particular icon to it and provide specific fields (for example, birth dates for the milestone of having a baby). On Pages, Facebook simply shows a generic milestone template and lets you edit it at will. You can create a title (for example: opened new offices downtown), then add photos, information about locations and dates, and provide an additional "story." When you're done, click the blue Save button and the milestone will be added to the proper place on your Page's Timeline.

TIP

If you are creating a lot of milestones as you set up a Page, make sure to check the Hide from News Feed button, which prevents those items from appearing as News Feed stories for people who have liked your Page.

Notes

Notes is Facebook's blogging feature. Notes look similar to the posts you might see on the blogging platform `Medium.com` — in other words, a big pretty photo on top and big centered text beneath. Previews of your notes appear as posts on your Page's Timeline. To create a note, click the Event, Products + tab in the Publisher, and then Write a Note. This opens the Create Note window. Click on the top gray section to add a photo to the top of the Note. Click on the Title to add a title to the note, and click where it says Write Something. . . to author your note or blog post.

While you are writing, you can click on the gray plus sign icon on the left side of your writing to add a photo to the text. You can also choose to embed photos and videos from popular sites such as YouTube, Instagram, and Soundcloud. You can click on the formatting icon (a series of parallel lines) to add formatting such as headers or bullet points to your text. When you're done, click the blue Publish button to publish your note. If you want to save and come back later to keep working on your note, click the gray Save button. You can access your draft from the Publishing Tools tab.

Using Facebook as Your Page

Part of using Facebook as a Page is being interactive. Pages aren't just ways for you to distribute information to people who like your business or band or book. Pages are a way for you to engage in conversation and be human (or as human as a Page can be) with people. Part of that is liking and commenting on behalf of your Page.

Liking, commenting on, and sharing posts

As a Page admin, when you're looking at posts on Facebook, you have the opportunity to like and comment on many of them *as* your Page. When you are looking at a public post from another Page, look in the top right corner of the post, where a tiny thumbnail of your (personal) profile picture appears next to a down arrow. Clicking that arrow opens a window for selecting who you want to comment as, shown in Figure 14-10.

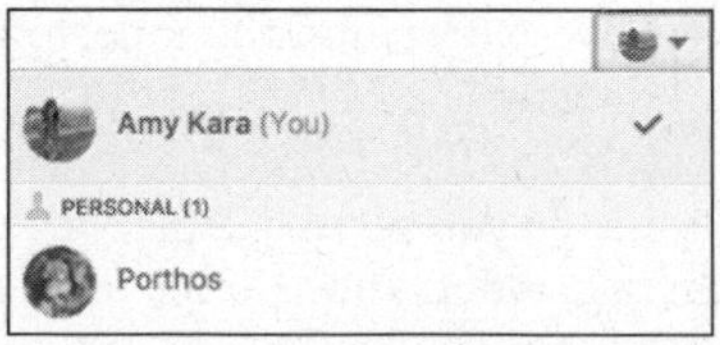

FIGURE 14-10:
Like or comment
as your Page.

Select the Page you would like to use to comment or like, and then click on any of the links at the bottom of the post to like, comment, or share that link on your Page.

When you like, comment, or share as a Page, changing who is commenting only works for that particular post. In other words, if there are ten articles you want to comment on as your Page, you will need to switch from your personal account to your Page, as described above, each of those ten times.

Liking other Pages

You can like other Pages as your Page. To do so, follow these steps. For clarity's sake, I reference your Page as LocalCoffeehouse and the Page you want to like as MajorCoffeeBrand.

1. **Go to the Page you want to like (MajorCoffeeBrand).**

2. **Click the More [. . .] button under the cover photo.**

   A menu of options opens.

3. **Click Like As Your Page.**

   A confirmation window appears where you can choose the Page you want to use to like MajorCoffeeBrand.

4. **Use the drop-down menu to choose LocalCoffeehouse.**

5. **Click Submit.**

Liking other Pages can be a great way to be involved with the other entities your Page interacts with in real life, and also a way to get ideas for what to post about. For example, if you are a restaurant and you like the Pages of other restaurants nearby, you might learn about local events that you also want to promote. There are so many possibilities for using your Page over time; this chapter really just gives you the basics. Other Pages can teach you a lot.

Managing a Page

The basics of using a Page are fairly simple: Pages are Timelines for non-people (or famous people); use them to share and interact with your customers and fans. Up to this point, this chapter has focused on those basics.

Once you have the basics down, however, it's worth noting that Pages is an incredibly powerful and diverse product. Pages can be created to represent the family dog or to represent the Smithsonian Museum. The needs for those two entities are pretty different, and yet Pages accommodates them both. In this section, I'm going to go over many of the settings and tools that Pages offers you beyond simple sharing. Some of these tools might seem superfluous to you. Some of the settings might not apply to you. I might miss certain settings that only apply to certain Page types (since my test Pages might be from different Page types). If you find yourself with a question I don't answer here, Facebook itself provides a lot of material for Page owners to explore and learn from. A good place to start is www. facebook.com/business/products/pages/.

You may notice that when you look at your Page, there is an additional menu bar across the page, right below the blue bar on top. Pictured in Figure 14-11, these tabs are only visible to you as the Page's admin. People who like the Page don't see this.

FIGURE 14-11: Page management tabs.

The first tab, Page, simply brings you back to your Page's Timeline. The other tabs are where you find options that help you get the most from your Page.

Inbox

Much like your personal Facebook account, Pages have an Inbox where you (and other admins) can respond to messages from people who encounter your Page. You will see a red box with a number indicating how many new messages you have. People don't have to like your Page to message it, and the sorts of messages you receive may vary. Figure 14-12 shows a sample Inbox, with an open message.

At first glance, this Inbox looks very similar to your personal message center, and it does have some similarities. Your message list is displayed on the left side of the page, with the newest messages appearing at the top of the list. Unread messages are in **bold.** The message you have open is displayed in the center of the page. You read a message thread from top to bottom (scroll up to see the oldest messages) and you can type your reply at the bottom of the thread.

Unlike your personal Inbox, the right side of the page displays any publicly available info about the person you are messaging with. This gives you a sense of whom you are talking to — where they are from, where they work, all the sorts of things that might be important to learn if someone is trying to contact you to make a professional connection.

FIGURE 14-12:
A Page Inbox.

Depending on what your Page represents, you might get a lot of "customer support" type questions in your messages as well. In those cases, it might be less important to know these biographical details about your customer, but it never hurts to put a name with a face when you are talking to your customers.

You can use the search box on the top left side of the page to search through your Page's messages by keyword or name.

Message options

When you are looking at the list of messages down the left side of the page, you have a few options for keeping track of messages. Hover over any individual thread and click the gear icon that appears to access these options:

» **Flag:** Flagging a message thread ads a tiny orange label that says "flagged" to that thread in the Inbox. You can flag a message for any reason and it's up to you and your fellow Page admins to decide what types of messages get flagged. You might choose to flag any message that requires a reply, or to flag messages that require urgent action. It's up to you.

» **Mark as Spam:** If you receive messages that are spam, click this option to remove them from the Inbox. Messages you mark as spam get moved to your Spam folder, which you can access by clicking the down arrow next to the word Inbox at the upper left corner of the Inbox.

» **Mark as Unread:** You can choose to mark messages as read or unread, again, signifying whatever you and your fellow admins agree upon. I usually mark messages as unread when I intend to reread them later.

>> **Archive:** Archiving a message moves it to the Archived folder, which you can access by clicking the down arrow next to the word Inbox at the upper left corner of the page. Archived messages reappear in the Inbox if either you or the other person adds another message to the thread.

Replying to messages

The basics for replying to messages as a Page are pretty much the same as any email, text, or instant message service. Type your response and click Send. Additionally, you can add attachments or stickers by clicking the paperclip or smiley icon, respectively.

Facebook also provides the ability to send what it calls *saved replies.* Saved replies are just what they sound like, common replies that you can save to more quickly send to people. Are people always writing in to ask what the delivery window is for your pizza shop? Create a saved reply explaining your policies. Then, anytime someone writes in asking that question, you can respond in just a few clicks; no typing necessary. Click the speech bubble icon to open the Saved Replies window, shown in Figure 14-13.

FIGURE 14-13: Create Saved replies here.

Saved replies are designated by titles (which the person you are messaging doesn't see). If you have a lot of saved replies, you can search through the options using the search box at the top of the Saved Replies window. To select one of the saved replies, simply click on the reply you want to send. This fills the reply box with the text from the saved reply. Then click Send.

You can click the blue link to Create New Reply. This opens a window for entering the title and text of the saved reply. Click to personalize the saved reply with things like the name of the admin who is replying, or the name of the person who originally sent the message. You can also add images from your computer's hard drive. Click Save Reply when you're done creating the reply.

Notifications

Whenever anything happens to your Page such as someone liking it, liking a post your Page made, commenting on a post, sharing a post, and more, it creates a notification. All the notifications about your Page are collected on the Notifications tab, shown in Figure 14-14.

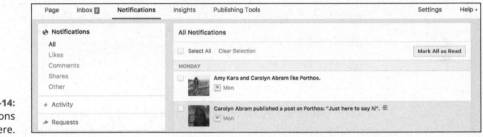

FIGURE 14-14: Notifications go here.

Notifications may or may not be something that winds up mattering to you as a Page owner. In general, evidence of people interacting with your Page and the content you post is considered to be a good sign of engagement, so if the amount of notifications suddenly change a lot or a little, that can be important to note. You can mark notifications as read or unread by selecting individual notifications (via the check box to each one's left), and then clicking the Mark as Read or Mark as Unread buttons.

In addition to notifications of actions, the Notifications tab shows you a record of *activity* and *information requests*. Activity includes things like people mentioning (or tagging) your Page in a post. Information Requests show up when someone comes to your Page and wants to find out something that isn't there. For example, if you didn't add a website to your Page when you set it up, people can click a link to ask for your website. Those requests come to this portion of your Page's Notifications tab.

You can control how you receive notifications from the Settings tab. I go over that later on in this chapter, in the section "Settings."

Publishing Tools

The Publishing Tools tab gives you the ability to quickly review your posts — ones you have already made, ones you have drafted, and ones you have scheduled. As shown in Figure 14-15, the Publishing Tools tab shows a list of your posts, along with some data about those posts.

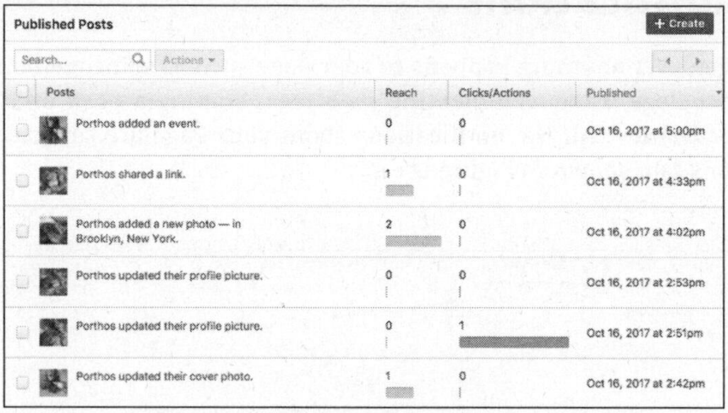

FIGURE 14-15: Review your posts and their impact.

The left side of the Publishing Tools tab categorizes your posts so you can quickly get to the type of post you want to review. For example, if you are logging in to see what posts other admins have scheduled for the upcoming week, you can click on Scheduled Posts to view only those posts. You can also use this menu to jump to your video library, to any forms you have created for Lead Ads, or any events you have planned.

When you are looking at Published Posts, you can see a thumbnail of whatever image accompanied the post and the title of it (if it had one). You can then view your *reach* for that post. Reach means the number of people who saw the post. Remember, News Feed (the main way your posts get distributed) works on an algorithm so that each person using Facebook sees what is most likely to be interesting to that person, so not all the people who have liked your Page will see your post. You can also see how many people liked or commented on your post. Finally, you can see when your post was published on the right side of the screen.

WARNING

It's worth noting here that as of time of publication of this book, Facebook has announced that going forward, News Feed will prioritize posts that are interactive and engaging to users. For the most part, this means posts from a user's family and friends will be prioritized while posts from Pages may see less traction than they're used to. The takeaway is that engagement is key — if your Page's post is receiving a lot of comments and likes, it's more likely to show up in your fans' feeds.

Settings

As I mentioned previously, Pages is a powerful and in many ways flexible system that accommodates virtually every type of entity that isn't a person. In order for a system to be that flexible, it needs to have a lot of options. And nowhere is the number of options available more apparent than on the Settings tab (see Figure 14-16). Here, I go through each setting. I try to include examples of how some of the more obscure settings might be used. Remember, depending on your Page and how you use it, many of these might not be relevant to you. Many settings will seem especially irrelevant if you're just starting out with your Page and don't have a lot of people who have liked it. If your Page has recently picked up in popularity and you are feeling overwhelmed by managing it, you may want to revisit some of the settings you had previously ignored.

Page	Inbox	Notifications	Insights	Publishing Tools		Settings	Help ▾
⚙ General		Page Visibility		Page published			Edit
🏴 Messaging		Visitor Posts		Anyone can publish to the Page / Anyone can add photos and videos to the Page			Edit
⚙ Edit Page		News Feed Audience and Visibility for Posts		The ability to narrow the potential audience for News Feed and limit visibility on your posts is turned off			Edit
🚩 Post Attribution		Messages		People can contact my Page privately.			Edit
🔔 Notifications		Tagging Ability		Only people who help manage my Page can tag photos posted on it.			Edit
💬 Messenger Platform		Others Tagging this Page		People and other Pages can tag my Page.			Edit
👤 Page Roles		Page Location for Frames		Other people can use your Page's location for photo and video frames.			Edit
👥 People and Other Pages		Country Restrictions		Page is visible to everyone.			Edit
👥 Preferred Page Audience		Age Restrictions		Page is shown to everyone.			Edit
⚙ Partner Apps and Services		Page Moderation		No words are being blocked from the Page.			Edit
▾ Branded Content		Profanity Filter		Turned off			Edit
📷 Instagram		Similar Page Suggestions		Choose whether your Page is recommended to others			Edit
★ Featured		Page Updates		Page posts are automatically published when you update Page Info, reach milestones, receive reviews and more.			Edit
🎬 Crossposting		Post in Multiple Languages		Ability to write posts in multiple languages is turned off			Edit
📋 Page Support Inbox		Translate Automatically		Your posts may show translations automatically for people who			● Chat

FIGURE 14-16:
Settings, so
many settings.

General

General settings include a variety of settings about how your Page posts and interacts with other people and Pages on Facebook. To open the settings related to these categories, click Edit to the right of each setting. When you adjust a setting, remember to click Save Changes.

>> **Page Visibility:** This controls whether or not your page is Published (publically visible) or not. If you want to make a lot of edits to your Page without people seeing those edits, you may want to opt to Unpublish the Page for a period of time while you make your changes.

>> **Visitor Posts:** By default, people can post to your Page as they would post on a friend's Timeline. You can disable this, or choose for people to be able to post text, but not photos and videos, or choose to review posts before they appear on your Page.

>> **Audience Optimization for Posts:** If you want the ability to "target" your post to certain demographics (for example, a post about your band's upcoming show in New York only being shown to people who live in New York), you can turn this setting on. Once it's turned on, you'll be able to access the Audience Selector by clicking the globe icon that appears in the Publisher.

>> **Messages:** If you don't want people to be able to message your Page, you can turn off that ability here. There are any number of reasons you might not want to use the message features — you don't think you'll have the time to respond to messages, or you would rather people contact you elsewhere, or you just don't think it makes sense for you.

>> **Tagging Ability:** You can choose to allow everyone to tag photos and videos you post, or you can choose to only let you and other admins tag photos and videos posted by your Page.

>> **Others Tagging this Page:** You can check this box to prevent people from tagging your Page in their own Timeline posts.

>> **Page Location for Frame:** This setting allows people to use your Page's location as a setting for a Frame they build using the Camera Effects Platform. This setting is fairly intricate in that it only applies to a small subset of Facebook users who create these frames.

>> **Country Restrictions:** By default, everyone the world over can find and view your Page. You can choose to hide it from certain countries, or only allow certain countries to see it.

>> **Age Restrictions:** By default, anyone of any age (well, older than 13, which is the youngest age at which you can use Facebook) can see your Page. You can choose to restrict this so that people under 17, 18, 19, or 21 can't see your Page. This is most relevant to you if you are creating a Page to represent a brand of alcohol or tobacco (and there is, in fact, an "Alcohol-related" setting that automatically adjusts the age restrictions for your Page).

>> **Page Moderation:** You can create a list of words that, if they are detected in a post, blocks that post from being posted.

>> **Profanity Filter:** You can choose to turn on Facebook's profanity filter, which has two settings: Medium or Strong. If someone tries to enter a post with a profanity, that person will be unable to add it to your Page.

- **Similar Page Suggestions:** This controls whether or not your Page will appear in Facebook's automatically generated "Page Suggestions." By default your Page appears in Page suggestions.

- **Page Updates:** If you update your Page's About section, achieve milestones, receive reviews, and so on, a post is automatically published on your behalf.

- **Post in Multiple Languages:** Allow other Page admins to post in multiple languages.

- **Translate Automatically:** People who use Facebook in another language will see your posts automatically translated into their language. Note that this feature isn't available to every single user.

- **Comment Ranking:** If you are a very popular Page that gets lots of comments and replies to every post you make, you may want to turn on comment ranking. This setting tries to determine the most relevant comments (as determined by people liking and replying to that comment) at the top of the comments section. If you don't turn this on, the most recent comments are displayed first.

- **Content Distribution:** Give users in some countries the option to download videos that you have added to your Page. Check this box to prohibit anyone from downloading your videos.

- **Download Page:** Click the Download Page link to receive a copy of your Page posts, videos, and Page Info. An email alerts you that the file is ready to download. This feature can be life-saving if content is accidentally deleted.

- **Merge Pages:** If you wind up with more than one Page for the same thing (it happens), you can merge the two so that it's easier to reach everyone who has liked either Page.

- **Remove Page:** If you want to delete your Page entirely from Facebook, follow the prompts in this setting. You have 14 days to change your mind and reactivate your Page.

Messaging

The Messaging section of your Page is where you'll go to communicate directly with customers and fans. Assuming you have kept your Page's ability to receive messages, you can adjust settings here. I go over the three most important ones:

- **Prompt Visitors to Send Messages:** If you want to encourage visitors to engage with you one on one, you can turn this setting on and they may see prominent reminders and prompts to send a message your way.

- **Response Time Display:** If you typically respond to 75% of your messages within a day or less, Facebook automatically displays your average response time to people who visit your Page. If you don't meet these two criteria, then no information is provided related to response time. You can choose to show either your average response time, or what you want people to expect as a response time (an hour, a few hours, a day).

>> **Instant Replies:** Even if you don't intend to respond to messages instantly, you can enable an *Instant Reply*, or auto-reply that gets sent to people whenever they write to you. Instant replies can include any information you think is relevant to messaging with your Page. Remember to click Save Reply when you're done writing your instant reply.

Edit Page

The Edit Page section is all about your Page's templates and tabs.

>> **Template:** By default, your Page uses the standard template, but if you click the Edit button next to this setting, you can choose from other pre-fab templates, including templates for venues, restaurants and cafes, or video creators.

>> **Tabs:** The rest of this page is devoted to the tabs on your Page. Click the Settings button next to each tab to get that tab's unique URL. This is useful if you want to send your Page's Photos to someone without asking them to wade through your Page to locate those photos. Some tabs also have additional settings. For example, the Review tab lets you choose whether fans are able to leave publicly visible reviews on your Page. The bottom of this page has a button to Add a Tab. Clicking this brings up a list of tabs you can choose to add to your Page, such as Offers or FAQ.

Post Attribution

Post Attribution settings dictate whether, by default, your posts to your Page will be attributed to you personally or to the persona of your Page. In other words, if I create a Page for my dog, Porthos, I can decide whether posts to Porthos' Page come from me, Amy, or from Porthos.

Notifications

Notifications always appear in your Notifications tab for your Page, but you can also choose if they go into your Facebook notifications (where notifications for your personal account also appear), your email, or via text message on your phone.

If you want to see Notifications on Facebook but are feeling overwhelmed by the sheer amount, you can choose to receive a summary of notifications every 12–24 hours. You can also choose to turn off specific types of notifications (for example, you might want to be notified about new comments, so you can reply right away, but you might not want to be notified whenever someone likes a post).

You can also turn off notifications about messages your Page receives. This can be helpful if most of the time you are using Facebook as yourself, and not your Page. Your Page's messages will always be available in the Messages tab.

Messenger Platform

This is an advanced group of settings that you'll use if you build or use apps or bots in the Messenger section of your Page. You can learn more about your options for using these apps and bots at `http://developers.facebook.com/docs/messenger-platform`.

The setting on this Page that applies to most people is Discover Visibility. By default this is set to Show, which means that people will be able to see your Page in a new Messenger section called Discover, which highlights local places and businesses they can message. If you find you're receiving too many irrelevant or spammy messages, toggle this setting to Hide.

Page Roles

Page Roles represent the different responsibilities that people who manage Pages may have. Often, you aren't the only person who represents your Page. You might have a small business and you may want all your employees to be able to post photos and announcements on behalf of your Page. Or you might need moderators to respond to people's comments and messages that you cannot respond to yourself. There are six different types of page roles, outlined below:

>> **Admin:** If you created a Page, you are automatically its admin, and you can control all aspects of your Page. That includes: adding other people as admins or other roles, editing your Page's settings, editing the Page, posting from the Page, sending messages as the Page, responding to and deleting comments and posts as the Page, removing and banning people from the Page, creating ads, viewing insights, and seeing who published as the Page.

>> **Editor:** Editors have all the same abilities as admins, but they *do not* have the ability to edit all of the Page's settings or assign Page roles to other people.

>> **Moderator:** Moderators have many of the same abilities as admins and editors, but they can't edit the Page or create posts as the Page.

>> **Advertiser:** Advertisers only have the ability to create ads, view insights, and see who published as the Page. Lots of companies specialize in helping people manage their online advertising presence, which is why this is a unique position you can assign out.

>> **Analysts:** Analysts can see your Page's insights and see who published as the Page.

>> **Live Contributor:** This role is for a person filming live video from a mobile device. They can post the content, but can't comment as the Page, create ads, access Publishing Tools, or see Insights.

As the admin, you can add someone to any of these roles from the Page Roles section of the Settings tab. Type a name or email address into the text field under the Assign a New Page Role section, then decide what type of role you would like that person to have in managing your Page. Click Add when you're done.

People and Other Pages

The People and Other Pages section of the Settings tab displays every person and Page who has liked your Page. Hover over any name and click on the gear icon that appears to take either of the following actions:

>> **Remove from Page Likes:** Removing people from Page likes means that person will no longer be shown as someone who likes your Page. It's basically a way to force someone to unlike your Page.

>> **Ban from Page:** If someone is being abusive or inappropriate on your Page, you can ban that person from ever interacting with your Page again.

Preferred Page Audience

Facebook recently removed this section to simplify settings. You may see a notice explaining the change.

Partner Apps and Services

Apps are a way for companies that are not Facebook to build functionality that works on Facebook. Apps for Pages often add specific functionalities to your Page for things like booking an appointment or ordering food from a delivery service. Click the blue Add Service button to scroll through a list of apps you can add to your Page. One way to get ideas for apps that might be useful to your Page is to look at similar Pages and see what apps they use.

The Partner Apps and Services section shows you all the applications your Page is using. If you no longer use some of these applications, click the gear icon next to their name and choose Remove Service.

Branded Content

Branded content is content you create to promote another company or product (it often resembles a regular piece of your content) in exchange for some kind of value to your company. As an example, if the popular website Buzzfeed decides to publish an article titled "10 Ways You Can Use Aluminum Foil That Will Blow Your Mind" and you notice that near the top it says "sponsored by Reynold's Wrap," that article is likely branded content.

From this Page, you can allow other Pages to tag your Page in a branded content post (this setting's default is off). You may want to toggle this setting to on if you think these tags can grow your Page's presence and fan number in a positive way. If you're a local coffee shop, you may appreciate the boost that comes from being tagged by a major coffee brand.

Once you turn this setting on, you can type the names of Approved Pages in the relevant field to ensure that only Pages you trust will be able to tag your Page.

Instagram

From the Instagram section, you can link your business' Instagram account to its Facebook Page. After you link these accounts, you can create ads on Facebook and show those same ads on Instagram as well as manage Instagram comments from the Pages Manager App.

Featured

The Featured section is where you can choose to feature certain Pages your Page has liked. A selection of Pages your Page has liked always appears on your Page, so choosing to feature some merely allows you to specify which ones you'd most want people to know you like.

Crossposting

Let's continue using the example of the local coffee shop. Perhaps the local coffee shop has partnered with a local artist to display her work on the walls of the shop. In order to promote the partnership, the coffee shop films the canvasses being hung and posts the video to their Page. In this scenario, the local artist may want to feature the same video on her own Page.

Here is the place to list the URLs or names of Pages you want to crosspost on. You can add any Page you want, but that Page has to add you as well before the ability to crosspost on that Page is available. If the other Page accepts your request to crosspost, you'll be able to see crosspost as an option when you choose Upload Photos/Videos from your Page's Publisher. Note that the other Page will be able to see the insights for that post (they will not be able to see insights for any posts that aren't crossposted).

Page Support Inbox

Page Support is a special Inbox for communicating with Facebook's Help Team about your Page. If you ever wind up needing help from Facebook with your Page (for things like resetting your password or following up on reported material), those messages can be found in the Page Support section of your Page.

Payments

A new feature lets fans make purchases directly from your Page. If you want to sell items on your Page, come to this section to connect a payment method via Stripe or PayPal. Note that Facebook does not charge a fee for any purchases made via your Page. You may also notice that you're unable to change the accepted currency – this is to help ensure that you are who you say you are in your personal account that manages the Page.

Calendar Settings

If you use Google Calendar to schedule your client appointments, this is a handy tool that syncs appointments made through your Page to your Google Calendar. Click Google Calendar and log in to your Google Account to add these appointments. Note that by logging in, you are giving Facebook permission to view your email address and manage your calendars – you will be prompted to click Allow to acknowledge this request before you finish logging in.

Activity Log

The Activity Log is a chronologically ordered list of every action your Page has taken (such as posting a photo) as well as every action involving your Page (such as being tagged in a status update).

Insights: Finding Out Who Is Using Your Page

After you create your Page, you might notice a tab at the top of your Page labeled Insights. The Insights tab contains all the data that Facebook can give you about who is looking at your Page, what they liked or didn't like, how they've been interacting with your Page, and how engagement has changed over time. You can see a sample Insights Overview in Figure 14-17.

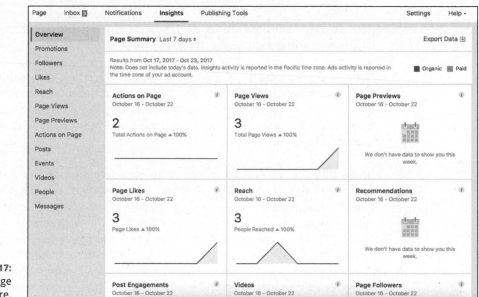

FIGURE 14-17:
View your Page
Insights here.

Similar to many of your Page's management tabs, a menu down the left side of the page lets you dig into different statistics: Likes, Reach, Page Views, Posts, Videos, and Followers. By default, you land on the Overview section, which gives you, well, an overview of all those different stats.

At the top of the Overview section the date range of the data is noted. Under are nine boxes, each with some numbers and graphs. I cover the three data points you'll be looking at the most.

>> **Page Likes:** Likes are the most basic metric for measuring how your Page is doing. Likes aren't everything; if you're trying to draw attention to your Page, someone clicking Like and then never visiting your Page again or reading anything you post isn't actually so useful. But your "Likes count" is a good baseline number to pay attention to. The Page Likes box shows you how many likes you have, and how much it's changed in the last week. If you notice a sudden uptick or downtick in likes, you might want to think about anything your Page has done or posted in the last week that might have mattered to people.

>> **Reach:** Reach shows you how many people have seen posts you've made in the last week.

>> **Post Engagements:** Post Engagements keeps track of how many people have liked, commented, shared, or clicked on one of your posts in the last week.

Click on any of the boxes to see a larger view of the graph as well as settings that let you toggle between weekly, monthly, and quarterly views.

None of these numbers, alone, really matter. Together, they paint a picture of what your customers and fans are doing, and if you are truly interacting with them, or simply shouting into the void. The way these numbers trend over time helps you learn more about your customers and fans and how they want you to interact with them.

Below the nine boxes are insights about your five most recent posts. Each post gets a row with a link to the post if you want to view it. You can see what type of post it is (link, picture, video, and so on), how it was targeted (everyone or a specific demographic), the reach of that post, and the engagement with that post. Again, you're not looking to achieve any one particular goal here, but you can learn a great deal. You might see that you have more engagement with photo posts, or greater reach when you target a post by demographic. Because managing a Page is an ongoing process, these types of insights let you make small adjustments to how you manage your Page and share with people who like your Page.

Chapter **15**

Using Facebook with Games, Websites, and Apps

This book spends a lot of time defining what Facebook is — it's a way to keep up with friends, it's a constantly updating newsletter about your friends, it's a way to share photos and posts. There's one more definition to add to the list: Facebook is a collection of information about you. It's not the cuddliest definition, but it's an important one to understand as you learn about *Facebook Platform.*

Facebook Platform is what Facebook uses to take your collection of information and (with your consent) make it available to other websites, game manufacturers, and app developers. What this means in practical, concrete terms is that you can choose to use your Facebook information to, for example, log in to a website like Pinterest and share your pins with Facebook friends. You can also use your Facebook information to start playing games like Candy Crush Saga or Bejeweled Blitz with your friends, both on Facebook and on your mobile phone.

The ways you'll see Facebook Platform integrating into your experience on Facebook may change over time. Right now, you'll likely see it mostly as games and as ways to log in to other websites to then post stories back to Facebook. No matter what forms it may take in the future, it's important to understand what you share with apps. In this chapter, I explain the more common examples of how you'll wind up using apps, and how to manage your apps and your information over time.

What Apps Need

For the purposes of this chapter, when I talk about apps, I'm talking about games and websites that were built by companies other than Facebook. But for the purposes of the next few sentences, I want to talk about an app that Facebook did build: Photos. As described in Chapter 11, Facebook Photos is an incredibly useful tool because it's easy for people to see your photos, as well as photos of you.

Photos works so well because Facebook knows some really important information about who you are (your name and face) and who your friends are (people who want to see your photos). Facebook also knows that you are okay sharing your photos through News Feed, because, hey, you're using Facebook to share your photos. In other words, Facebook uses your information — who you are, who your friends are — to create a useful experience — sharing photos.

Other apps, ones not built by Facebook, require the same things to work. They need to know who you are and who your friends are. Some of them may need to know when your birthday is or the type of music you like. An app like Photos has your permission as soon as you start using Facebook, but websites, games, and apps need to obtain your permission before they can get this information. Here's how to think about the information apps need and get when you use a game or outside website.

The basics

All apps need your basic information, also known as your Public Profile, if you want to use them. In other words, if you're not comfortable sharing this information with an app, you can't use it. Your *basic information* refers, in this case, to any information about you that is set to Public. For everyone on Facebook, this includes:

>> Your name

>> Your profile picture

>> Your gender

- » Your age range (ex: 21+ years old)

- » Networks (including professional and educational)

- » Language and country

- » Your user ID (This is the number associated with your Facebook account; everyone has a unique ID.)

- » Any other information you have shared publicly

In addition to this, when you start using a game or app, most will request that you share your contact email address with them. The app can store that email address in order to contact you in the future. This allows you to establish a direct relationship with the app so that the developers can always get in touch with you, without Facebook acting as an intermediary.

Giving your email to an application means you can get email newsletters and other updates direct from the source without logging in to Facebook. If at any time you don't want to share your email address with a certain application anymore, you need to unsubscribe from its email list through *the app developer* (in other words, through whatever company makes the app) as opposed to through Facebook.

The slightly less basic

In addition to basic information, apps might require information that is not publicly available. What information this includes depends entirely on the app and what it does. Here are some examples of information an app might want to use:

- » Your list of friends

- » Things you like (books, music, movies, Pages, and so on)

- » Things your friends like (books, music, movies, Pages, and so on)

- » Location information (Hometown, Current City)

- » Your birthday

- » Your photos

- » Your posts

- » Posts that have been shared with you

Permission to act

In addition to all the types of information apps need from you, apps also need permission to take certain actions, including things such as the following:

>> **Posting to your Timeline on your behalf** (for example, creating a post when you win a game). You can choose who can see these posts using the regular Privacy menu, which is covered in Chapter 6.

>> **Sending you notifications.** Notifications are like the notifications you receive from Facebook about being tagged in a photo or invited to an event. Games or apps may send you notifications when it's your turn in a game or when you're receiving a game challenge from another player.

Games on Facebook

The most common type of app on Facebook now is a game. Games can range from matching games like Bejeweled Blitz or Candy Crush Saga to casino games like Texas HoldEm or Bingo Blitz. Whenever you click to play a game on Facebook, you see the Continue to Game window, shown in Figure 15-1.

FIGURE 15-1:
Continue to play
your game?

The moment you see this window is the moment of truth in terms of deciding whether you want to share your information with the game to play it. The window provides a few pieces of information to pay attention to:

>> **Your Name:** If you share your computer with other people, when you see this window you want to make sure that your name is the one you are looking at. Look for the blue button that says Continues as *<Your Name>*.

>> **What the app receives:** Facebook provides a list of the information the app will receive when you click Continue as *<Your Name>*. Often that is just the Public Profile I mentioned earlier. Sometimes it will include other pieces of information such as your email address, birthday, or Friend List. You can choose to edit what you provide to an app by clicking either Edit This or Review the Info You Provide. Clicking the latter link opens a list of information that the app has requested (shown in Figure 15-2). Uncheck the circle to the right of any piece of information to prevent that info being shared with the game.

You can't uncheck sharing your Public Profile with a game. If you don't want to share your basic information with a game, you can't play it.

REMEMBER

>> **Permission to Act information:** Most games have a notice at the bottom of the Continue to Game window that says, "This doesn't let the app post to Facebook." Many games will ask for permission to post later, once you've already started playing. If this notice does ever say that it will allow the game to post to Facebook, make sure you are comfortable with that happening before you click Continue as *<Your Name>*.

When you have reviewed this information and are comfortable with what you are about to share with the game, click the Continue as *<Your Name>* button to go to the game's Home page.

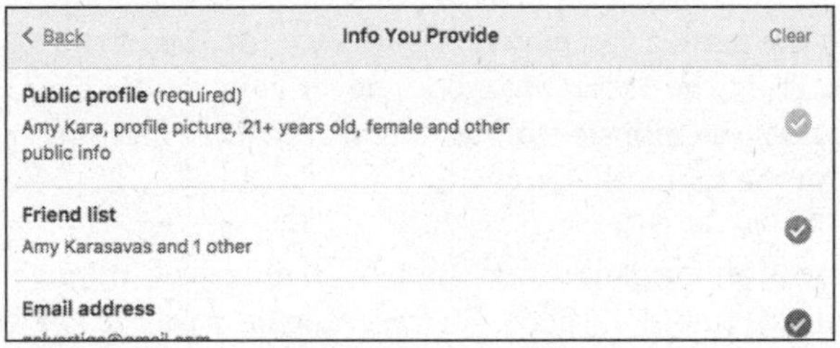

< Back	Info You Provide	Clear
Public profile (required) Amy Kara, profile picture, 21+ years old, female and other public info		⊘
Friend list Amy Karasavas and 1 other		⊘
Email address		⊘

FIGURE 15-2:
Info that your
game requests.

Game Home pages on Facebook

You can see a sample Home page (for Candy Crush Saga) in Figure 15-3. Its Home page basically prompts you to start playing the game. Notice that the big blue bar is still at the top of the screen, which means that if you get bored playing this game, you can easily go to your Facebook Home page or Timeline.

FIGURE 15-3:
The Home page for Candy Crush Saga.

Some games don't have Home pages within Facebook; instead when you click on them you're taken to a new browser window or tab to play your game on the game's website. Depending on what game you're playing, you can follow that game's prompts to learn how to make matches, find the bad guy, or win the poker pot!

Sidebar links

The left-side menu on your Home page is where you go to get to different parts of Facebook: your groups, News Feed, events, and so on. Links to the games you play most often will appear in the Shortcuts section of the side menu.

You can pin the games you play most often to the top of the Shortcuts section for easy access. From the Shortcuts menu, hover your mouse over the game you want to add and click the ellipsis icon that appears next to it. You can then select "Pin to Top" from the menu that appears.

TIP

If you've used lots of games and apps over time, you might not see all of them listed in the side menu. If this is the case, the best way to see all your games is to click on Settings from the Account menu (down arrow) in the blue bar. Continue to the Apps section to see every game or app you've ever given access to.

Invitations and notifications

Just like you can invite friends to events, you can also invite friends to play games with you. After your friends are playing the same game as you or using the same application, you can send them requests for specific actions. App invites and requests appear in your friend's notifications on the friend's Home page.

Often, when you send a request or invitation through a game, a preview window appears, as shown in Figure 15-4. This shows you what your friend will see in his notifications and asks you to confirm that you want to send the invitation or request. Click the blue Send Request button if you're happy with the invite.

WARNING

In Figure 15-4, note the Don't Ask Again Before Sending Requests To *<friend>* From This App check box below the preview. If you leave this check box selected, the app will be able to send that friend requests on your behalf as often as it wants. Uncheck this box so that you always know when an app is sending your friend a request.

Posts

As you play games, you may be prompted to post things to your Timeline. Figure 15-5 shows what one such prompt might look like. In this case, it's a game prompting you to share that you completed another level. If you want to share these achievements with friends, that's great. Click the Post to Facebook button and feel free to add your own comments to the text field.

If you'd rather not post to your Timeline about something like this, just click Cancel and continue with whatever it was you were doing.

The Game Store

If you find yourself really into playing games on Facebook, the Game Store can be a great place to find out about new games. To get there, click on the Games link in the left-side menu (in the Explore section of the Home page) and then click on Game Store from the left menu of the Games page. Figure 15-6 shows the Game Store.

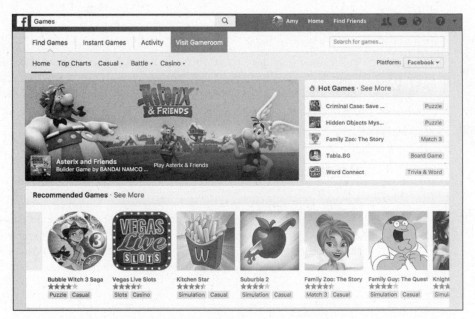

FIGURE 15-6:
The Game Store.

The top portion of the Game Store showcases a rotating list of "Featured" games. You can also see "Hot Games" listed on the right side of the page. Click to look at games by category (Casual, Battle, or Casino), or scroll down to see recommended games. You can search for games in the upper-right corner of the page.

At the very top of the page, right below the blue bar, are four tabs. By default, whenever you click to go to the Game Store you arrive on the Find Games tab, where you can search for a game to play. The Activity tab displays any requests or invites you've been sent from friends playing a game. A red flag indicates how many unread items await. Instant Games are games that are available to play immediately in your Facebook messenger – no loading necessary. Clicking the blue Play button launches a version of the Continue to Game window that shows which information of yours the game will have access to. Click Play Now to continue or navigate away from the game if you decide against it. The last tab is Gameroom, which is software you can install on your PC desktop or laptop to play games off Facebook. This option is geared to avid gamers.

Whenever you click on a game from the Find Games tab, a Continue to Game window opens as seen in Figure 15-7. If you want to learn more about the game, click on the arrows in the upper portion of the window to page through a slide show with screen shots and information about how to play the game. You can use the buttons at the top of the window to like or share the game, or to visit the game's Page on Facebook. If you decide you don't want to play the game after all, click on the X in the upper right corner to close the window and return to the Game Store.

FIGURE 15-7:
Continue to Game from the Game Store.

Using Facebook Outside of Facebook

Believe it or not, there are websites out there that aren't Facebook. Websites like Yelp can help you find a place to eat. Or you might watch television at www.hulu.com. Or you might create pin boards of interests on www.pinterest.com. Many of the most popular websites allow you to use your Facebook credentials to speed up the process of getting started on a new site, as well as to share activity more widely with your friends on Facebook.

Figure 15-8 shows the landing page for www.pinterest.com. Pinterest is a website that allows you to create collections (called boards) of interesting links or images you find on the web. For example, if you're planning to get a haircut, you could create a board where you "pin" images of hairstyles you like. What's important in Figure 15-8 is that there are a few ways to get started on Pinterest — you can enter your email and create a password, log in with your Google account, or you can click the big blue Continue with Facebook button. On some websites, this might say Log in with Facebook, but the effect is the same; clicking it brings up the Log in with Facebook window, shown in Figure 15-9.

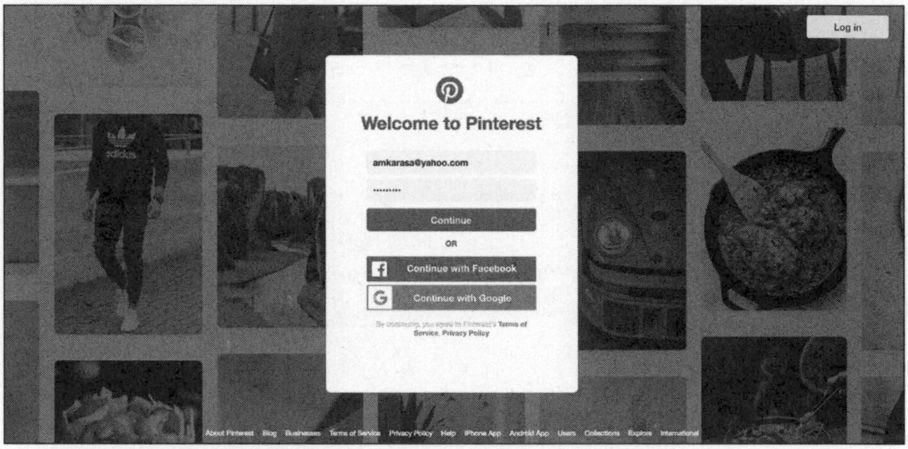

FIGURE 15-8:
A few ways to join.

FIGURE 15-9:
Log in with Facebook.

If this looks familiar, that's because it's more or less the same as the Continue to Game window shown in Figure 15-1. And that's because the same thing is happening here: You are deciding if you want to share your Facebook information with a company that is not Facebook. Just like the Continue to Game window, the Log in with Facebook window tells you the following information:

>> **Your name:** *Your name* is your first name that you use on Facebook and you'll see it in the blue Continue as <*Your Name*> button.

>> **The name of the website you are about to log in to:** In this example, Pinterest is the website you are about to log in to.

>> **The information that website will receive:** Click the Edit This link to change the information that you allow the website to get, but at a minimum you are required to share your Public Profile.

>> **Information about permission to act:** In other words, it tells you whether clicking Continue will allow the website to post information back to Facebook on your behalf.

If you're okay sharing this information, click Continue as <*Your Name*> to start using the website. Some websites may ask you to enter your email address after this step so that they can contact you directly instead of through Facebook.

I chose Pinterest as an example because it shows some of the ways you might find it convenient to use your Facebook account to log in. At its most simple, signing up through Facebook saves you the time it takes to create a new account. When you first join, most websites ask you to enter your name, birthday, create a password, add a profile picture, and so on and so on. Signing up through Facebook takes care of that for you (in fact, you can see your Facebook profile picture appear on the site you are using).

Perhaps more important, sites like Pinterest have a social element to them: You likely care about the things your friends have pinned, reviewed, watched, and so on. By logging in with Facebook and giving access to information like your Friend List, Pinterest can quickly help you find people you want to follow or invite to join Pinterest, by matching your Friend List to their own list of users.

You can also choose to share your Pinterest boards on Facebook, which means even if your Facebook friends don't use Pinterest themselves, they'll be able to see when you've created a new collection you want them to know about.

Mobile Apps and Facebook

If you have an iPhone, Android, or other smartphone that uses apps, you can connect your Facebook account with mobile apps. This is very similar to the way you connect your account with websites. In fact, because many websites, like Pinterest, also have mobile apps, you may wind up signing up with Facebook on the web, only to use an app on your phone, or vice versa. Similarly, many games you play on Facebook have mobile app counterparts, so you can continue a game on your phone whenever you are forced to step away from your computer.

REMEMBER

Figure 15-10 shows an example of the mobile Log In with Facebook screen. Like the Log in with Facebook screens you would see when using Facebook on the web, the moment you tap Continue as <Your Name> on this screen on your mobile device is the moment you share your information with the app and link your Facebook account to the app.

And like the permission windows you see on your computer screen, this screen on your mobile shows the following information:

>> The app's name

>> Your name

>> The information the app will receive

>> Information about whether the app can post to Facebook

FIGURE 15-10:
Logging in to an
app with
Facebook from
your smartphone.

When you use Facebook to log in to an app on your phone, you reap the same ben-efits as using it to log in to a website:

» Automatic creation of your account and profile without having to enter in your details

» Use your Facebook Friend List to find friends within the app

» Share content from the app back to Facebook quickly and easily when you want to

Managing Your Games, Websites, and Apps

There are so many apps and games out there that I couldn't even begin to write "Apps and Games For Dummies." You'll need to learn about the games you choose to use by playing them, and the websites you log in to by using them. At the same time, because you are using Facebook with these games, websites, and apps, you still control your Facebook information and how it gets used.

For the purposes of discussing how you can change settings related to games, websites, and mobile apps, I will be referring to all these incarnations as *apps*. You can view your current settings for any app by following the steps below:

1. **From any page on Facebook, click the Account menu (down arrow) in the big blue bar at the top of the page.**

2. **Click Settings from the menu that opens.**

   This brings you to the Settings pages.

3. **On the left side of the page, click Apps.**

   This opens the App Settings page. The top portion of the page displays the games you've used, websites you have connected to your account, and mobile apps you have logged in to with your account.

4. **Hover your mouse cursor over the app you want to review and click the pencil icon that appears.**

   This opens a window, shown in Figure 15-11, that displays information about that app and your information.

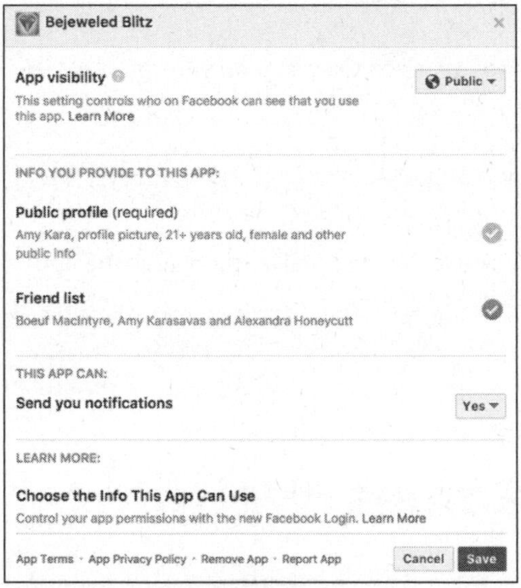

FIGURE 15-11: Edit what permissions the app has here.

App visibility

The top portion of the App Settings window displays the current *visibility* of the app. In this case, visibility refers to who can see that you use the app in question. The visibility is controlled by the same privacy menu that you use to choose who can see posts you make. Click on the drop-down menu to choose whether this information is visible publicly, to just friends, or to a custom set of people.

TIP

Many apps automatically set their visibility to Only Me. So if your friend Tammy is also playing Candy Crush Saga, but she can't locate your account in the game, try changing this setting to Public or Friends.

Info you provide to this app

The bulk of the App Settings window reviews the information that you shared with the app when you started using it. Each type of information the app requested is listed here, and a blue check mark signifies that it is currently being shared. Beneath the information type, you can see specifically what is shared. For example, you might see that you share your Likes with an app, and those likes include the TV show Parks and Recreation, Barack Obama, and 21 other Pages.

You can click to uncheck any type of information from the list except your Public Profile (which, remember, includes your name, profile picture, age bracket, gender, and other information you share publicly).

This app can

The This App Can section reviews what permissions the app has, usually whether it can post to your Timeline on your behalf, and if it can send you notifications. Use the drop-down menus to change these permissions to yes or no.

Learn more

The Learn More section provides links to the Help Center where you can learn about many of the topics covered in this chapter, including how to get in touch with the developers of the app.

REMEMBER

If you change any of the settings in the Edit App Settings window, click the blue Save button at the bottom of the window to make sure the new settings stick.

Removing apps

The simplest way to adjust how an app interacts with your information is simply to revoke its ability to interact with your information. This option makes sense only if you are 100 percent finished with an app — that is, you don't plan to use it again in the future.

To remove an app, go to the App Settings page (as described in the section "Managing Your Games, Websites, and Apps") and hover your mouse cursor over the app you want to remove. Click the X that appears in the upper right corner. A window pops up explaining that doing so removes it from your Facebook account, but that the app may still have some of the data you shared with it (it just won't get any new data going forward). You can then choose to delete all the app's activity on Facebook by selecting the Delete All Your <app> Activities Including Posts, Photos, and Videos On Facebook check box. Clicking the Remove button finishes the process.

When you remove an app, you will no longer be able to use the app, and it won't be able to send any information or posts to your Timeline or invitations to your friends. At the same time, because so many apps exist outside of Facebook, you have to keep in mind that it will still be able to contact you via your email address, and it may still have an account for you created via Facebook. If you want to cut off an app completely, you may need to delete your information and close your account on another website separate from Facebook.

Apps others use

When your friends use other websites and apps in conjunction with Facebook, they may find it useful to see their friends' (in this case, your) information — for example, a game might want to know if your friend's friends (for example, you) are online so they can challenge someone to a new round of the game. This information can be made available through your friend even if you are not a user of that game, app, or website.

To control what information apps can see about you through your friends, click Edit in the Apps Others Use section of the Apps Settings tab. In the window that opens, use check boxes to select (or deselect) what information can be made available to apps through your friends. Click the Save button when you're finished.

Opting out

If you've been reading this chapter and you're getting more and more queasy about the idea of using games and apps, you can consider opting out of using apps entirely. This isn't a step I personally recommend because applications can be a lot of fun and very useful. But if you're very protective of your information, you can effectively turn off apps.

From the App Settings page, click Edit in the Apps, Websites, and Plugins section of the page. The window that opens explains what Platform is and how you can use it, as well as what you will and won't be able to do if you turn it off. If you are confident in your decision, click the blue Disable Platform button.

Clicking this button effectively removes all the apps you have used and prevents your account information from being used by any application ever again. If, at some point in the future, you find an app you do want to use and click any of the Play Now buttons, you will be prompted to turn Platform back on.

Controlling what you see from friends

News Feed can be a great way to discover what apps your friends use, but it can be overrun with app stories, blocking out the interesting content that's not related to those games and apps. Here are a few tips to keep your News Feed (and the rest of your Facebook) from being cluttered by apps:

>> **Hide from News Feed.** If your News Feed is inundated with posts from apps, click the gray ellipsis or down arrow at the top right of the post. A menu of options appears, including Hide All From <app>. When you click Hide, the post disappears from News Feed and is replaced by text confirming that it has been hidden.

>> **Block an app.** If you find an app offensive or it keeps sending you invites or requests, you can block it. From the Settings page, navigate to the Blocking tab using the left menu and enter the app's name in the text field in the Block Apps section. The app will no longer be able to contact you via Facebook or see any of your info.

>> **Block a friend's invites.** Sometimes just one person is the problem. The person may be sending you invites or requests from multiple apps, and it's driving you nuts. Navigate to the Blocking section of the Settings page and enter your friend's name into the text field in the Block App Invites section. Then, any invites or requests she sends you will automatically be ignored and won't generate any notifications on your Home page or in your email. You'll still be friends with her, and you'll still see posts from her such as status updates and photos; you just won't get the app stuff anymore.

TIP

If you don't want to see app stories in your News Feed, but still want to know what your friends are up to, Games Feed may be for you. Click on Games Feed from the Explore section of the left-side menu of your Home page to see a list of actions your friends have taken within apps and games.

Reporting offensive apps

If you are using an app and you think it's offensive, using your information inappropriately, spammy, experiencing bugs, or not working properly, you can send a report to either Facebook or the app developer. Follow the steps at the beginning of this section to open that app's App Settings window. At the very bottom of the window are links, including one to Report App.

Once you click that link, a window opens with possible reasons that you are reporting the app. Depending on what you choose, you will be prompted to send the report either to Facebook or to the app developers.

5

The Part of Tens

Chapter **16**

Ten Ways to Make the Most of Your Facebook Content

I spend a lot of time in this book emphasizing how easy things are to do or reminding you of the simplest way to do things. Want to update your status? Click, type, post. Want to post a picture from your phone? Tap, select, post. Using Facebook is meant to be easy and seamless when you want. This chapter, however, is about some of the ways you can go beyond the basics. Some of these things are ways to make your content a little more special, a little less rushed. Others are ways to take stock of your history on Facebook, organize it, and get nostalgic for it. These are the kinds of things that when I've seen them on Facebook, I think to myself: How do I do that? Well, here's how.

Remember the Past

Quick, what were you doing a year ago? Not, like, in general. But exactly 365 days ago. Were you having a good day or a bad one? Did you go to the grocery or to a party or just to work like normal? If you've been using Facebook for over a year, and like most people, use it every day, you can find out using the On This Day app. On This Day is an app created by Facebook and is available to you as soon as you create your Facebook account. You can find it by looking in the Apps section of the left sidebar and clicking On This Day.

On This Day is simple: It resurfaces posts you made on this day in the past. Depending on how long you've been on Facebook, it could be from several years ago or from just last year. Your memory might be a photo you shared or a status post or a wall post someone left for you. Sometimes it might be a bit boring, but at the same time it's fascinating to see how things have or haven't changed. And sometimes it brings up something so delightful you can't believe you've forgotten it — a funny photo you took or the sweet words of a friend. You can repost or comment on these types of discoveries and share the memory that way. You can also choose to be notified about your On This Day memories or you can just check out the app whenever you're in need of a bit of nostalgia. Facebook will also occasionally post a memory to the top of your News Feed (it won't be shared with your friends unless you choose to share it with them).

Scrapbook Your Baby Photos

If you're the parent of young kids and you choose to share photos of them on Facebook, you might run into a problem where you and your spouse or partner are constantly adding one-off photos of the cuteness, but then it's hard to find a photo on Facebook when you want to. Facebook created a special way to compile photos of your kids called Scrapbook. Scrapbook lets you create a tag for your child without creating a profile for them. You can then tag your kid in photos. Only you and your partner can tag your child, so you don't have to worry about them being tagged in photos without your permission.

To create a scrapbook, navigate to the About section of your Timeline and click to add a family member in the Family and Relationships section. When you add your son or daughter, you can click a box to "Add Scrapbook." Once you've saved the relationship, the scrapbook is created and you will be prompted to tag photos you've already added to Facebook. After you've created your scrapbook you can keep adding to it by continuing to tag your child in posts about her. Click on your child's name to view all the photos in their scrapbook

Say Thanks

Facebook's Say Thanks feature allows you to create a quick little video to thank a friend for being, well, your friend. Videos scan through a few photos with text interwoven to tell your friend thanks for just being them. You can choose from three basic scripts: Old Friend, Friend, or Family.

To create your Say Thanks video, go to www.facebook.com/thanks. There, you can choose the friend you'd like to say thanks to. Once you've chosen the friend, Facebook displays a collection of photos you've both been tagged in. You can choose the photos you want in your video by clicking on them. Preview your video and then click the green Share Video button at the top of the page to add it to Facebook. All your friends will be able to see the video. If you're someone who is prone to crying, don't forget the tissues.

Give Your Photos Some Flair

Whenever you add a photo from the Publisher, you can add some creative touches to the photo by clicking the "Edit Photo" paintbrush icon. These editing options are just that — options. They aren't required, and no one will mind if you just post your photo as a photo. At the same time, these options can just make your photo a little more . . . exceptional.

Options include adding filters, cropping and rotating your photo, adding text to your photo, and adding stickers to your photo. If you want more specifics on how, exactly, to add these pieces of flair to your photos, check out Chapter 11.

Review the Last Year (or Years)

Every winter Facebook offers the ability to look back on everything that's happened to you in the last year. Often played as a slide show, Year in Review videos highlight the most important parts of your year — the milestones compiled into a digital album, no trip to the scrapbook store required.

Facebook periodically makes other sorts of review videos for various occasions. On its birthday (February 4) it often offers the ability to "Look Back" through everything that you've ever done since you joined Facebook. Keep your eyes peeled for Facebook promoting these sorts of videos at the top of your News Feed. You aren't required to make one, but they can be fun.

Make your status stand out

By default, your status posts get displayed as simple black text in a white box. Nothing wrong with that. But if you want to draw a little more attention to your post, you can easily add a background to it. When you add a background, your post is displayed centered and bolded with the background you choose behind it.

To add a background to your post, click any of the colorful boxes that you see beneath your text when you're typing your status. Some backgrounds have designs such as fall leaves or standing stones, and others are simply a color. When you're happy with both your background and your text, click Post.

Add Tags

In addition to tagging friends in photos and posts, you can tag almost any *thing* in your posts. You can tag famous people, television shows, movies, bands, companies. Honestly, almost anything. To start tagging, simply type the @ symbol and begin typing the name of the person, place, or thing you want to tag. As you type, Facebook will auto-complete with suggestions. When you see the one you want, click on it. So if you're excited for the new *Star Wars*, you can tag it, and when friends mouse over the tag, they will see a preview of its Page. They can then click on the tag to view the *Star Wars* Page and check out all the cool movie posters. You don't have to have previously liked a Page to tag it; just type @ and go.

Go Live

Facebook Live Video is a feature you can find when you're using the Facebook app on your iPhone or Android smartphone. Live Videos are just what they sound like — a video that broadcasts exactly what you're doing right now. Going live gives people a peek into your life and a chance to connect in real time to your Facebook friends. You can choose to save live videos to your Timeline permanently or simply let them disappear when you're done broadcasting. To get started, tap the Live button in the bottom of the publisher in your Facebook app. Tap the red Live button and your friends will be able to see . . . whatever it is you want to share.

Use Stickers or GIFs in Your Messages

In conversations, there's so much more going on than what's said. There are gestures, expressions, emphasis. No matter how fast we get at communicating via text, there's always something that gets left behind. While that gap can't quite be fixed by using stickers and GIFs, it can be made a little less wide by doing so. Stickers and GIFs are visual ways to represent sentiments, and using them can function as a sort of punctuation to the messages you send to friends. Click on the Sticker or GIF buttons at the bottom of a chat window to browse the hundreds upon hundreds of options Facebook offers you. Stickers and GIFs can represent emotions, activities, people, places . . . anything really. You can also choose from sticker packs or GIF libraries that have been created by companies other than Facebook.

Friend-a-versaries

One of the On This Day memories you may occasionally see is the memory of the day you first became friends with someone important in your life. Congratulations, you can celebrate your friend-a-versary on Facebook! The easiest way to celebrate is to share the post about your friendship's ripe old age and include a little note about why that friend is important to you, or what you think about the fact that you guys have been friends for so many years.

It's important to note that Facebook only marks the anniversary of the day you became friends on Facebook. If you were actually friends long before that, your friend-a-versary might seem a bit inaccurate. Still, it never hurts to tell a friend how happy you are to be friends with them.

Chapter **17**

Ten Ways Facebook Uniquely Impacts Lives

Sometimes people are dismissive of Facebook, saying, "I keep up with my friends by calling them and visiting them. I don't need a website to do that for me." And you don't *need* a website to do that for you. At the same time, though, Facebook can supplement your existing relationships in very real ways. Here are some ways that maintaining a friendship on Facebook can have big impacts in the real world.

Keeping in Touch with Far-Away Friends

I once spent a summer leading a troop of sixth graders into the wild. After two weeks of backpacking, kayaking, climbing, and bonding, the kids were given a big list of email addresses and phone numbers, said their goodbyes, and were packed off to their respective homes. I, about to head out west to work at Facebook, lamented the fact that the kids were too young to be on Facebook because they almost assuredly would lose that sheet of paper. I quickly friended my co-counselors (who were all old enough to be on Facebook) and kept up with them through photo albums, messages, and posts. As an added bonus, years later, when one of my co-counselors needed a reference, he knew exactly where to find me.

Facebook is not just useful for keeping in touch with summer friends; it can be a really nice way to deepen ties to the people you meet at conferences, retreats, vacations, and so on. I've never met any of my editors for this book in person, yet because of our Facebook friendships I've watched their kids grow up and know about the other projects they are working on.

Preparing to Head Off to School

Everyone has a story about leaving for college. Whether they're dropping off a child or an older sister or heading off themselves, people remember some form of anxiety, nervousness, or blinding fear of the unknown. Who were these people in the hallway or sharing the bathroom? Who was this so-called roommate?

In fact, there are special groups on Facebook for colleges and universities that only students and faculty can join. As soon as incoming freshmen receive their .edu email addresses, they can join this group and start connecting with other students. As they get to know the people in the group, they may find that by the time they arrive on campus, they already know some people. Instead of wandering into the great unknown, college students go off to school having been introduced to their future roommates, classmates, and friends.

Going on Not-So-Blind Dates

Ever been a matchmaker? Ever had a particularly difficult "client" — a friend who has a million requirements for "the one"? Ever been embarrassed because you didn't realize just how picky your friend was until after the date? Enter Facebook. Now, "He's smart, funny, has a great job, lots of cool hobbies, a nice family, and nice friends" can be condensed into a Facebook message with a shared Timeline. From there, both parties can decide based on the Timelines — looks, interests, or the combination of all the information — whether they want to go on a date. In fact, many dating apps work by importing (with your permission) information from your Facebook profile to try to find you matches.

TIP

While showing a friend someone else's Timeline can be the right way to prevent a complete disaster, don't let your friend get too picky with the information there ("I could never date someone who didn't listen to Bowie!"). Encourage her to take a glance at a few photos, point out some of the things the two have in common, and then point them to a coffee shop or bar where they can meet in person.

Meeting People in Your New City or Town

Heading off to college isn't the only time in people's lives that they find themselves someplace new without a lot of friends. But active Facebook users often find that there are many ways Facebook can help alleviate the confusion. Whether it's searching for old friends who may have wound up in your new home, or getting some introductions from mutual friends, Facebook makes moving less of an ordeal — a neighborhood is waiting for you when you arrive. When I arrived in Seattle from California, I quickly learned that many friends from college and people I used to work with had settled here, as well. It was wonderful to feel like I wasn't surrounded by strangers but by friends.

Reconnecting with Old Friends

Long-lost friends. The one who got away. I wonder whatever happened to her. Have you heard about him? These are just some of the ways people talk about the people they somehow lost track of along the way. Whatever the reason for the loss, this sort of regret can be undone on Facebook. Finding people is easy, and getting in touch is, too.

Many recent graduates exclaim that going to a reunion is unnecessary — you already know what everyone is doing five years later; you found out from Facebook. But even for the not-so-young alums, the Find Classmates and Find Coworkers features provide a direct line to search anyone who's on Facebook that you remember from way back (or not so way back) when.

Facebook gets emails every so often about people who find birth parents or biological siblings on Facebook. However, the majority of the time, people are looking for and finding their old classmates and reminiscing about the good old days. Better yet, they are re-igniting a spark in a friendship that can last far into the future.

Keeping Up with the 'Rents . . . or the Kids

Face it: Keeping your parents in touch with everything that's going on is difficult. However often you speak, it sometimes feels as though you're forgetting something. And visits often feel rushed, as though you don't have enough time to truly catch up.

I've found that Facebook Photos is one of the best ways to easily and quickly share my life with my parents. Because I can upload photos so quickly — both from my mobile phone and from my computer — they can feel as though they were present at the *<insert activity here>*. Whether that's the walk I took around the lake, the concert I attended, or the really tasty pie I made, it's as though I called to tell them about it right after it happened. And of course this can happen in the other direction as well: I can see when my parents post photos of their own adventures in the world.

For new parents, Facebook is invaluable for connecting kids with their grandparents. There are few things grandparents like more than photos of their grandkids being brilliant, and you can have those in spades on Facebook. The more generations you have on Facebook, the more fun it can be for all.

Facebook Networking

If you've ever found yourself job hunting, you probably are acquainted with the real-world version of *networking.* You ask friends for their friends' numbers and job titles; you take people out to coffee; you go on interviews; you decide whether the company is right for you; you repeat the whole process.

Although finding the right job hasn't gotten any easier with Facebook, a lot of the intermediate steps have. Asking your friends for their friends' info is as easy as posting a status. You can also search for people who work at companies that interest you, and see if you have any mutual friends who can introduce you. After you receive some names, send them a Facebook message (or an email, whichever is more appropriate) to set up the requisite "informational coffee date."

After interviewing, a great way to get information about a company is to talk to people who work there. Use Find Coworkers to search for friends who've listed that company in their Timelines.

WARNING

The only caveat to this approach is that you're now using Facebook to represent a professional portion of your life. If you contact people via Facebook and they feel a little uncomfortable with the content in your Timeline, whether that's your profile picture, a recent status that can be easily misinterpreted, or a post from a friend that reveals just a little too much information, it could make a bad first impression — just as if you'd shown up to the interview in torn jeans and the shirt you slept in. As a well-educated user of Facebook (because you *have* read all previous 15 chapters without just skipping directly to this one, right?), you're well aware of the myriad privacy settings that enable you to tailor what different parties see and don't see. However, if anything on your Timeline might be particularly misunderstood, simply hide it until you sign your offer letter.

Facebook for Good

Facebook has always been impressive at gaining support for important causes. Whether it's a monk-led protest in Myanmar, raising money for Puerto Rico after a hurricane, creating a massive rally in Colombia denouncing a terrorist organization, or raising Autism Awareness in the United States, Facebook lets ideas spread from friend to friend to friend. Sometimes groups are the tools used, sometimes it's encouraging people to change their profile pictures to a specific image in support of their cause. There's no perfect formula for creating a Facebook revolution, but don't hesitate to share your beliefs on your Timeline or express support for causes around the world.

As I edit this chapter, it is Giving Tuesday — the Tuesday after Thanksgiving when people are encouraged to donate to charity. This year, Facebook announced that it has partnered with the Gates Foundation to match up to two million dollars in donations to nonprofits through Facebook fundraisers. People all over the country have created fundraisers to take Facebook up on this offer and make the holiday season a little bit brighter for all sorts of different organizations.

Going to the Chapel

A small bit of Facebook trivia: There has, in many circles, arisen the idea of *Facebook Official (FBO)* — the act of moving from *single* to *in a relationship* and listing the person that you're in a relationship with on your Timeline. For any fledgling couple, this is a big deal for their personal lives; however, becoming Facebook Official also serves notice to friends and anyone who happens upon one's Timeline: I'm taken.

Because of this relationship function, Facebook has become the fastest way to spread a wedding announcement to extended friend groups. Of course, people still call their parents and their closest friends, but *everyone* can find out and share in the happiness via News Feed. Congratulatory Timeline posts ensue, as do copious numbers of photos with *the ring* tagged front and center.

After the wedding has taken place, Facebook becomes a wonderland of virtual congratulations as well as photos of the big day. And in case anyone missed it, he can share in the after-party online.

Hey, Facebook Me!

Before Facebook, in both romantic and platonic contexts, it was hard to get from "Nice to meet you" to "Will you be my friend?" Now, the simple phrase, "Facebook me!" expresses this sentiment and so much more. "Facebook me!" can mean *get in touch, look me up,* or *I want you to know more about me* but in a pressure-free way. It doesn't mean *take me to dinner,* or *let's be best friends forever and ever.* It's simply a way to acknowledge a budding friendship.

"Facebook me!" can also be how good friends say, "Keep up with my life; I want you to know about it," which acknowledges that people are busy and that it's difficult to find time to see each other or talk on the phone. However, even when you're incredibly busy, a quick check on Facebook can make you feel connected again.

Chapter **18**

Ten Frequently Asked Questions

Having worked for Facebook and on this book for several years, we know a lot about the specific complications, confusions, and pain-points people come across while using Facebook. At dinner parties, group functions, family events, or even walking across the street wearing a Facebook hoodie, someone always has a suggestion or a question about how to use the site. It's understandable. Facebook is a complex and powerful tool with a ton of social nuances, many of which have yet to be standardized. There are a lot of different features, and Facebook changes a lot. Each year, Facebook modifies parts of the site, redesigns how certain pages look and feel, and adds features. To keep up on what's happening with Facebook, you can like the official Facebook Page, found at www.facebook.com/facebook, and you'll get updates straight from the horse's mouth.

What follows are the questions I hear most often from friends and family (and the occasional message from a stranger who really needs help), often with strain in their voices or pain in their eyes. The goal of highlighting the more complicated questions is to save you the stress of encountering these issues and wondering whether you're the only one who just doesn't get it.

Do People Know When I Look at Their Timelines?

No. No. No. When people see stories about their friends pop up on their Home page, they sometimes get a little anxious that this means Facebook is tracking everything everyone does and publishing it to everyone else. That's not true. Consider two types of actions on Facebook: creating content and viewing it. Creating content means you've intentionally added something to Facebook for others to look at or read, such as uploading a photo or a video, commenting on or liking something, or posting a status. These types of actions are all publishable posts — that is, stories about them may end up on your Timeline or in your friends' News Feeds — although you have direct control over exactly who gets to see these posts.

The other type of action on Facebook is viewing content such as flipping through photos, watching a video, clicking a link your friend has liked, or viewing someone's Timeline. Unless someone is looking over your shoulder as you browse, these types of actions are strictly private. No one is ever directly notified about them, and no trace of the fact that you took that action is left on your Timeline or in your friends' News Feeds. So now you can check people out to your heart's content.

I Friended Too Many People and Now I Don't Like Sharing Stuff — What Can I Do?

Having a big friend list is a very sad reason to not be sharing with people you *want* to share with. You can fix this by using privacy settings, which are covered in detail in Chapter 6. Here's an overview for how to change who can see a post you are making.

1. **When you have completed with your post, click the Privacy menu in the lower-right corner of the Publisher.**

   It usually says "Public" or "Friends" by default. This opens a menu of options.

2. **Choose Friends Except. . .**

   This opens a window for choosing people from your friend list.

3. **Click on the faces of any friends you *don't* want to see your post.**

   You can scroll up and down or type friends' names into the search box at the top to find specific people. You can select as many people as you want.

4. **When you're done choosing people, click Save Changes.**

This is now your new default for when you share posts with people.

Another thing you can do is start to remove excess people from your friend list if you don't think it will cause you social awkwardness in real life. I've found that people I used to work with and never see in real life anymore rarely notice when I've removed them from my friend list.

What's with the New Facebook — Can I Change It Back?

Inevitably, Facebook is going to change the way it looks. You're going to log in one day, and things will look different — the things you were used to seeing on the left will now be on the right, or gone completely, or someplace hidden . . . it's confusing. Facebook changes the look and feel of either the Home page or the Timeline about once per year. And trust me when I say that when you log in and this has happened to you, you're going to hate it.

Unfortunately, no matter what you do, no matter how much you hate it, Facebook rarely goes back on a redesign like that. You won't be able to change it back, and the best thing you can do is try to figure out the new site. Check out the Help Center (click the Quick Help menu in the big blue bar on top, and then click Help Center in the upper-right corner of the menu that opens) or Facebook's Page (www.facebook.com/facebook) to read about the layout changes and how the site works. And then try to use Facebook a few minutes a day until you get used to it. Over time, it won't seem so bad any more. You'll look at a photo of the old Facebook, and you'll think how ugly it looks by comparison.

So, short answer: *No, you can't change it back.* But I have complete confidence in your ability to adapt to the new Facebook.

I Have a Problem with My Account — Can You Help Me?

I wish I could. Unfortunately, I am but a user like you, and that means although I can help diagnose the issue, I can't usually treat it. Sometimes the problems are Facebook's fault, and sometimes they are user errors, but either way, I don't really have the tools required to fix them. Most account problems can be resolved only by Facebook employees with special access to the specific tool required to fix an account. Here are a few of the account questions I've received recently, and the answers given:

>> **I can't remember my password. Can you reset it for me?** *Answer:* No can do. Click the Forgot Account link on the login page to start the reset process, which entails Facebook sending a password reset code to your email or Google account.

>> **My account was deactivated because it said I was sending too many messages. Why? Can you fix it?** *Answer:* I recently had this happen to two friends: one who was using his account to promote his music career, and one who was distributing his poetry to many, many friends through messages. This is Facebook spam detection at work. When an account starts sending a lot of messages in quick succession, especially when those messages contain links, this looks a lot like spam to the system. In most cases, the person is warned first, but if the behavior continues, his account is disabled. The only way to have this action reversed is to write in to Facebook's Help Team and request reactivation. To write in to Facebook, go to the Help Center (www. facebook.com/help) and search for a FAQ entitled My Personal Facebook Account Is Disabled. Follow the instructions for contacting Facebook. The process of getting your account reactivated can sometimes take several days.

What Do I Do with Friend Requests I Don't Want to Accept?

This is a tough question. As far as I know, there isn't exactly a social convention for this yet, so the answer to this question is pretty personal. Just know that there are several actions you can take:

>> **Click Delete Request.** Remember, people are never notified if you have rejected their friend request. If you don't want to be their friend, you don't have to be.

>> **Many people just leave the request sitting there forever.** I admit I am guilty of this. If you don't want to accept because you don't want that person having access to your Timeline, you can accept the request and then add him to a special restricted Friend List. You can go into your Privacy settings and exclude that Friend List from seeing any parts of your Timeline that aren't set

to Public. Then anyone you add to that list will be restricted. In this way, you can accept the Friend Request without giving up access to your Timeline.

>> **If you don't want to accept because you don't want to read about that person in your News Feed, no problem!** Simply click Confirm. The first time she shows up in News Feed, hover over the story and click the ellipsis (or down arrow) in the upper-right of the story. Choose Unfollow *<Friend's Name>* in the menu that opens to prevent any future stories from that person from appearing in your News Feed.

Why Can't I Find My Friend?

I'm assuming you're asking this question after exhausting every possibility for finding friends, as described in Chapter 8. And I'm also assuming you're looking for a specific person, not friends in general.

You won't be able to find a friend for the following few reasons:

>> **She hasn't joined Facebook.** Shocking, I know. If you think she'd enjoy it, you can always invite her to join and be your friend as long as you have her email address.

>> **She goes by a different name on Facebook to protect her privacy.** For example, if her name is Jane Smith, she may list her name as Janie S. Try searching for her by her email address or phone number.

>> **She has a common name.** Facebook Search tries to get you to the right Jane Smith by looking at things like friends in common and shared hometowns, but sometimes it comes up empty.

>> **She doesn't have much information filled out on her Timeline.** If you're looking for a high school classmate, but she never entered her high school information, you're going to have a hard time finding her.

>> **She blocked you.** Yes, this one is harsh. I put it on the list only because I've seen it happen before. Someone says to me, "I *know* she's on Facebook. And I *know* she's friends with my friend. But when I go to find her she's not there."

While it hurts to be blocked by someone, don't drive yourself crazy looking for reasons why it happened. If she doesn't want to connect with you on Facebook, that's her loss; move on to your other friends and all the things you can share with them.

Will Facebook Start Charging Me to Use the Site?

Another simple answer: *No.*

This rumor is a particularly nasty one that makes the rounds every now and again via people's statuses. There are several variations, but they always seem to involve asking you to repost the status that Facebook is shutting down/going to start charging/running out of names. Don't fall victim to this ruse. Facebook has long maintained that it will always be free to users. Unless you're advertising something, Facebook will always have space for you for free.

How Do I Convince My Friends to Join Facebook?

While the obvious answer to this question is to give them a copy of this brilliant book about how to use Facebook, there are a few other things you can try. You can tell her anecdotally the ways in which Facebook has enriched your life. Maybe you're interacting with your kids more, you're keeping in touch with friends you thought were lost, or you have a place to put your thoughts and photos where your friends might see them. You can let her look over your shoulder as you use the site so that she can see the experience herself — ask her questions about whether there's anyone she'd like to look up. The more information she sees about the people she cares about, the more likely she is to take the next step.

One common complaint from people who haven't joined the site is that they "don't have time for yet another computer thing." To this concern, one common response is that Facebook is an efficiency tool that often saves a person time compared to using old-school methods of communication. Messaging can often replace email, and events are easier to coordinate over Facebook. Sharing phone numbers is easier. Sending and receiving links is easier. Finding rides to the airport, restaurant recommendations, and who is heading to the park on Saturday are all faster and easier than trying to use email, phone, or other methods of communication.

REMEMBER

Finally, for some people, it's just not their time. No matter what you say, they'll stick their fingers in their ears and sing *la-la-la* until you start talking about sports or the weather or the circus coming to town next week. You can't force them to Facebook; you have to let Facebook come to them. Over the years, I've watched many a nonbeliever eventually cross over and discover the value. Patience may be your only weapon for these diehards.

What If I Don't Want Everyone Knowing My Business?

To those who ask that question and don't have time to read Chapter 6 of this book, which goes into detail about how to be a private person on Facebook, I simply try to impart the following message: You can be an extremely private person and still derive nearly all the same value out of Facebook as anyone else. All you have to do is learn how to use the Privacy controls and lock down all your information and access to your Timeline, ensuring that only those you trust can see your info. From there, you can interact in all the same ways as anyone else without feeling like your privacy is being compromised.

Note: Besides understanding the Privacy settings and taking the initial time to adjust yours until they feel just right, you will have to do a little extra work to be private on Facebook and still derive comparable value. You'll likely have to put in extra effort connecting with friends, because the more locked-down your information is, the harder you make it for not-yet-Facebook-friends to find your Timeline, and the harder it is for your friends to find you, identify you, and connect with you. If you're willing to do the work of seeking out your friends and connecting with them, however, your experience should be nearly identical with everyone else's.

Does Facebook Have a Feature That Lets Me Lock Myself Out for a Few Hours?

Short answer: *Not really.*

Long answer: Many people do *deactivate* their accounts. Deactivation is a way of shutting down your account temporarily. It means that no one will see your Timeline or be able to interact with you on Facebook. Some people will deactivate their accounts, their reason being "I spend too much time using Facebook." The benefit of such an action is that you're guaranteed not to get notifications about messages, picture tags, Timeline posts, or anything else. The downside is that it will cause a lot of confusion among your friends who suddenly can't message you, tag you, or write on your Timeline. If they have your email address, they're likely to bug you anyway to ask why you disappeared from Facebook.

The reason it's not a real solution is because all you must do to reactivate at any time is to enter your password (just like signing in), and you're completely back to normal. So if you're remotely curious how your social group has evolved without you, you may have trouble truly staying away.

Just like many good things in life, the key to keeping them good is moderation. French fries are delicious, but too many give you a tummy ache. Dancing is a blast 'til your feet are covered with blisters. Television is educational and entertaining until it's 3 a.m., you're watching your fifth infomercial, you forgot to feed the cat and put out the trash, and you find yourself wondering what life is all about. Facebook is no different. It's a brilliant utility when used to make your life easier and your social interactions richer. When you find yourself flipping through two-year-old vacation photos of a friend of a friend of a friend of a friend, it's time to blink a few times, step away from the mouse, and go out for ice cream, or dancing, or whatever else it is that gives you joy.

Chapter **19**

Ten Tips for Parents of Teens on Facebook

t's hard to put the word *teenager* together with the phrase *social media* and not get just the teensiest bit anxious. A lot of horror stories are out there about cyberbullying and online predators. Any parent is likely to be a bit worried.

However, it's unreasonable to think you can keep your teen away from Facebook, much less the Internet. That's where their friends are and that's where they want to be. So here are some tips I hope will be useful in navigating the waters of Facebook and the Internet at large.

I should acknowledge here that I'm neither a parent of a teen nor a teenager, so I don't pretend to know everything about what's going on in your family or in your teen's life. Think of these tips as a useful jumping-off place for figuring out how to keep your teen safe online.

Talk to Teens about General Internet Safety

Here are some general Internet safety tips that apply no matter what kind of website you're using:

>> Don't share any personal identifying info (address, phone number, credit card info, and so on) with anyone you don't know.

>> Create different passwords for all the sites you use. Passwords should also be difficult to guess and contain a mix of numbers, upper- and lowercase letters, and symbols.

>> Don't share your passwords with anyone, even boyfriends/girlfriends or best friends. (This is one that teenagers tend to struggle with.)

>> Click only those links you trust; be wary of scammy-sounding advertisements. They are usually scams.

Beware of Strangers

On Facebook, in general, people are who they say they are and tend to have only one account that links to their real email address and contains only real information about them. Unfortunately, like the real world, Facebook isn't completely free of malicious people who lie to take advantage of someone else.

The good news is that it's easy to keep your experience free of people like this by accepting only Friend Requests from people you know in real life. Talk to your teen about the importance of sharing information only with people they actually know and telling you when someone they don't know contacts them.

Teach Teens How to Report Abuse

Virtually every piece of content on Facebook has a Report link. These include photos, videos, messages, Timelines, groups, posts, and events. If you or your child comes across content that is abusive or offensive, report it by clicking any of the Report links located near these pieces of content. Facebook investigates all abuse reports and removes content that violates its Statement of Rights and Responsibilities. You can report Timelines for being fake or posts for being harassing.

TIP

The only caveat is that some stuff that may be offensive to you or your teen may not be considered offensive by Facebook's staff. For example, you can't report a photo for being unflattering — you can only ask that the person who posted it take it down.

Teach Teens How to Block People

Certain kinds of behaviors can eventually lead to someone being kicked off Facebook, but you (and your teen) might not want to wait around until the offender is out for good. If someone is bothering your teen (or you) and won't leave your teen (or you) alone, don't hesitate to block the person from the Privacy Shortcuts menu. Blocking someone almost has the effect of making it seem like that person isn't on Facebook. Neither of you will be able to see each other in searches, to message each other, or to look at each other's Timeline.

Personally, I block strangers early and often. I receive my share of junk mail, and anytime a stranger sends me a weird link or comments on my looks, I both report and block the person. It just gives me peace of mind to do so. To block someone, follow these steps:

1. **Click the question mark in the circle icon in the big blue bar on top and choose Privacy Shortcuts from the drop-down menu.**

2. **In the Privacy Shortcuts menu, click the How Do I Stop Someone from Bothering Me section.**

This expands an interface for adding people to your blocklist.

3. **Type a name or email address in the Add Name or Email text box.**

4. **Click Block.**

The person is then added to your blocklist. Repeat Steps 3 and 4 as needed to block more people.

Learn to Use Privacy Settings

This book contains an entire chapter on privacy. You can rest easier if you go through your teen's Privacy settings with her and agree on settings that allow her to share more safely. In general, sharing only with friends or, better yet, creating a list of close friends can quickly ensure that fewer people are seeing your child's information and that, at all times, you both have a complete list of who those people are. If you have a question about anything, refer to Chapter 6 for help.

Talk about Posts and Consequences

Even with good Privacy settings, teenagers often struggle with the idea that once something is shared, it's hard to undo. This is extremely true of things like Facebook photos or posts. Encourage your teens to think about how something might be seen and interpreted by people who aren't their closest friends. Would they want a college admissions officer to see that photo? Would they want their boss to read that post? Both situations have happened with real consequences. The college admissions officer might decide you aren't really "Hah-vahrd" material, or the boss may fire you for complaining on Facebook about her way of speaking. The things that happen on Facebook don't always stay on Facebook; they have a way of spreading. Remind your teen to think before he posts.

Remember the Golden Rule

As much as many parents worry about their kids being the victims of cyberbullying, you must also consider that kids can be the perpetrators of cyberbullying. Talk to your kids about the behaviors that might affect others, whether known or unknown. This includes things like creating hateful Facebook groups targeting a teacher or peer, as well as going into a forum somewhere else on the Internet and posting something inflammatory or offensive under the protection of anonymity (although, on the Internet, anonymity doesn't usually last).

The Golden Rule applies to your child just as much in adolescence as when she was in kindergarten: Do unto others as you would have them do unto you. Would you want someone saying something bad about you online? How would you feel if you posted something personal, and people made fun of you? Part of being part of Facebook (and other online communities) is being a good citizen. That makes Facebook Nation a safe place for all.

Respect Teens' Boundaries

After you get them set up on Facebook and talk about all the general ideas for Internet and Facebook safety, you need to give them some space. As one of my teenage cousins said to me, "They should be my friend, and that's it."

Some kids are comfortable interacting with their parents; others think it is the most embarrassing thing in the world. Hey, that's okay. When you were a teen, did you like it when your parents came along with you and your friends when you went out? Did you like it when they listened in on your phone calls or read your diary? That's what it can feel like to some teenagers when they're asked to be friends with their parents: like you're invading their space.

You can talk to them about some of the things you see on Facebook (both the good and the bad; trust me, there are both!), but commenting on their stuff and posting on their Timeline are likely to get you unfriended. As long as you let them know they can come tell you whenever they're having some sort of problem (and that they always tell you when they're contacted by a stranger), it's important to let them know that you trust them to make smart choices.

Don't Send Friend Requests to Teens' Friends

If their friends friend you, it's probably okay to accept those requests (though you may want to check with your teen first; see the previous section, "Respect Teens' Boundaries"). However, it's generally considered weird and pushy for you to reach out to their friends.

Make Space for Your Own Social Life, and Your Family Life, on Facebook

If you joined Facebook just to understand what's going on in your teen's life, that's great. But now, having read this book, I hope you can see that there's a lot Facebook can offer you and your friends, with or without your children present. Share photos. Coordinate events with your friends. Post statuses about what's going on with you. It doesn't always have to be about them.

One way to keep your social life separate from your teen's social life, but still have a little interaction on Facebook, is to create a group for your family. You can add lots of different family members, and everyone can share the sort of stuff family members like to know: holiday newsletter–type stuff. It creates a space where it's okay for you and your son or daughter to interact on Facebook. Hopefully, it's a way to bring you both a little closer.

One parent I spoke to mentioned that he likes to send his teen messages on Facebook letting her know he loves her. It's just another way for them to connect where his daughter is comfortable, and it has strengthened their relationship.

Index

About the Authors

Carolyn Abram is a writer. She was the first user of Facebook at Stanford in 2004 and worked for Facebook from 2006-2009. She has used Facebook every day for most of her adult life, acquiring 805 Facebook friends. Despite that, she managed to receive a BA from Stanford ('06) and an MFA from California College of the Arts ('12). Her short fiction has appeared in *New California Writing 2013*, *Switchback*, and *The Offbeat*. She currently lives in Seattle with her husband, children, and dog.

Amy Karasavas is a writer and marketing consultant. She was an early employee of Facebook, working there from 2007 to 2010. She is currently training to become a sommelier (a departure from her days working at start-ups). She lives with her partner Michael and their two dogs in Brooklyn, NY.

Authors' Acknowledgments

Carolyn: A huge thank you to Amy Karasavas for signing on to working on this edition; your feedback and comments have been invaluable. As usual, thanks to the flexibility and support of the Wiley Team, especially Steve Hayes, who did not know ten years ago that he would still be stuck with me today.

On the home front, I want to thank Eric, Connor, and Lina for simply being. Our family is a delight to me. I also want to acknowledge the enormous web of people who actually make it possible for me to get work done by helping care for my children: the staff at SEED Early Childhood School, a rotating cast of babysitters, our friends, and our families.

In closing, I'd like to thank the billions of Facebook users around the world who are busy connecting, sharing, and generally having fun on Facebook. Keep on signin' on.

Amy: I can't say thank you enough to Steve Hayes and Colleen Diamond for their assistance and their wisdom in guiding this process throughout. Also a huge thank you to the rest of the Wiley crew. And to Carolyn for answering my questions and for her excellent work — she sets the bar high.

I need to thank my partner Michael for his love, his jokes, and his continual support (and for keeping me plied with lattes). And to our two dogs we adopted this year — they have filled our lives with mayhem and delight.

I'm thankful to have been a part of Facebook's early days and to watch it continue to be so impactful.

Publisher's Acknowledgments

Acquisitions Editor: Steve Hayes

Project Manager: Colleen Diamond

Development Editor: Colleen Diamond

Copy Editor: Colleen Diamond

Technical Editors: Carolyn Abram and Amy Karasavas

Editorial Assistant: Owen Kaelble

Production Editor: G. Vasanth Koilraj

Cover Image: © enisaksoy/iStockphoto

Leverage the power

Dummies is the global leader in the reference category and one of the most trusted and highly regarded brands in the world. No longer just focused on books, customers now have access to the dummies content they need in the format they want. Together we'll craft a solution that engages your customers, stands out from the competition, and helps you meet your goals.

Advertising & Sponsorships

Connect with an engaged audience on a powerful multimedia site, and position your message alongside expert how-to content. Dummies.com is a one-stop shop for free, online information and know-how curated by a team of experts.

- Targeted ads
- Video
- Email Marketing
- Microsites
- Sweepstakes sponsorship

20 MILLION PAGE VIEWS EVERY SINGLE MONTH

15 MILLION UNIQUE VISITORS PER MONTH

43% OF ALL VISITORS ACCESS THE SITE VIA THEIR MOBILE DEVICES

700,000 NEWSLETTER SUBSCRIPTIONS TO THE INBOXES OF *300,000* UNIQUE INDIVIDUALS EVERY WEEK

PERSONAL ENRICHMENT

Staying Sharp
9781119187790
USA $26.00
CAN $31.99
UK £19.99

Facebook
9781119179030
USA $21.99
CAN $25.99
UK £16.99

Guitar
9781119293354
USA $24.99
CAN $29.99
UK £17.99

Investing
9781119293347
USA $22.99
CAN $27.99
UK £16.99

Beekeeping
9781119310068
USA $22.99
CAN $27.99
UK £16.99

Digital Photography
9781119235606
USA $24.99
CAN $29.99
UK £17.99

Meditation
9781119251163
USA $24.99
CAN $29.99
UK £17.99

Pregnancy
9781119235491
USA $26.99
CAN $31.99
UK £19.99

Samsung Galaxy S7
9781119279952
USA $24.99
CAN $29.99
UK £17.99

iPhone
9781119283133
USA $24.99
CAN $29.99
UK £17.99

Crocheting
9781119287117
USA $24.99
CAN $29.99
UK £16.99

Nutrition
9781119130246
USA $22.99
CAN $27.99
UK £16.99

PROFESSIONAL DEVELOPMENT

Windows 10
9781119311041
USA $24.99
CAN $29.99
UK £17.99

AutoCAD
9781119255796
USA $39.99
CAN $47.99
UK £27.99

Excel 2016
9781119293439
USA $26.99
CAN $31.99
UK £19.99

QuickBooks 2017
9781119281467
USA $26.99
CAN $31.99
UK £19.99

macOS Sierra
9781119280651
USA $29.99
CAN $35.99
UK £21.99

LinkedIn
9781119251132
USA $24.99
CAN $29.99
UK £17.99

Windows 10
9781119310563
USA $34.00
CAN $41.99
UK £24.99

SharePoint 2016
9781119181705
USA $29.99
CAN $35.99
UK £21.99

Fundamental Analysis
9781119263593
USA $26.99
CAN $31.99
UK £19.99

Networking
9781119257769
USA $29.99
CAN $35.99
UK £21.99

Office 2016
9781119293477
USA $26.99
CAN $31.99
UK £19.99

Office 365
9781119265313
USA $24.99
CAN $29.99
UK £17.99

Salesforce.com
9781119239314
USA $29.99
CAN $35.99
UK £21.99

Coding
9781119293323
USA $29.99
CAN $35.99
UK £21.99

dummies.com

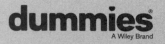
dummies
A Wiley Brand